THE ECONOMY OF BRAZIL

BRAZIL: STATES AND REGIONS

Source: Map by James A. Bier from the *Library Guide for Brazilian Studies* (University of Pittsburgh Book Centers, 1964), page 5. Reproduced and corrected with the permission of the author, William Vernon Jackson.

Key to Regions: 1. North 2. Northeast 3. East 4. South 5. Center-South

THE

ECONOMY OF

Brazil

Edited by HOWARD S. ELLIS

Foreword by LINCOLN GORDON

UNIVERSITY OF CALIFORNIA PRESS

Berkeley and Los Angeles / 1969

University of California Press
Berkeley and Los Angeles, California

University of California Press, Ltd.
London, England

Contents

Tables

Figures

Foreword

This volume presents a series of penetrating essays on Brazil's economic development during the postwar period by a group of exceptionally well-informed Brazilian and American authors. It reaches more deeply into key aspects of a transitional economy than much of the literature on developing countries which deals only with broad macro-economic aggregates. The Brazilian authors include professional economists who have been at the center of national policy formation and execution, as well as some of the best trained representatives of the younger generation. On the American side, all the contributors have had the benefit of intimate contact with the complexities of Brazilian economic life.

The postwar decades have been a period of dramatic change in the Brazilian economy, marked by rapid industrialization, urbanization, inflation sometimes approaching monetary chaos, and a kaleidoscopic overlay of shifting political forces. The old cliché of the "sleeping giant," with an ever-receding potential for a never-realized future, has totally disappeared. These have been years of early adolescence in Brazil's struggle for economic maturity, and the imbalances and growing pains of adolescence are still much in evidence. There remain immense challenges in the needs for institutional modernization in agriculture and education, the efficient diversification of export products and markets, and the simulation of investment and job creation to match the heavy pressures of demographic growth and migration to the cities.

Nevertheless, the Brazilian economy is clearly in motion,

even though its destiny remains uncertain. These essays should help both professional economists and the wider public to understand some of the processes and problems being faced in deciding that destiny.

LINCOLN GORDON

President, The Johns Hopkins University,
U.S. Ambassador to Brazil, 1961–1966

The Contributors

Alan Abouchar, b. 1932, New York, New York. Transport Advisor, Brazil Development Assistance Program, University of California, Rio de Janeiro, 1965–1968; Berkeley, since 1968. DEGREES: Bachelor of Arts, Economics, New York University, 1954. Master of Arts, Economics, New York University, 1960. Master of Arts, Statistics, University of California, Berkeley, 1963. Doctor of Philosophy, Economics, University of California, Berkeley, 1966. EARLIER POSITIONS: Research Associate, The Brookings Institution, 1963–1965. Free lance translator (Russian), U.S. Department of Commerce, 1961–1963. AUTHOR: *The Transport Sector in Brazil* (Rio de Janeiro, EPEA, 1967), mimeographed. "Rationality in the Prewar Soviet Cement Industry," *Soviet Studies*, 1967. "Inflation and Transport Policy in Brazil," *Economic Development and Cultural Change*, 1968. "Comercio e Transporte na ALALC," *Revista Brasileira de Economia*, 1967. "Distância de Transporte, Custos Operacionais, e Tarifas de Carga nas Ferrovias Brasileiras," *Revista Brasileira de Transportes*, third quarter, 1966.

Werner Baer, b. 1931, Germany. Associate Professor, Vanderbilt University, since 1965. DEGREES: Bachelor of Arts, Queens College, 1953. Master of Arts, Harvard University, 1955. Doctor of Philosophy, Harvard University, 1958. EARLIER POSITIONS: Instructor, Harvard University, 1958–1961. Assistant Professor, Yale University, 1961–1965. Visiting Ford Foundation Professor, University of São Paulo, 1966–1968. Ford Foundation Economics Advisor in Brazil,

1967–. AUTHOR: *The Puerto Rican Economy and United States Economic Fluctuations*, 1962. With Issac Kerstenetsky: *Inflation and Growth in Latin America*, 1964. *Industrialization and Economic Development in Brazil*, 1965. Journal articles on trade and development.

Donald W. Baerresen, b. 1928, Los Angeles, California. Associate Research Economist, Brazil Development Assistance Program, University of California, Rio de Janeiro, 1965–1967; Berkeley, 1967–1968. DEGREES: Bachelor of Arts, University of California, Los Angeles, 1950. University of California exchange student in Colombia, 1959. Master of Arts, University of California, Los Angeles, 1961. Doctor of Philosophy, University of California, Los Angeles, 1963. EARLIER POSITIONS: Research Associate, The Brookings Institution, Washington, D.C., 1963–1964. Economist, Organization of American States, 1964–1965. AUTHOR: Co-author: *Latin American Trade Patterns* (Washington, D.C.: The Brookings Institution, 1965). *An Analysis of Tax Policy of the Ecuadorean Central Government* (Washington, D.C.: Organization of American States, May 1968). "A Method for Planning Economic Integration for Specific Industries," *Journal of Common Market Studies*, September 1967. HONORS: Earhart Research Fellowship, Santiago, Chile, 1961–1962. Ford Foundation Doctoral Fellowship (2 years).

Joel Bergsman, b. 1936, Wilkes-Barre, Pennsylvania. Visiting Associate Research Economist, Brazil Development Assistance Program, University of California, Rio de Janeiro, 1966–1967; Berkeley, 1967–1969. DEGREES: Bachelor of Electrical Engineering, Cornell University, 1959, Master of Business Administration, Stanford University, 1961. Doctor of Philosophy, Stanford University, 1963. EARLIER POSITION: USAID, Washington, Office of Program Coordination, 1963–1965. AUTHOR: "Electric Power Systems Planning Using Linear Programming," IEEE *Transactions on Military Electronics*, April 1964. With Alan S. Manne: "An Almost Consistent Model for India's Fourth and Fifth Plans," *The Economic Weekly*, November 20, 1965. Reprinted in Irma Adelman and Erik Thorbecke (eds.); *The*

Theory and Design of Economic Development (Baltimore: Johns Hopkins Press, 1966).

Octavio Gouveia de Bulhões, b. 1906, Rio de Janeiro. Professor, National Faculty of Economic Sciences, Rio de Janeiro. DEGREES: Bachelor of Legal and Social Sciences, Rio de Janeiro, Doctor of Legal and Social Sciences, Rio de Janeiro. Courses in Economics, American University, Washington, D.C. EARLIER POSITIONS: Chief, Section of Economic and Financial Studies, Ministry of Finance, 1939–1951. Representative of Brazil in Conferences on Monetary Stabilization, 1943; and delegate to Breton Woods Conference, 1944. Alternate Executive Director, International Monetary Fund, 1946. President, Joint Brazilian-American Commission (Abbink Commission), 1948. President, National Economic Council, 1954. Interim Minister of Finance, 1954. Director of SUMOC, 1961. Minister of Finance, 1964. AUTHOR: *Marginal Comment on a Report*, in Portuguese (Rio de Janeiro: 1950). *Economics and Political Economy*, in Portuguese (Rio de Janeiro: 1960).

Arthur Candal, b. 1935, Porto Alegre, Brazil. Senior staff member, IPEA, Ministry of Planning, Rio de Janeiro. DEGREES: Bachelor of Law and Social Sciences, University of Rio Grande do Sul, Brazil, 1958. Diploma, Latin American Institute, Santiago de Chile, 1963. Diploma, National Economic Planning, Warsaw, 1964. EARLIER POSITIONS: Senior staff member, Office of Administration and Planning, Rio Grande do Sul, 1963–1965. Project Evaluation Expert, ECLA, TAO, FAO; La Paz, 1966.

Julian M. Chacel, b. 1928, Rio de Janeiro. Director General, Instituto Brasileiro de Economia, Fundação Getúlio Vargas. Member of the Economic Council, Confederação Nacional da Indústria. Assistant Professor, Federal University, Rio de Janeiro. DEGREES: Bachelor of Economic Science, Rio de Janeiro, 1949. University Doctorate, Faculty of Law, Paris, 1951. EARLIER POSITIONS: Chief of Centers of IBRE: National Accounts, 1956–1958, Agricultural Studies, 1960–1963. Brazilian delegate to the VII, VIII and IX Latin American Regional Conference of FAO, and to the XIII World Conference. AUTHOR: "Implicações Econômicas de Reforma Agrária," *Instituto Interamericano de*

Ciências Agrícolas, 1963. Contribution to the *Programa de Ação Econômica do Govêrno,* 1964–1966. *Projeções de Oferta e Demanda de Produtos Agrícolas para Brasil,* 1967. Various articles in *Revista Brasileira de Economia.* HONORS: Eisenhower Fellow, 1958. Visiting Scholar, Columbia University, 1964.

Howard S. Ellis, b. 1898, Denver, Colorado. Flood Professor of Economics, Emeritus, University of California, Berkeley. Chief of Party, Brazil Development Assistance Program, University of California, Rio de Janeiro, 1965–1967. DEGREES: Bachelor of Arts, University of Iowa, 1920. Master of Arts, University of Michigan, 1922. Doctor of Philosophy, Harvard University, 1929. Doctor of Laws, University of Michigan, 1951; University of California, 1968. EARLIER POSITIONS: Instructor to Professor, University of Michigan, 1920–1938. Flood Professor, University of California, Berkeley, 1938–1965. Visiting Professor, Columbia University, 1944–1945, 1949–1950; Tokyo, 1951; Bombay, 1958–1959; Center of Economic Research, Athens, 1963. Assistant Director of Research and Statistics, Board of Governors, Federal Reserve System, Washington, D.C., 1943–1945. Economic Policy Committee, U.S. Chamber of Commerce, 1945–1946. AUTHOR: *German Monetary Theory* (Cambridge, Mass.: Harvard University Press, 1934). *Exchange Control in Central Europe* (Cambridge, Mass.: Harvard University Press, 1941). *Industrial Capital in Greek Development* (Athens: Center of Economic Research, 1964). *A Survey of Contemporary Economics* (Philadelphia: Blakiston, 1948) [Editor]. With N. S. Buchanan: *Approaches to Economic Development* (New York: Twentieth Century Fund, 1955). *Economic Development for Latin America* (New York: Macmillan, 1961). Spanish edition (Mexico, D.F.: Fondo de Cultura, 1960). HONORS: American Economic Association: President 1949. International Economic Association: President, 1953–1965; honorary President, 1957–.

Eugenio Gudin, b. 1886, Rio de Janeiro. Professor Emeritus, University of Brazil, Rio de Janeiro. President of the Brazilian Society of Political Economy. President of the Brazilian Economic Institute, Getúlio Vargas Institute, Rio de Janeiro, 1946–. DEGREES: Degree in Civil Engineering, University of Brazil, 1905. Doctor Honoris Causa: Dijon, 1957, Bahia, 1957. EARLIER POSITIONS: Delegate to Breton Woods International Monetary Conference, 1944. Brazilian Governor of the IMF and IBRD, 1951–1955. Minister of Finance, Government of Brazil, 1954–1955. Member of the Council (1956) and Vice President (1959); International Economic Association. AUTHOR: *Capitalism and its Evolution* (Portuguese), 1935. *Principles of Monetary Economics* (Portuguese), 2 volumes, 1943. *Collected Essays* (Portuguese), 1944. *Inflation, Credit, and Economic Development* (Portuguese), 1956. *Analysis of Brazilian Problems, 1958–1964* (Portuguese), 1965. HONORS: Officer of the French Legion of Honor, 1952. Peruvian Order of Merit, 1955. Correspondent, Institute de France, 1961. Grand Cross of the Brazilian National Order of Merit (1967).

Samuel A. Morley, b. 1934, Aberdeen, Washington. Assistant Research Economist, Brazil Development Assistance Program, University of California, Rio de Janeiro, 1965–1967; Project Coordinator, Berkeley, 1967–1968. DEGREES: Bachelor of Arts, Yale University, 1956. Doctor of Philosophy, University of California, Berkeley, 1965. EARLIER POSITIONS: Research Assistant, University of California, Berkeley, 1962. Teaching Assistant, University of California, Berkeley, 1962–1963. AUTHOR: "The Determinants of the Demand for Imports in Brazil," article to be submitted to the *Review of Economics and Statistics*. HONORS: *Magna Cum Laude*, Yale University, 1956. National Science Foundation Fellow, 1963–1965.

Roberto de Oliviera Campos, b. 1917, Cuiabá, Brazil. President, INVESTIBANCO (Banco de Investimento e Desenvolvimento, S.A.), since 1967. President, CICYP (Conselho Interamericano de Comércio e Producão). DEGREES: Bachelor's Degree, Catholic Seminaries of Guaxape and Belo Horizonte, 1934. Master of Arts, George Washington University, Graduate studies, Columbia University. EARLIER POSITIONS: Professor of Money and Banking and Business Cycles at the School of Economics, University of Brasil, 1956–1961. Economic Counsellor of the Brazil-United States Economic Development Commission,

1951–1953. Director, General Manager and President of the National Economic Development Bank, 1952–1959. Secretary General of the National Development Council, 1956–1959. Roving Ambassador for financial negotiations in Western Europe, 1961. Ambassador of Brazil to the United States, 1961–1963. Minister for Planning and Coordination, 1964–1967. Member of the Inter-American Committee for the Alliance for Progress, representing Brazil, Ecuador and Haiti, 1964–1967. AUTHOR: "Inflation and Balanced Growth," pp. 82–103, in *Economic Development for Latin America*, ed., H. S. Ellis (London: Macmillan, 1961). Portuguese edition (Mexico, D.F.: Fondo de Cultura, 1960). "Two Views on Inflation in Latin America," in *Latin American Issues*, ed., A. O. Hirschman (New York: Twentieth Century Fund, 1961). *Reflections on Latin American Development* (Austin, Texas: University of Texas Press, 1967). Numerous articles in Brazilian daily papers. Numerous contributions to APEC, 1963–1968. HONORS: Honorary LL.D., New York University.

Mário Henrique Simonsen, b. 1935, State of Guanabara, Brazil. Professor in the Analytical Economics course, Conselho Nacional de Economia, since 1959. Professor and consultant in the Instituto Brasileiro de Economia, Fundação Getúilo Vargas, since 1959 and 1961, respectively; and Director of the School of Postgraduate Studies, the same, since 1965. DEGREES: Degree of Civil Engineering, University of Brazil, 1957. Degree of Economist, University of Rio de Janeiro, 1963. EARLIER POSITIONS: Technical consultant, Economic Department of the National Confederation of Industry, 1961–65. Director of CREDISAN, 1962–63. Consultant of CONSULTEC, since 1960. AUTHOR: "Notes on the Controversy between Monetarists and Structuralists" (presented to the 1963 Conference on Inflation and Growth, Rio de Janeiro) in *Inflation in Latin America* (New Haven: Yale University Press, 1964). *The Experience of Inflation in Brazil* (Rio de Janeiro: Instituto de Pesquisa e Estudos Sociais, 1964). *The Brazilian Capital Market* (Rio de Janeiro: Escritorio de Pesquisa Aplicada, 1965). *Micro-economic Theory*, Vol. I and II (Rio de Janeiro: Fundação Getúlio Vargas, 1968). Numerous articles in newspapers and journals.

Gordon W. Smith, b. 1934, Pittsfield, Illinois. Assistant Research Economist, Brazil Development Assistance Program, University of California, Rio de Janeiro, 1965–1967; Berkeley, 1967–1968. DEGREES: Bachelor of Arts, Washington University, St. Louis, Missouri, 1956. Doctor of Philosophy, Harvard University, 1966. EARLIER POSITIONS: Research Assistant, Washington University, 1958–1959. Research Assistant, Harvard University, 1959. Teaching Fellow, Harvard University, 1959–1961. AUTHOR: *Marketing and Economic Development: A Brazilian Case Study* (Rio de Janeiro: Fundação Getúlio Vargas, 1968). "Agricultura e O Plano Trienal," *Revista Brasileira de Economia*, December 1962. HONORS: Phi Beta Kappa, Arnold J. Lien prize, Washington University, 1956. Earhart Fellow in Economics, 1959–1960. Bliss Fellow in Latin American Studies, Harvard University, 1961–1965.

Willy van Rijckeghem, b. 1935, Ghent, Belgium. Visiting Associate Research Economist, Brazil Development Assistance Program, University of California, Rio de Janeiro, 1965–1967. DEGREES: Bachelor of Economics, University of Ghent, 1956. Master of Economics, University of Ghent, 1958. Doctor of Economics, University of Ghent, 1961. EARLIER POSITIONS: Research Fellow, Centre National de la Recherche Scientifique, Paris, 1961. Visiting Research Associate, University of Oslo, 1963. Visiting Assocate Professor, University of North Carolina, 1963–1964. Research Director, University of Ghent, 1964. Advisor, Consejo Nacional de Desarrollo, Buenos Aires, Harvard University Development Advisory Service Project, 1964–1965. AUTHOR: *De meting van het publiciteitseffekt* (Ghent, 1961). With G. Maynard: "Stabilization Policy in an Inflationary Economy: The Argentine Case," *Development Policy, Theory and Practice*, ed., G. Papanek (Cambridge, Mass.: Harvard University Press, 1968). Articles in *Cahiers Economiques de Bruxelles, Weltwirtschaftliches Archiv, Southern Economic Journal, Applied Statistics, Econometrica. Review of Economics and Statistics*. HONORS: Honorary Fellow, Belgian American Educational Foundation, 1964. Prize of Vereniging voor Economie, 1967 (Belgium).

Preface

Howard S. Ellis

The present volume was occasioned by the presence in
Rio de Janeiro over the period 1965–1967 of a group of pre-
dominantly young economists who constituted a mission of the
United States Agency for International Development and the
University of California at Berkeley. The main purposes of
the mission were to assist an agency of the government of Brazil,
the Office (now Institute) of Applied Economic Research, in
the gathering and analysis of economic facts for the use of the
Ministry of Planning and Economic Coordination and in formulating the Ten Year Economic Plan. The aspirations, frustra-
tions, and accomplishments of this vast and many-hued
country in its pursuit of development stirred the imagination of
these scholars. This book of essays is the outcome of a desire on
their part and on the part of the cooperating Brazilian economists to set down some of the results of their experience and
studies for the possible benefit of the economic progress and
welfare of the country, the largest and in some crucial respects
the most richly endowed of Latin America.

Being fully cognizant of the limits upon knowledge of a
country's economy, on the part of foreigners, and of the number
of facets which any one person or any half-dozen persons could
treat authoritatively, the members of the "California group"
resolved to enlist the help of Brazilian economists. This re-
cruiting venture proved to be most successful, the cooperating

Brazilians ranging from a young economist, who collaborated
in the writing of one essay, to a former Minister of Finance,
the acknowledged dean of the economic profession in Brazil,
if not very probably of Latin America. Included in this company is a former Brazilian ambassador to the United States
who was Minister of Planning and Economic Coordination
1964–1967; an eminent professor, Minister of Finance during
those same years, which figure so largely in the essays; and
two other economists, variously distinguished, but having in
common their high positions in the leading economic research
institution of Brazil. Still another is an American economist,
not improperly thought of also as "Brazilian" through several
years' residence in that country, author of books and articles
pertaining to its economic development.

The qualifications of the American contributors to the
undertaking, one may perhaps venture to suggest, are not
limited to enthusiasm and imagination, essential though these
attributes be. All American participants have been special stu-
dents of economic development in the academic sense; all
have written articles, and some a book or books, on the subject;
all have had some previous contact with Latin American problems through research and study in the field or through the
literature; and several have some direct acquaintance with
countries in other continents and with their economic problems. The interested reader will find biographical notes on all
contributors, native and foreign, later in the book.

The title of the book indicates that it is not designed as
an encyclopedia or handbook. Indeed, it represents no pre-
conceived scheme; the participants were invited to choose a
theme of lively interest to themselves. Despite this latitude it
is evident, as the table of contents indicates, that there are
several definite foci of interest. But, to repeat, the volume is
not an encyclopedia; it does not pretend to cover the whole
economy of Brazil, and the essays are not mere recitations of
economic fact — however important it may be to distinguish
facts from conjectures or wishes — but in most cases present
a thesis or some challenging ideas concerning the meaning of
the facts and their significance for policy. Thus the book does
not represent any single methodology, style and organization,

or economic philosophy. Such diversity is able to portray the multifaceted Brazilian economic life more richly than if all contributions had been poured from the same mold.

These characteristics are evident from the outset, in Professor Gudin's sketch of Brazil's recent economic history. From the perspective of his 82 years, an analytical economist as well as an active participant in the economic development of his country, he regards that development as marked chiefly by industrialization, inflation, and government paternalism, all of which have failed to bring to the average Brazilian the benefits to be expected of development.

Part II presents an array of factual information on the structure of Brazilian economy, both industrial and agricultural, but each essay embodies some challenging ideas. For industry, Dr. Bergsman points to its extraordinary growth in Brazil as a factor in gross domestic product, attributing this growth to protection against foreign competition, public investment, and investment subsidies, working through import substitution and the building-up of infrastructure. Thus Dr. Bergsman shares much common ground with Professor Gudin as to moving causes; but while Gudin decries this nexus, Bergsman finds that it gave rise to reasonably balanced growth. Both writers deplore the small degree to which industrialization improved the employment and real-wage situation.

Another generally optimistic retrospective of recent Brazilian economic history is presented in Professor Werner Baer's inquiry into the steel industry. Over the past two decades, this industry has risen from small beginnings to a viable level of efficiency compared with foreign sources, and the indications are for a thriving future. This is the more important for Brazil, Professor Baer demonstrates, because of the strongly favorable stimuli of steel production (forward and backward linkages, in the economist's jargon) on the rest of the economy.

Professor Chacel's extensive statistical study of agriculture leads to the conclusion — at variance with an indictment of the latifundia for uneconomical operation which has been widespread in Latin America — that the minifundia are equally inefficient. Also at variance with another bit of orthodoxy is Chacel's finding that agricultural production in Brazil is much more a function of expanding area under cultivation than of capital intensity.

While Parts I and II are concerned with some of the central substance of development itself, Part III looks first into some of the distortions of the economy which have resulted from inflation and growth, and, second, into certain foreign trade factors which have helped or hindered development and which may do so in the future.

First come three essays which treat the monetary, financial, and price aspects of inflation, which has been — for better or for worse — the constant companion of Brazil's efforts toward economic progress. Professor Simonsen, reviewing the history of inflation and the character of Brazilian credit institutions, finds that the irrational and crippling maximum-interest law has been in large measure circumvented in the short-term-capital market by various devices of the banks and by the famous *letras de câmbio* of the credit and finance companies. But the long-term capital market has been devastated by the risks imposed by inflation, partly rectified recently by "monetary correction." The stock market suffers from numerous fundamental defects, intensified by inflation.

Professor Bulhões confronts the same problems from the vantage point of the Ministry of Finance. He shows that the new, highly successful Treasury Obligations with monetary correction have not adversely competed with private securities. On the contrary, their effect should be beneficial on the capital markets if the proceeds of Treasury Obligations with monetary correction are not simply dissipated in increased central government expenditure. Monetary correction has been helpful in many contexts but is not a cure-all for the evils attending inflation.

The essay written by the editor presents the thesis that "corrective inflation" under the Castello Branco government was a success. That it could have succeeded in still greater degree can scarcely be denied, but economic policy was not directed to checking inflation alone. Much effort was also expended upon correcting price distortions over a wide range (commodity prices, utility rates, exchange rates, interest, etc.) and this involved, in some cases, raising a price faster than the average inflation. Also, much attention was given to basic institutional reforms for the long run. The leading roles in reducing inflation were played by fiscal measures and wage restraints.

Dr. Gordon Smith advances the thesis that Brazilian agricultural policy has relied excessively upon market stimuli, to the almost complete neglect of education, research, land reform, and other structural factors. He proceeds to an analysis of four parts of government policy, all expected to improve agriculture through market stimuli. First, the efforts to improve marketing through cheaper transportation and better storage facilities did raise output significantly. Second, the substantial sums for fertilizer subsidies paid off quite meagerly in direct influence on production; the increased level of output after the subsidies was largely due to a learning-by-doing process induced by lower fertilizer prices. A third part of the program, subsidized credit for agriculture, would have yielded considerably more if it had been correlated with technological supervision. Finally, the minimum price program after 1963 was too erratic to be effective.

Part III concludes with two essays which explore some of the foreign-trade aspects of economic development. Dr. Baerresen's study of the participation of Brazil in the Latin American Free Trade Association comes to a favorable judgment with regard to its influence on Brazil's economic growth. The test period, 1962–1965, yielded positive results (except for 1963) as to the relative volume of Brazil's trade with the LAFTA region when compared with that of other Latin American countries. Also, with respect to the portion of the study devoted to commodity categories, again a favorable result emerges (except for 1963) regarding Brazil's exports of manufactures. This augurs well for a successful changeover from exclusive reliance upon import substitution to export promotion for economic development in the future.

Since the rapid growth of the Brazilian economy in recent decades has been chiefly related to import substitution, Dr. Morley's econometric study of import-demand functions supplies the quantitative explanation of the relations between imports and economic development. One of the more important implications of his analysis is the demonstration of the sensitivity of imports to the growth rate of the economy. Since imports tend to grow somewhat more rapidly than output, even a considerable expansion of exports will still leave a certain margin to be covered by import substitution, for example in petroleum production and wheat. Another important finding is the low price elasticity of imports, for which he offers plausible explanations. This low elasticity, he believes, would point to the dubious efficacy of devaluations in reducing balance of payments deficits. However, Morley's analysis does not extend to the effect of devaluation in encouraging exports.

A chief link between past and future is formed by economic planning, the subject matter of Part IV, within which the progression is from past to present to future. Ambassador Campos' essay presents the retrospect from the vantage point of one who has been engaged in planning and the execution of plans. After delineating the ideological, technical, and institutional obstacles and objectives of planning, he reviews specific Brazilian plans from the Second World War to the present. These include the "bottleneck" approach of the Joint Brazil-United States Development Commission (1949–1953); the "growing points" line of the National Bank for Economic Development (1952); Kubitschek's National Development Council (1956); Goulart's Plano Trienal (1962–1964); and the Castello Branco Program for Government Economic Action and his Ten-Year Plan (1964–1967). In his concluding section, "The Road Ahead," the author draws together the lessons of experience, emphasizing the human factors which condition the success of economic planning.

The present time is the focus of Dr. Abouchar's research into the transportation situation in Brazil. In a preliminary analysis, he compares three types of economy — mature market, Soviet type, and underdeveloped market — concluding that a rate structure based upon full costs is the appropriate one. This judgment is borne out with specific reference to Brazil when the operation of this principle is compared with other conceivable pricing rules, such as average and marginal cost, and the encouragement of infant industries. Abouchar appraises the present rate structure of railroad, motor vehicle, coastal, and air transport, concluding with the benefits to be had by putting each on a basis of self-support.

Professor van Rijckeghem's essay is marked by two distinctive features: it incorporates the first complete input-output table for the Brazilian economy, based on 1959 data; and it is unique among the essays in this book in presenting conclusions regarding the character of the Three-Year Plan for 1968–1970. The consistency model itself, which could be applied to other countries besides Brazil, includes consumption functions, product and distribution matrices, input-output elasticities, and capital-output elasticities. Applying the apparatus to Brazilian data, van Rijckeghem provides the "happy ending" to the story of these essays by his conclusion that the planned acceleration of growth to 7 percent per annum seems realistically attainable.

In conclusion, the editor wishes to bespeak his obligation and thanks in several quarters. Special acknowledgment is due to Professor Gudin for his encouragement and sage advice. Professor Werner Baer played an important role in the initiation and early evolution of the volume. To Dr. Alan Abouchar belong my thanks for carrying on direct communication with writers and the publisher in Rio de Janeiro after my departure. Antecedent to the making of this book lie the support of the California project by USAID, and the wise counsel and cooperation of its officials, especially Dr. John H. Kaufmann. Warm thanks are due to various Brazilian government officials, including those of IPEA, and to Brazilian economists, including those participating as authors of essays in this volume. The views expressed in these essays are those of the individual authors and do not necessarily reflect the opinions of the IPEA or USAID. In the preparation of the manuscript, the secretaries in the Brazil Development Assistance Program in Berkeley, Mrs. Julia Cleland and Mrs. Janie Prior, displayed exemplary concern and fortitude. Last, but only chronologically, the editors of the University of California Press, Dr. Grant Barnes and Dr. Max Knight, have contributed to the final product in several important respects. The figures were prepared by Mrs. Frances Pemantle.

Commonly Abbreviated Names
of Brazilian Government Agencies,
Other Public Organizations, etc.

ABCAR: Associação Brazileira de Crédito e Assistência Rural
Brazilian Association for Rural Credit and Technical Assistance

BNDE: Banco Nacional de Desenvolvimento Econômico
National Bank for Economic Development

CACEX: Carteira de Comércio Exterior
Department [of the Banco do Brasil] for Foreign Commerce

CADE: Comissão Administrativo para Defesa Econômico
Administrative Committee for Economic Protection

CFP: Comissão de Financiamento de Produção
Committee for the Financing of Production

CONEP: Comissão Nacional de Estimulo a Estabilização de Preços
National Committee to Promote Price Stabilization

CONSPLAN: Conselho para Planejamento
Advisory Planning Council

COPLAN: Comissão para Planejamento
Planning Committee

CPA: Conselho Política de Aduaneira
Council on Tariff Policy

CREAI: Carteira de Crédito Agricola e Industrial
Department [of the Banco do Brasil] for Agricultural and Industrial Credit

CREGI: Carteira de Crédito Geral
Department [of the Banco do Brasil] for General Credit

DASP: Departamento Administrativo de Serviço Público
Administrative Department for Public Service

DNER: Departamento Nacional de Estradas de Rodagem
National Highway Department

EPEA: Escritório [later Instituto] de Pesquisa Econômica Aplicada
Office [later Institute] of Applied Economic Research

FINAME: Fundo de Financiamento para Aquisição de Máquinas de Equipamento Industriais
Fund for Financing the Acquisition of Industrial Machines and Equipment
Fund for Financing the Acquisition of Industrial Machines and Equipment

FINEP: Fundo de Financiamento de Estudos de Projetos e Programmas
Fund for Financing the Study of Projects and Programs

FGV: Fundação Getúlio Vargas
Getulio Vargas Foundation

FUNDECE: Fundo de Democratização do Capital das Emprésas
Fund for Democratizing the Capital of Firms

FUNFERTIL: Fundo de Estímulo Financeiro au Uso de Fertilizantes e Supplimentos Minerais

IBE: Instituto Brasileiro de Economia
         Brazilian Institute of Economics

IBGE: Instituto Brasileiro de Geografia e Estatistica
         Brazilian Institute of Geography and Statistics

IBRA: Instituto Brasileiro para Reforma Agraria
         Brazilian Institute for Agrarian Reform

ORTN: Obrigações Reajustáveis de Tesouro Nacional
         Adjustable Bonds of the National Treasury

PAEG: Plano de Ação Econômico do Govêrno
         Government Plan for Economic Action

RFFSA: Rêde Ferroviaria Federal, S.A.
         Federal Railway System, Inc.

SEEF: Serviço de Estatistica Econômica e Financiera
         Service of Economic and Financial Statistics

SNI: Servicio Nacional de Investimentos
         National Investment Service

SUDENE: Superintêndencia do Desenvolvimento do
         Nordeste
         Superintendency of Development of the
         Northeast

SUMOC: Superintêndencia de Moeda e do Crédito
         Superintendency of Money and Credit

SUNAB: Superintêndencia Nacional do Abasticimento
         National Superintendency of Food Supply

Throughout the book, GNP has been used in place of PIB (Producto Interno Bruto), the usual designation in Brazil. They are conceptually the same, but statistical interpretations differ slightly.

All cruzeiro figures, unless otherwise noted, are in terms of the "old" cruzeiro, i.e. at the exchange rate of Cr$2200 = U.S.$ 1.00 prevailing before the devaluation of February 1967.

Part I

CHAPTER 1

The Chief Characteristics of the
Postwar Economic Development of Brazil

Eugenio Gudin

The purpose of this essay is to outline the salient trends of the post-World-War-II economic history of Brazil: industrialization, inflation, and the growing predominance of government in economic life.

INDUSTRIALIZATION

The postwar years, especially 1950–1962, mark the most intensive industrial development of the Brazilian economy. The index of gross national product (in real terms) rose from 100 in 1949 to 211 in 1963; the index of industrial production rose to 318, that of agricultural production to only 178.[1]

The extent to which imported industrial goods were replaced by those produced domestically is shown in Table 1. Imports of nondurable consumer goods declined from 7.5 percent of total imports in 1948 to between 5 and 6 percent in 1958–1960, while imports of durable consumer goods fell precipitiously from 9.8 percent in 1948 to 1.2 percent in 1961, and imports of capital goods from 39.3 percent in 1948 to 31.6 percent in 1961.

[1] *Revista Brasileira de Economia*, March 1966.

Equipment imports (Table 2) fell from 24 percent in 1947 to 15.6 percent in 1959, while domestic production of equipment rose from 29.9 percent to 46.8 percent.

The categories of industrial production that more than doubled from 1950 to 1960 were metallurgy, machinery, elec-

TABLE 1. IMPORTS BY MAJOR CATEGORIES
(percent)

	Consumer Goods		Producer Goods			
Year	Durable	Non-durable	Fuels and lubricants	Raw materials and intermediate products	Capital goods	Total
1948	9.8	7.5	13.0	30.4	39.3	100.0
1949	8.2	7.4	13.4	34.3	36.7	100.0
1950	6.4	7.0	13.7	35.9	37.0	100.0
1951	9.3	6.6	11.4	31.9	40.8	100.0
1952	6.0	6.8	13.1	28.2	45.9	100.0
1953	2.1	7.4	20.1	38.4	32.0	100.0
1954	2.6	6.4	18.3	42.3	30.4	100.0
1955	1.7	7.6	22.8	40.7	27.2	100.0
1956	1.7	7.9	24.6	39.3	26.5	100.0
1957	1.9	6.4	19.0	35.6	37.1	100.0
1958	2.1	4.7	21.7	33.2	38.3	100.0
1959	2.0	4.3	16.3	32.7	41.7	100.0
1960	1.4	5.6	22.2	37.4	33.4	100.0
1961	1.2	6.2	22.7	38.3	31.6	100.0

Source: ECLA, *Economic Bulletin for Latin America*, May 1964.

trical equipment, transportation equipment, paper, and rubber. In some cases (for example, durable consumer goods), imports ceased almost entirely. In these and other categories, possibilities for import substitution have been exhausted, and further development now depends on the capacity to export.

The proclamation of the republic in 1889 was followed by serious political and economic disturbances that lasted for more that ten years. Then, from 1902 to 1910, Brazil went through a period of extraordinary development: yellow fever was suppressed, the first large hydroelectric plants in Rio de Janeiro and São Paulo were built, industrialization began, mainly in textiles,[2] important ports were constructed, an exten-

---

[2] Editor's comment: One reader has pointed out, however, that a sub-

sive railway system was developed, the capital (Rio de Janeiro) was transformed into a modern city, and so forth. Some industries, especially textiles, shoes, and other consumer goods, developed considerably. The number of industrial employees almost doubled from 1907 to 1918, but the patterns of industrial production were more or less unchanged by growth. In

TABLE 2. FORMATION OF FIXED CAPITAL
(percent)

			Equipment		
Year	Total	Construction	Total	Domestic production	Imports
1947	100.0	46.1	53.9	29.9	24.0
1948	100.0	42.3	57.7	35.4	22.3
1949	100.0	40.6	59.4	39.0	20.4
1950	100.0	38.1	61.9	43.7	18.2
1951	100.0	37.8	62.2	40.4	21.8
1952	100.0	38.8	61.2	39.9	21.3
1953	100.0	42.8	57.2	43.7	13.5
1954	100.0	35.8	64.2	46.3	17.9
1955	100.0	37.2	62.8	47.8	15.0
1956	100.0	33.1	66.9	53.1	13.8
1957	100.0	34.9	65.1	45.7	19.4
1958	100.0	37.3	62.7	45.4	17.3
1959	100.0	37.6	62.4	46.8	15.6

Source: Instituto Brasileiro de Economia, Fundação Getúlio Vargas.

1914, the country was not yet ready to "take off" industrially, and World War I had an unfavorable effect on Brazil's exports as well as on the inflow of foreign capital.

The Great Depression of the 1930's also affected the Brazilian economy adversely, especially the value of Brazil's coffee exports. In 1928 Brazil exported some 15 million bags of coffee at about US$ 23 cents a pound; in 1931–1932 about 15 million bags were again exported, but at 7 to 9 cents a pound. Brazil, during the 1930's, amply confirmed the belief that during a serious depression the industrialized countries suffer from unemployment and curtailment of production, but not from a large reduction in prices; while the primary producing coun-

stantial industrial beginning had been made in textiles in the nineteenth century.

tries do not experience a large reduction in production or employment, but a very serious decline in the prices of their exports. Brazil's coffee exports did not diminish appreciably, but the fall in price of about two-thirds seriously worsened the terms of trade and Brazil's capacity to import. The 1930 rate of exchange, Cr$8.3 per dollar,* fell to Cr$18.7 in 1939 (when, with the cooperation of the Export-Import Bank of Washington, the construction of the Volta Redonda steel plant was begun).

During World War II the heavy demand for exports, coupled with the impossibility of importing substantially, resulted in an increase in Brazil's foreign reserves, from about US$ 70 million to some US$ 700 million in 1945. The rate of exchange of Cr$18 to the dollar was kept unaltered, because of the belief (later vindicated) that with the ending of the war it would have to be raised again. In fact, in 1945-1947, imports increased by 40 percent in quantity and 80 percent in dollar value, with an appreciable deficit in the balance of payments.

Out of the US$ 700 million reserves available to Brazil in 1946, about US$ 350 million were in gold, US$ 262 million in sterling, and the rest in dollars and other currencies. The amount in sterling was not freely usable, Great Britain having declared its inability to pay except by transferring its capital investments; and the Brazilian government, pressed by public opinion, did not touch the gold reserve. On the other hand, the wholesale price index in the United States rose from around 43 (1957-1959 = 100) in 1940 to 81.2 in 1947, so that the purchasing power of Brazil's reserves was reduced in real value by nearly 50 percent. This reduction, coupled with Great Britain's inability to pay, explains why Brazil benefited little from its war exports and accumulation of foreign reserves.

These circumstances led to the meetings during 1949 and 1950, in Rio de Janeiro, between the Brazilian foreign minister, Raul Fernandes, and the American ambassador, Herschell Johnson. Their conversations resulted in the creation of the

* If not otherwise noted, all cruzeiro figures throughout this volume are in terms of the "old" cruzeiro, i.e. at the exchange rate of Cr$2200 = U.S. $1.00 prevailing before the devaluation of February 1967.

Brazilian-American Mixed Committee (Comissão Mixta Brasil–Estados Unidos) to study and promote Brazil's economic development. The committee was not directed to plan Brazil's industrialization; its main object was the development of the country's infrastructure: railways, electric power, and so forth. In fact, it may be said that Brazilian industrialization was not planned; it grew from a set of circumstances, the first of which was exchange control and the special preference given to imports of equipment and machinery. Exchange control was established in June 1947 and lasted in its original form until January 1953. During that time, the exchange rate was kept at 18.7 to the dollar in spite of a rise of 67 percent in the cost of living; imports were strictly controlled by the concession of "licenses," which naturally acquired a high value. Incidentally, it is remarkable that under such control corruption was kept at a minimum.

With the outbreak of the Korean War, because of the fear that it would turn into a new world war, imports were demanded in excess of available resources. Imports grew from US$ 950 million in 1949 to 1,703 million in 1951 and 1,702 in 1952. Compensatory financing for the corresponding balance-of-payments deficits amounted to US$ 291 million in 1951 and 615 million in 1952. A good deal of the increased imports were for industrial machinery and equipment. This marked the beginning of the industrialization period.

Thus it came about that Brazilian industrialization during the 1950's was paid for not out of the reserves accumulated during World War II, but by the haphazard financing that followed it from 1950 onward.

In October 1953 a new system of multiple exchange rates was adopted; import licenses were eliminated and replaced by auction sales of exchange. Imports were divided into five categories according to need, and each auction corresponded to a specific category. However, some imports were put in a "special category" outside the auction system, and were entitled to the "official rate of exchange." "Surtaxes" might be added in some cases, as determined by the Superintendency of Money and Credit (SUMOC). "Equipment considered essential for economic development" was included in this special category. When the auction system was put into force in 1953, the basic rate for the dollar was Cr$18.72, while the free market rate (created in January 1953) was Cr$43.32.

In 1953, imports fell to US$ 1,116 million, compared to US$ 1,703 and US$ 1,702 million in 1951 and 1952. The deficit of the balance of payments on current account fell to US$ 31 million, compared to US$ 468 and US$ 707 million in 1951 and 1952. At the end of the Vargas government (August 1954), the exchange situation was desperate. A Vargas Eximbank loan (1953) of US$ 300 million, plus a post-Vargas (November 1954) loan of $200 million granted by a group of American bankers and guaranteed by Brazilian gold reserves, were barely sufficient to cover the most pressing debts. (These data on the Brazilian exchange situation in the years 1947–1955 are presented as the basis of the argument which follows, to show how costly industrialization was to Brazil.)

Imports of equipment and machinery were largely responsible for the extraordinarily high import levels of 1951 and 1952, and for the corresponding deficits in the Brazilian balance of payments on current account covered by "compensatory financing." These deficits were US$ 291 million in 1951, US$ 615 million in 1952, and US$ 203 million in 1954, a heavy burden to be supported by the country in later years.

Late in 1954, and in 1955, the scarcity of foreign exchange was further aggravated by the collapse of coffee sales: coffee was allowed to reach very high quotations in the New York market, which subsequently violently declined. However, the firm financial policies against inflation and toward achieving an equilibrium in the balance of payments adopted by the new government (under President Café Filho) created a feeling of confidence in the economy, and inspired an increase in foreign private investments. To ease the free entry of these investments, the government issued a Money and Credit Instruction, numbred 113, early in 1955. This Instruction granted no exchange subsidy whatsoever, nor any subsidy either in customs duties or in any other way, but simply removed bureaucratic and other obstacles then prevailing against the entry of foreign investments.[3] Several foreign firms, among them Mercedes-

---

[3] Editor's comment: An alternative view is that SUMOC 113 did grant an exchange subsidy. See Lincoln Gordon and Engelbert L. Grom-

Benz, Volkswagen, Dunlop, and Platt, proceeded with their schemes for investment in Brazil. Instruction 113 was slightly modified two years later by Decree 42,820. The value of foreign investments made under Instruction 113 is shown in Table 3. These investments were pure entries of foreign capital, not involving any provision of exchange whatsoever. They certainly did not add to the burdens that resulted from the imports of industrial machinery in the period 1951–1954.

TABLE 3. FOREIGN INVESTMENTS UNDER INSTRUCTION 113
(thousands of US$)

1955	31,315	1958	82,504
1956	55,793	1959	65,844
1957	108,184	1960	106,823

Source: SUMOC *Bulletin*, May 1961, Table 5.1.

Brazilian industrialists, however, protested against Instruction 113 as discriminatory, favoring foreign industrialists over Brazilians. They maintained that if the foregn investor were obliged first to transfer his funds to Brazil at the free market rate and then to bid for exchange under one of the above-mentioned "categories of import," he would suffer a loss that would make his investment less attractive. In other words, they considered that a sort of punishment in the form of a loss in exchange should be forced on the foreign investor for the privilege of investing in Brazil, though he was not concerned with any exchange transaction at all (he simply brought in machinery and equipment).

The exchange situation in 1955 did not permit the supply of foreign exchange to Brazilian industrialists on the terms they wished, but with the resurgence of coffee exports in 1956 the Kubitschek government granted extraordinary facilities for industrialization, although again, as in 1951–1954, at the expense of the nation. The scheme consisted in the government's guaranteeing to importers of industrial machinery and equipment (through "suppliers' credits" payable in installments over

mers, *United States Manufacturing Investment in Brazil: The Impact of Brazilian Government Policies 1946–1960* (Cambridge, Mass.: Harvard University Press (1962).

a period of from three to seven years) not only assurance of
the supply of exchange, but an especially favorable rate of
exchange, the "cost of exchange," basically the exchange rate
paid to coffee exporters for their bills.[4]

The exchange advantage granted holders of these suppliers' credits can be measured by taking the difference be-

TABLE 4. FINANCING AT "COST OF EXCHANGE RATE"
(thousands of US$)

1957	260,505
1958	396,987
1959	326,801
1960	242,051
Total	1,226,344

Source: Computed by the author.

TABLE 5. DIFFERENCE BETWEEN MARKET RATE AND
COST OF EXCHANGE RATE (PLUS SURTAXES)

Year	Market rate	Cost of exchange rate plus surtax		Difference
1955	73.54	(3–23–55)	33.82	39.72
1956	75.67	(for the year)	33.82	41.85
1957	78.00	(9–12–57)	43.83	86.18
1958	130.00	(5– 9–58)	51.82	78.18
1958	130.00	(10– 3–58)	70.00	60.00
1959	159.83	(1– 9–59)	80.00	79.83
1960	199.26	(12–31–60)	100.00	99.26

Source: Computed by the author.

tween the market rate of exchange and the cost of exchange
rate, plus surtaxes established by SUMOC. These figures show
that, during the period 1955–1960, nearly one-half of the cruzeiro cost of the equipment and machinery imported by Brazilian industry was paid by the nation.

The resulting subsidy can be measured by multiplying
the differences in rates by the value of the suppliers' credits
imports shown in Table 6. This subsidy, amounting to nearly

[4] The foreign price of coffee, if fully paid to the coffee producer,
would not only cause an excess of production still worse than it already
was, but a terrific inflation. Hence the especially low rate of exchange for
coffee export bills.

one billion dollars, does not include the benefits of the same nature mentioned above for the period 1951–1953, through the grant of import licenses for machinery and equipment at the parity rate (Cr$18.72 to the dollars, when the free rate was twice as much).

Such was one of the costs paid by the nation, by consumers in general and by agriculturists in particular, for industrialization. But that was not all. Other costs were entailed by guaranteeing domestic industry a monopoly on the domestic market. This monopoly was assured by the customs tariff wall,

TABLE 6. SUBSIDY TO INDUSTRY
(millions; new cruzeiros converted to US$ at market rate)

Year	Cr$	US$
1955	3.178	43.2
1956	10.588	139.9
1957	22.493	172.7
1958	27.429	211.0
1959	26.104	163.2
1960	24.021	120.6
	Total US$	850.6

Source: Computed by the author.

which made imports prohibitively expensive, and by the prevailing inflation (in which demand largely exceeded available output).

Until 1957, customs duties were regulated by the 1934 tariff expressed in specific sums of cruzeiros. With the depreciation of the cruzeiro from 1940 onward, the protection provided by this specific tariff gradually diminished; but this hardly reduced tariff protection in general because exchange controls and import licenses never permitted imports to compete with domestic production. However, the new 1957 ad valorem tariff (anything from 60 to 100 percent) legally consolidated domestic industry's monopoly of the Brazilian market. This monopoly is largely responsible for the high prices of most industrial products in Brazil—when compared, on a stable-currency basis, with other countries. It would, however, be unfair not to mention that taxation by the federal and state governments also contributes to high prices. The automobile industry claims that nearly 50 percent of its costs consists in taxes and interest on turnover capital. It is most regrettable that the Ministry of Industry and Commerce has never properly investigated and clarified this important point.

The growth of long- and short-term Brazilian foreign liabilities during the main period of industrialization is shown in Tables 7 and 8. The tables reveal an increase of about one billion dollars in long-term liabilities, and of about half a billion in short-term ones, from 1956 to 1963.

TABLE 7. LONG-TERM LIABILITIES
(millions of US$)

Year end	Compensatory financing	Suppliers credits	Total
1955	1,044	683	1,682
1956	918	780	1,698
1957	862	962	1,824
1958	999	1,011	2,010
1959	902	1,126	2,028
1960	913	1,115	2,027
1961	1,153	1,326	2,479
1962	1,203	1,394	2,597
1963	1,221	1,431	2,652
1964	1,190	1,441	2,631
1965	1,350	1,487	2,837
1966	1,285	1,655	2,940

Source: Central Bank, *Reports to IMF.*

This heavy burden is not all attributable to industrialization. The construction of Brasília (even though it was financed almost entirely in cruzeiros, through large government internal deficits) and other ventures have their share in the violent aggravation of external indebtedness.

Brazilian industrialization thus far has not been an indisputable step in the direction of improving the standard of living of the Brazilian people. Imported articles have been replaced by those domestically produced, but at much higher prices. Under the inflationary demand that has prevailed in Brazil for the last fifteen years, the Brazilian consumer is at the mercy of the producer where price is concerned. That almost every industrial product, from ordinary textiles to heavy machinery, is now produced in the country may be very comforting to the pride of the nationalists, who often refer to this fact as Brazil's "economic liberation." But if the meaning of economic development is the gradual improvement of the people's standard of living, the industrialization thus far realized is of doubtful worth.

It should be said, of course, that the costs and prices of any industrial products could be considerably reduced if taxes were not so heavy and rates of interest not so high. Be that as it may, there is no doubt that, if Brazil wishes to foster

TABLE 8. SHORT-TERM LIABILITIES
(*millions of US$*)

Year end	Swaps	Commercial arrears	Oil companies	Credit lines	Others	Total
1955	143.3	n.a.	n.a.	3.5	103.1	249.9
1956	122.7	n.a.	n.a.	n.a.	119.8	242.5
1957	143.1	n.a.	n.a.	21.0	84.2	248.3
1958	112.7	n.a.	n.a.	52.9	101.7	267.3
1959	227.7	n.a.	n.a.	28.5	152.8	409.0
1960	275.4	68.0	n.a.	52.0	232.4	627.8
1961	347.6	183.7	n.a.	50.5	166.1	747.9
1962	394.2	128.0	35.4	15.5	58.0	631.1
1963	364.2	121.8	55.1	n.a.	99.5	640.6
1964	312.7	228.8	5.5	0.6	17.9	565.5

Source: Central Bank, *Reports to IMF.*

its economic development, sooner or later it will have to face the second step of its industrialization, reducing costs and prices (including refund of taxes) in order to be able to compete in the field of exports. This is why analysis of costs, and of the possibilities of improving productivity, should be the most pressing item for the joint efforts of the government and the industrialists.

INFLATION

Political Causes

In his paper for the 1956 Rome Congress of the International Economic Association, Professor Gottfried Haberler writes: "It is not surprising that poor and backward countries, when they make up and set their minds to develop in a hurry and catch up with the more developed countries, are continually tempted to overspend their meagre resources and to live beyond their means."[5]

Postwar inflation in Brazil, however, is fundamentally a by-product of the political evolution that has taken place during the past twenty or thirty years, as the old oligarchical type of government has been replaced by governments truly elected by the masses.

In the old type of government the president, in whose hands a great deal of power was and still is vested, was chosen

TABLE 9. COST OF LIVING
(STATE OF GUANABARA)

Year	Index (December)	Annual rate of increase (percent)	Year	Index (December)	Annual rate of increase (percent)
1947	56.7	6.0	1957	224.0	13.4
1948	58.7	3.5	1958	262.7	17.3
1949	62.2	6.0	1959	399.4	52.0
1950	69.1	11.1	1960	494.3	23.8
1951	76.6	10.9	1961	707.7	43.2
1952	92.5	20.8	1962	1,099.0	55.3
1953	108.0	16.8	1963	1,985.0	80.6
1954	136.3	26.2	1964	3,704.0	86.0
1955	162.4	19.1	1965	5,385.0	45.0
1956	197.6	21.7	1966	7,600.0	41.0

Source: Fundação Getúlio Vargas.

by agreement between the oligarchical groups of the most influential states. Elections were a pure formality. Public opinion found expression in a free press and a small but vociferous minority in Congress. The president was not only automatically assured of the support of a large majority in Congress, but was entirely free from pressures coming from demagogues or labor syndicates.

Although this type of political structure could not last forever, it must be said that while it did last the integrity of administrations and of Congress was much superior to that of the elected democratic governments of today.

Today, governments can come into power only through

[5] In International Economic Association, *Stability and Progress in the World Economy*, Douglas Hague, editor (London: Macmillan, 1958), pp. 151–179.

genuine elections, that is, through intense electoral campaigns in which all kinds of promises to better the lot of the people are made. A candidate for the presidency has little chance to succeed without making many promises to influential members of his own party, and entering into quid pro quo arrangements with the many other parties.

This explains why the type and quality of government has deteriorated during the political evolution of Latin America. The worth of a president or a governor of a state, apart from

TABLE 10. MEANS OF PAYMENT

Year end	Millions of NCr$	Percentage increase	Year end	Millions of NCr$	Percentage increase
1947	46.538	—	1957	290.938	33.9
1948	50.063	7.6	1958	333.138	21.4
1949	58.265	16.4	1959	500.572	41.7
1950	78.322	34.4	1960	692.032	38.2
1951	90.749	15.1	1961	1,041.842	50.5
1952	104.052	14.8	1962	1,702.305	63.4
1953	124.069	19.1	1963	2,792.183	64.0
1954	151.474	22.1	1964	5,191.000	85.9
1955	177.922	17.4	1965	9,104.000	75.4
1956	217.283	22.1	1966	10,815.000	18.8

Source: Banco Central.

his political ability, is measured by what is called his "capacity to accomplish," that is, his ability to build or at least start the construction of roads, stadia, power plants, palaces, and so forth, *no matter what the price* in terms of increased indebtedness, distortion, and disorganization of the country's economy. Seriously unbalanced budgets are a natural consequence, and the mainspring of inflation.

During the early years of the Great Depression (1930–1936), in spite of a marked increase in means of payment prices did not rise appreciably. From 1936 to 1941 increases were quite moderate. It may be said that Brazilian inflation dates from 1941; the cost of living rose from 107 in 1940 (1938 = 100) to 190 in 1945, between 10 and 20 percent per year. It proceeded more or less at that rate until 1959 when (as a result of Kubitschek's extravagances) it jumped to 30 and 40 percent per year. With Goulart it rose to 50 percent in 1962, to more than 70 percent in 1963, and to 80 percent in 1964, when the revolution took place.

Taking 1953 = 100, the cost of living behaved as shown in Table 9. The evolution of the means of payment is shown in Table 10.

Structural Causes

It is alleged in some quarters, especially in the Economic Commission for Latin America (ECLA), that "for structural reasons" inflation in Latin America differs from that occurring in developed countries. Basically, the phenomenon of inflation is the same everywhere; inflation is the result of excessive expenditure compared to supply somewhere within the system. The main argument of the "structuralists" is that economic development leads to a change in relative prices because of structural transformation in the economic system. It would not be difficult, however, to show that even if such changes took place their impact on the rate of inflation would be negligible.

The only "structural" feature that may in fact contribute to inflation in the underdeveloped countries is their inelasticity of supply. In the developed countries, industry does not normally operate at 100 percent of capacity. The economic system can therefore respond to the inflationary impact of additional demand by increasing its industrial output. In the under-

TABLE 11. GOVERNMENT RECEIPTS, EXPENDITURES, AND CASH DEFICIT
(percent of GNP)

Year	Expenditures NCr$ millions	Receipts NCr$ millions	Deficit NCr$ millions	GNP NCr$ millions	Expenditures (percent of GNP)	Deficit (percent of GNP)
1954	50.5	46.5	4.0	552.2	9.1	0.7
1955	61.4	55.7	5.7	691.7	8.9	0.8
1956	93.4	74.1	19.3	884.4	10.6	2.2
1957	126.7	85.8	40.9	1,056.6	12.0	3.9
1958	146.2	117.8	28.4	1,310.0	11.2	2.2
1959	211.5	157.8	53.7	1,788.9	11.8	3.0
1960	297.5	219.8	77.7	2,385.6	12.5	3.3
1961	447.9	317.5	130.4	3,522.0	12.7	3.7
1962	778.7	497.8	280.9	5,586.8	13.9	5.0
1963	1,435.0	930.8	504.7	9,847.0	14.6	5.1

Source: Government accounts and Instituto Brasileiro de Economia.

TABLE 12. MINIMUM WAGE (STATE OF GUANABARA)

Date of readjustment		Minimum wage (NCr$ per month)	Increase as percent of previous wage	Increase (percent) in cost of living since previous readjustment
Jan.	1952	1.20	—	—
July	1954	2.40	100.0	54.4
Aug.	1956	3.80	58.3	51.4
Jan.	1959	6.00	57.9	47.8
Oct.	1960	9.60	60.0	70.0
Oct.	1961	13.44	40.0	42.2
Jan.	1963	21.00	56.3	67.1
Feb.	1964	42.00	100.0	109.5

Source: Fundação Getúlio Vargas.

developed countries, however, due to capital scarcity and normal full employment, appreciable spare capacity is not available in industry, the transportation system, or the power supply. Agricultural output, as is well known, is not elastic either. This is why underdeveloped countries may be somewhat more vulnerable to inflation than developed countries.

Direct Causes

As to the direct causes of inflation in Brazil, the figures already cited in this essay are sufficiently revealing. The main cause (Table 11) was the excess of federal expenditures over receipts. The construction of Brasília alone is estimated to have cost around one billion dollars.

Of the two other causes of inflation — expansion of credit and wage inflation — it may be said, generally, that they resulted from the increase in means of payment, which in turn resulted from the government's printing money. In fact, bank credit in real terms remained practically stationary from 1951 to 1964, as shown in Table 17 below. It may also be said of wages that they rose with the increases in the cost of living resulting from federal deficits (see Table 12). Except for the 1954 wage push (forced by Goulart under the Vargas administration) discrepancies in the readjustment of minimum wages were not important.

Goulart's demagogic influence made itself felt long before 1961 when he reached the presidency; during both the Vargas

and the Kubitschek presidencies (1951–1960) he was busy
building personal support among workers in the sectors he
considered vital for political domination. These were mainly
oil (Petrobrás) and transport, both maritime (including ports)
and rail. Through control of these industries he could, if he
so wished, paralyze the country, by stopping all means of transportation and ceasing to supply gasoline and oil even to the
army. In these sectors Goulart made sure wages were double
or more than double wages in similar activities in other sectors.

Effects

The postwar inflation was very harmful to private enterprise in Brazil. Profits in depreciated cruzeiros were compared
with capital expressed in cruzeiros of much greater value, of
ten or more years earlier, and income tax was thus often
charged on illusory "extraordinary profits." Income-tax authorities allowed no provision for the depreciation of the cruzeiro,
while commercial bank credit, as mentioned above, was kept
scarce. Capital depreciation, calculated on "historical" capital
figures, was also completely inadequate. When the principle
of "monetary correction" of capital was introduced by the
revolutionary government, a tax of 10 and later 5 percent was
collected on the amount readjusted. Even the most prosperous
enterprises found it difficult to pay interest on a capital readjusted in current cruzeiros and over and above that, to pay
reasonable dividends, while fresh capital was scarce, largely
because of government competition. The economic restoration
of Brazilian private enterprise will take years, even assuming
government willingness to cooperate.

Many Brazilians believe that inflation is not particularly
harmful to economic development, and are inclined to proceed
with plans for development without first overcoming inflation.
But it may be well to remember what Hans Singer, the well-
known United Nations economist, said in one of his Brazilian
lectures: "There never was to my knowledge a successful case
of economic development coupled with inflation. There was no
inflation in Great Britain during the period of economic development (1789–1914); neither was it in the years of marked
United States development; there was no inflation coupled

with economic development in Japan and no inflation in the economic process of the Soviets."[6]

Singer has not made year-by-year comparisons of rates of development and rates of inflation; his statement refers to the long periods during which these countries developed economically. In this sense it may be said, though reliable statistics are lacking, that the years of Brazil's greatest economic progress, 1902–1912, were not accompanied by inflation.[7]

It is one thing to show, as Singer did, that there was no inflation in the decades of marked economic development; it is another to try to find a year-by-year correlation between the rates of inflation and economic development. I have found no year-by-year correlation between rates of economic development and rates of inflation in the cases of Argentina, Brazil, Chile, Ecuador, Guatemala, or Mexico.[8] The reason is that inflationary forces in any one year do not generally affect economic development in that same year; the effect may even be favorable if there are unused factors of production. The evil consequences come later, when the government is forced to adopt restrictive measures and correct distortions. Inflation in year 1 affects economic development in years 3, 4, or 5. The recessions that Brazil suffered in early 1965 and late 1966, entailing a decline in the rate of development in these two years, are to be debited to the inflation prevailing in early 1964. It is also difficult to determine how much the present rate of economic development is affected by disorganization and inefficiency in electric power, maritime and railway transportation, and telephone communications caused by the lack of adjust-

[6] See *United Nations Development Projects, 1951.*

[7] Following the proclamation of the republic in 1889, Brazil went through a period of political disorder culminating in a civil war that lasted from September 1893 to March 1894. Not until the third term of civilian government (Rodrigues Alves) was the country in financial shape for economic development. During this period (1902–1906) the country, through a conjunction of favorable factors, entered into a phase of unfettered economic prosperity. The trend continued to 1912. The volume of paper money of 670 million of new cruzeiros in 1900 grew to only 702 in 1906 and 897 in 1913.

[8] Eugenio Gudin, paper submitted to the Elsinore conference of the International Economic Association.

ment of the rates for these services during the inflation of the past ten years.

NATIONALIZATION

The third major characteristic of Brazilian postwar economy was the large expansion of the public sector relative to the private sector. Not only have several new industries been directly developed by the state, but some that had been in the private sector have been nationalized ("statization" is the Brazilian expression) in some significant meaning of the term. The

TABLE 13. GOVERNMENT EXPENDITURE
(percent of GNP)

Year	Percent	Year	Percent
1956	26.8	1960	34.4
1957	29.4	1961	36.6
1958	30.7	1962	38.3
1959	31.4		

Source: Instituto Brasileiro de Economia, Fundação Getúlio Vargas.

extent of this phenomenon is shown in Table 13. In six years the public sector's share of the gross domestic product grew from 26.8 percent to 38.3 percent, an increase of nearly 50 percent.

The main items were:

(1) Oil. A monopoly on crude oil production was granted in 1948 to a public company called Petrobrás, which today is the largest enterprise in Brazil and perhaps in Latin America. Its activities cover not only crude oil, but almost all refining and transporting of petroleum products, including asphalt, synthetic rubber, and so on.

(2) Steel. The first steel plant in Brazil, Volta Redonda, in the state of Rio, was begun on government initiative in 1939 with the collaboration of the Export-Import Bank of the United States. It began production two years after the end of World War II. After World War I, the Itabira Iron Ore Company had made several attempts to build a steel plant in the Rio Doce valley, down which iron ore was to be carried from the mines

to the sea. Due partly to "nationalistic" opposition, and partly to the fact that the company's main interest was centered on the export of ore, negotiations never succeeded. A plant for the manufacture of "special steels" (Acesita) had been built by the Itabira Company, but lack of capital had made it necessary for the government to take over. Besides Volta Redonda, two other large plants were started: Cosipa in the port of Santos in the state of São Paulo, and Usiminas in the state of Minas Gerais. Brazilian private capital partially financed Cosipa; Usiminas was financed by Japanese and Brazilian government capital.

Over 90 percent of iron ore exports are in the hands of another large government enterprise, the Companhia Vale do Rio Doce, to which the Itabira Company mines were transferred. The construction of a steel-pellet plant has just been started near the port of shipping. Only the mining and export of manganese ore from the northern state of Pará (Amapá), and the minor export business from the port of Rio, are in private hands. It may therefore be said that 90 percent of siderurgical activities in Brazil are the hands of the government.

(3) Electric Power. A very large part of this industry has been nationalized during the past ten to fifteen years owing to a combination of inflation and demagoguery. Although inflation made it essential for electric light and power rates to be readjusted, the government not only refused to approve the readjustments (which were, naturally, unpopular) but, for demagogic purposes, raised salaries and wages, often beyond the rate of inflation. As a result, no more foreign capital was invested in these industries, and development of power-generating capacity for the two large systems, São Paulo and Rio Light, practically ceased; instead, large hydroelectric plants (Furnas, Cemig, and so on) were built by the government. The large plant in the Northeast at Paulo Affonso Falls on the lower São Francisco River was a government undertaking from the start, because its low rentability could not attract private capital. A large group of electric power companies operating in various states and controlled by the American and Foreign Power Company was taken over by the government; it is now the largest part (though not the only one) of the second government "colossus," Electrobrás, which comprises all govern-

ment electric power enterprises, including the São Francisco Company.

(4) Railways. The government's refusal to grant rate increases necessary to meet the rise in prices and wages was at the root of nationalization. Wages were raised rather freely, but not rates. Rapidly growing competition from the highways also weakened the economic condition of the railways. The nationalization of three of the most important railway systems of the country — the São Paulo Railway (from Santos to Jundiaí), the Leopoldina Railway, and the Great Western of Brazil in the Northeast — was made easy when in 1945 Great Britain declared her inability to pay war debts except through her foreign investments. The railways were all British-owned.

In São Paulo, where government railways functioned effectively in interchange traffic with the best Brazilian private railways, such as the admirably run Paulista Railway, the rise of wages to the level prevailing in the government forced the private lines into the general nationalization scheme. The São Paulo–Rio Grande do Sul railway, which had been occupied by the revolutionaries in 1930, was never returned to the owners and was finally nationalized. Deficits of hundreds of billions of cruzeiros pere year, coupled with deterioration of railway

TABLE 14. TAX RECEIPTS
(percent of GNP)

Year	Direct taxes	Indirect taxes	Total taxes
1947	5.1	9.6	14.7
1948	5.1	10.2	15.3
1949	5.2	10.7	15.9
1950	5.3	10.5	15.8
1951	5.8	11.9	17.7
1952	6.1	11.4	17.5
1953	5.8	11.1	16.9
1954	5.6	13.1	18.7
1955	5.9	11.5	17.4
1956	6.2	12.6	18.8
1957	6.4	13.0	19.4
1958	6.4	15.5	21.9
1959	6.4	16.5	22.9
1960	6.2	16.7	22.9

Source: Centro de Estudos Fiscais, Fundação Getúlio Vargas.

TABLE 15. GOVERNMENT EXPENDITURE
(percent of GNP)

Country	Government expenditure *(percent of GNP)*
Netherlands	36.1
Sweden	34.4
Brazil	34.4
Great Britain	32.2
Canada	30.1
Belgium	27.6
U.S.A.	26.4
Australia	24.2
Japan	21.7
Ecuador	21.3
Costa Rica	18.4

Source: *Statistical Yearbook,* 1960.

service, were and still are a serious burden on the nation's budget and economy.

(5) Coastal Shipping. Until the 1940's this activity was largely in the hands of a private Brazilian company, Companhia Costeira, which operated very efficiently. It fell into the hands of the government after the death of the company's president and main owner, Henrique Lage. The terrific demagoguery prevailing during the Kubitschek and Goulart governments (1956–1964) had the effect of nearly doing away with coastwise shipping. The tonnage of dry cargo in the main port of Santos fell from 1,300,000 tons in 1956 to 120,000 in 1964. Merchandise is now transported from the extreme south (Rio Grande do Sul) to the extreme north (Pará) by road, at a cost more than ten times that of normal ocean-shipping freight. The port of Pará was also taken over by the government, for no apparently justifiable reason.

The *Diário Oficial* of July 7, 1966, published a list drawn up by the "Administrative Committee for Economic Defense" (CADE) naming 207 companies controlled by federal, state, and municipal governments.

Since the end of World War II, taxation (federal, state, and municipal), including welfare contribution and coffee financial surplus, has evolved as shown in Table 14. Taxes grew from 14.7 percent of GNP to 22.9 percent in thirteen years. The ratio between state expenditure and GNP in Brazil, as compared with other countries, is shown in Table 15.

Table 16 shows the public and private sectors' shares in fixed-capital formation, that is, investment. The private share fell from 84.2 percent to 65.2 percent from 1947 to 1964, while that of the public sector grew from 15.8 percent to 34.8 percent. It is estimated that, in 1966, two-thirds of the 16 percent of savings in the GNP was absorbed by the public sector. Meanwhile, bank credit to the private sector remained unaltered in real terms for fifteen years (Table 17), while the GNP doubled.

TABLE 16. FIXED-CAPITAL FORMATION
(percent of total capital formation)

Year	Public sector	Private sector
1947	15.8	84.2
1952	26.8	73.2
1957	37.0	63.0
1960	38.4	61.6
1964	34.8	65.2

Source: Ministry of Planning, 1966.

TABLE 17. BANK LOANS TO THE PRIVATE SECTOR
(in NCr$)

Year end	Loans to private sector	Wholesale price index (1953 = 100)	Loans in real terms (NCr$ of 1953)
1951	85.647	83.5	103.815
1952	102.279	90.4	104.898
1953	120.360	113.2	106.325
1954	152.194	140.3	108.478
1955	171.405	153.5	111.664
1956	205.449	192.9	106.505
1957	254.509	199.4	127.637
1958	311.577	255.0	122.187
1959	400.839	347.1	115.488
1960	565.044	460.8	112.622
1961	781.422	691.6	112.988
1962	1,254.472	1,037.0	120.971
1963	1,945.848	1,886.0	103.173
1964	3,666.592	3,556.2	103.104

Source: SUMOC and Fundação Getúlio Vargas.

Average quotations on stock exchange securities in real terms were:

Year	Average
1961	100
1962	98
1963	119
1964	66
1965	49
1966 (June)	51
1966 (August)	43

The conclusion seems amply warranted that one of the main characteristics of the Brazilian economy in the postwar period has been hypertrophy of the public sector at the expense of private enterprise. The recovery of the private sector will take years. Expectations for transfer of economic activities from the public to the private sector are quite uncertain, an unfortunate position for the country's economy, for, as the well-known economist and statesman Roberto Campos recently said, "public enterprises are immune to bankruptcy, while having the greatest contempt for costs of production."

Part II

CHAPTER 2

Industrialization: Past Success and Future Problems

Joel Bergsman and Arthur Candal

Most of the developed countries followed a model of development in which gradual industrialization was the basic element in the creation, growth, and structural change of the whole fabric of modern institutions and modern individuals. Countries now developing are, for the most part, not following this model. Brazil, which presents a well-known example of both rapid economic growth and persistent difficulties, is also an outstanding example of a modern model of rapid development through import substituting industrialization.[1]

Whatever success Brazil has achieved by following this model was made possible by three basic factors. First, export

[1] There are three published works on the subject of industrialization in Brazil to which the authors owe a great debt. These works are required reading for anyone interested in Brazilian economic problems: Werner Baer, *Industrialization and Economic Development in Brazil* (Homewood, Ill.: Richard D. Irwin, 1965); Maria de Conceição Tavares, "The Growth and Decline of Import Substitution in Brazil." ECLA, *Economic Bulletin for Latin America*, IX, No. 1, March 1964; Carlos Lessa, "Fifteen Years of Economic Policy in Brazil," ECLA, *Economic Bulletin for Latin America*, IX, No. 2, Nov. 1964. We are also grateful for helpful comments from Gordon Smith, Maria da Conceição Tavares, Judith Tendler, and Rosemary Thorp.

production had allowed the creation of a modest industrial sector and a part of the population with some modern institutions and attitudes by the time import-substituting industrialization began. Second, the great size of the country partially counteracted the low income level and other "low-level equilibrium trap" problems, and permitted a more diversified and probably less costly industrial development than is possible in smaller countries. Third, difficulties with the balance of payments furnished a strong economic and psychological motive to take advantage of these favorable factors. The result was the creation of the largest and most diversified industrial sector in Latin America.

Perhaps the outstanding characteristic of the import-substitution model is that it permits rapid growth independent of the overall growth of income and of consumer demand. Once in motion, the process generates its own growth in demand, and can thus be self-sustaining until the structure of imports itself restricts further opportunities for new import-substituting investment.

The rapidity of the process, the degree to which it fed on itself, and its foundation in preexisting modernized enclaves resulted in a tremendous gap between the modern industrial sector and the traditional sector, which was left behind. The development of the modern economic, social, and psychological characteristics that normally result from gradual industrial development did not occur in much of Brazil. The duality of Brazil exists not only between the city and the countryside, but also between different economic sectors, social classes, regions, and institutions.

These persistent problems and imbalances, which may appear to be impediments to development, should be seen rather as guideposts for current action and future progress.

A BRIEF HISTORICAL REVIEW

From the 1850's to the early twentieth century, Brazilian industry was technologically and structurally much closer to their contemporary industry in countries that are now developed than it is today. There was significant early development in textiles, iron, and shipbuilding. Brazil was also richly endowed with most of the natural resources needed for industry. For two main reasons Brazilian industry did not develop more rapidly. First, very profitable opportunities appeared for what are now traditional commodity exports; thus investment resources and talent were diverted from less profitable industrial activities. Second, the social-institutional structure did not develop in a way that facilitated continuing industrialization. The profitability of the primary exports created power groups that influenced exchange policy, education, labor policy, and fiscal policy in favor of their own interests, which were generally incompatible with industrialization. Only the recurring crises in markets for these traditional exports (World War I, the 1930's, and World War II) led Brazil to adopt industrialization as the means to further development.

Brazilian industry before World War II was typical of a country in the early stages of industrialization. The leading sectors were traditional industries such as textiles and food products. Brazil had been an important exporter of textiles around the turn of the century, and was again during World War II.

After a short period of free imports with an overvalued cruzeiro (1945–1947) that resulted in the expenditure of the foreign exchange reserves accumulated during World War II (largely in an ineffective attempt to curb inflation and, again, to protect coffee-export earnings) Brazil embarked on a de facto protectionist policy. A strict licensing system was used to limit imports. Industrialization was not consciously a high-priority goal. However, the combination of inflation and a fixed exchange rate made the licensing system the effective allocator of foreign exchange; imports of consumer goods were drastically curtailed and the import-substitution process started in earnest.

The inauguration of a state-owned 270,000-ton integrated steel mill at Volta Redonda in 1946, the foundation of the National Economic Development Bank (BNDE) in 1952, and the foundation of the state-owned petroleum monopoly, Petrobrás, in 1954 were important beginnings in public investment and investment subsidies in infrastructure and basic industries. Volta Redonda was soon expanded to a capacity of over one million tons, and it, together with other steel mills and basic industries, provided domestically available inputs for the automobile, capital-goods, and other industries. The BNDE in its early years concentrated on electric power and transportation. Petrobrás began building refineries and exploring for domestic petroleum fields to reduce the demand for imported petroleum and petroleum products.

Throughout the period of postwar growth, protection, public investment, and investment subsidies generally complemented each other. Protection created a favorable atmosphere for import-substitution investment, while public investment and investment subsidies helped to provide the infrastructure and investments in heavy industry to complement and increase private investment. Tariff protection and other subsidies to private investment seem to have had their greatest effect on growth from the late 1940's through 1952, while investment in public and "mixed" enterprises grew fastest in the Kubitschek period of the late 1950's. A rough indication of this is shown in Figure 1, which gives the level and structure of real gross fixed investment.

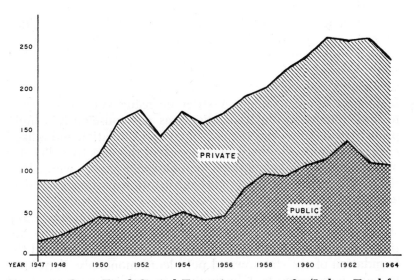

FIGURE 1: Gross Fixed Capital Formation, 1947–1964 (Index: Total for 1949 = 100) Source: Center for Fiscal Studies, Fundação Getúlio Vargas

The import-licensing system in effect until 1953 resulted, among other things, in the loss of a significant potential source of public revenue. Benefits derived from the shortage of foreign exchange went to those who received import licenses, whereas under a tariff system these benefits would have gone to the government. Thus the management of the external sector was far from efficient in providing government resources. During this period (1948–1952) investment in infrastructure lagged greatly behind what was needed, and inflation proceeded at an average rate of 11 percent per year.

In 1953 the import-licensing system was abolished and a multiple-category exchange-auction system was established as the principal means of controlling imports.[2] This system, and the modified auction-tariff system that replaced it in 1957, contributed over 10 percent of total government revenues.

From 1954 through 1964, the system of multiple exchange rates and tariffs gave a bias to import substitution in manufacturing of well over 100 percent.[3] Exports were discouraged not only by the bias in exchange rates, but also by fluctuations in the real export exchange rate, since the nominal rate was adjusted infrequently in the face of a continuous inflation. The average month-to-month fluctuation in the real rate was over 3.8 percent, and in 49 months during the period 1948–1966 inclusive the fluctuation was over 5 percent.

The management of the import side of the foreign sector, at least, was providing public revenue as well as protecting import substituting investments. From 1953 until about 1960, public investment in physical infrastructure kept pace with industrial growth, although it did not close the initial gap. Investment in social infrastructure, especially education, lagged farther and farther behind, and today is one of the most glaringly backward aspects of Brazil. On balance, public expenditure was growing faster than public revenue, and this combined with other factors continued to cause inflation. From 1954

[2] See A. Kafka, "The Brazilian Exchange Auction System," *Review of Economics and Statistics*, August 1965, pp. 308–322.

[3] See J. Bergsman, *Brazil's Industrialization and Trade Policies*, Oxford University Press to appear.

through 1960 inflation ranged between 12 and 26 percent per year, averaging 20 percent.

The interaction between inflation and industrialization is complex, and not completely understood.[4] Several industrialization effects tended to feed inflation in Brazil. First, intersectoral imbalances between supply and demand appeared continually during the rapid structural change. The imbalances caused shifts in relative prices, which, as always in a growing economy, moved upward more readily than downward. Second, many new industries were monopolistic or oligopolistic in structure and, since they were strongly protected from foreign competition, tended to sell at high prices relative to imports. Thus the continuing substitution introduced more and more price increases as supply shifted from imported products to higher-priced domestic ones. Third, inflation made cost accounting extremely difficult. Even in a competitive market structure, businessmen may tend to adopt price leadership behavior if they don't know what their costs are. If one sees his competitor raising prices, he can't say, "I'm making money at the old price; I'll just stay there and take his customers away," if he doesn't know whether he is making profits at the old price, and is also a little bit afraid of "spoiling the market."

At the same time, inflation played several important roles in industrialization. Perhaps the most important of these was to facilitate the transfer of resources from wages to profits, and from the private sector to the public. These transfers increased the resources for investment in industry and related infrastructure. In the 1949–1959 period, physical production per worker increased 90 percent, real wages per worker increased 26 percent, and wages as a percentage of value added decreased 18 percent. The government share in GNP rose from 17 to 20 percent in the same period.[5] The inflation certainly was partly

---

[4] For three interesting analyses of Brazilian inflation, see Antonio Delfim Netto and others, *Alguns Aspectos da Inflação Brasileira*, Estudos Anpes No. 1 (São Paulo, 1965); Mario Henrique Simonsen, EPEA, Ministry of Planning, *Aspectos da Inflação Brasileira* (Rio de Janerio, 1964), mimeographed; Baer, *op. cit.*, chap. 5.

[5] Data from Industrial Censuses of 1950 and 1960, *Conjuntura Econômica*, and Center for Fiscal Studies, Fundação Getúlio Vargas. In *Bases Macroeconômicas do Plano Decenal* (Rio de Janeiro: EPEA, Min-

caused by this increase in government spending. By inflation-ary financing in the face of rising prices the government could achieve its desired real expenditures more easily than the pri-vate sector. As to the transfer from wages to profits, it surely would have been harder to keep real wages from rising as fast as they did if nominal wages had not been rising so fast. There is some evidence that this "illusion" effect, if it did exist, was discovered; in the early 1960's wages rose fast enough to make up almost all of the losses suffered during the 1950's.

It is also likely — although we have no quantitative data to show this effect — that the inflation increased the income of the upper-income classes more than that of the lower. This would have increased the demand for many industrialized consumer products that would have been consumed very little by the lower-income classes in any case. A similar effect, of which we can be more certain, is that the inflation increased the demand for durable consumer goods as a store of assets, and for inven-tories as a simple way to make a profit. The use of housing as a store of private assets, so often observed in inflationary situa-tions, was somewhat suppressed by rent controls.

Around 1955, rapid and diversified industrialization be-came a primary, conscious goal of the government. Subsidies and special treatment for both foreign and domestic private investment were widely used to help attain this goal. These incentives included loans at low or negative real-interest rates, tariff exemption and lower exchange rates for a significant quantity of imported capital goods,[6] and liberal profit-remit-tance regulations. Foreign private investment was seen not only as a source of savings but also as a source of even more important "know-how." Another device used to facilitate new investment was the executive group (*Grupo Executivo*) formed in various industries. Such groups combined planning and execution; formed by representatives of cabinet ministers and of the heads of other important institutions such as the BNDE and CPA (Tariff Council), they worked intimately with manu-facturers and had the power to implement their plans for in-

istry of Planning, 1967) it is estimated that, for the entire economy, the share of labor in production fell 8 percent during the 1949–1959 period.

[6] See Bergsman, *op. cit.*

vestment and production in various industries, such as automobiles, chemicals, shipbuilding, and capital machinery and equipment.

The subsidies to investment caused overbuilding, and probably increased the use of more capital intensive technology in newly established industries. The negative-interest loans and subsidized imports of capital goods were exploited in full measure. Overcapacity is hard to measure, but it certainly occurred in many industries, such as automobiles, shipbuilding, some chemicals, and most traditional consumer goods. The effect of the bias toward capital intensive technology is even harder to estimate, but the abnormally high productivity of Brazilian industrial labor (discussed below) indicates that it might have been significant.

MODIFICATIONS IN THE INDUSTRIAL STRUCTURE

Industry in the Economy

In 1949, Brazilian industry accounted for 26 percent of GNP, in 1964, 35 percent.[7] This increase, brought about by a growth of over 8 percent per year in industrial value added, points up the dynamic nature of Brazilian industrial growth, which brought about one of the most rapid and radical structural modifications recently observed in an underdeveloped country. This degree of industrialization would not be surprising in a country with much higher per-capita income than Brazil. One factor that partly explains its occurrence in Brazil is the country's great size; when both per-capita income and population are taken into account, the degree of industrialization in Brazil is only about 15 percent above the intercountry pattern.[8] Industry's share in employment is only about 8 percent of the total. As is shown in Table 1, this is far below its share in other countries with similar degrees of industrialization.

There are some statistical problems in the intercountry comparisons in Table 1, the main one being that the data for

[7] In current prices. Prices of industrial goods went up at a slower rate than prices in general; thus industry's share in physical output rose even faster.

[8] See the appendix to this chapter, pp. 60–72.

TABLE 1. INDUSTRY'S SHARE IN PRODUCTION AND EMPLOYMENT

Country	Industrial production (percent of GNP)	Industrial employment (percent of total)
Brazil 1949	26	8[a]
Brazil 1964	35	8[a]
Argentina	34	25[a]
Mexico	25	16[a]
Canada	28	26
Denmark	27	30
Greece	18	16[a]
Ireland	19	16[a]
Italy	31	30
Netherlands	30	25
Norway	28	23
Portugal	35	20[a]
Spain	23	18[a]
United States	30	26

Source: *Some Factors in Economic Growth in Europe During the 1950's* (United Nations, 1964).
[a] Refers to economically active population.

some countries refer to persons actually employed, and those for others refer to the "economically active population." However, the intercountry difference is so great that the greater relative productivity of Brazilian industrial labor is beyond doubt. In the typical developed country, a high percentage of workers is employed in high-productivity occupations (industry and some services), but in Brazil only a very small percentage is in these sectors. The differences in productivity between the sectors are also much greater in Brazil. This situation makes growth through development of mass markets extremely difficult. Most Brazilian workers are just too far below the income levels that would make them significant consumers of a rapidly growing industrial output.

The post-World-War-II development of Brazilian industry has only aggravated the difficulty by increasing the gap between the lower and the higher productivity sectors, as can be clearly seen by analyzing the elements of the growth of productivity.[9] In this analysis we divide total productivity

[9] This analysis follows the general idea of the UN analysis, *Some Factors in Economic Growth in Europe During the 1950's*, United Nations, 1964.

growth into two components, "structural" and "technological."
The structural component is defined as the increase that would
have occurred if productivity in each sector remained constant,
with only the structure of employment changing. The technological component, defined as the part of the total increase not
accounted for by the structural component, is mainly that part
caused by productivity increases in each sector, assuming a
constant structure of employment. A breakdown into these
two components of the overall increase in Brazilian labor productivity from 1950 to 1960 is shown in Table 2.

TABLE 2. INCREASE IN LABOR PRODUCTIVITY, 1950–1960
(share of overall percentage increase, by sector)

Sector	Technological	Structural
Agriculture	8.1	4.0
Manufacturing	20.3	−1.6
Mining	0.6	0.0
Construction	0.6	0.0
Electric Power	0.2	0.3
Commerce	3.0	1.7
Transport and Communication	2.7	0.8
Services	−2.4	−0.2
Government	−4.6	−0.8
Total	28.4	4.1

Source: Calculations based on data from Demographic
Census of 1950 and 1960, and *Revista Brasileira
de Economia*, March 1962.

Increasing productivity in a small part of the labor force,
while leaving the rest stagnant, is hardly good development.
Instead of concentrating more and more capital on the same
small portion of the labor force, genuine development must include a shift of an ever-growing percentage of the labor force
to the more productive occupations.[10]

A policy of increasing productivity purely by "technological" means is unsatisfactory in itself: it carries part of the
population into the modern world and leaves the rest behind.

[10] This follows one of the basic ideas in J. C. H. Fei and G. Ranis,
Development of the Labor Surplus Economy (Homewood, Ill.: Richard D.
Irwin, 1964).

Moreover, such a policy is unlikely to be self-sustaining; with most of the economy stagnant, the growing sectors will run out of markets for their products. Exportation can alleviate this problem to some extent, but a continental country such as Brazil not only should, but in fact cannot avoid basing sustained growth principally on expanding its domestic markets.

Thus a balance is required: some of the capital-intensive, modern, industrial sectors are highly profitable and have both rapidly growing demand and dynamic effects on other sectors. These sectors will and should grow rapidly, but will not absorb much labor. However, development cannot take place without an increase in the percentage of the labor force engaged in higher-productivity sectors — most of industry, and part of agriculture and services.

As Table 2 shows, most of the recent increases in productivity in Brazil have been "technological": of the overall labor productivity increase of 32 percent from 1950 to 1960, 20 percent in industry and 8 percent in agriculture was due to "technological" increase. The "structural" component in agriculture was only 4 percent, and in industry it was negative. The Brazilian labor force has not been shifting into high-productivity industrial activities, and it is likely that reliance on continued productivity increases in small sections of the labor force contributed to the economic stagnation of the early 1960's. The weakness of consumer demand as a factor in the recession of the 60's, the abnormally high consumption of food products relative to other industrial goods, and the generally obvious existence of a dichotomy between the stagnant, poor Brazil and the developing, prosperous Brazil indicate that both industry and modern agriculture must be induced to absorb labor somewhat more rapidly than they have in the past — and perhaps also that the laborers should be allowed to retain a higher percentage of their productivity increases.

Perhaps one of the reasons why highly productive sectors have not absorbed more labor is that Brazil's famous cheap labor is not cheap at all, but simply low in price. With half of the population illiterate, and another large group without the basic education needed even to start on-the-job training in modern industry, it may indeed be more economical to apply more and more physical capital to a small modernized labor

force than to absorb more and more new workers with less capital per worker. The best way to begin spreading capital over
more workers may be through education. Providing today's chil-
dren with the abilities and attitudes needed to work in modern
industry should make tomorrow's industry more willing to employ them.

In addition to a poorly prepared working population and
high fringe-benefit labor costs, government policies of subsidized loans and tariff exemptions for imports of many capital
goods biased the capital-labor ratio still further.

Intra-Industrial Developments

Structural modifications within Brazilian industry took
place in the context of sustained rapid growth. The overall
level of industrial activity rose an average of 7.2 percent per
year from 1939 to 1949, 8.5 percent per year from 1949 to 1959,
8.5 percent per year from 1949 to 1959, and 9.7 percent per
year from 1959 to 1964. The average annual growth for the
twenty-five-year period was an impressive 8.3 percent.[11]

The early structure was heavily concentrated on producing
food products and textiles. These activities are still important
but have been joined by diversified chemicals, metallurgy, and
machinery and equipment. Paper and rubber products, though
much less important, have also been dynamic sectors. In the
most general terms evolution has been more or less typical,
with emphasis shifting from consumer goods to producer goods,

[11] These estimates are based on the data in Table 3. Current cruzeiros were changed to constant dollars by applying the purchasing-power
parity rate calculated by the United Nations for 1953 of US$ 0.0292 per
cruzeiro (quoted in A Study of Industrial Growth, 1963, 63.II.B.2.,
page 55) and the implicit GNP deflator from the Brazilian National
Accounts. No deflator was available for 1939; we used the Fundação
Getúlio Vargas estimate that real production in all manufacturing in 1939
was .499 times that of 1949. Revista Brasileira de Económia, March 1967.)
The sectoral distribution for 1939 was taken from the Brazilian industrial
census of 1940. The physical-product indices of the Fundação Getúlio
Vargas show manufacturing growing at 9.4 percent per year from 1949 to
1959, and 6.8 percent per year from 1959 to 1964. The average physical-
product growth from 1939 to 1964 would therefore be 8.0 percent per
year.

and from traditional to modern industries. This history is summarized in Table 3.

Many aspects of the structural changes become clearer when the evolution of production is considered according to classifications by use: consumer durables, consumer nondurables, intermediate goods, and capital goods (Table 4). The outstanding aspects are the growth in importance of capital goods and consumer durables; and the maintenance of the position of intermediate goods. This points up the integrated nature of the import-substitution process; not only finished goods but also the components and raw materials were produced more and more in Brazil.

The nondurable consumer goods industry, as shown in Table 5 and in the comparisons with international patterns in the appendix to this chapter (pp. 60–72), was already well developed by the late 1930's. The rapid growth of the durable consumer-goods and capital-goods industries indicates that growth was led by elements that had little to do with the overall growth of income and purchasing power in the economy: import substitution, public investments, and investment subsidies. Import substitution affected every industrial sector, and almost completely eliminated imports in most. Public investment and subsidies were important to the development of electric power, roads, railroads, and to such basic industries as steel, petroleum, chemicals, nonferrous metals, heavy machinery, automobiles, and shipbuilding. The complementary action of import substitution, an already substantial industrial tradition, importable "know-how," and public investment and investment subsidies made possible in fifteen years a structural change that took many decades in countries now developed.

The changing industrial structure must be studied in conjunction with the import substitution process, which gave it its main impulse and also its internal logic. Total imports fell from an average of 16 percent of GNP in 1947–1949 to 9½ percent in 1962–1964. The share of industrial products in total imports fell from 87 percent in 1953 to 58 percent in 1965.[12]

---

[12] Data from national accounts, and from IBGE, *Números Índices Anuais dos Preços e das Quantidades no Comércio Exterior e de Cabota-*

TABLE 3. EVOLUTION OF THE STRUCTURE OF BRAZILIAN INDUSTRY, 1939–1964

Sector	ISIC	Value added (millions of 1953 US$)				Distribution (percent)				Average annual Growth rates (percent)			
		1939	1949	1959	1964	1939	1949	1959	1964	39–49	49–59	59–64	39–64
Food, Beverages, & Tobacco	(20–22)	345	612	1,118	1,859	30	27	21	22	5.9	6.2	10.6	7.0
Textiles, Clothing, & Footwear	(23–24)	307	537	815	1,164	27	23	16	14	5.7	4.3	7.4	5.5
Wood, Paper, & Products	(25–27)	79	200	456	519	6	8	8	6	9.8	8.6	2.6	7.8
Leather & Rubber Products	(29–30)	26	75	181	239	3	3	3	3	11.2	9.2	5.8	9.3
Chemicals	(31–32)	124	230	723	1,386	11	10	14	17	5.6	12.2	13.8	10.2
Nonmetallic Mineral Products	(33)	61	165	356	355	5	7	7	4	10.5	8.0	nil	7.3
Metals & Metal Products	(34–38)	150	349	1,437	2,547	13	16	27	31	8.8	15.2	12.0	12.0
Others	(28, 39)	54	129	247	288	5	6	4	3	9.1	6.8	3.0	6.9
Total Manufacturing	(20–39)	1,146	2,297	5,333	8,357	100	100	100	100	7.2	8.5	9.4	8.3

Source: Industrial Censuses for 1939, 1949, and 1959; IBGE, *Industrias de Transformação, Dados Gerais — 1963/64*, April 1966 for 1964. Adjustments for comparability made by the authors.

Outstanding in this switch of imports from manufactured products to new materials is the behavior of fuels and lubricants. Refined petroleum products fell from 21 percent of total imports in 1953 to 5 percent in 1965, while crude oil increased from virtually zero in 1953 to 30 percent of total imports by 1965. Industrial growth was sufficiently rapid and diversified to keep the absolute value of manufactured imports roughly constant, liberating foreign exchange to allow nonindustrial raw-

TABLE 4. TOTAL OUTPUT BY MAJOR TYPE OF PRODUCT
(percent)

	1939	1949	1955	1959	1964
Consumer durables	} 80.1	{ 2.4	5.5	8.3	12.5
Consumer nondurables		{ 67.9	58.8	49.6	42.3
Intermediate goods	} 19.9	{ 25.3	30.4	30.7	34.6
Capital goods		{ 4.4	5.3	11.4	10.6
	100.0	100.0	100.0	100.0	100.0

Source: Same as for Table 3.

material imports. This could only have happened with a "big push" type of industrialization on a broad front. On the other hand, this continuing reduction of the import structure toward ever larger quantities of a few basic raw materials which Brazil as yet cannot supply causes increasing rigidity in import demand and makes industrial production in a way even more dependent on capacity to import.

Table 5 shows the interaction between changes in the structure of production and changes in the structure of imports. Only imports of industrialized products are considered. Figure 2 is a graph of the results. The reduction of imports as a percentage of total supply is especially striking when industrial goods alone are considered. The data for 1964 are somewhat distorted because the recession that started in 1963 affected import demand more than demand for domestic products; in particular, capital-goods imports for 1964 were abnormally low. The picture is nevertheless clear: Brazil imports

gem. This latter source for detailed import statistics unfortunately goes back only as far as 1953.

far fewer industrial products than she used to, and at present there is little room left for substitution except in capital goods and some chemicals.

Three stages are roughly distinguishable within the 1949–1964 period. During the first, the outstanding progress in import substitution was made in consumer durables. Consumer nondurables had already been almost completely substituted, and by the late 1950's most durables as well were produced domestically. As imports of consumer goods were reduced, the import-substitution process entered the second phase: completing the establishment of Brazil's diversified, highly integrated, and almost self-sufficient industry. Thus, both domestic production and imports of capital goods increased rapidly during this period (roughly 1955–1959). Domestic production of intermediate goods also expanded rapidly, so rapidly that imports of intermediate goods remained at a more or less constant

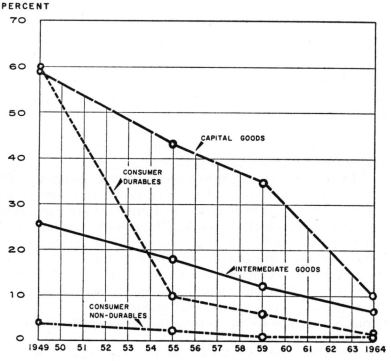

FIGURE 2: Imports as Percent of Total Supply of Industrial Products

absolute level. The third phase started about 1959, when the investments made during the second phase entered into full-scale operation. In this phase total industrial imports shrank rapidly as a percentage of total imports, since more and more imports of unprocessed raw materials were needed by the new industrial structure.

TABLE 5. STRUCTURE OF IMPORTS AND DOMESTIC PRODUCTION OF INDUSTRIAL PRODUCTS, BY USE

	Consumer goods		Producer goods		All industrial goods
	Durables	Nondurables	Intermediate	Capital	
	A. *Imports* (billion cruzeiros of 1955)				
1949	8.9	5.4	18.2	15.8	48.3
1955	2.1	4.5	22.6	13.7	42.9
1959	2.9	2.8	21.2	29.2	56.1
1964	1.5	3.9	18.6	8.7	32.7
	B. *Domestic production* (billion cruzeiros of 1955)				
1949	4.9	140.0	52.1	9.0	206.0
1955	19.0	200.9	104.0	18.0	341.9
1959	43.1	258.0	159.6	59.5	520.2
1964	93.8	319.5	261.2	79.7	754.2
	C. *Imports as percentage of total supply*				
1949	60.1	3.7	25.9	59.0	19.0
1955	10.0	2.2	17.9	43.2	11.1
1959	6.3	1.1	11.7	34.5	9.7
1964	1.6	1.2	6.6	9.8	4.2

Source: Imports from IBGE, *Números Índices . . .* , *op. cit.* Gross value of industrial production from Industrial Census, *Registro Industrial,* and indices of physical production from *Conjuntura Econômica.* Imports of 1949 projected backward using data in ECLA, "The Growth and Decline . . . ," *op. cit.*

Until the early 1960's the process of progressive vertical integration and self-sustaining growth can be seen. The investments of the 1950's had high linkage effects and constituted the simultaneous creation of both demand and supply for a wide variety of industrial products. As Baer concluded, "The picture which emerges . . . from the simultaneous growth of industries which to a large extent are each other's customers is that of a remarkably balanced growth. . . . Many complementary industries grew up simultaneously and acted as self-reenforcing factors." [13]

EVALUATION

We have seen that Brazilian industrial growth after World War II was largely led by import substitution. This growth was not limited by growth in final demand, but to a great extent was based on shifting the satisfaction of total demand from imports to domestic production, plus the increase in the producers'-goods component of that demand induced by the shift.

Being largely independent of growth in final demand, rapid industrial growth could proceed in the face of rather small increases in real disposable personal income. In fact, the slow rise in real wages in all sectors of the economy aided industrial growth by restricting demand for consumer goods and permitting more investment. Higher nominal wages would probably have been largely dissipated by inflation; it is doubtful that the government would have sacrificed its real share in expenditure, although real investment would probably have fallen somewhat in response to higher nominal wages.

We have also seen that imports of almost all types of industrial products fell nearly to zero, and almost all components of these products came to be produced in Brazil. Thus the process sustained itself throughout a long period; it created and satisfied its own demand, at least from 1947 through about 1961. One cost of thus integrating the industrial structure has been increased susceptibility to cyclical behavior: weakness in demand now affects domestic activity as well as imports. An offsetting benefit, of course, is reduced dependence on export earnings. This net saving in foreign exchange on merchandise account has in turn been partially offset by a rise in short-term obligations incurred to pay for capital-goods imports, as well as in payments of interest and profits. These rose to levels that caused repeated problems in the 1960's.

The extensive import substitution did create a few very high-cost industries. This had some interesting negative effects;

[13] Baer, *op. cit.*, p. 142.

for example, the external effects were counterproductive in these cases, since high-cost domestic production took the place of imports, thus raising costs, contributing to inflation, and allowing the establishment of inefficient plants that are still problems and obstacles to future growth.

Industrialization on a broad front, with widespread tariff protection, investment subsidies, and tariff exemption for "essential" inputs that had to be imported, was easier to sell politically and psychologically than narrower efforts might have been. Since the mid-1950's, there has been a strong public spirit of industrialization, and there have been few complaints that some sectors have been developed at the expense of others, because virtually all industrialization efforts have received public support. Adverse reaction from the large agricultural sector was reduced by partially subsidized imports of tractors, fertilizers, and other agricultural inputs, as well as by separate policies for coffee and cocoa, two of the main export crops.

The Brazilian economy entered the 1960's with one of the biggest and most diversified industrial sectors of the underdeveloped world, which was kept going with the aid of a large and well diversified set of distortions in relative prices. These distortions (caused principally by tariffs, other protective devices, and investment subsidies to certain sectors at certain times) protected both infant and mature industries, permitted the establishment of a few manufacturing processes that should never have been installed as they were and some others that should have been postponed, and allowed efficient industries either to earn high profits or to become less and less efficient.

Hindsight makes it easy to point out specific mistakes, even to suggest some modifications in policy that clearly would have avoided the greatest inefficiencies. It is much harder to compare actual results with those that might have come from some totally different policy that would not have included industrialization. On balance, we think that industrialization as it happened was better for Brazil than no industrialization at all, or than what might have resulted from a policy of noninterference with a market that was far from perfect. Brazil's industrialization through import substitution compares favorably with the experiences of most other underdeveloped countries in at least one important respect: Brazil succeeded in severely limiting industrial imports — in fact, in slightly reducing them in absolute value — while the economy grew at 6 percent per year for fifteen years. In other countries (Argentina and India are good examples) a less complete industrialization has only increased demand for imported industrial products, and aggravated balance-of-payments problems. Brazil's very extensive growth was vertically integrated almost completely; it hurt mostly the few very inefficient industries that were established. Given the inherent uncertainty and the deficiencies in data needed to plan efficient industrial growth, it is difficult to conclude that Brazil would in fact have been better off today if more selective policies had been adopted and the risk of failing to reduce import demand had been increased.

We have been discussing the main aspects and broad effects of industrialization. On a more tactical level, we observe that the instruments were more or less well chosen and efficiently used. The goals of extensive, diversified, and rapid industrialization and relaxation of balance-of-payments problems were achieved. The multiple rate and tariff system worked much better than systems in other countries that rely principally on quantitative restriction and licenses: the monopoly profit went to the government rather than to the importer, and great flexibility was permitted. On the other hand, a more uniform structure of protection with a lower maximum level would probably have avoided the worst inefficiencies while still inducing almost all the other substitutions. The strong bias in favor of import substitution resulted in a very inward-looking development, little concerned with internationally competitive costs. Public investment and investment subsidies complemented the protective system and resulted in many efficient heavy industries and much of the necessary infrastructure. However, subsidies to capital equipment probably increased both the capital intensity and the capacity of industry beyond the optimum. Tariff exemptions for required imported inputs, the many ways in which the interministerial executive groups oiled the bureaucratic machinery, and the favorable climate for foreign investment, all helped to create a supportive environment for new industries. Brazil did not exhibit the ambivalent "We need you but we don't like you" attitude toward industry seen in some other countries, which seems to result only in even higher-cost operation.[14]

THE CRISES OF THE 1960'S
AND CHOICES FOR THE FUTURE

The year 1962 was the last year of sustained industrial growth. The average annual industrial growth rate during the fifteen-year period 1948–1962 had been 9.8 percent, never falling below 5 percent. The contrast since 1962 is shown in Table 6.

TABLE 6. GROWTH OF INDUSTRIAL PRODUCTION

Period	Annual growth (percent)	Period	Annual growth (percent)
1948–62	9.8	1964	5.0
1962	8.2	1965	−4.7
1963	0.	1966	12.1

Source: Fundação Getúlio Vargas.

The stagnation during 1963–1965 was caused by a combination of factors, some acting throughout the period and others only at times. We believe that four factors explain the decline in growth: the reduction in opportunities for continued import substitution; a sharp drop in foreign private investment; political instability; and the end of high priority given to industrial growth in setting government policies.

Reduced Opportunities for Import Substitution

By the early 1960's most industrial products were supplied domestically. Opportunities for import substitution of industrial goods were almost exclusively in the capital-goods and chemicals sectors (including synthetic rubber). The structure of total supply in 1949 and 1961 is shown in Table 7 (see also Table 5).

Most of the metals imported were metals of which Brazil did not have sufficient ore deposits to exploit economically. Most of the chemicals were products of processes that likewise,

[14] For a further evaluation, see Bergman, *op. cit.*

TABLE 7. IMPORTS AS PERCENT OF TOTAL SUPPLY
OF MANUFACTURED GOODS

Sector	1949	1961
Metallurgy	22	12
Machinery	64	46
Electrical and communication equipment	45	17
Transport equipment	57	19
Chemicals and pharmaceuticals	29	17
Nonmetallic mineral products	10	4
Paper and products	10	7
Rubber and products	1	15
Wood products	1	1
Textiles	6	1
Clothing	0	0
Food products	4	2
Beverages	2	3
Tobacco, printing and publishing, furniture, and leather products	2	1
Total	16	10

Source: ECLA, "The Growth and Decline . . ." *op. cit.*, p. 40.

because of the small scale of the domestic market, were not economical. With the significant exception of capital goods, by 1961 technical factors had placed severe limitations on the rate of future industrial growth through import substitution. Development could continue at a rate faster than the growth rate of future industrial growth through import substitution. These, however, were limited in part by high manufacturing costs (notably in durable consumer-goods, rubber, textiles, clothing, and some chemicals), in part by an export exchange rate that was discriminatorily low and was subject to considerable uncertainty in real terms due to inflation, and in part by the general absence of an export mentality on the part of most Brazilian manufacturers. Restrictive policies by the developed countries on imports of industrial products were also a factor.

Drop in Foreign Private Investment

The high levels of foreign private investment of the late 1950's started to fall off in 1962 and dropped very sharply in 1963. The overall picture is shown in Table 8.

TABLE 8. DIRECT FOREIGN PRIVATE INVESTMENT
(annual average in millions of US$)

Period	Amount
1947–54	13
1955–61	102
1962	69
1963	30
1964	28

Source: SUMOC bulletins.

Total levels of investment in the economy as a whole were not noticeably affected by the fall in direct foreign private investment. In industry, however, this investment had been important both in amount and as a dynamic force that created new industries and thus more demand for other new products. It also induced, and required, a significant amount of complementary domestically financed capital formation. Unfortunately, no detailed estimates of investment by sector of destination exist. We can roughly estimate that annual gross investment in industry was about one-third of total investment, or about US$ 1,100 million per year. Thus just the amount of the fall in foreign investment (which in the late 1950's had been directed principally to industry) must have been significant, and its indirect effects were probably even more so. The decline in foreign private investment itself was probably caused largely by declining opportunities for import substitution, and by the political factors discussed below.

Total foreign exchange availability does not appear to have been a problem for industry during the early 1960's. Imports of industrial inputs — raw materials and intermediate goods — rose before and during the first year of the decline in industrial growth.[15]

[15] There are three sources of estimates of these data. Both the ECLA data (*Statistical Bulletin for Latin America*, II, No. 1, 1965, pp. 226–227) and the Brazilian Census Bureau data (IBGE, *Números Índices* . . . , *op. cit.*, p. 12) show imports of industrial inputs steadily rising. The index published by the Getúlio Vargas Foundation in *Conjuntura Econômica* shows imports of industrial inputs falling 13 percent in 1962, and rising 27 percent in 1963. For discussion of a contrary view see N. H. Leff, "Import Constraints and Development: Causes of the Recent Decline of

*General Political Instability and the Lower Priority Given to
Industrial Growth*

At the beginning of 1961, with the advent of the administration of President Jânio Quadros, the high priority given to
industrial growth gave way to other goals. As a study by
ECLA concluded, ". . . the swelling proportions assumed by
the inflation problem [in 1961–1963] shifted the center of attention from industrial development to the control of the inflationary process. . . . No longer were exchange, monetary, and
fiscal measures placed at the service of industrialization without due thought . . ."[16] In 1961 the annual rate of inflation
rose above 30 percent for the first time. It increased steadily
through 1964, as shown in Table 9.

TABLE 9. ANNUAL RATE OF INFLATION
(GNP implicit deflator)

Period	Annual rate (percent)
1955–60	20
1961	35
1962	49
1963	72
1964	91
1965	57
1966	38

Sources: National Accounts, Fundação Getúlio Vargas.

The political situation did not permit a coherent, continuous anti-inflation program. From time to time, half-way measures were taken, without much success or lasting effect. In
August 1961, Quadros resigned the presidency, precipitating a
short crisis caused by opposition to the succession of his vice-
president, João Goulart. Goulart was allowed to assume the
presidency, but with reduced powers. Lacking a stable political
base (and a coherent economic policy), Goulart tried to increase and consolidate his power by catering first to one group

Brazilian Economic Growth," *Review of Economics and Statistics,* February 1968, and the comment by J. Bergsman and S. A. Morley and the
reply by Leff in the same journal, February 1969.

[16] ECLA, "Fifteen Years . . .", *op. cit.,* p. 199.

and then to another. He adopted some measures aimed at supporting growth, some at combating inflation, some at increasing real wages, a few at agrarian reform, and so forth. Their total effect was contradictory, vacillating, and unsuccessful at either stabilizing prices or sustaining economic growth. The poor economic results of 1963 (which included stagnation in industry and a runaway inflation), together with Goulart's demagogic and left-leaning political style, finally proved too much for Brazil's more conservative power-groups, and at the beginning of April 1964 Goulart was ousted by a military coup that had wide support from urban middle-class, business, and landholding interests.[17]

Whatever utility inflation or inflationary policies may have had in the 1950's seems to have disappeared as its rate increased in the 1960's. Wage increases in industry, which had been held well below productivity increases during the 1950's, reached 18 percent in 1963, and another 9 percent in 1964.[18] A stabilization program was attempted from March to May in 1963, relying mostly on credit and government deficit control. Wages kept rising throughout the period, and the attempt probably caused more harm by its upsetting effect on expectations and current business operations than it did good. The year 1963 was also marked by widespread strikes and labor unrest. Add severe power-rationing caused by a drought in the Rio-São Paulo region, and one can only wonder why industrial production did not fall, rather than remain at the 1962 level as it did.

One of the causes of the drop in foreign private investment mentioned above was a new law controlling profit remittances that went into effect in September 1962. Remittances were limited to 10 percent of officially registered capital, and royalty payments to foreign parent firms were prohibited.[19] There was

---

[17] For an interesting account of this period, see Thomas Skidmore, *Politics in Brazil* (New York: Oxford University Press, 1967).

[18] EPEA, *Diagnóstico Preliminar, Mão-de-Obra*, Preliminary version, p. 241. Wage and productivity data from IBGE, *Registros Industriais*. Wages deflated by cost-of-living index for São Paulo from *Conjuntura Econômica*.

[19] Law No. 4131, Sept. 3, 1962.

also some nationalization of foreign investments in power and transportation during the Goulart administration. Generally, the political tone of the government was hostile to foreign capital.

The government that replaced Goulart's gave first priority on the economic front to braking the runaway inflation, using the traditional means of controlling credit, government deficits, and wages. The goal was to achieve relative stability in about three years, avoiding the hardships that would have resulted from a more rapid program. Nevertheless, even the "gradualist" stabilization from mid-1964 to June 1967 was no exception to the rule that stabilization in the short run has negative effects on growth.

CHOICES FOR THE FUTURE

As a prelude to examining alternatives for the future, we will discuss a more general problem, one that lies behind many of the causes in the decline of industrial growth discussed above, one that some Brazilian economists think may be crucial in the future. This is the problem of demand, as it applies to industrial growth.

By 1961, import substitution of industrial products had already reduced the potential for rapid future growth based on demand for imported products (see Tables 5 and 7 above). Although we cannot be sure, we believe it likely that industrial growth in the 1960's would have fallen short of that in the 1950's even if the other disturbing factors discussed above had not been present. Moreover, foreign private investment was in large part motivated by the Brazilian government's policy of substituting domestic production for imports; foreign firms that had been exporting to Brazil were faced with the choice of producing in Brazil or losing the market.[20] We believe it probable that foreign private investment would have fallen below the very high levels of the late 1950's simply because of reduced investment opportunities. If Brazil is able to maintain

[20] See Lincoln Gordon and Engelbert Grommers, *United States Manufacturing Investment in Brazil: The Impact of Brazilian Government Policies 1946–1960* (Cambridge, Mass.: Harvard University Press, 1962).

a more or less stable and healthy economic and political environment, the future may provide a test of this hypothesis.

Another possible cause of a demand problem lies in the distribution of income. There is some indication that weakening consumer demand has already played a role in the decline of the early 1960's. This is indicated by the structure of the decline in production, and by the real levels of wages, disposable income, and personal consumption. Domestic production of consumer goods *fell* by an average of 1.3 percent per year in the three-year period 1963–1965. Imports of consumer goods, which are not very significant anyway, also fell in the same period.[21] This means that the per-capita total supply of industrially produced consumer goods fell by an average of over 4 percent per year for the three years 1963–1965. The only significant part of this decline attributable to a supply constraint is the stagnation in production of agricultural raw materials during 1963.

The second indication of possible demand problems is the prolonged squeeze on wages and personal consumption throughout the 1950's and 1960's. Average wages in industry, as we have mentioned earlier, rose only by about 2 or 3 percent per year from 1949 to 1964.[22] Per-capita personal consumption rose by less than one-half of one percent per year from 1950 to 1964. As a percentage of total domestic expenditure, personal consumption fell from about 77 percent in the late 1940's to a range of 68–71 percent in 1951–1959, and fell again to a range of 64–66 percent in 1960–1964.[23]

None of this is conclusive. But the long-continued squeeze on wages and consumption, coupled with the fall in per-capita consumption of industrialized consumer goods in the early 1960's, suggests that industrial growth might have continued

[21] Data on production from CEPAL, *Brasil 1966* (Rio de Janeiro; March 14, 1967), p. 38. Data on imports from IBGE, *Números Índices . . . , op. cit.*

[22] Average wages from *Industrial Census of 1950 and 1960*, and *Registro Industrial* for other years. Deflated by cost-of-living index for São Paulo.

[23] Data from national accounts. Deflated by cost-of-living index for São Paulo. Personal consumption is estimated as a residual in the national accounts, and is perhaps more subject to error than other estimates.

more strongly if there had been faster growing consumer demand to take the place of import substitution as a leading factor. The main points, however, are that

the chief dynamic elements in the past were import substitution and the new demands it induced for intermediate and capital goods;

import substitution can no longer play this dynamic role;

Brazil has not yet found a policy capable of creating or supporting other dynamic factors to induce further rapid growth.

This does not mean that no room exists for additional import substitution. Import substitution may still play two significant roles: first, a diminished continuation of its past dynamic role, as the domestic market expands and new activities become possible at economic scales of production; second, as a means of avoiding or bypassing future balance-of-payments problems.

Another factor influencing the future course of industrial growth is policy concerning minimum levels of productivity to be required in new activities. Since 1964, government policy has required domestic industry to be more competitive in international markets. Tariffs have been reduced; competitive price has come to play a more important role in obtaining protection under the Law of Similars, and consideration is now being given to relaxing the extreme requirements for high domestic content in automobiles and other products. The consensus apparently is that productivity in industry should be increased — an emphasis important to increasing exports of industrial products. In the short run, industrial exports cannot be expected to play an important role. They now compose a very small part of either total exports or total industrial production (about 6 percent and 2 percent respectively). Most Brazilian industry is unable to compete in international markets, both because of its own low productivity and because of institutional restrictions outside Brazil. In the long run, however, Brazil should look more and more to exports of industrial goods as a source of foreign exchange, as well as a dynamic internal element. Imports as a percentage of GNP cannot be much further reduced; exports will therefore have to increase at least as fast as the GNP. The current low level of industrial exports is all the more reason to emphasize measures to increase them.

All things considered — the reduced possibilities for additional import substitution, the difficulties of increasing industrial exports, the great size of the country — we conclude that the key to Brazil's future industrial growth is the domestic market. Current thought about future growth seems to follow one or the other of two models.[24] One emphasizes public spending as a leading factor, and implies increasing government investment and consumption, with the government active not only throughout the infrastructure (power, transportation) but in manufacturing as well. This model emphasizes favorable conditions for investments, rather than increased productivity. The alternative model emphasizes consumer demand as the leading factor, and implies constant or reduced participation of the public sector in total demand. The emphasis is on increased consumer purchasing-power and improvements in productivity.

To a certain extent, actual policy can follow both these models. For example, current government policy seems to indicate increased emphasis on public investment, but also involves reduced tariff protection and increased emphasis on cost-cutting. But in many important aspects the two models are mutually inconsistent. The basic conflict is one of income distribution; the first model implies more income for government and for capital, and the second more for the private sector and labor. The first model probably implies turning the internal terms of trade against agriculture, at least in the short run. The second model, because of the large percentage of agricultural workers in the labor force, implies turning the internal terms of trade in favor of agriculture.

The first model, which might be called the "investment" or "autarkic" model, requires less change from the import-substitution model of the past. The major difference is that, in the past, demand was present before domestic supply, in the form of imports. In the investment model, new demand

[24] For an early discussion along this line, see ECLA, "The Growth and Decline . . . ," *op. cit.*, pp. 56–59. Both models are simplified here, not, we hope, excessively.

comes from increasing public spending and from investments in general. Even if the resources for this spending can be gathered, it is not clear whether this model can be self-sustaining in the long run.

The second model, which might be called the "consumption" or "more open" model, requires a much sharper break with the import-substitution model. Given the present structure of the Brazilian economy, the consumption model seems more likely to be self-sustaining eventually, but much more difficult to put into practice. How to transfer Brazilian industry from highly protected to more competitive, lower cost production? How to increase the income, the productivity, and thus the purchasing power of the mass of agricultural workers ?

Nevertheless, we believe that something like the consumption model offers better prospects for Brazil in the long run — not only because it seems to be more likely to be self-sustaining and appeals more to our sense of equity, but because it seems to offer greater chances of reducing the tremendous gap between the modern Brazil and the underdeveloped Brazil. We fear the social effects of continued rapid development for only a small part of the country, while the rest is left behind. The investment model implies such a continuation; the consumption model implies a reversal. It implies seeking widespread productivity increases for the mass of Brazilian workers in all sectors, rather than heavy investment and rapid productivity increases for a small part of the labor force. The differences in productivity implied by the data in Table 1, aggravated by the trends shown in Table 2, would not be allowed to persist.

How can the consumption model of industrialization be implemented? Changing the present industrial (and total economic) structure to a mass-consumption structure would require a transition period during which many policies from the investment model would be used. These policies would be changed as widespread productivity increases made consumer-led growth feasible. Initially, resource allocation would emphasize the provision of complementary capital needed for productivity increases. This complementary capital would be applied to physical infrastructure, where the greatest lacks seem to be in communications, agricultural marketing facilities, and transportation. It would be applied to social infrastructure, where the greatest deficiencies are in education and health. Improvement in education is probably the most important requirement for attaining the widespread productivity increases required for the consumption model.[25]

In industry, policies would aim at a steady decrease in protection, at programs to assist business in meeting stronger competition, and probably at elimination of the subsidies for the purchase of capital goods that have probably biased technology toward more capital-intensive forms. The reduction in protection has already been started in 1967, with a reduction in tariffs, elimination of the special category of imports, and greater attention to competitive price in granting protection under the Law of Similars. The government should attempt, wherever possible, to counter demands for restoring higher protection with proposals to assist in improving efficiency and lowering costs of production. Some such programs are already under way, and others are in the planning stage; examples are the subsidized loans for replacing obsolete equipment in the textile industry, and the planned Productivity Center, which will offer training and technical assistance in various techniques of management and administration, mainly to smaller firms in "traditional" industries. Removing subsidies for purchases of capital goods would imply increasing protection to some capital goods that are now virtually unprotected, and eliminating tariff exemption for certain importers of these goods. (Continued subsidies for capital equipment for agriculture may still be a good idea; removing subsidies applies more to capital goods for industry.)

There are many difficulties, political as well as economic, in achieving this kind of development in Brazil. But development consists of more than ten more years of rapid growth of GNP. The contrasts between São Paulo and the Northeast, between *favelas* and luxury apartments in Copacabana, are not only undesirable but indeed unstable. Brazil has created the most modern and diversified industry in Latin America. Perhaps the new goal should be to increase the number of

[25] For studies of the deficiencies in these sectors, the reader is referred to the EPEA *Diagnósticos* on those subjects, published by the Ministry of Planning of the Government of Brazil in 1966 and 1967.

Brazilians this industry serves. Such a goal appears not only to be equitable, but also to offer the best chances for self-sustaining economic and social progress.

APPENDIX TO CHAPTER 2

COMPARISON WITH AN INTERCOUNTRY PATTERN

Studying one case history can be more meaningful if we have similar histories in mind. How does the evolution of Brazil's industrial structure compare with the experience of other countries? For comparison, we shall use the results of a study published by the United Nations showing that a strong relation exists between the structure of industry in a given country and the per-capita income and population of that country.[1] In other words, if we know the levels of per-capita income and population, we can do a pretty good job of predicting the level added in each branch of industry.

The existence of this relationship does not imply that the levels of income and populations cause the levels of industrial production to be as they are. Nor does it imply that, for any particular country, the pattern of industrial activity should be as predicted. Natural resource endowments, demand patterns, trading relationships, and other factors may and do cause particular patterns to differ from the average intercountry tendency.

Apart from the peculiarities of individual countries, the normal evolution of the pattern of industrial production over time may not follow the path predicted by the cross-section study. Variance between time series and cross-section behavior is common in economic activity; savings functions are a common example. The data in the UN study are consistent with the possibility that the cross-section pattern is shifting over time.[2] Thus, even the "normal" evolution of value added in a sector may not be that predicted by inserting

[1] A Study of Industrial Growth, 1963. Sales No. 63.II.B.2. The UN study is essentially a re-estimation of the original work by Hollis B. Chenery, "Patterns of Industrial Growth," American Economic Review, Sept. 1960.

[2] See the Study, pages 43–52.

time series of the income and population variables and deriving time series of industrial value added from the equations based on the cross section.

Another of the problems of comparing time series and cross-section behavior is that of changing relative prices. Relative prices have shifted significantly in Brazil in recent decades, and patterns of growth look quite different if one attempts to hold relative prices constant. The correct way to treat this problem is not perfectly clear, but we believe the best way is to let relative prices vary. The major reason for this is that there was no correction made for different relative prices in the observations in the original UN study.

These problems of possible time shifts in the cross-section pattern and changing relative prices imply that the changes over time — that is, the growth rates — apparently predicted by the results of the UN study may not really represent the average intercountry tendency. The absolute magnitudes predicted for any particular year are also subject to some difficulties. The most serious of these is probably the choice of an exchange rate for "value added"; another is differences in industrial classifications. We have tried to minimize such distortions but must point out that a margin of uncertainty remains.

Having stated all these qualifications, we present on the following graphs of the behavior of nine selected sectors of the Brazilian economy relative to the behavior predicted by the UN study. Each graph shows the deviations from the predicted value added as percentages of the predicted value added. We also present two tables, one a comparison of the predicted and actual structures of the Brazilian economy for 1949 and 1964 (Table A-1), the other a comparison of predicted and actual growth during the 1949–1964 period (Table A-2).

We can draw several conclusions from these results. First, a set of methodological implications: the results of the UN study predict Brazil's industrial structure only roughly. Actual value added deviates considerably from predicted value added in many sectors, and in the total. In general structure, the predictions were fairly accurate, but the actual growth of each sector during the 1949–1964 period bore little resemblance to the predictions.

If we had used the cross-section results in, say, 1949 to predict

TABLE A-1. ACTUAL AND PREDICTED INDUSTRIAL STRUCTURE
(percent of total) [a]

Sector	ISIC classification	1949 Actual	1949 Predicted	1964 Actual	1964 Predicted
Food, beverages, and tobacco	(20–22)	27	23	22	15
Textiles	(23)	19	14	11	13
Clothing and footwear	(24)	4	5	3	4
Wood products	(25–26)	6	4	4	4
Paper and products	(27)	2	2	2	2
Printing and publishing	(28)	4	3	2	3
Leather products	(29)	1	1	1	1
Rubber products	(30)	2	2	2	1
Chemicals	(31–32)	10	14	17	14
Nonmetallic mineral products	(33)	7	6	4	5
Basic metals	(34)	6	5	9	10
Metal products	(35–38)	10	18	22	25
Miscellaneous	(39)	2	2	1	2
Total	(20–39)	100	100	100	100
Total (million U.S.$)		$2,295	$2,845	$8,620	$7,420

Source: "Predicted" values calculated by the authors from the equations in the
UN *Study.* Actual values from Industrial Census for 1949; *Industrias
de Transformação, Dados Gerais* — 1963/64, IBGE, April 1966 for 1964.
[a] Details may not add to totals because of rounding.

TABLE A-2. ACTUAL AND PREDICTED SECTORAL GROWTH, 1949–1964

Sector	ISIC classification	Percentages Actual	Percentages Predicted	Percentages Difference
Food, beverages, and tobacco	(20–22)	7.7	6.9	12%
Textiles	(23)	4.9	9.2	−47
Clothing and footwear	(24)	6.9	8.1	−15
Wood products	(25–26)	5.2	9.6	−46
Paper and products	(27)	9.5	12.3	−23
Printing and publishing	(28)	4.2	9.5	−56
Leather products	(29)	5.5	7.3	−25
Rubber products	(30)	9.4	7.8	20
Chemicals	(31–32)	12.8	8.8	45
Nonmetallic mineral products	(33)	5.2	8.2	−37
Basic metals	(34)	12.4	14.1	−12
Metal products	(35–38)	15.2	12.1	26

Source: See Table A-1.

DEVIATIONS FROM INTERCOUNTRY PATTERN

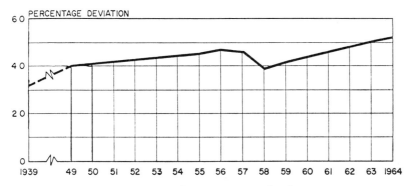

FIGURE A1: Food, Beverages, and Tobacco

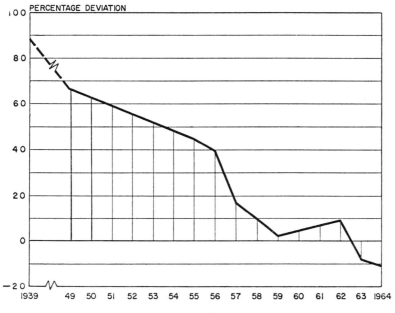

FIGURE A2: Textiles

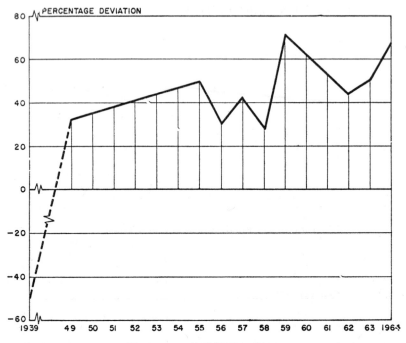

FIGURE A3: Rubber Products

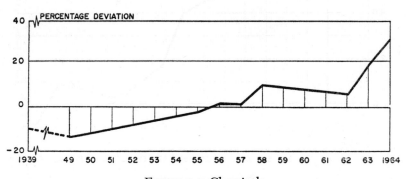

FIGURE A4: Chemicals

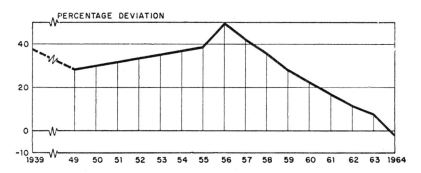

FIGURE A5: Nonmetallic Mineral Products

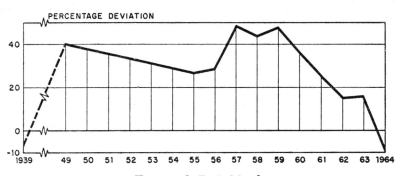

FIGURE A6: Basic Metals

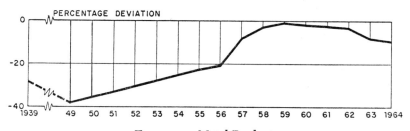

FIGURE A7: Metal Products

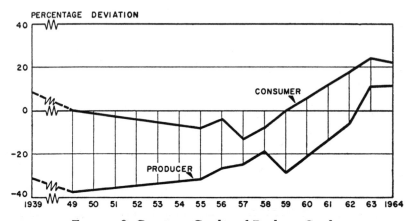

FIGURE A8: Consumer Goods and Producer Goods

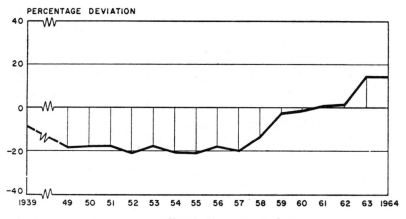

FIGURE A9: All Manufacturing Industry

either the levels of value added in, say, 1964, or the future growth rate of each sector, we would have done a pretty poor job. Thus, the usefulness of cross-section results for making sectoral projections of growth, investment requirements, and so forth is seriously in doubt. The cross-section results not only do not tell us what should happen; neither do they tell us with any useful degree of precision what will happen.

If we had further information about the context in which the observed patterns evolved, and some confidence in an idea of how that context might look in the future, the cross-section results might be useful as one way of projecting future growth, the results to be compared with other projections to arrive at a final set of predictions. Some of this type of analysis is presented below, where we discuss the results for each sector in turn.

Food, Beverages, and Tobacco
(International Standard Industrial Classification 20–22)

Production in this sector has been consistently above the "normal" level, with a slightly rising trend. We can speculatively explain this greater-than-expected activity in two ways. The first is the relatively good performance of Brazilian agriculture, which has provided a very elastic (that is, easily expandable) supply of raw materials. This is no doubt largely due to the plentiful supply of land. A second, less certain, is that a relatively high degree of income inequality may be hidden behind the average per-capita income figures for Brazil. If income distribution is more skewed in Brazil than in countries with similar incomes and populations, we would expect the consumption of food products to be relatively higher.

In a study of the relative efficiency of various Brazilian industries, we found that many branches of this sector ranked very high. The overall picture of this sector is thus one of efficient production, adequate raw material supplies, and perhaps a stronger demand than Brazil's average per-capita income would indicate.

Textiles (ISIC 23)

The textile industry presents a dramatic picture of a once-healthy but now sick industry. Before and during World War II,

Brazil was one of the world's principle producers and exporters of textiles. Today a large part of the industry is extremely inefficient and produces almost exclusively for domestic consumption, at high prices permitted by a tariff which until March 1967 averaged over 200 percent.[3] There seems to be no natural or fixed technological reason for the decline and present state of the textile industry. A few Brazilian producers are able to export. The value of present production is more or less at the level of the international pattern, but this is partially a statistical phenomenon resulting from high prices.

The industry can be thought of as composed of two parts. One produces synthetic and high-quality natural textiles for higher-income domestic consumers and for export. Most firms in this part of the industry are either quite young or have recently invested heavily in modern equipment. The other part of the industry produces lower quality natural textiles, in conditions of great inefficiency. This part is faced with weakening demand and overcapacity because of the shift in demand to synthetics and because of the decreasing or stagnant purchasing power of the lower-income groups. Many firms in this part of the industry are trapped in a vicious cycle of low sales, low profits, and inability to finance the modernization needed to increase sales and profits.[4]

Customs tariffs on textiles and on clothing were and are higher than in any other sector — averaging 20 percent. In the revised tariff schedule adopted in early 1967, they still average about 100 percent. Lowering this extreme barrier to competition, in conjunction with a reequipment and reorganization program that has already been started, would probably be a good idea.

Rubber Products (ISIC 30)

A large part of the recent growth of this sector is explained by greater demand for tires for Brazil's automobile industry.

---

[3] See Bergsman and Malan, "A Estrutura de Proteção no Brasil," *Revista Brasileira de Economia*, Sept. 1967. Brazil's textile industry has been frequently studied. See the EPEA *Diagnóstico* and the studies cited there.

[4] See J. Bergsman, *"Brazil's Industrialization and Trade Policies,* Oxford University Press, to appear.

Chemicals (ISIC 31–32)

One of the most dynamic in any developing economy, the chemical sector has grown even more rapidly than normal in Brazil. Analysis of this extremely heterogeneous sector is very difficult at this level, but one may note generally low tariff protection, preferential treatment of investment by the government, and a relatively mature consumer-oriented branch of the sector (soaps, pharmaceuticals, and so on). Remaining opportunities for import substitution lead us to expect growth in this industry to continue at a rapid pace.

Nonmetallic Mineral Products

This sector produces mostly construction materials. Its decline in the early 1960's is due to the falling off of both residential construction and public investment. The former declined because rent controls reduced the profitability of building to rent, and scarcity of home financing reduced the demand for homes to buy. The latter declined as the government cut investment to try to reduce inflationary pressures.

Basic Metals (ISIC 34) and Metal Products (ISIC 35–38) [5]

Both basic metals and metal products have been tending towards the "normal" level of production. The basic metals sector had been above the normal level, probably reflecting Brazil's comparative advantages, principally in iron and steel. Iron and steel is one of the most efficient of Brazil's industries, relative to international patterns; nonferrous metals are relatively inefficient but rapidly becoming more efficient. Metal products, which includes all capital and consumer durable goods, electrical and transportation equipment, and semifinished metal products as low on the scale as foundry products and forgings, has been below the "normal" level but has recently caught up. This recent growth is due in large part to the automobile industry, started in the mid-1950's.

[5] There is a significant difference between the Brazilian and the ISIC classifications of these two sectors, and we have adjusted the original data as best we could. The difference is that many activities in ISIC 35 are included in the Brazilian sector "Metalúrgica." We are indebted to Walter Ferri for pointing this out to us.

In the drive to industrialize, imports of capital goods were often permitted with low or zero customs duties, and with other special benefits as well. This naturally retarded growth in the domestic capital-goods industry. Even so, the domestic industry is reasonably well developed, and with the recent "Buy Brazilian Act," limiting special treatment for imports, the whole metal and metal-products sector will probably grow quite rapidly.

Consumer and Producer Goods

Consumer-oriented goods and producer-oriented goods followed a similar trend. Consumer goods were more or less at the level of the international pattern, rising steeply since the mid-1950's to about 25 percent above the "normal" level in 1963–1964. Producer goods were well below the "normal" level until the early 1960's, and in 1963–1964 were only about 10 percent above it. This means that the declining importance of consumer goods and growing importance of producer goods was quite consistent with their typical behavior in other countries. Moreover, compared to average intercountry tendencies, Brazil's consumer-goods industries appear to be relatively more important than her producer-goods industries. This may be partly explained by the higher relative price of consumer goods, which receive far more tariff protection than producer goods.[6]

Total Manufacturing

The sustained, strong growth of industry in Brazil is a justly well-known and much-discussed phenomenon. As we noted earlier, growth averaged over 8 percent per year for the entire period 1939–1964, the rate rising more or less steadily throughout. This is an experience that few now less-developed countries have matched.

If we compare this performance with that predicted by the UN study (Figure A-9), we see that the actual growth rate was less than would be expected for a country with Brazil's income and population growth during the 1940's, and barely equal to the expected rate from 1950 to around 1955–1957. Only since the mid-1950's has Brazilian industry grown faster than "normal." And if we can accept

[6] See Bergsman, *op.cit.*

our exchange rate, only around 1960 did the level of industrial activity reach "normal"; it was around 20 percent below normal from 1949 through the mid-1950's.

Brazil's industrialization, viewed in this light, does not appear excessive or overdone. A thorough evaluation of every policy that affected industrialization, and of every relevant investment, would surely disclose some wise decisions and some not so wise. But the present evidence indicates that the overall level of industrial activity reached in the early 1960's was appropriate for a country the size of Brazil.

For the information of interested readers, we present in Tables A-3 and A-4 the basic results of this comparison: the actual and predicted value added for each year and for each sector studied.

TABLE A-3. ACTUAL VALUE ADDED
(according to the ISIC, in million 1953 US$)

Sector	1939	1949	1955	1956	1957	1958	1959	1962	1963	1964
20–22	345	612	799	861	874	958	1118	1496	1811	1859
23	252	440	562	587	511	568	625	914	884	898
24	55	97	144	156	157	170	190	245	268	266
25–26	62	148	205	206	199	233	292	319	338	316
27	17	52	99	94	89	116	164	196	228	203
28	41	92	108	106	120	136	162	175	200	170
29	19	31	40	44	45	51	59	71	65	69
30	7	44	75	67	81	75	122	136	151	170
31–32	124	230	404	429	486	566	723	957	1215	1386
33	61	165	192	213	256	289	356	367	432	355
34	53	129	222	283	277	344	442	634	773	744
35–38	97	220	408	466	568	756	995	1484	1736	1803
39	13	37	73	84	89	111	85	122	114	118
Total	1146	2297	3331	3596	3752	4373	5333	7116	8215	8357

Source: Calculated by the authors from Industrial Censuses for 1939, 1949, and 1959; Industrial Register, 1955 and 1958; Industrías de Transformação, Dados Gerais – 1963/64, IBGE, April 1966 for 1964.

TABLE A-4. PREDICTED VALUE ADDED
(million 1953 US$)

Sector	1939	1949	1955	1956	1957	1958	1959	1962	1963	1964
20–22	259	423	552	590	601	685	791	1005	1128	1156
23	134	265	388	421	438	513	614	834	954	992
24	52	101	143	152	158	183	215	285	318	328
25–26	40	84	123	132	137	162	194	265	300	310
27	12	29	45	50	51	65	85	130	158	165
28	24	56	85	90	96	112	134	184	205	212
29	12	19	23	25	25	30	35	41	54	55
30	14	33	50	51	56	63	71	94	99	102
31–32	114	272	415	441	475	553	652	906	1005	1042
33	66	117	154	168	171	200	240	319	369	380
34	39	103	162	188	194	254	344	556	710	748
35–38	137	348	529	592	615	776	1010	1540	1865	1940
39	16	40	62	67	71	86	106	153	176	183
Total	919	1890	2731	2967	3088	3682	4491	6128	7341	7613

Source: Calculated from the equations in the UN *Study of Industrial Growth*, Table 1, page 7.

CHAPTER 3

Steel and the Brazilian Economy

Werner Baer

The development of the Brazilian economy after World War II was dominated by industrial growth.[1] While the real Gross Domestic Product grew at an annual rate of close to 6 percent from the early 1950's to the early 1960's, industrial production grew at an annual rate of close to 10 percent. The main impulse behind the industrialization was government policies encouraging import substitution. From the very beginning, one of the chief characteristics of these policies was the stimulation of vertical integration within the developing industrial complex. That is, the government tried to stimulate a maximum amount of forward and backward linkages within the economy.[2] It is thus not surprising to find that the steel industry was

[1] This essay is based on material from my forthcoming monograph *The Development of the Brazilian Steel Industry.* I would like to thank J. Almeida, M. Falcão, I. Kerstenetzky, and W. O. Thweatt for helpful suggestions in writing this essay. My steel study was made possible by support from the Social Science Research Council and the Instituto Brasileiro de Economia of the *Fundação Getúlio Vargas.* Space does not allow me to mention the many economists and engineers who were instrumental in helping me to obtain data and in shaping my ideas. They will all be credited in my forthcoming monograph.

[2] For a detailed description and analysis of this policy see Werner Baer, *Industrialization and Economic Development in Brazil* (Homewood, Ill.: Richard D. Irwin, 1965), chaps. 3 and 6.

one of the most dynamic industries, its output growing at an annual rate more than 50 percent higher than the growth rate of industrial production.

An industrialization policy maximizing internal linkages can be criticized as being autarkic in nature, as placing no emphasis on selecting sectors with the greatest potential comparative advantage, and thus as being wasteful of scarce investment resources. It has also been claimed that maximizing linkages within an economy will result in production on too small a scale in most industries, thus depriving most industries of economies of scale. Two main counterarguments have been developed. First, it is often difficult to know ahead of time where a country's potential comparative advantages really are; only after the opportunity has existed for a broad spectrum of industries to develop over a period of time can one make some judgment about which industries deserve to survive. Second, given the restrictive policies of the developed countries with regard to imports of manufactures from developing countries together with the difficulties of creating effectively integrated regional markets, many countries had no choice but to promote the development of well-balanced industrial parks.

The critics of industrialization policies emphasizing linkages have usually singled out the heavier industries, such as steel, for their attack. They have developed a conventional wisdom that stresses the development of lighter industries as more within the legitimate sphere of activity of developing nations. Steel mills and other heavy industries are thought to be too complex for the labor and managerial talents available. Where such projects have been developed, they have usually been dismissed by these critics as wasteful prestige projects. These criticisms are not legitimate, since they assume that all developing countries are homogeneous, that grand generalizations can be made and all-inclusive theories can be constructed. They do not take into account the differences in resources, geography, and population of the developing countries.

In this paper I shall review the growth of the Brazilian steel industry and its effect on the growth of the economy, and I shall try to analyze some indicators of its performance. From the data presented, I hope to draw some conclusions about the role of heavy industry in the process of economic development.

STEEL TECHNOLOGY AND BRAZIL'S RESOURCES FOR STEELMAKING

Brazil possesses most of the raw materials and other natural resources necessary for the manufacture of steel products: iron ore, limestone, manganese, water, and a huge hydro-electric-power potential. The country has one of the world's largest and highest-quality iron ore reserves (known reserves in 1966 amounted to more than 27 billion tons, the iron content varying between 58 and 66 percent). Most of the ore is mined in the state of Minas Gerais. Coal is the only main raw material input lacking. The only coal deposits in Brazil are in the south, mainly in the state of Santa Catarina. However, this coal is of poor quality, has a high ash content, and cannot be relied on exclusively for producing coke. Thus, ever since the introduction of coke-using blast furnaces in Brazil, the major imported input has been coal. Until the end of 1966, Brazilian mills using coke were forced by the government to consume 40 percent domestic coal to protect the domestic coal industry.[3]

The making of final steel products involves four basic stages of production: the mining and treatment of raw materials, the reduction of iron ore into pig iron, the transformation (or refining) of pig iron into steel, and the rolling of steel ingots into final steel products.[4]

A fully integrated mill includes all of these stages. The final products coming out of the rolling mill can be divided into two basic types: flat and nonflat. The former include such

[3] In the decade from the mid-1950's to the mid-1960's, Brazil has become a major iron-ore exporter. The coal used by the steel industry is usually shipped in the empty returning ore vessels. The use of domestic coal substantially lowered the productivity of the blast furnaces until the government lowered the requirement of domestic coal inputs in 1966.

[4] My forthcoming monograph will contain a more detailed description of steelmaking processes and the economics of steel technology. One of the standard reference works for steelmaking is Harold E. McGannon, ed., *The Making, Shaping, and Treating of Steel*, eighth edition (Pittsburg, Pa.: United States Steel Corporation, 1964).

products as sheets and tin plate, that is, products used in the automobile, shipbuilding, canning, boiler-making, and many other industries. Nonflat products include bars, rods, rails, seamless tubes, heavy sections, and so on. Many of the latter are associated with the housing and to a large extent the road-building industry.

Besides fully integrated firms, one finds in Brazil many semi-integrated firms. These may be firms specializing in the production of pig iron and pig-iron products; or firms making steel ingots from pig iron bought from outside or from scrap, and rolling these ingots into final products (some of these firms specialize in "special steels"); or firms specializing only in rolling steel ingots bought from other firms.

The production of pig iron with blast furnaces using charcoal rather than coke is still widespread in Brazil (in the mid-1960's about 40 percent of the country's pig-iron production was based on charcoal). Charcoal comes mainly from the natural forests or eucalyptus plantations in Minas Gerais. It is relatively cheap because of the low-wage rural labor employed and the cheapness of the land. The use of charcoal permits substantial capital savings, since the costly coke ovens and their ancillary units are not needed. Belgo-Mineira, with an output of about 400,000 tons annually, is the world's largest integrated steel firm based on charcoal.[5]

The economist's traditional concern with capital vs. labor-intensive techniques of production is usually not especially relevant in choosing steel technology. For example, the blast furnaces of large firms producing 700 tons or more of pig iron a day cannot rely on labor-intensive methods of charging the furnace. The use of fairly automatized techniques becomes inevitable. Of course, charcoal-using furnaces have a greater labor-absorption capacity, given the labor-intensive methods of collecting wood and making charcoal. The same situation holds for the steel-shop section of a firm. The efficiency of the

[5] The future of charcoal-based steel production in Brazil is limited. With the natural wood supply close to the plants vanishing, the possibility of rising labor costs, and the costs of establishing eucalyptus plantations, the cost advantages of charcoal-based production may soon disappear. For firms with no plantations the cost of charcoal is already increasing, since the natural forests are farther and farther from the mills.

Linz Donawitz or oxygen method is now generally recognized as being superior to the older open-hearth method, and every new large plant will adopt it. Smaller firms, especially those producing specialty steels, will use electric furnaces. The rolling mills have even fewer options. Older mills still use semi-automatized equipment. In smaller Brazilian mills one can still find workers pushing billets back and forth through rollers, but this is an inefficient method that cannot be used at all in the production of flat products.

This does not mean that the steel industry has a small direct-employment impact. Much labor is absorbed in a whole series of ancillary activities. Foundries making ingot molds are usually an integral part of a firm, and in Brazil the methods used are not overly automatized; maintenance workshops producing parts for all sections are labor-intensive in nature, and are larger in Brazil than in more industrially advanced countries as a result of the difficulty of obtaining spare parts; the frequent relining (especially in the steel shop) of vessels and ladles with refractory bricks is by its nature labor-intensive. Thus in 1964, when output was over 3 million tons of ingot steel, the industry directly employed about 80,000 workers (not counting charcoal workers, office workers in headquarters and commercial branches of the firms, coal workers in Santa Catarina, and so on).

HISTORICAL SUMMARY

Ironworking activities in Brazil can be traced back to the mid-sixteenth century. Forges operated in what is now the state of São Paulo in the sixteenth and seventeenth centuries, and in Minas Gerais during the gold rush in the eighteenth century, producing utensils for the mines.[6] In the early nineteenth century, with the arrival of the Portuguese royal family in Brazil, official stimulus was given to iron-smelting operations. Foreign experts were brought to Brazil to supervise the build-

[6] Until the nineteenth century the mercantilistic policies of the Portuguese government did not permit the establishment of any manufacturing operations in the Brazilian colonies; thus all these early efforts were clandestine in nature.

ing and operation of establishments that produced weapons for the military and utensils for diamond mining in Minas Gerais and for farming. However, most of these establishments were closed as the century wore on.

Although iron production never completely ceased in the nineteenth century, it took place only in small shops. In 1964, 120 forges were reported in operation, producing about 1,550 tons annually. Scientific interest in iron ore and iron and steel production was maintained throughout the century. In 1879 the School of Mines at Ouro Prêto, Minas Gerais, was founded for the training of geologists and metallurgical engineers; and a little later the Escola Politécnica of São Paulo was founded. The Brazilian army also showed a keen interest in metallurgy throughout the nineteenth century, as well as in the twentieth. It was especially interested in the growth of iron and steel production. In 1930 the army founded the Escola de Engenharia do Exército, which was to produce some of Brazil's finest metallurgical engineers. (Many of today's top men in the steel industry are graduates of this institute.) Thus, it is interesting to note that although steel production in Brazil was not significant until the fourth decade of the twentieth century, the country had long accepted the fact of Brazil's future destiny as a large steel producer — hence the great emphasis on the training of metallurgical engineers even before the surge in demand for their services.

As Brazil entered the twentieth century, pig-iron production had reached only 2,000 tons, most of which was used to make tools and spare parts for the railroads, large coffee plantations, and sugar mills. Production grew little in the next ten years; imports of rolled-steel products averaged 272,500 tons in the period 1908–12. In 1924, the earliest date for steel-production statistics, total output was only 4,492 tons.

With growing steel imports in the first decades of the twentieth century, government circles became increasingly interested in establishing large-scale steel production. The problem was lack of government or private capital. Although World War I stimulated industrial growth, its effect on iron and steel output was not pronounced.[7] Iron production reached

---

[7] The major growth was in the textile, food products, and other light industries. See Baer, *op. cit.*, chap. 2.

about 10,000 tons in 1919. Steel output was still negligible, and up to the mid-1920's almost all rolled-steel products were still imported.

What growth there was in iron and steel production in the first three decades of the twentieth century was mainly on the initiative of private entrepreneurs. In 1921 foreign capital and know-how entered the picture when the Belgian-Luxembourg ARBED group, at the invitation of the governor of Minas Gerais, absorbed a small steel shop and founded the Companhia Siderúrgica Belgo-Mineira. Other small firms were founded in the 1920's, especially in the São Paulo area, turning out steel and steel products destined for the manufacture of equipment for the sugar industry. Some of these firms constructed relatively primitive rolling facilities to produce bars and rods for the construction industry.

In the mid-1930's Belgo-Mineira built an integrated steel mill at Monlevade, Minas Gerais, and by the end of that decade the steel industry had made substantial progress. Pig-iron production reached 185,000 tons in 1940, steel-ingot production, 141,200 tons. Brazil no longer directly imported pig iron and steel ingots, though it still imported 70 percent of the rolled products it consumed.

Throughout the 1930's there was a powerful movement within the government to create a large-scale fully integrated steel mill based on coke,[8] and later in the decade, Getúlio Vargas became increasingly committed to build such a firm either by stimulating private enterprise (foreign or domestic) or by government intervention. When the U.S. Steel Corporation decided not to build a plant (though the report of its experts had made a favorable recommendation), the government decided to build an integrated steel mill itself.[9] After a

[8] Up to that time all fully integrated firms used charcoal, while semi-integrated firms used scrap-consuming electric steel furnaces.

[9] My forthcoming monograph will go in much greater detail into the circumstances that led the government to enter the picture. I have also omitted in this narrative the Farquhar controversy. Farquhar, an American entrepreneur, had a scheme for establishing a large firm exporting iron ore and building a steel mill. The latter would have used imported coal brought back by empty iron-ore boats. For political reasons, his scheme was never realized.

period of negotiation, in which the Brazilians used the interest of the Germans in building a plant in Brazil as an implied threat, the U.S. Export-Import Bank agreed to finance the building of the steel works at Volta Redonda.[10] The plant was built in the years 1940–1946; because of wartime conditions construction took longer than originally expected. In April 1946 Volta Redonda began to produce coke, and in June of that year the blast furnace and steel shop began to function. The rolling mills, however, were not finished until late 1947. When they began to operate in 1948, Brazil became the first Latin-American country to have a fully integrated coke-based steel mill.

Throughout the 1930's and 1940's smaller firms were founded, many of a semi-integrated nature (firms producing steel using electric furnaces to melt down scrap). Often these operations began as subsidiaries of firms producing various types of equipment that wanted to integrate backward. Other steel mills were founded by private entrepreneurs, but were taken over by the government as a result of their indebtedness. A case in point is the fully integrated specialized-steel firm Acesita, founded privately but eventually passing into the control of its principal creditor, the Banco do Brasil.

The industrial growth of the post-World-War-II period, and especially the emphasis in the 1950's on the vertical integration of Brazil's industrial complex, led to the expansion of existing steel-producing facilities and the creation of new enterprises, both private and governmental. Volta Redonda, whose ingot capacity was 270,000 tons when it opened in 1946, went through successive expansions until in 1965 its capacity was approximately 1,400,00 ingot tons. Belgo-Mineira's successive expansions resulted in a capacity of 450,000 tons in 1965. Many of the smaller private firms, both semi-integrated and fully integrated, also expanded with the growth of the internal market.[11] More small firms also sprang up in the 1950's. The

[10] Documentation for this episode can be obtained in *Foreign Relations of the United States, Diplomatic Papers, 1940*, Volume V, "The American Republics" (Washington: United States Government Printing Office, 1961), pp. 600–614.

[11] The industry was protected through tariffs and direct controls. That is, a customer had to prove first that local firms could not supply his

largest of the new firms of the 1950's was the German concern Mannesmann, which constructed a fully integrated mill specializing in the production of seamless tubes and various types of special steels.

During the 1950's two new large integrated mills were conceived, Usiminas and Cosipa. The basic idea for the creation of these firms was that of local private and governmental interests. Usiminas was constructed by a Japanese steel consortium, which originally participated with 40 percent ownership. The Brazilian ownership was originally divided between the state of Minas Gerais, the Government Economic Development Bank (BNDE), some other state-owned companies, and a smaller group of private interests. As the project's costs increased during construction beyond what was originally planned, the BNDE, through its contributions, gradually became the majority owner, Japanese interest shrinking to about 20 percent. Cosipa was originally created by private interests. However, by the late 1950's the government of the state of São Paulo and the BNDE had to enter the picture to get the project under way. Gradually the BNDE achieved the controlling interest in the company. Both Usiminas and Cosipa are fully integrated coke-based plants, specializing in flat products. Usiminas began operation in October 1962, when its first blast furnace began to produce pig iron; its steel furnaces and rolling mills started to function in mid-1963. Cosipa, which began operating its rolling mills in December 1963 (rolling ingots from Volta Redonda), started to function as a fully integrated mill in early 1966.

In 1965 about two-thirds of Brazil's steel-producing capacity was in the hands of government-controlled firms. It is interesting to note that in each case the government came in reluctantly. A private solution was first contemplated in the case of Volta Redonda; this failed mainly with the bowing-out of U.S. Steel. Cosipa was the brainchild of private groups, Usiminas of local private and government groups. In each instance the costs proved too high for any one private group, and since the government emphasized import-substitution in

needs before receiving permission to import. For certain products, the Companhia Siderúrgica Nacional had an import monopoly.

basic industries, it made its development bank underwrite the successful conclusion of these projects.[12]

STEEL AND THE REST OF THE ECONOMY

The growth of the iron and steel industry in absolute terms is summarized in Table 1, which shows the production and total apparent consumption of iron, steel ingots, and rolled-steel products for selected years, also the ratio of imports of each of these items to total apparent consumption. It would seem, from the data, that by the early 1930's Brazil was completely self-sufficient in producing pig-iron, and that by the early 1950's self-sufficiency in ingot-steel production had also been achieved. This, however, is an illusion. A detailed analysis of rolled-steel product imports would show that many of these imports were semifinished products destined for rerolling operations in Brazil, which would indicate that Brazil had not become completely self-sufficient in pig-iron or ingot-steel production. Import substitution of rolled-steel products was much slower. Only with the full operation of Volta Redonda in the late 1940's did Brazil begin to rely on its own rolled products for almost 70 percent of its needs. When Usiminas and Cosipa came into operation in the 1960's, Brazil supplied itself with about 90 percent of the steel products it needed.

A comparison of the growth rates of ingot and rolled-steel production with various aggregates is shown in Table 2. The yearly growth rate of the real Gross National Product in the period 1947–1961 was smaller than the yearly growth rate of industrial production, and the yearly growth rates of steel-ingot and rolled-steel production were substantially higher than the growth rates of industrial production. Thus, iron and steel production was one of the leading subsectors of industry, which

---

[12] During the 1950's, as industrialization snowballed, pig iron came into short supply. This gave rise to blast-furnace construction in various parts of Minas Gerais by individuals who owned land with iron-ore deposits. The total capacity of these operations rose to almost 900,000 tons. By the early 1960's, however, more than half of this capacity was idle, since the larger firms' pig-iron production capacity had substantially increased.

TABLE 1. Brazilian Production of Iron and Steel
(tons)

Year	Pig iron			Steel ingot			Rolled steel products		
	Production	Apparent consumption	Imports (percent of consumption)	Production	Apparent consumption	Imports (percent of consumption)	Production	Apparent consumption	Imports (percent of consumption)
1925	30,046	41,760	28.0	7,559	14,123	46.5	283	373,485	99.9
1930	35,305	37,258	5.2	20,985	24,766	15.3	25,895	259,224	90.0
1940	185,570	185,570	0.0	141,201	147,810	4.5	135,293	414,519	69.4
1945	259,909	259,909	0.0	205,935	233,474	11.8	165,805	465,639	67.5
1950	728,979	728,979	0.0	788,557	803,119	1.8	572,489	843,049	32.6
1960	1,749,848	1,749,848	0.0	1,843,019	1,843,019	0.0	1,712,289	2,128,331	20.4
1964	2,445,525	2,445,525	0.0	3,043,749	3,043,749	0.0	2,377,000	2,595,000	11.5
1965	2,258,529	2,258,529	0.0	2,978,122	2,978,122	0.0	2,302,400	2,166,300	8.6
1966	2,939,230	2,939,230	0.0	3,775,104	3,775,104	0.0	2,903,828	n.a.	n.a.

Source: CEPAL, A Economia Siderúrgica da América Latina: Monografia do Brasil, Santiago: Dec. 1964 (mimeographed, prepared by Dr. M. Falcão); Instituto Brasileiro de Siderúrgica, Boletim IBS; IBGE, O Brasil em Números; import data for iron and steel from IBRE, Fundação Getúlio Vargas.

was the leading sector of the economy. These growth rates cannot be dismissed as being high because of a tiny base: Table 1 shows that iron and steel production at the beginning of the post-World-War-II period was not negligible. Table 2 also shows the growth rates of apparent consumption of steel-ingot and rolled-steel products as being smaller than the production growth rates which indicates substantial import substitution of steel products. The apparent growth rate of ingot-steel consumption is still higher than the industrial production growth

TABLE 2. GROWTH RATES OF STEEL AND STEEL PRODUCTS
(*percent*)

Year	Real GDP	Indus-trial pro-duction	Steel-ingot pro-duction	Rolled-steel pro-duction	Steel-ingot apparent con-sumption	Rolled-steel apparent con-sumption
1947–61	6.00	9.50	13.50	15.30	12.50	9.25
1947–55	5.75	9.00	14.50	16.00	13.50	8.50
1956–61	6.75	11.00	10.50	12.50	11.00	11.00
1962–64	3.50	4.40	10.00	7.25	10.00	4.80

Source: Calculated from the sources mentioned in Table 1.

rate, while the apparent growth rate of rolled-steel product consumption is slightly lower than the industrial production growth rate. However, since the industrial production index includes a substantial proportion of production directly substituting imports, steel may still be considered one of the leading net-growth industries within the general industrial sector.

The cause of the high growth rates of steel consumption in Brazil is basically the policies adopted by the government to maximize the vertical integration of the industrialization process within the country. There exists substantial evidence to show that when most linkages of an industrialization process occur within a country (another way of describing vertical integration) steel production is affected more than other sectors. In a ranking of forward linkages in fourteen major industrial sectors in the United States, for example, the iron and steel industry came out first; in backward linkages, it came out fifth.[13] In absolute terms, the power of forward linkage was

[13] Baer, *op. cit.*, pp. 138–144.

about twice as strong in iron and steel as in the second-ranking industrial group, while in backward linkages iron and steel was less than 15 percent behind the first-ranking industry. In total repercussion effect — a weighted average of forward and backward linkages — iron and steel had the highest ranking. Since Brazil aims at producing a fairly self-sufficient industrial complex, maximizing internal linkages, the relative ranking of industries in terms of linkage effects can be considered similar in both economies (not, of course, the absolute values, which are not comparable).

Another insight into the large growth rates of steel relative to other sectors of the economy can be gained from the well-known United Nations study on industrial growth.[14] Taking a combined cross-section of fifty-three countries in 1953 and forty-eight countries in 1958, a regression analysis was made to determine the influence of per-capita income and population on the degree of industrialization; this was followed by a regression analysis to determine the output values of thirteen different sectors, using per-capita income, population, and degree of industrialization as independent variables. It was found that the income elasticity of total industrial output was 1.37, while income elasticity for the basic-metals sector was 1.99 (a figure topped only by the paper-products sector, which reached 2.03). Basic metals had the highest population elasticity and also the highest proportional response to the variable "degree of industrialization." The very high response of the basic-metals sector in the cross-section study shows that the high growth rate of the Brazilian steel sector, relative to industrial production and GNP growth rates, is consistent with observed trends throughout the world.

As a matter of fact, an experiment made for the year 1962, in which Brazilian data for per-capita income, population, and degree of industrialization were used to "predict" the "normal" pattern of Brazil's industrial structure within the framework of the U.N. model, showed that the actual contribution of the basic-metals sector was much smaller than expected.[15] It was predicted that basic metals would make up 9.7 percent of the

[14] United Nations, A Study of Industrial Growth (New York, 1963).
[15] Baer, op. cit., p. 145.

industrial sector's total value added, but the actual contribution amounted to only 5.7 percent. The explanation could be that the basic-metals sector comprises more than just the iron and steel industry. However, it should also be noted that 1962 imports of steel products were about 15 percent (by weight) of total steel-products consumption (they would have made up a higher percentage of consumption by value, being of a specialized nature). Whatever the accuracy of this experiment, the results indicate that the growth of Brazil's steel output was not out of proportion to general industrial growth, and that one might even suggest that the sector should have grown at an even faster rate.

Table 3 shows per-capita ingot-steel consumption for selected Latin-American countries. Despite the fact that Brazil is Latin America's major steel producer, per-capita consumption is less than in Argentina, Chile, and Mexico, and even smaller than the average for Latin America. This indicates that continued industrialization and per-capita income growth in Brazil will lead to substantial increases in the market for steel, and thus to the expansion of steel production.

Besides observing the aggregative growth rate of steel pro-

TABLE 3. APPARENT STEEL CONSUMPTION AND GROSS DOMESTIC
PRODUCT FOR SELECTED COUNTRIES

Country	Apparent steel ingot consumption (kg. per capita)			Gross national product (US$ per capita)	
	1952	1964[a]		1953	1964
Brazil	26.2	44.2	(3,222)	250	325
Argentina	46.7	108.0	(1,833)	n.a.	616
Colombia	13.0	33.5	(264)	n.a.	301 (1958)
Chile	47.5	86.4	(611)	n.a.	411 (1958)
Mexico	34.1	61.6	(2,402)	232	400
Peru	14.4	23.7	(87)	n.a.	250
Latin America	29.3	49.5	(8,793)	n.a.	n.a.
United States		615.0	(118,067)	2,080	2,900

Source: United Nations, *Statistical Yearbook*, 1965; United Nations, *Yearbook of National Accounts Statistics*, 1964; CEPAL, "La Economia Siderúrgica de América Latina," Feb. 1966 (mimeographed).
[a] Figures in parentheses represent total ingot-steel production in thousands of tons; the Brazilian figures are not accurate, but were not changed since the CEPAL document did not mention how the estimates were arrived at for each country. These aggregates should, however, give an idea of the relative magnitude of each country's steel capacity.

duction, it is also instructive to note the changes that have taken place in the nature of Brazil's steel production and consumption. One would expect an industrializing country to use an increasingly high proportion of flat products, which are used mostly in manufacturing. Table 4 shows production and con-

TABLE 4. PRODUCTION AND CONSUMPTION
OF FLAT PRODUCTS

Year	Production (percent of total steel production)	Consumption (percent of rolled-steel consumption)
1925	0.0	22.8
1930	0.0	25.0
1940	0.0	35.3
1945	0.0	26.5
1950	34.4	34.5
1960	41.3	41.6
1964	40.8	41.2

Source: Calculated from the sources used in Table 1.

TABLE 5. SECTORAL USE OF
STEEL PRODUCTS, 1964
(percent)

Automotive	6.4
Civil Construction	27.9
Railroads	4.4
Naval	6.9
Machine	6.3
Metallurgical Industries	31.5
Other	16.6
Total	100.0

Source: Estimated from data of Tecnometal study for BNDE (unpublished).

sumption of flat products as related to total production and consumption, and indicates the expected trend. Until the late 1940's hardly any flat products were produced in Brazil, but by the 1960's they composed over 40 percent of total output. The proportion of flat products consumed also rose drastically after World War II, which is easily explained by the nature of Brazil's industrialization in the 1950's and 1960's, when the emphasis was on stimulating such flat-product-using industries as automobiles and shipbuilding, and on the vertical integration of economic activity. One should thus have expected these changes in the structure of steel production and consumption.[16]

In Table 5, I have reproduced an estimate of the sectoral distribution of steel sales in Brazil for the year 1964. The automobile, naval, and metallurgical industries together use a percentage greater than the proportion of flats produced. The consumer of nonflat products is the construction industry. The small share of the automobile industry is because these are estimates of direct steel consumption, and the automobile industry buys its parts from many subcontractors who fall into the category "metallurgical industry."

It is not surprising that the steel industry should have a most powerful forward-linkage effect, since its output is rarely a final product, but rather an input into another industrial sector. Until the mid-1960's, most of Brazil's steel output was used domestically and the full linkage effect of the industry was felt internally. It is probable that the repercussion or linkage effect on the economy of flat products is considerable, since these products undergo many transformations in the process of being turned into final products and thus receive more value added than such items as rails, construction rods, and so on. Thus, the larger the value of flat products produced, the greater will be the repercussion effect of steel production on the economy.

FOREIGN EXCHANGE SAVINGS

It is very difficult to estimate the foreign exchange savings a country makes when import-substitution industries are established. Should one just compare the new domestically produced output with direct new imported inputs? Should one also take into account the foreign exchange used to pay the interest and amortization of foreign loans used to construct

[16] Steel experts have told me that the long-run equilibrium ratio of flats to nonflats for an industrialized country is about 50–50. As industrialization proceeds, at first the use of flats rises much faster than nonflats. But once a certain level of industrialization is reached, a country tends to consume more and more nonflat special steels.

the industry? And what about the indirect imported inputs the growth of the industry stimulates? Since these problems can never be satisfactorily resolved. I have made some arbitrary decisions in my calculations. I did not take into account the repayment of loans, since they should be linked to the general capacity of the economy to earn foreign exchange and since these loans, once repaid, are not of long-run interest in terms of the new structure of the economy and its operation.

I have measured the foreign exchange saved in the following manner. If O^{47} and O^{64} are steel outputs for the years 1947 and 1964, and if C^{47} and C^{64} and M^{47} and M^{64} represent steel consumption and imports respectively for the years indicated, then

$$C^{47} = O^{47} + M^{47}$$
$$\text{and}$$
$$C^{64} = O^{64} + M^{64}$$

If the steel output of 1947 had remained unchanged while steel consumption rose to the 1964 levels, then the additional steel imports that would have been needed in 1964 would have been equal to

$$\triangle M^{64} = C^{64} - O^{47} - M^{64}$$

Although I am fully aware that 1964 steel consumption would have been different if the 1947 steel-production level had not changed (though I assume that the growth of the economy would have been the same as it actually was, even without the development of the steel industry), I thought that the order of magnitude involved would be of interest. Multiplying $\triangle M^{64}$ by the per-ton steel price of imports in 1964, I obtained the product US$ 473.8 million. This would be the foreign exchange savings in 1964, given all my heroic assumptions. This has to be counterbalanced by the imported inputs of the steel industry. A rough estimate I made shows that the 1964 coal bill for the steel industry (coal being the chief imported input) amounted to US$ 24.4 million. Other imported inputs, such as various oils consumed, electrodes, and so on, can be assumed to be equal to coal imports. Foreign interest payments of the industry amounted to approximately US$ 35 million. No matter what alternatives one presents to the method used to make these estimates (even lowering the average import price used and assuming a lower growth rate of the economy than actually occurred), the foreign exchange savings implied are indeed impressive.

EFFICIENCY

A close examination of the steel industry has led me to conclude that an analysis of the productivity of labor is not very relevant in trying to evaluate the performance of the industry. In my cost estimates I have found that direct labor input in the blast furnaces of large integrated mills never amounted to more than 2 to 3 percent of the total cost of one ton of pig iron (in smaller establishments it was about 5 to 7 percent). The percentage was no bigger for the steel furnaces, and even smaller (around 1 percent) in the rolling mills.[17] This implies that even large proportional variations (ranging from 50 to 100 percent) in the labor-input price will not have appreciable effects on costs. I am not trying to say that total labor employed does not substantially affect total costs of the firm: there can be no doubt that Brazilian steel firms employ more labor in auxiliary activities and in office work than American or European firms. Also, many Brazilian steel firms have had to build towns for their workers, with all sorts of required social investments.[18] I would argue, however, that

[17] My forthcoming monograph on the Brazilian steel industry will include a more detailed presentation of cost estimates, especially the proportion of costs attributable to raw material, labor, and capital inputs. Another economist, studying labor productivity in the steel industries of various European countries, came to the same conclusion. He found that "in the steel industry labor cost is only a rather small part of total cost" and that "the figures on labor requirements are certainly elements of total efficiencies by which the steel industries could be compared, but they do not by themselves give the complete picture of the situation." See Erik Ruist, "Comparative Productivity in the Steel Industry," in *Labor Productivity*, John T. Dunlop and Vasilii P. Diatchenko, eds. (New York: McGraw-Hill, 1964), pp. 175–176.

[18] For example, the firms of Volta Redonda, Usiminas, Belgo-Mineira, Acesita, and others are all located in areas where the land was completely unimproved before the establishment of these plants. Given Brazil's social legislation and political pressures, each firm had to build

though these factors are a substantial cost burden to steel firms, they do not affect the basic productivity of these firms. When the pressure of competing against free imports or for exports becomes heavy, a society has many means to eliminate the drag of very expensive social-overhead subsidies.

A most relevant measure of the efficiency or productivity of a steel operation is the coke rate of blast furnaces, that is, the amount of coke consumed per ton of pig iron produced. Since coke is the most important input of the blast furnace (amounting to about 70 percent of the total value of raw material inputs), a steel mill will attempt to consume as little coke per ton of pig iron produced as possible. There are many techniques to bring the coke rate down: using sinter or pellets instead of iron ore,[19] injecting oil into the blast furnace, or improving the quality of the coke used. It is thus most important, when analyzing the performance of a blast furnace over time, to be aware of changes in techniques that decrease coke rates. Table 6 shows the coke rates of some selected Brazilian and other Latin-American firms. The Belgo-Mineira and Ferro Brasileiro firms operate charcoal furnaces, and what is of interest here is the change over time in the "charcoal rate." The most efficient blast furnaces operate in Japan, where a coke rate of 450 kg. per ton of pig iron has already been attained; in the United States coke rates of 550 to 570 kg. are presently the norm.

When examining Brazilian coke rates it should be kept in mind that until recently coke-based steel firms were required by law to use 40 percent domestic coal. The poor quality of this coal has been prejudicial to the achievement of high productivity rates in blast furnaces. Technical studies have estimated that Brazilian coke rates could be brought down to about 520–

substantial social-overhead facilities. At Volta Redonda, for example, the rents paid by workers in company houses are purely nominal; most of the housing expenses are subsidized. This does not mean that the subsidies are counterbalancing factors to a lower relative wage.

[19] Sinter results from the fusion of fine iron ores and fine iron-bearing particles with powdered coal and some other fluxes. Pellets are agglomerates hardened after being formed into balls; they are used specially where ores are extremely fine. The coke rate can also be brought down by reducing the size of the particles in the solid charge.

TABLE 6. BLAST FURNACE PRODUCTIVITY
(consumption in kgs per ton)

	Year	Iron Ore	Sinter	Coke	
Brazil					
Volta Redonda	1960	1,416	101	815	
	1964	911	635	656	
Usiminas	1964	102	1,495	592	
	1966	334	1,205	623	
Chile					
Huachipato	1963	1,613	n.a.	601	
Argentina					
San Nicolas	1963	1,570	n.a.	700	
Mexico					
Monclova	1963	1,060	n.a.	830	
Brazil — Charcoal Furnaces				*Charcoal (m³/ton)*[a]	
Belgo-Mineira					
at Monlevade	1940	1,592	n.a.	4.1	(943)
	1956	200	1,369	3.2	(736)
	1964	844	626	3.0	(690)
Cia. Ferro					
Brasileiro	1939	1,829	n.a.	4.9	(1,127)
	1955	1,692	n.a.	4.0	(920)
	1964	801	820	3.7	(851)

Sources: Calculated from materials made available directly by firms; for non-Brazilian firms, see CEPAL, *La Economia Siderúrgica de América Latina*, Feb. 1966 (mimeographed).

[a] Numbers in parentheses are estimates of equivalents in coke, multiplying the cubic meters of charcoal by 230 kg. However, comparison is meaningless for cost purposes.

550 kg. of coke per ton of pig iron if imported coal were used exclusively.[20] That is, given the excellent quality of Brazil's iron ore and the techniques of production now used, the country could lower its coke rate below the levels attained in the United States and many European countries.

Table 6 shows that Brazil has a satisfactory coke rate compared to other Latin-American plants.[21] The decline in the

[20] Amaro Lanari Junior, "Consumo de Carvão Nacional na Siderurgia," in *Metalurgia*, XXI, No. 93, Aug. 1965, p. 646. Another Brazilian steel expert has told me that, according to his calculations, Brazilian firms could even bring their coke rates down to 500 kg.

[21] The coke rate in Indian steel mills in 1960 was approximately 900

Brazilian coke rate, especially at Volta Redonda, can to a large extent be attributed to the increasing use of sinter. The substantial decline in the charcoal rates of Belgo-Mineira and Ferro Brasileiro are also due to the increasing use of sinter. With the decline in the use of domestic coal and the injection of oil into blast furnaces, Brazil could easily become one of the most efficient pig-iron producers in the world. Since liquid pig iron is one of the major inputs of the steel furnace, a low coke rate obviously makes substantial cuts in the cost of steel ingot production, which in turn produces substantial savings in the rolling mill.

Information on production costs is most relevant for evaluating the degree of efficiency of an industry; it is also one of the most difficult kinds of information to obtain or to estimate. Table 7 contains some of my own cost estimates for various types of Brazilian firms, as well as ECLA cost estimates for Volta Redonda and a selection of other Latin American firms.[22] Except for my estimates of the cost of pig-iron production, Brazil has lower costs than other Latin American plants. One should note especially the low cost of pig-iron production of medium firms, since they all utilize charcoal.

All cost estimates are reached indirectly. Usually information about physical and labor inputs is obtained directly; prices of inputs are sometimes furnished directly, and sometimes have to be obtained through reports in trade journals. Capital costs are, as usual, the most tricky part of cost estimating. In my own calculations I have used capital charges estimated by ECLA for Latin American plants, with special adjustments made for Brazilian firms. Taking into account the excess capacity an integrated steel mill will necessarily have for years after its inauguration, the capital costs should probably be higher than the ones actually imputed. The rolling-mill section is usually the most lumpy part of the investment; it is rarely used at full capacity in the initial stages of production. Although fixed capi-

kg. per ton. See William A. Johnson, *The Steel Industry of India* (Cambridge, Mass.: Harvard University Press, 1966), p. 206n.

[22] A detailed description of how my cost estimates were arrived at will appear in my forthcoming monograph. Given the confidential nature of the information I obtained from many firms, I have listed my findings by types of firms, using averages for firms in each category.

TABLE 7. COST ESTIMATES, BRAZILIAN AND OTHER LATIN
AMERICAN IRON AND STEEL FIRMS
(US$ per ton)[a]

	Author's estimates	CEPAL estimates			
Type of firm	Brazil	Brazil (Volta Redonda)	Argentina (San Nicolas)	Chile (Huachipato)	Mexico (Monclova)
Blast Furnace (Pig Iron)					
Large integrated (coke-based)	48.49–50.32	40.50	56.72	45.96	43.11
Medium (charcoal-using)	34.49–38.93	n.a.	n.a.	n.a.	n.a.
Steel Furnace					
Large Siemens Martin	67.36–71.85	71.75	85.37	73.91	71.23
Medium Siemens Martin	65.35–71.03	n.a.	n.a.	n.a.	n.a.
Large Linz Donawitz	68.85–73.44	n.a.	n.a.	n.a.	n.a.
Medium Linz Donawitz	60.86–64.92	n.a.	n.a.	n.a.	n.a.
Medium electric	64.95–72.75	n.a.	n.a.	n.a.	n.a.
Rolling Mills					
Large flat	120.63	156.24	180.99	187.46	172.67
Large nonflat	101.98	115.34	n.a.	118.70	n.a.
Medium nonflat	103.77	n.a.	n.a.	n.a.	n.a.
Medium flat	147.27	n.a.	n.a.	n.a.	n.a.

Sources: First column estimates based on direct information obtained from various steel firms. CEPAL estimates from the same
source as Table 6.
[a] "Large" or "Medium" refers to large or medium integrated firms, except for medium electric steel furnace. When two numbers are cited in first column, they refer to cost ranges, i.e., the highest and the lowest cost estimated.

tal costs will thus be rather high in the beginning, I have chosen not to take them into account. The main reason is that I am interested in the ultimate feasibility or comparative advantage of producing steel in the country. If the market is large enough and growing rapidly enough, the problem of high fixed capital costs will disappear.

Other independent cost estimates are even lower than those in Table 7. For example, the estimates of a consulting firm for the Brazilian development bank (BNDE) and for the World Bank (IBRD) show costs of pig iron varying between US$ 31.50 and 40.00 for large-scale integrated mills and costs as low as US$ 23.60 for charcoal-based pig iron. And a direct confidential report by one of the large integrated steel producers revealed a pig-iron cost of US$ 44.38 in April 1966.

When examining the cost data one should also keep in mind the handicap under which the Brazilian coke-based firms are operating when they use low-grade Brazilian coal. It has been estimated that this raises the cost of producing pig iron by about US$ 12 a ton, thus in turn raising the cost of producing steel ingots by about US$ 11 and of rolled products by between US$ 14 and 18 a ton.[23] Even if these estimates are a little high, it should be obvious that the exclusive use of imported coal could substantially lower the costs per ton relative to other Latin American countries. Also, applying these cost-reduction figures to the large integrated coke-cased plants in Table 7 brings their cost figures much more into line with the cost estimates for charcoal-using plants.

The possible cost reductions stemming from economies of scale seem quite substantial according to studies made by ECLA experts.[24] For example, it has been estimated that the value of installed blast furnace capacity per ton of pig-iron output falls by about 35 percent when comparing a blast furnace plant of 400-thousand-ton with one of 1.5-million-ton capacity; for a Siemens-Martin steel furnace the cost of installed steel section capacity per ton of ingot falls by 48 percent; and for flat rolled products the cost of installed rolling mill capacity

[23] Amaro Lanari Junior, *op. cit.*, p. 646.
[24] Comisión Econômica para America Latina, *La Economia Siderúrgica de América Latina*, Feb. 1966 (mimeographed), pp. 208–211.

per ton falls by 42 percent. As a result of these economies (again when increasing output from 400 thousand to 1.5 million tons), the cost of production per ton of pig iron, steel ingots, and flat rolled products is cut by 1.28, 16.5, and 28.7 percent respectively. Since all large coke-based plants of Brazil aim at production levels of 1.5 million tons or more in the early 1970's, they will obviously benefit considerably from economies of scale attributable to fixed-capacity costs.

TABLE 8. STEEL PRICES IN LATIN AMERICAN
AND EUROPEAN COUNTRIES
(US$ per ton, August 1965)

Country	Concrete rods	Cold-Rolled sheets
Argentina	238	287
Brazil	139	243
Colombia	122	165
Chile	164	298
Mexico	154	208
Peru	206	—
Venezuela	148	—
West Germany	108	158
Belgium	99	153
France	104	149

Source: CEPAL, *La Economia Siderúrgica de América Latina,* Feb. 1966 (mimeographed), p. 170.

In its study of the Latin American steel industry, ECLA tried, among other things, to make some international steel price comparisons in order to get some idea of the relative efficiency of steel industries. Table 8 shows two of their estimates of dollar prices for steel products in various countries. Although Brazil turns out in most cases to be the second-lowest-price producer in Latin America, these figures are suspect, because in most cases Colombia, which is known to have one of the less efficient steel mills in Latin America, is the lowest-price producer. Obviously one runs into the exchange rate problem: Which is the correct one to use at which time? Table 9 shows internal Brazilian steel prices converted into US$ at various times at the prevailing exchange rates. One should note especially the prices in October 1965, the month before a devaluation from Cr$1,850 to Cr$2,200 to the dollar,

TABLE 9. BRAZILIAN STEEL PRICE ESTIMATES
(US$ per ton)[a]

Date	Round bars	Cold-rolled sheets
Oct. 1964	230–270	250–310
June 1964	190–230	220–280
Jan. 1965	190–220	210–270
Oct. 1965	130–150[b] 110–130[c]	n.a.
Oct. 1966	n.a.	220–240
March 1967	n.a.	170–230[d] 150–210[e]

Source: Calculated from prices listed in *Máquinas & Metais* of CSN.
  [a] The price range in each category represents the cheapest and
  the most expensive product. Except as noted, the rate of exchange prevailing on the given date has been used.
  [b] At the rate of Cr$1,850/US$.
  [c] At the rate of Cr$2,200/US$.
  [d] At the rate of Cr$2,700/US$.
  [e] At the rate of Cr$3,000/US$.

TABLE 10. BRAZILIAN STEEL PRICE ESTIMATES,
OCTOBER–NOVEMBER 1965
(US$ per ton)[a]

Concrete rods	89–127
Rolled bars	94–142
Cold-rolled sheets	98–145

Source: Unpublished study for BNDE and
  World Bank by Booz Allen.
  [a] Prices were estimated for various firms;
  ranges represent cheapest and dearest
  prices. Rolled bars exclude bars of special steels.

and March 1967, the month in which the cruzeiro was devalued
from Cr$2,200 to Cr$2,700 to the dollar. For October 1965 I
used both the October rate and the one instituted in November
1965. For March 1967 I used both the new Cr$2,700 rate and
the rate of Cr$3,000, since it has been claimed that the March
1967 devaluation was not big enough when compared to
changes in the domestic price level. Tables 8 and 9 clearly
reveal how sensitive prices are to the exchange rate one
chooses, and how close the Brazilian price sometimes comes to
European prices. Table 10 shows prices ranges in October–
November 1965 for some products, as estimated by a special
study group that obtained direct price information from firms.
These prices are perhaps a little on the low side (though they

might contain special reductions offered to customers, but not listed), and are prices at the mill rather than at the places of consumption.[25]

The data indicate that Brazil's prices are among the lowest in Latin America and, depending on what exchange rate one chooses, are not necessarily out of line with European prices. Taking into account the cost reductions attainable by increasing the use of imported coal and by economies of scale, one is led to conclude that Brazil has a comparative advantage in the production of steel.

MANPOWER, TECHNOLOGY, AND QUALITY OF OUTPUT

As I mentioned above, various institutions in Brazil have been training metallurgical engineers for decades; and when the spurt in steel production occurred, there was an adequate supply of top professional people. The greatest manpower shortage is of specialized workers, a shortage that forces plants to work below capacity, since much on-the-job training must take place. I have been told by many section supervisors that untrained workers adapt themselves very rapidly to the requirements of specialized work; but efficiency could doubtless be greater with a better trained labor force. There would be fewer losses due to machinery breakdowns, production slowdowns, and so on.

Steel technology was imported from abroad. Each of the large plants was built by foreign specialized construction firms. Volta Redonda was planned and its building supervised by Arthur McKee; Cosipa by Kaiser; Usiminas by a group of Japanese firms; Mannesmann by the parant company in Germany.

[25] I have not mentioned the degree of protection enjoyed by the Brazilian steel industry, since tariff levels have no real importance. No steel product that can be produced domestically is imported. If the demand for common steel products is greater than the supply, the relevant products are imported through a subsidiary of the Cia. Siderúrgica Nacional, which has an import monopoly. Special steels can be imported by individual firms only if the firms can show authorities that they cannot obtain the product domestically.

The plants, however, were run by Brazilian manpower after a fairly short period of time. A larger proportion of the plants to be erected in the late 1960's and 1970's will be produced in Brazil. Brazil already has the capacity to build large blast furnaces, many parts of rolling mills, many technical installations (such as various types of cranes), and so on. Moreover, most large Brazilian firms support research, and some contributions have already been made in the making of various types of steel.

Over the last two decades the quality of Brazil's steel has been substantially improved. One of the main reasons has been the nature of the postwar industrialization process. For example, the specifications on steel quality are much more rigorous in the automobile and machine-tool industries than in the construction industry. When these industries first appeared and were forced to buy their steel domestically, the reject rate was very high. This forced steel firms to establish rigorous quality control. The improvement in steel quality has been notable, according to most experts, and obviously this will help the country in entering the international steel market.

EXPANSION PLANS AND EXPORT POSSIBILITIES

In 1966 ingot-steel production was almost 3.8 million tons, and rolled-steel production 2.9 million tons. Demand projections for 1975 for ingot steel have varied between 7.3 and 12.7 million tons. The most reasonable projection to me seems to be for a demand of about 10 million ingot tons in the mid-1970's, since it assumes a growth rate of industrial production of about 8 percent a year. Of course, this does not take into account the possible growth of exports. Steel exports jumped from about 10 thousand tons in 1962 to 482 thousand in 1965, but fell again in 1966. The increase in 1965 was mainly due to the industrial recession in Brazil, which resulted in substantial exports of steel products (often below cost), especially to Argentina. Argentina produces less than its rolling capacity, but plans to increase production in the near future, thus eliminating a market for Brazil. However, discussions are already taking place between a Brazilian industrial group and a foreign consortium about the possibility of constructing a large integrated tidewater mill in Brazil (probably in Vitória) that would produce semifinished products for export to Europe or the United States for final rolling into finished products. This type of vertical division of labor between Brazil and some developed countries could open new vistas for Brazil's participation in the international steel market. Since Brazil has a comparative advantage in the production of steel, export possibilities will depend on the development of an effective export credit mechanism.

The expansion plans of major firms would lead to production levels that would permit full economies of scale. Volta Redonda plans to expand capacity to 3.5 million tons, though as this is written financing is available only for an expansion to 2.5 million tons.[26] Usiminas and Cosipa are aiming for expansion to 1.5 million tons each, and Belgo-Mineira to approximately 600 thousand tons. Economies of scale will also substantially reduce the marginal capital/output ratio in the Brazilian steel industry. The cost of new facilities in the 1950's and early 1960's, and the value of the marginal output achieved, resulted in a ratio of approximately 3.5. It was so high because of the necessity for lumpy initial investment expenditures for the rolling mills, and for some other ancillary sections that had to operate below full capacity for a long time. The ratio will be lower in the future because only the blast furnaces and steel furnaces will have to expand to increase rolled-steel production. This is especially true of Usiminas and Cosipa. Some engineers have estimated that the capital/output ratio for the industry as a whole might fall to about 2.8 in the decade 1965–1975.

CONCLUSION

The Brazilian experience in establishing a steel industry should make it clear that the usual condescending cliché about the wastefulness of implanting a heavy industry in a developing country does not state a universal truth. Given the natural

[26] One expert has argued that it might be more economical for the company to build a second integrated steel works at an entirely new site rather than to expand the existing plant.

resources, a large market, and a technical elite already trained in technology, it is perfectly possible for a developing country to establish a steel industry with comparative advantage. Also, given new technologies that make steel production in many older industrial areas of the world obsolete, it makes sense for the developed world to leave some of the markets to countries like Brazil. In other words, given the changes in world trading patterns (and a diminishing participation of primary products in world trade), which call for a redivision of labor between the developed and the developing world, steel output could be partially taken over by some of the developing countries.

It could still be argued that the resources invested in building up the Brazilian steel industry might better have been used to build up an alternative sector, say a new agricultural export sector (like meat) or a lighter industry (like textiles or food products). But an attempt to calculate what might have happened if resources used in steel had been employed differently would mean making so many assumptions about markets, prices, technology, and so on, that such an exercise would not be very meaningful. Given the existing import restrictions in the developed countries against many light manufactured products, especially from Latin America, a substantial expansion of light manufactured products capacity would not have made much sense. It is also most doubtful that the development of the steel industry used resources that might have been applied to the agricultural export sector.

Finally, I believe I have shown that in Brazil, with its natural advantages for steel production and large internal market, the growth of the steel industry had a substantial impact for growth through its high linkages with other industries. Given the complexity of a steel operation, the planning necessary for the building of its numerous sections, the infrastructure in transportation and power supply associated with it, and the training its many specialized shops give to the labor force, I believe the development impact of steel through external economies is extremely high, though, of course, difficult to calculate.

CHAPTER 4

The Principal Characteristics of the
Agrarian Structure and
Agricultural Production in Brazil

Julian Chacel

Brazil is one of the countries that has made the most use of import-substitution industrialization to propel its economic growth. The process, resumed after World War II with emphasis on the substitution of capital goods, produced highly satisfactory rates of economic progress in the second half of the last decade. Today, however, there is a feeling, common in Latin America, that this process no longer has the same potential to push economic expansion. It is argued that the "margin" for import substitution has been substantially reduced, leaving primarily sectors with highly advanced technologies, high capital intensities, and low employment multipliers.

Because the rates of progress of the last decade are believed no longer possible without a change in the propulsion mechanism, we see today a return to emphasis on agricultural activities in Latin American economic thought. Thus, as in classical antiquity the great poets sang the praises of rural life, economists and planners today emphasize land reform in the search for new stimulants to growth.

In the hope of reaching some general policy recommendations for agricultural development, in this paper I intend to analyze empirical data on two important aspects of Brazilian agriculture: the agrarian structure, and the level and structure of agricultural technology.

THE AGRARIAN STRUCTURE

The most recent and complete data on Brazil's agrarian structure [1] are contained in the cadastre compiled by the Brazilian Agrarian Reform Institute (IBRA) as a basis for the tax on rural properties. This tax is an important part of the recent land-reform law, the Land Statute (*Estatuto da Terra*); it is designed to modify rural property relations through its principle of tax-rate progression in accordance with property size and utilization. The cadastre itself was compiled from detailed questionnaires filled in by rural landowners in December 1965. The owners of 3.4 million properties with a total area of 307 million hectares responded, making this the most extensive survey of rural landholdings yet undertaken in Brazil. (The 1960 census included 265 million hectares; 232 million were surveyed in the 1950 census.) The magnitude of the response is explained by the requirement that landowners present certificates of registration with IBRA in order to receive bank credit, especially from the official banks, which are the principal sources of long-term loans and the agents for the minimum-price program.

My analysis uses the tabulations of cadastral data made by IBRA. Unfortunately, the data are still provisional, though up to date and complete, and an examination in depth of the agrarian structure is therefore limited. In the rush to process the questionnaires for tax purposes, a careful critique of the consistency of the information was pushed into the background. Analysis is also limited by the fact that the class intervals of property size used in the IBRA tabulations are too wide to allow one to relate variations in the size of property to

[1] When the concept of the production establishment is adjusted to the concept of the property, the agrarian structure can be examined through Agricultural Census data. It so happens that the results of the 1960 Agricultural Census have not yet been entirely tabulated, and as of this date (1967) the most recent complete information still comes from the 1950 Census.

changes in the structure of the production process. Without a finer stratification only very broad generalizations are possible, and indications of the most desirable property sizes can be obtained only tentatively and indirectly.

General Aspects of Agrarian Structure

Table 1 shows agricultural properties by area for those cases in which the informant declared total area.

The Lorenz curve of the cumulative frequencies of the number of properties and of total area appears in Figure 1, and clearly shows the inequality in the distribution of land ownership. Another measure of concentration is given by the Gini index, which in this case is .78, quite high and very near the same measure calculated using the census distributions.

TABLE 1. AGRICULTURAL PROPERTIES BY AREA, 1965

Area (hectares)	Number of properties	Percentages	Total area (1,000 hectares)	Percentages
Less than 10	1,201,863	35.92	5,565	1.81
10–100	1,727,469	51.63	57,072	18.58
100–1,000	375,804	11.23	105,825	34.46
1,000–10,000	39,269	1.17	97,342	31.69
10,000–100,000	1,627	0.05	35,925	11.70
100,000 and over	27	0.00	5,400	1.76
Total	3,346,059	100.00	307,132	100.00

Source: Cadastral survey of the Brazilian Agrarian Reform Institute (IBRA).

The data show that 2.8 percent of the properties contain 50.0 percent of the total area. The size range can be judged from the means of the two extreme classes of property size, showing that the largest properties are 4,350 times the size of the smallest. The strong asymmetry of the distribution reflects the twofold nature of the Brazilian agrarian problem: alongside the "latifúndio" (very large property) the "minifúndio" (very small property) appears with great frequency. 35.9 percent of the total number of properties are smaller than 10 hectares, but they make up only 1.8 percent of the total area recorded in the cadastre.

To complete this picture, sharecropping and rentals (held by many to be socially undesirable) occur on 318,000 and 109,000 properties, respectively. Sharecropping is practiced on

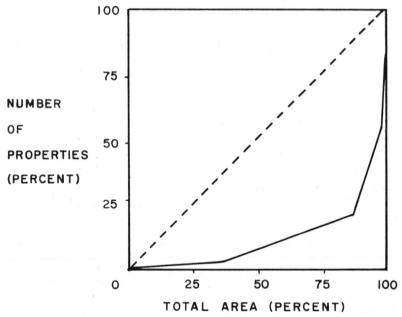

Fig. 1. Concentration of Agricultural Land Ownership, 1965. The Lorenz
curve shows what percentage of properties own what percentage
of land. If all properties were the same size, the Lorenz curve
would be the 45-degree broken line. The actual situation in Brazil,
where land ownership is concentrated in a small number of large
properties, is shown by the solid line.

9.5 percent of the total area, and 3.2 percent is rented. Sharecroppers and renters number a little less than 1 million persons,
between 20 and 25 percent of the managerial force in farming
in Brazil.

Projections to 1965 of rural population using the preliminary results of the 1960 Demographic Census show an active
population in rural areas of 15.7 million persons 20 years of
age or older (the legal minimum age for owning land).[2] Assuming an equal distribution of population by sex and bearing in
mind the small number of women among the ranks of rural

[2] In *Projeções de Oferta e Demanda de Produtos Agrícolas no
Brasil* (Instituto Brasileiro de Economia, Fundação Getúlio Vargas), I,
p. 33.

entrepreneurs, 4.6 million potential landowners are landless. Now, although this figure probably overstates the number of potential candidates for land ownership under a land reform program — it includes all rural adult males — it still gives a first approximation of the human dimension of the agrarian problem in Brazil. Despite their imprecision, these numbers cast strong doubt upon the efficacy of Brazil's agrarian reform, which uses taxation as its fundamental instrument to modify the agrarian structure. The slowness of the process seems incompatible with the magnitude of the problem.

Table 2 shows land use by size. The declarations of the landowners themselves show that the land in productive activities ("exploração"), including forest reserves and timber, has not reached 50 percent of the usable area.

The distribution of land in use, as a percentage of the total area in use and of total potentially usable area is as follows:

Activity	Percent of area in use	Percent of usable area
Crops	19.5	9.6
Livestock	63.9	31.6
Forests	16.6	8.2
Total	100.0	49.4

Taking usable land as the point of reference, the best coefficient of utilization in productive activities (croplands, pastures, and forests) does not occur, as one might expect, in properties of smaller size, but rather in the area class of 100–1,000 hectares. Smaller properties are in crops more than the larger ones, but the larger are more used for pasture. Table 3 shows land use by property size.

The patterns of land use indicated by the IBRA data differ widely from those of the 1950 agricultural census, which show much more land in use in all size categories. According to the 1950 census, which uses the productive establishment rather than the property as the basic organizational unit, the lowest use-rate (75.2 percent) is in the 100–1,000-hectare class. The highest rates (over 90 percent) are on establishments larger than 10,000 hectares. This is not the place to discuss these differences in detail. The census, limited to establishments in production at the time, excluded many unused properties that would have been included in the IBRA survey, which would

TABLE 2. LAND USE BY AREA, 1965
(1,000 hectares)

Area (hectares)	Total land area	Area Usable for Agriculture in Brazil						Unusable area
		Total	Utilized area				Unused	
			Total	Crops	Live-stock	Forests		
Less than 10	5,565	5,052	2,355	1,361	709	284	2,697	513
10–100	57,075	52,060	27,379	10,912	12,775	3,692	24,681	5,015
100–1,000	105,825	96,335	52,154	9,647	35,357	7,149	44,181	9,490
1,000–10,000	97,342	87,993	42,135	4,085	30,660	7,389	45,858	9,349
10,000–100,000	35,925	31,904	11,848	769	7,731	3,347	20,056	4,021
100,000 and over	5,400	4,939	1,853	40	742	1,071	3,086	461
Total	307,132	278,282	137,722	26,814	87,975	22,933	140,560	28,851

Source: IBRA Cadastral Survey.

tend to raise the percentage of land in use above that shown by IBRA. On the other hand, the lower the percentage of usable are in use, the higher the Land Statute's tax — so landowners probably overstated the amount of land in use when reporting to IBRA. The IBRA ratio of area in use to total area may thus be distorted, but should give a more accurate picture than the census of the important potential of still unutilized lands.

TABLE 3. USABLE AREA BY SIZE AND USE
(*percent*)

Area (hectares)	Usable area	Utilized area	Crops	Livestock	Forests
Less than 10	100.0	46.6	26.9	14.0	5.7
10–100	100.0	52.6	21.0	24.5	7.1
100–1,000	100.0	54.1	10.0	36.7	7.4
1,000–10,000	100.0	47.9	4.6	34.8	8.5
10,000–100,000	100.0	37.1	2.4	24.2	10.5
100,000 and over	100.0	37.5	0.8	15.0	21.7

Source: Same as Table 2.

As was noted earlier, the size categories used in the IBRA tabulations are too broad to tell where the change in the composition of agricultural production occurs. However, there is no reason to believe that the IBRA data differ on this question from the census data. In the latter, pasture lands begin to exceed crop lands in the 50–100-hectare category, and large-scale cattle-raising occurs beginning with the 200-hectare class, where pastures are more than 50 percent of usable land. Forests begin to exceed croplands at the 100-hectare level, but exceed pastures only in the over-100,000-hectare class. There is no doubt, however, that the dominant characteristic of agricultural activity in Brazil is its extensive nature, which appears in properties and establishments of comparatively modest size.

A study was made some years ago for the state of São Paulo from a sample of 1,500 farms grouped in seven area classes, the largest being 3,000 hectares and larger.[3] This study showed that the proportion of the property's total area in crops and pasture (excluding forests) was greatest in the 100–300

[3] "Pesquisa Agrícola em São Paulo," *Revista Brasileira de Economia*, XVI, No. 2, p. 15.

hectare group (78.5 percent). In the two adjacent classes, 30–100 hectares and 300–1,000 hectares, these percentages were 77.1 and 74.1 percent respectively.

The relation between usable land and land in use gives no indication of the intensity of production. The little statistical evidence there is on the subject in Brazil shows that output per unit of land declines constantly as size of property increases, and that net product per person on the property grows rapidly beginning with the 100–1,000-hectare class, where there is a change in the structure of production from crops to livestock.

Table 4 shows IBRA's data on the agricultural investment situation. About 10.8 percent of investment is in buildings, 30.4 in equipment, 14.8 in perennial crops, 30.5 in animals, and 13.8 in other items.

Properties of 10–10,000 hectares systematically account for more than two-thirds of each type of agricultural investment. This is confirmed by the 1950 census data; however, there are important substantive differences between the census and the IBRA survey concerning the composition of total investment, specifically the ratio of building and improvement to equipment investments. The IBRA ratio varies around 1:3 in all area classes, with a decline at the extremes. The 1950 census ratio varies around 2:1, with a tendency to diminish as the size of the production establishment increases. It is very difficult to judge which source is preferable in this case. It could well be that the rapid industrialization of the 1950's made the landowners the best judges of the replacement costs of equipment, and that the severity of the inflation could have enormously increased the difference between the real value and the historical costs of improvements on the land, which have a much slower turnover rate than equipment. If this has been the case, the IBRA data substantially understate the capital/output and capital/land ratios, mainly by underestimating the value of investment in buildings and improvements on the land.

At the present stage of Brazilian agricultural development, there seems to be little meaningful correlation between capital intensity per unit of land and size of property and structure of production. For all types of investment, the cadastral survey and the census show a systematic decline in capital applied per

TABLE 4. AGRICULTURAL INVESTMENT, 1965
(NCr$)

Area (hectares)	All improvements	Buildings	Equipment	Perennial crops	Medium and large animals	Other
Less than 10	1,032,865	131,804	427,276	166,430	215,415	91,940
10–100	4,916,380	610,032	1,602,191	898,947	1,248,057	557,153
100–1,000	5,008,513	500,761	1,479,051	641,494	1,714,330	672,878
1,000–10,000	2,253,821	202,488	558,623	231,058	823,607	438,046
10,000–100,000	320,972	20,139	57,992	23,395	112,519	106,927
100,000 and over	13,810	760	2,656	3,765	5,870	759
Total	13,546,360	1,465,984	4,127,788	1,965,088	4,119,797	1,867,703

Source: Same as Table 2.

TABLE 5. AGRICULTURAL LABOR FORCE

Area (hectares)	Properties with wage workers	Permanent wage workers	Maximum wage workers	Properties with renters	Renters	Properties with share-croppers	Share-croppers
Less than 10	188,059	236,747	791,984	20,461	25,286	41,423	54,600
10–100	395,760	510,090	2,296,438	60,387	97,095	198,765	366,427
100–1,000	166,361	566,456	1,770,145	24,147	74,556	71,260	287,778
1,000–10,000	21,376	209,386	426,503	2,945	22,719	6,672	60,214
10,000–100,000	969	26,764	40,390	137	1,624	161	4,744
100,000 and over	14	744	960	2	10	1	22
Total	772,539	1,550,187	5,326,420	108,079	221,290	318,282	773,785

Source: Same as Table 2.

hectare as the size of property increases. The finer stratification of the census shows, however, that the fall in capital/land ratio begins with the establishments of extremely small size (between 1 and 2 hectares) and continues through the whole spectrum. The rate of decline diminishes, however, as size increases. Furthermore, a scatter diagram of 180 pairs of observations from the IBRA cadastre, with capital improvements on land and equipment plotted against property size, suggests a non-linear negative correlation for both cases.

At first sight such observations might appear to commend the minifúndio, with its high capital/land ratio, a conclusion that obviously collides with the necessity for the amortization of fixed costs and with arguments for economies of scale. For a definitive judgment on the relation between fixed capital and property size, greater details about the nature of the investment are needed (for example, what construction materials are used in improvements, whether the equipment is powered, and so on). The best inference to be drawn from these rather confusing considerations is that capital is not a significant factor in Brazilian agricultural production. Taking buildings and equipment into account the capital/output ratio for 1965 (IBRA) is about .78, which obviously does not signify a high average productivity of capital, but only the great importance of the land factor in the production processes of agriculture.

If, however, for the reasons set forth above concerning the evaluation of investments by landowners, the value of equipment declared to IBRA is accepted and the 2:1 ratio found in the 1950 census is used to estimate the value of improvements on the land, the capital/output ratio is 1.72. This ratio, even though probably overestimated, is closer to the empirical evidence of other statistical inquiries, and does not substantially alter the importance of land as a production factor.[4]

Table 5 shows a breakdown of the agricultural labor force by type, omitting landowners and their families. The insta-

---

[4] In the agricultural survey already mentioned for São Paulo, the capital/output ratio was found to be 1.50. São Paulo, however, has a greater concentration of agricultural investment in fixed capital than the rest of the country. But it is still difficult to accept the ratio of .78, as will be seen from other data in this paper.

bility of the wage worker ("assalariado") group, less than one-third of which is composed of permanent laborers, is obviously due largely to the seasonality of agricultural activity; but it is also clear that the ratio could be higher were it not for known deficiencies in the organization of production. It is also notable that sharecroppers and renters are two-thirds as numerous as permanent wage laborers.

Landowners and their families, though not included in the IBRA data, are the most important part of the labor force.

TABLE 6. LANDOWNING LABOR FORCE

Area (hectares)	Landowners and members of their families[a]
Less than 10	3,661,200
10–100	5,773,200
100–1,000	10,300
1,000–10,000	800
10,000–100,000	0
100,000	0
Total	9,445,700

[a] Items do not add precisely to total because of rounding.

We can roughly estimate their number by assuming that relations between types of labor have not changed since the 1950 census, and by making a few slight conceptual adjustments between the census data and the IBRA cadastre. The results are shown in Table 6.

This in turn makes it possible to estimate the total effectively employed labor force. Some double counting is unavoidable because temporary wage laborers migrate from property to property during a single year.[5] All things considered, however, I estimate the effectively employed labor force at approximately 16.2 million.

[5] The census records the production establishment, and includes renters and their active dependents in the group of 9.4 million landowners (IBRA counted 220,000 renters in 1965). Instead of using IBRA's total for the number of sharecroppers — which showed an improbably large decline from 1950 to 1965 — I assumed that this group grew at the same rate as the total number of permanent workers, and thus got 1,358,000 sharecroppers rather than the 774,000 shown by IBRA.

The figures seem to indicate some structural underemployment in agriculture. According to the population projections mentioned above, the total rural population between the ages of 10 and 59 was probably about 25.1 million in 1965.[6] Since the coefficient of participation of the Brazilian rural population in agriculture is estimated at about .67, the potential labor supply should be about 16.8 millon people.

Labor effectively employed per property unit obviously increases with property size; however, labor employed per hectare of land in use decreases. Thus, on the large properties, a low average intensity in labor use per land unit is joined to low intensity in the use of capital. In the agrarian structure as a whole, extensive production techniques are a dominant characteristic.

Regional Aspects

Table 7 shows regional differences in agrarian structure, which are marked enough so that any program of land reform and technological change in Brazil must be adapted to them.[7]

Properties of less than 10 hectares are concentrated in the Northeast and the South, with 40.5 and 38.9 percent, respectively, of the total for Brazil. Properties larger than 10,000 hectares are mostly in the Center-West, though relatively frequent in the Northeast and North. Since the North and Center-West still have extensive, unsettled agricultural frontiers, concentration seems most intensive in the Northeast. A policy of consolidating the minifúndios and redistributing land will have more effect on the 1,000–10,000-hectare properties in the traditional agricultural areas than on the great expanses of unoccupied space in the frontier regions. The latter do not yet constitute critical economic and social problems.

There are also large regional differences in the degree to which usable land is actually used (see Table 8). The South has about 40 percent of Brazil's croplands, but extensive live-

---

[6] *Projeções* . . . , *op. cit.*, p. 33.

[7] The geo-physiographical regions used here are those of the Brazilian Institute of Geography and Statistics with two alterations: the states of Bahia and Sergipe are put in the Northeast rather than the East; and a Center-East region is introduced that includes Minas Gerais, Espírito Santo, Rio de Janeiro, and Guanabara.

TABLE 7. AGRICULTURAL PROPERTIES BY REGION, 1965

Area (hectares)	Brazil	North	Northeast	Center-East	South	Center-West
Less than 10	1,201,863	10,209	486,688	222,258	467,089	15,619
10–100	1,727,469	32,559	461,589	334,635	823,562	75,124
100–1,000	375,804	11,625	125,984	88,538	94,696	54,961
1,000–10,000	39,269	3,668	9,484	5,267	7,413	13,437
10,000–100,000	1,627	223	235	106	142	921
100,000 and over	27	16	1	0	1	9
Total	3,346,059	57,300	1,083,981	650,804	1,392,903	160,071

Source: Same as Table 2.

TABLE 8. LAND USE BY REGION, 1965
(1,000 hectares)

Region	Total area of proper- ties	Land usable for agricultural activities						Unusable	Land in use (percent of usable land)
		Total	Used			Unused			
			Crops	Livestock	Forest				
Brazil	307,132.4	278,281.7	137,722.1	26,814.5	87,974.5	22,933.1	140,559.6	28,850.7	49.5
North	24,978.7	23,175.6	8,706.0	1,042.6	2,016.7	5,646.7	14,469.6	1,803.1	37.6
North- east	79,198.6	68,181.3	33,214.0	8,792.9	17,861.5	6,559.7	34,967.3	11,017.3	48.7
Center- East	49,101.7	44,313.6	28,928.9	4,588.1	21,858.0	2,482.8	15,384.7	4,788.1	65.3
South	69,332.6	64,807.4	37,498.0	10,642.3	21,715.2	5,140.5	27,309.4	4,525.2	57.9
Center- West	84,520.8	77,803.8	29,375.2	1,748.6	24,523.1	3,103.4	48,428.6	6,717.0	37.8

Source: Same as Table 2.

stock raising in the Center-East region gives it the highest apparent coefficient of land utilization. However, the Center-East also contains most of the Brazilian "cerrado,"[8] where acid soils restrict pasture lands to low productivity. It is impossible to decide what causes the differences in the degree of land utilization without further information on soil quality, access to markets, degree of settlement, and so forth.

Data on the regional distribution of investments in agriculture (see Table 9) show an immense gap between the South and the rest of the country. Agricultural land in use in the South makes up 27.2 percent of Brazil's total agricultural land in use, but the South has 78 percent of the total investment in construction, 46 percent of the total in equipment, 65 percent of the total in perennial crops, and 44 percent of the total in livestock. The Northeast, perhaps because of its sugar plantations, has 27 percent of the equipment investment and 22 percent of the investment in perennial crops. The structure of the labor force in the South is also different: in other regions, the ratio of permanent wage workers to temporary labor varies between 1:2.48 and 1:5.62, but in the South it is as low as 1:1.38, according to IBRA. This greater stability can perhaps be explained by the importance of the region's permanent crops, the greater diversification of its farm enterprises, its comparatively intensive cattle industry, and its greater concentration of investment — that is, by the South's higher technological development.

A breakdown by region of several important characteristics of the agrarian structure is shown in Table 10.

THE STRUCTURE OF PRODUCTION

This examination of the technical structure of production is based on data from a farm survey carried out in 1962–1963 by the Brazilian Institute of Economics (IBRE) of the Getúlio Vargas Foundation. The survey covered 2,500 production establishments sampled in clusters in parts of seven agriculturally important states. From 1960 to 1963 these states ac-

[8] *Translator's note*: The broad expanse of highly acid brushlands located mainly in Minas Gerais, Goiás, and Mato Grosso, and deficient in most chemicals necessary for productive farming.

TABLE 9. AGRICULTURAL INVESTMENT BY REGION, 1965
(1000 NCr$)

Region	Total investment		Buildings	Equipment	Perennial crops	Medium and large animals	Other
	(percent)	(1000 NCr$)					
Brazil	100.00	13,546,360	1,465,984	4,127,788	1,965,088	4,119,797	1,867,703
North	1.69	229,330	11,539	44,967	38,554	77,434	56,836
Northeast	19.77	2,677,646	96,697	1,127,463	424,516	762,926	266,044
Center-East	17.16	2,325,103	159,296	725,743	232,354	936,859	270,851
South	53.84	7,293,213	1,137,973	1,915,050	1,217,721	1,831,159	1,191,310
Center-West	7.54	1,021,068	60,479	314,565	51,943	511,419	82,662

Source: Same as Table 2.

TABLE 10. AGRARIAN STRUCTURE OF BRAZIL
(percent of total in category)

Category	North	Northeast	Center-West	Center-East	South
Unusable land	8.13	25.78	27.53	15.99	22.57
Usable land	8.33	24.50	27.96	15.92	23.29
Area in use	6.32	24.12	21.33	21.00	27.23
Cultivated land	3.89	32.79	6.52	17.11	39.69
Pasture	2.29	20.30	27.88	24.85	24.68
Investments	1.69	19.77	7.54	17.16	53.84
Work force	2.63	41.38	8.59	21.16	26.58

Source: Same as Table 2.

counted for 66 percent of the total cotton production of Brazil, 58 percent of the rice, 46 percent of the coffee, 66 percent of the sugar cane, 53 percent of the beans, and 70 percent of the corn. In livestock, they produced 55 percent of the pork, 59 percent of the poultry, and 75 percent of the milk.

Table 11 shows technical coefficients of production for Brazil as a whole. These coefficients are the ratio between a given input and a unit of output, and indicate both level of technology and average productivity of each productive element.[9] The land-area coefficients measure the number of hec-

[9] In estimating the production functions, three forms of equation were considered: Cobb-Douglas, semilogarithmic, and quadratic. The Cobb-Douglas form, $X_1 = 10^a \cdot X_2^b \cdot X_3^c \ldots X_n^h$ was chosen, since it yielded coefficients of multiple correlation higher than the semilogarithmic form, and since the quadratic form had too many variables for the available computers to handle. Cobb-Douglas functions are not restricted to constant returns to scale; nevertheless, for all practical purposes the functions both for crops and for the agricultural sector as a whole are homogeneous to the first degree. Only in the case of livestock production were there nonconstant (negative) returns to scale, probably because livestock production never occurs separate from cropping. As a result, pasture area, for example, showed negative regression coefficients. Since the concept of production used is that of gross value, the negative coefficient is in agreement with the fact that, as the importance of livestock increases in the productive unit, the gross value of production falls. This does not signify, however, a decline in net product, because the operating costs of livestock production are relatively lower than those in crop production. The significance levels of the regression coefficients are indicated in *Projeções . . . , op. cit.*, which is being being published in English by the United States Department of Agriculture.

tares per 100 old cruzeiros of total production; the others are expenditures per old cruzeiro of agricultural production.

The most important expenditure is always for labor, which is most intensive in crop raising. Neither fertilizer and insecticides nor vaccines and medicine constitute an important expense, since they are used in small quantities. Taking fixed capital in the narrow sense, the capital/output ratio is 1.40 for the agricultural sector as a whole, 1.37 for crops, and 1.47 for livestock production. Adding the value of cropland and pasture

TABLE 11. TECHNICAL COEFFICIENTS OF BRAZILIAN
AGRICULTURAL PRODUCTION, 1962[a]

	Total agriculture[b]	*Crop raising*	*Livestock production*
Total area of establishment	0.006892	—	—
Area of perennial and annual crops	—	0.002089	—
Natural and artificial pasture land	—	—	0.003245
Seeds and seedlings	0.019601	0.025021	—
Feed of agricultural and industrial origin consumed	0.052047	—	0.075582
Organic and chemical fertilizers consumed	0.003226	0.003936	—
Insecticides, raticides, germicides, herbicides, formicides, and similar products	0.002024	0.002281	—
Vaccines, medicines, and disinfectants purchased	0.000815	—	0.001271
Labor used, including that supplied by manager's family	0.489356	0.524541	0.395425
Total value of land and perennial crops	4.129035	4.132814	4.034549
Total value of construction, improvements, machines, vehicles, equipment, and work animals	1.402839	1.368743	1.470409
Brood cows	0.040194	—	0.152945
Brood sows	0.003355	—	0.002443
Cattle (excepting brood cows), hogs (excepting brood sows), sheep, goats, poultry, horses, asses, and mules (excepting work mules)	0.196062	—	0.421183

Source: IBE.

[a] Coefficients for crop and livestock production are calculated from samples. Coefficients for total agriculture may reflect different samples.

[b] Total agriculture coefficients for area of perennial and annual crops and natural and artificial pasture land not calculated in the original data source and hence are not available.

TABLE 12. DEVIATIONS OF TECHNICAL COEFFICIENTS
OF PRODUCTION BY STATE, 1962
(percent deviation from average)

Input	Ceará	Pernambuco	Minas Gerais	Espírito Santo	São Paulo	Santa Catarina	Rio Grande do Sul
Total area of establishment	+70.69	+15.42	+29.56	+76.39	−34.16	−17.38	−1.93
Seeds and seedlings	−59.54	+47.04	−2.13	+10.31	−52.74	+18.16	+90.75
Feed of agricultural and industrial origin consumed	−37.44	−72.15	+5.38	−33.73	−64.75	+96.59	+22.38
Organic and chemical fertilizers consumed	−75.76	−52.51	−13.17	−71.64	+5.30	−42.10	+63.70
Insecticides, herbicides, and similar products	−58.79	−32.76	−8.84	−5.39	+14.53	−17.64	+17.54
Vaccines, medicines, and disinfectants purchased	+20.12	−15.21	+16.20	+33.86	−53.37	+58.28	+56.81
Labor used, including that supplied by manager's family	+20.01	+44.88	+8.66	+5.68	−32.76	−30.33	+34.33
Total value of land and perennial crops	+14.73	+1.78	−9.59	+40.35	+28.43	−37.78	−38.89
Total value of construction, improvements, machines, vehicles, equipment, and work animals	−3.79	+6.16	+21.88	−9.70	−30.70	−19.90	+34.93
Brood cows	+50.20	+73.53	+23.75	−24.98	−64.62	+49.42	+88.15
Brood sows	−21.91	+74.81	−73.89	−16.48	n.a.	+7.90	+88.14
Cattle (excepting brood cows), hogs (excepting brood sows), sheep, goats, poultry, horses, asses, mules (excepting work mules)	+57.93	+40.17	+9.02	−4.32	−55.58	+8.70	+83.33

Source: IBE.

area to capital, the ratio increases to 5.50 in the three cases considered.

The differences in general level of technology between the states surveyed is indicated in Table 12, which shows each state's deviations from the average coefficients for the whole samples. There is an inverse relation in the use of some inputs; for example, states that use more fertilizers, insecticides, and vaccines (measured in currency) also use comparatively less land area per monetary unit of output.

The labor coefficient as measured in currency is probably somewhat distorted, because it is likely that the greater the productivity of labor in a given region, the greater its price. Despite this distortion, São Paulo's labor coefficients are the lowest of the seven states. This is not due to substitution of capital for labor, since São Paulo's capital/output ratio is also the lowest of the group. Hence the average efficiency of agriculture in São Paulo is much greater than in the rest of the country, partly because of the state's large comparative advantage in coffee production. The labor and capital coefficients for Rio Grande do Sul are high because of its many small properties, and because cattle raising is more intensive in that part of the country than in other areas (reflected in use of more labor and in greater investments in fences for division of pastures).

Production Elasticities

Production elasticities (the coefficients of the Cobb-Douglas function, see note 3) measure the variation in output associated with variation in a given input, all else being constant. Table 13 shows estimated elasticities for crops and livestock in Brazil as a whole. According to Table 13, doubling the area planted in crops would increase output by about 48 percent, while putting 100 percent more labor into the same area would increase production by only 12 percent. Probably the biggest factor affecting productivity is still the natural fertility of the soil; since modern technology has not been much applied to Brazilian agriculture, the survey data do not reflect its influence. Thus, if the use of fertilizer or insecticide were doubled, production would increase by about 6 percent; if

TABLE 13. PRODUCTION ELASTICITIES IN BRAZILIAN AGRICULTURE, 1962
(dash indicates category not applicable)

Input	Crops	Livestock
Area of perennial and annual crops	0.4765	—
Natural and artificial pasture land	—	0.0666
Seeds and seedlings	0.1074	—
Feed of agricultural and industrial origin consumed	—	0.1502
Organic and chemical fertilizers consumed	0.0569	—
Insecticides, herbicides and similar products	0.0582	—
Vaccines, medicines and disinfectants purchased	—	0.0700
Labor used, including that supplied by manager's family	0.1167	0.1839
Total value of land and perennial crops	0.0643	0.2574
Total value of construction, improvements, machines, vehicles, equipment and work animals	0.1291	0.1118
Brood cows	—	−0.0145
Brood sows	—	0.0140
Cattle (excepting brood cows), hogs, (excepting brood sows), sheep, goats, poultry, horses, asses and mules (excepting work mules)	—	0.0913

Source: IBE.

investments in fixed capital (buildings, machines, and vehicles) were doubled, production would increase about 13 percent. Additional use of pasture lands would cause little increase in livestock production. Livestock would be more sensitive than crops to increases in labor, or to the use of better technology. The increased diversification of production attendant on doubling areas in crops would affect output more than a one hundred percent increase in any other factor of production.

Tables 14 and 15 show estimated production elasticities for crops and livestock by states. Production is most sensitive to variations in area planted in Pernambuco and Espírito Santo. This is a curious result for two geographical areas characterized by a monoculture of perennial crops (sugar and coffee, respectively) and costs noncompetitive with the rest of the country. Crops are most responsive to fertilizers in Minas Gerais and in São Paulo. The greatest response to the use of both seeds and seedlings and equipment is in Rio Grande do Sul, perhaps be-

TABLE 14. PRODUCTION ELASTICITIES FOR CROPS BY STATE, 1962

Input	Ceará	Pernam-buco	Minas Gerais	Espírito Santo	São Paulo	Santa Catarina	Rio Grande do Sul
Area of perennial and annual crops	0.4699	0.5716	0.4918	0.5455	0.4771	0.4118	0.4300
Seeds and seedlings	0.1135	0.0607	0.0342	0.0560	0.0752	0.1164	0.2639
Organic and chemical fertilizers consumed	0.0394	0.0214	0.0815	0.0749	0.0650	0.0742	0.0326
Insecticides, herbicides, and similar products	0.0296	0.0671	0.1179	0.0126	0.0559	0.0591	0.0149
Labor used, including that supplied by manager's family	0.0753	0.1943	0.1311	0.1489	0.1498	0.0297	0.0389
Total value of land and perennial crops	0.0950	0.1100	0.0394	0.0166	0.1083	0.1052	0.0442
Total value of construction, improvements, machines, vehicles, equipment, and work animals	0.2175	0.0353	0.1788	0.1710	0.0490	0.0939	0.2494

Source: IBE.

TABLE 15. PRODUCTION ELASTICITIES FOR LIVESTOCK BY STATE, 1962

Input	Ceará	Pernambuco	Minas Gerais	Espírito Santo	São Paulo	Santa Catarina	Rio Grande do Sul
Natural and articial pasture land	0.0007	0.0141	0.0030	0.1563	0.1652	0.0102	0.0455
Feed consumed of agricultural and industrial origin	0.1889	0.0212	0.1932	0.1522	0.0057	0.3531	0.3022
Vaccines, medicines, and disinfectants purchased	0.0786	0.0808	0.0503	0.0840	0.0196	−0.0296	0.1885
Labor used, including that supplied by manager's family	0.1204	0.0446	0.2234	0.1824	0.2499	0.0186	0.1026
Total value of land and perennial crops	0.1637	0.1050	0.0385	0.1235	0.5701	0.1348	0.1139
Total value of construction, improvements, machines, vehicles, equipment, and work animals	0.2734	0.4144	0.1602	0.1642	0.0696	−0.0013	0.0551
Brood cows	−0.0058	0.0508	0.0087	0.0769	−0.0366	−0.0832	−0.0160
Brood sows	−0.0281	0.0208	0.0127	0.0243	0.0073	−0.0721	0.0472
Cattle (excepting brood cows), hogs, (excepting brood sows), sheep, goats, poultry, horses, asses, mules (excepting work mules)	−0.0266	0.0651	0.0083	−0.0033	0.1593	0.1171	0.1106

Source: IBE.

cause of the presence of wheat and irrigated rice, crops with high capital intensity. Pernambuco, São Paulo, and Espírito Santo, the areas of the sample where perennial crops are most important, were more sensitive to the use of additional labor. In the states of the extreme south, where the family farms of European origin have been fragmented into minifúndios by inheritance, additional labor would have little or no impact on output.

Perhaps the most important observation on animal raising was that no major increase would result from expanding pasture area in the traditional cattle-raising states. The greatest effects on production would be felt in Espírito Santo and São Paulo. But it is important that increasing land in crops, which implies the introduction of a system of more diversified production, would greatly increase output in São Paulo. This variable has the most production elasticity. Improving management techniques (more intense feeding of animals) would produce the greatest effects in Santa Catarina and Rio Grande do Sul. Additional labor would have the greatest impact on production in São Paulo and Minas Gerais. More capital would have great effect on output in the states of the Northeast, especially Pernambuco. An increase in the number of brood cows seem to be irrelevant, or even an excess, when the effects of increases in the use of other factors are taken into account. Finally, increasing the stock of animals (all types) would have the greatest impact on production in the southern states.

Even if the technical coefficients of production and the estimated production elasticities are only approximate, which is not improbable given the circumstances of the field investigation, some implications are unmistakable. Among the general characteristics of agricultural production, the great differences from state to state in the technical structure stand out. Consequently the responses of production to changes in inputs vary widely.

SOME CONCLUSIONS

Some general conclusions that future agricultural policy should take heed of can be made, despite the preliminary character of some of the data on agrarian structure and despite the incompleteness of the data on the technical structure of production. There is little doubt that the agrarian structure's malformation has two aspects: the minifúndio and the latifúndio. The high proportion of proprietors and members of their families in the work force is no sign of a tendency toward a sociologically ideal situation, but simply a reflection of the many small properties (less than 20 hectares). On the other hand, the concentration indices of landholdings give a very clear idea of the extent of the latifúndio.

Action to correct the malformation of the land structure ought consequently to consider both consolidating and dividing landholdings. On the regional level, in the Northeast and Center-East consolidation and land redistribution, together with interregional migration, would probably be in order. In the South, policy should center on consolidation of small properties and shifting population to the Center-West region through regulating and accelerating movements that until now have been spontaneous. The problem of correcting the agrarian structure would require careful government action in these regions, because consolidation involves much more difficult technical and juridical problems than property fragmentation. In contrast, the policy required in the North and Center-West regions would be more preventive than corrective. Regulation of territorial settlement would aim at preventing the deformations of structure that would otherwise arise within the next two decades.

The intensity of use of labor and capital is a constantly declining function of property size, beginning with small farms. Extensive production processes dominate where land is the most important influence on production. This makes some sense as long as there is an agricultural frontier, and as long as the coefficient of land use is low in long-settled regions. In Brazil it is not a question, as some sectors of Chilean public opinion facetiously assert, of building a second story on the country, so that agrarian reform does not provoke a collapse of production. Since the supply of land is reasonably elastic, what matters is the degree of modernization that one wants to accompany agrarian reform. It would seem that the first priority is an increase in the intensity of labor per unit of land as a means of improving labor productivity.

The celebrated Latin American concept of "total" land reform does not appear to offer the best solution for present Brazilian conditions. Such reform is equivalent, in my judgment, to putting the farm into a system of total adjustment in which labor and capital per unit of land are made to increase at the same time, while the farm derives external economies from improvements in the infrastructure. The most important aspect of a mass solution in Brazil, however, should be to combine man and the land in such a way as to increase employment.

An examination of the technical structure of production shows the lack of modern factor-combinations, with a low capital/output ratio and infrequent use of fertilizers, insecticides, and vaccines and other medicines. Up to a certain point this is explained by the large potential supply of cultivable lands. A policy aimed at expanding production, however, ought to distinguish between degrees of modernization in crop and in livestock production. In crop raising, expansion should be based on increasing the relatively more abundant factor, land.

The introduction of some crop raising into livestock farms would greatly affect their net product and would guarantee a greater use of labor. Furthermore, livestock production output would respond more than that of crops to higher technology (industrial feed, use of vaccines and other medicines), and the intensification of production per hectare would require investments in fixed capital that would stimulate employment. In short, modernizing livestock production should take precedence over modernizing crop raising in order to ensure better mobilization of scarce productive resources and of relatively abundant labor.

Part III

Part VI

CHAPTER 5

Inflation and the Money and
Capital Markets of Brazil

Mário Henrique Simonsen

One of most interesting examples of the way Brazilian institutions adapted to inflation is furnished by the money and capital markets. In the 1930's two laws were framed, dominated entirely by money illusion, that if followed to the letter during periods of inflation would virtually have prevented equilibrium of these markets. These laws were never repealed, and persisted as difficult-to-modify taboos; as a result, a series of makeshift devices developed that tended more or less to equilibrate these markets. It is interesting to examine how such devices emerged, and what distortions in the financial system of the country were created by the inflation.

The two traditional laws that would have impeded the adjustment of the money market to inflation were promulgated in 1933, during a time of monetary stability. The usury law prohibited interest charges above 12 percent per year. The gold clause law forbade contractual payments except in domestic currency at its legal value. It was generally understood that the usury law dealt with nominal (and not real) interest rates, and that the gold clause law prohibited any agreement with monetary correction (that is, in which payments are readjusted in proportion to the general rise in prices). Thus the two laws, interpreted literally, implied a negative real rate of interest whenever inflation exceeded 12 percent per year — which it has never failed to do since 1950. Since the annual rate of inflation was over 80 percent in 1963 and 1964, it is easy to see that if these laws had been rigorously obeyed, the money market would have suffered incredible distortions.

Neither of these laws has yet been explicitly revoked. The banking reform law, promulgated in 1964, made the regulation of maximum interest rates the exclusive power of the Monetary Council, but the general understanding is, at least as long as the word "interest" is used, that the 12 percent annual limit is still in effect. The devices used to get around the usury law are innumerable, but all of them are based on some legal fiction that avoids the term "interest." As to the gold clause prohibition, it is still in operation in the sense that two parties in Brazilian territory cannot, for example, contract a loan in dollars. Nevertheless, credit operations with monetary correction have been permitted in numerous cases since 1964 and 1965. In these cases the 12 percent annual limit applies to the real, not the nominal, interest rate. However, this admission of monetary correction is quite recent, and not yet of much influence. Most of the country's financial institutions, with the exception of the private investment banks and the real estate credit companies, have adapted themselves to the old legislation vitiated by money illusion. In examining how this adaptation took place, we must pay special attention to the distortions in the financial structure caused by the interaction of the law of usury, the prohibition of monetary correction, and inflation.

THE EVOLUTION OF THE RATE OF INFLATION

Since the greatest distortions now seen in the money and capital markets in Brazil result in the last analysis from the severity of the inflationary process, it is important, before examining the main problem, to set forth quantitatively the evolution of the rates of price increases. One of the curious aspects of Brazilian economic history is the upward trend in prices recorded ever since the first years of the Empire. Probably because of the chronic tendency toward budgetary deficits, Brazil did not experience price cycles similar to those of the United States, where long periods of inflation alternated with long periods of price declines. Brazilian history records some years of deflation, but never a long period of falling prices.

Little is known quantitatively about Brazilian inflation before World War I. Indications are that in the period of the Empire, 1822–1889, prices probably rose very gently, perhaps at an average rate of 1.5 percent per year. The first years of the Republic brought an inflationary wave, associated with the heavy emissions of paper money during that time. Between 1896 and 1900 prices again fell, because of the deflationary policy of the Campos Salles government, and thereafter remained practically stable until 1914. Judging by the cost-of-living indices constructed for the city of Rio de Janeiro, prices probably rose on the average of 8 percent per year between 1914 and 1927. Between 1927 and 1933, the cost of living fell by 15 percent, mostly because of the Depression. From that time until the beginning of World War II, prices rose again, at an annual rate of 7 percent — with a certain dampening tendency in the years just before the war.

For the period after 1939, much more satisfactory statistical information about Brazilian inflation is available. Tables 1 and 2 show the two most popular indicators, the cost-of-living index for the state of Guanabra and the wholesales price index, both constructed by the Getúlio Vargas Foundation. According to these indices, between 1939 and 1946 prices rose 15 percent per year on the average — largely because of supply difficulties during wartime and the inflationary impact of Brazil's balance-of-payments surpluses. Between 1947 and 1949, the rise in prices slowed down perceptibly, since the cost of living had almost stabilized. Nevertheless, in 1950 prices again began rapidly rising, and from then until 1958 the rate of inflation oscillated more or less irregularly around an average of 17 percent, with no explosive tendency.

The inflationary gallop of recent years apparently began in 1959, when the government decided to abandon the promising program of monetary stabilization prepared at the end of 1958. In 1959 prices rose some 40 to 50 percent. In 1960 inflation relented a bit; prices rose only 25 to 30 percent. But in 1961 they jumped again, 40 to 50 percent, and in 1962 even higher, 50 to 60 percent. In 1963 the situation grew even worse. The cash deficit of the federal government reached unprece-

dented levels, and the executive branch gave the nod to extrava-
gance in wages. As a result, prices rose 80 percent. In the
first three months of 1964, the last months of the Goulart government, prices rose 25 percent—extrapolated geometrically,
a rate of 144 percent in one year. In fact, effort on the part
of the Castello Branco government not exactly to combat inflation, but to escape hyperinflation, succeeded in reducing the
effective rate of price increases to about 90 percent in 1964.
In 1965 and 1966, as a result of the gradualist policy of combating inflation, the rate fell to around 40 percent per year.

TABLE 1. COST-OF-LIVING INDEX, THE STATE OF GUANABARA
(1953 = 100)

Year	Annual average		December	
	Index	Annual change (percent)	Index	Annual change (percent)
1939	21.6	—	23.1	—
1940	22.2	4.2	24.7	6.9
1941	24.6	10.8	27.7	12.1
1942	27.4	11.4	32.4	17.0
1943	30.3	16.6	33.8	4.3
1944	34.1	12.5	38.7	14.4
1945	39.7	16.4	44.1	14.0
1946	46.3	16.6	53.5	12.1
1947	56.4	21.8	56.7	6.0
1948	58.3	3.4	58.7	3.5
1949	60.9	4.5	62.2	6.0
1950	66.5	9.2	69.1	11.1
1951	74.5	12.0	76.6	10.9
1952	87.4	17.3	92.5	20.8
1953	100.0	14.4	108.0	16.8
1954	122.4	22.4	136.3	26.2
1955	150.7	23.1	162.4	19.1
1956	182.2	20.9	197.6	21.7
1957	211.9	16.3	224.0	13.4
1958	242.9	14.6	262.7	17.3
1959	338.0	39.1	399.4	52.0
1960	437.4	29.4	494.3	23.8
1961	582.9	33.3	707.7	43.2
1962	884.0	51.7	1099.0	55.3
1963	1507.0	70.4	1985.0	80.6
1964	2889.0	91.7	3704.0	86.6
1965	4787.0	65.7	5385.0	45.4
1966	6764.0	41.3	7600.0	41.1

Source: Fundação Getúlio Vargas.

Although any forecast on the subject is difficult, there are strong hopes that the rate will continue to fall during the Costa e Silva administration.

THE STRUCTURE OF THE FINANCIAL SYSTEM

The financial system of Brazil is composed of the Central Bank, the commercial banks, the Bank of Brazil, the credit and finance companies, the development banks (bancos de fomento), the private investment banks, the savings banks

TABLE 2. GENERAL WHOLESALE PRICE INDEX
(1953 = 100)

| Year | Annual average | | December | |
	Index	Annual change (percent)	Index	Annual change (percent)
1939	17.4	—	19.0	—
1940	18.5	6.3	18.8	−1.1
1941	21.5	16.2	23.6	25.5
1942	25.4	18.1	27.7	17.4
1943	30.3	19.3	31.7	14.4
1944	34.5	13.9	36.8	16.1
1945	39.7	15.1	40.7	10.6
1946	45.8	14.5	49.6	21.9
1947	48.7	6.3	49.1	−1.0
1948	53.2	9.2	55.0	12.0
1949	58.0	9.0	64.2	16.7
1950	65.8	13.4	73.4	14.3
1951	78.8	19.8	82.5	2.4
1952	86.9	10.3	90.4	9.6
1953	100.0	15.1	113.2	25.2
1954	130.3	30.3	140.3	23.9
1955	147.4	13.1	153.5	9.4
1956	175.7	19.2	192.9	25.7
1957	197.6	12.5	199.4	3.4
1958	221.8	12.2	255.0	27.0
1959	305.5	37.7	347.1	36.1
1960	399.8	30.9	460.8	32.8
1961	552.1	38.1	691.6	50.1
1962	846.0	53.2	1037.0	49.9
1963	1468.0	73.5	1886.0	81.9
1964	2813.0	91.6	3645.0	93.3
1965	4254.0	51.2	4676.0	28.3
1966	5787.0	36.0	6413.0	37.1

Source: Fundação Getúlio Vargas.

(caixas econômicas), the National Housing Bank (Banco Nacional de Habitação), and of several specialized entities such as the real estate finance companies (sociedades imobiliárias), credit cooperatives, insurance and capitalization companies (companhias de seguros e capitalização), social welfare institutes (institutos de previdência social), Fund for Financing the Acquisition of Industrial Machinery and Equipment (FINAME), and so on. Several intermediary institutions also exist in the capital market, such as the stock exchanges, mutual funds, and companies specializing in the distribution of stocks, bills, and other paper. The Central Bank performs the classical functions of bank for the government, bank for the banks, and bank of emission. The commercial banks operate almost exclusively in the field of short-term loans, above all in the form of discounts of *duplicatas* trade acceptances, which are seldom for more than 120 days. The credit and finance corporations extend loans for terms that vary from six months to two years, generally on the basis of acceptance of *letras de câmbio* (real bills of exchange). The Bank of Brazil combines the operations of a commercial bank with those of an agricultural bank, entering even into some lines of investment banking. The savings banks attract lower- and middle-income savings (and, in some cases, public resources) and grant personal, commercial, and mortgage loans. The most important of the development banks is the National Economic Development Bank (BNDE), the function of which is long-term financing of fixed capital investment in basic sectors. The National Housing Bank, founded in 1964, regulates and refinances housing credit. The first private investment banks were founded in 1966; their objective is to extend long-term industrial financing. Until now, however, their operations have been limited almost entirely to the acceptance of bills of exchange typical of finance corporations.

Table 3 shows the distribution of loans and financing on December 31, 1966.[1] Two facts — that short-term loans showed more than four times the total of long-term loans, and that the latter came almost exclusively from goverment institutions — are characteristic of the financial system of Brazil. This is

[1] The data relative to the National Economic Development Bank also include the stock holdings of that institution.

TABLE 3. LOANS AND FINANCING TO THE PRIVATE SECTOR

Classification	Balance, December 31, 1966 (million NCr$)	Percentage of total
Short-Term		
Commercial and development banks	5,214.9	48.9
Bank of Brazil and CACEX	2,141.1	20.1
Finance companies	1,031.0	9.7
Savings banks	280.0	2.6
National Cooperative Credit Bank	17.7	0.2
Social welfare institutes and Insurance companies	18.0	0.2
SUBTOTAL	8,702.7	81.7
Long-Term		
National Economic Development Bank	858.0	8.1
Bank of Brazil	594.8	5.6
FINAME	114.8	1.1
Savings banks	250.0	2.3
National Housing Bank	88.5	0.8
National Cooperative Credit Bank and others	22.6	0.2
Social welfare institutes and Insurance companies	26.0	0.2
SUBTOTAL	1,954.7	18.3
GRAND TOTAL	10,657.4	100.0

Source: Central Bank. Includes mixed corporations and producing autarchies.

largely a result of inflation, as will be discussed farther on. The largest part of the short-term loans is granted by the commercial banks, followed by the Bank of Brazil and the credit and finance corporations. A much smaller part is made up of the loans (mostly personal) of the savings banks. A minute share is left for the insurance companies, social welfare institutes, and the national cooperative credit banks. Table 3 makes it clear that the country's major source of long-term loans is the National Economic Development Bank (although a good part of its operations have been in the form of stock participation). The Bank of Brazil also maintains some important lines of long-term credit, principally in financing agriculture (for example, for reducing the number of coffee trees) and industry. Real estate credit is extended mostly by the savings banks and the National Housing Bank (the latter operating through several other institutions). The Fundo de Financiamento para Aquisição de Maquinas e Equipamento Industriais (FINAME) is an institution that specializes in financing the domestic machinery industry. It has been operating since 1965 through the commercial banks and finance corporations, with counterpart funds of foreign aid as its financial base. Finally, a small part of the long-term loans is extended by the social welfare institutes, insurance companies (mortgage credit), and the National Cooperative Credit Bank.

COMMERCIAL BANKS AND THE SHORT-TERM CREDIT MARKET

The tradition of Brazilian commercial banks always was to extend short-term loans rarely exceeding 180 days, generally in the form of the discount of *duplicatas*.[2] This tradition was based partly on the desire for security, inasmuch as these loans were based primarily on demand deposits, and partly on the fact that sales on time by industry and commerce (before the appearance of installment plans) rarely exceeded this term. In the last few years, with inflation, the term of commercial bank loans has shortened even more, and today does not go beyond 90 to 120 days.

Commercial banks were probably the institutions that suffered the greatest distortion from the conjunction of inflation and the law of usury. Interest rates paid depositors rarely went over 6 percent per year, which obviously meant a strongly negative real rate. Interest rates charged to borrowers, however, increased considerably by means of several devices for getting around the law of usury; in some periods they were as high as 4 percent a month. The enormous gap consequently opened between interest rates charged and those paid is responsible for the deep distortions in the system.

Except for occasional irregularities, the banks meticulously obeyed the usury law as it applied to the payment of interest to their depositors. The monetary authorities system-

---

[2] The *duplicata* is a credit instrument specially created by Brazilian commercial legislation; it corresponds to the sale of goods on time.

atically prohibited this rate from exceeding 6 percent per year, and in 1966 they went so far as to withdraw permission to pay interest on demand deposits (except on lower-income personal accounts, for which a limit of 3 percent per year was fixed). This situation, quite artificial from the standpoint of real interest, was sustained partly because of strict enforcement by the government, partly because it was harder to circumvent the usury law on deposits than on loans, but above all because the system was able to continue functioning in spite of this artificiality. Indeed, although time deposits have waned considerably in real terms, demand deposits have kept up with inflation perfectly. Both of these results are easily explained: with strongly negative interest rates in real terms, it was natural that the holders of savings would be uninterested in putting them in time deposits. Demand deposits withstood inflation because individuals and firms could not dispense with cash for transactions, and the bank continued to be the best place to keep it. Hence commercial banks could respect the usury law in the payment of interest to their depositors. Were demand deposits to diminish in the same manner as time deposits, the system would be so shaken that the usury law would have to be either revoked or circumvented by some device.

Table 4 shows how demand and time deposits in commercial banks evolved in nominal and real terms between 1951 and 1966. Between 1951 and 1965 demand deposits almost doubled in real terms. On the other hand, time deposits were reduced to a quarter of their initial level, falling from 24.4 percent of total deposits in 1951 to only 4.0 percent in 1965. It is interesting that in 1966 there was a notable increase in time deposits; they tripled in nominal value and doubled in real terms. In part this is due to the banks' opening of fixed-term time-deposit accounts with prestipulated monetary correction that yield 20 to 22 percent per year; in part it is due to the abolition of interest on demand deposits (except in limited lower- and middle-income personal accounts). The latter action probably led several banks to classify as time deposits many accounts that had previously been registered as demand deposits. Banks observed the limits of the usury law on loan rates until the beginning of the 1950's. Thereafter, however, a great variety of

TABLE 4. COMMERCIAL BANKS, DEMAND AND TIME DEPOSITS
(year-end balances in million NCr$)

Year	Deposits in current cruzeiros				General wholesale price index (1953 = 100)	Deposits in 1953 cruzeiros	
	Demand (1)	Time (2)	Total (3)	Percentage (2) of (3)		Demand	Time
1951	52.2	16.9	69.1	24.4	82.5	63.3	20.5
1952	60.3	16.9	72.2	23.4	90.4	66.7	18.7
1953	71.2	17.7	88.9	19.9	113.2	62.9	15.6
1954	84.9	20.4	105.3	19.3	140.3	60.5	14.5
1955	102.4	19.8	122.2	16.2	153.5	66.7	12.9
1956	126.6	21.1	147.7	14.3	192.9	65.6	10.9
1957	176.1	24.3	200.4	12.1	199.4	88.3	12.2
1958	216.1	25.8	241.9	10.6	255.0	84.7	10.1
1959	321.6	30.8	352.4	8.7	347.1	92.7	8.9
1960	438.2	47.4	485.6	9.8	460.8	95.1	10.3
1961	610.8	55.2	666.0	8.3	691.6	88.3	8.0
1962	1037.7	56.3	1094.0	5.1	1037.0	100.0	5.4
1963	1703.9	89.4	1793.3	5.0	1886.0	90.3	4.7
1964	3069.6	148.3	3217.9	4.6	3645.0	84.2	4.1
1965	5799.7	241.7	6041.4	4.0	4676.0	124.0	5.2
1966	6390.0	696.0	7086.0	9.8	6413.0	99.6	10.9

Source: Central Bank.

devices were invented to bypass the legal limit of 12 percent per year.[3] Among the most popular are the following:

Interest "on the outside." This is the crudest system, used on a small scale because it compromise the capacity of the bank and the accounts of the borrower. It consists simply of collecting, in addition to the interest permitted by law, an extra rate not entered in the books.

The surcharge of banking commissions. This is the most common system. It consists of collecting, in addition to official interest, several commissions for services rendered, such as the opening of credit, collections, and so on. These commissions, duly inflated, elevate the effective cost of money to the desired level.

Tied accounts. This rather ingenious system consists of obliging the borrower to take out a loan greater than that desired, to pay interest on the whole, and to leave part of the funds in the bank in a tied account that pays no interest.

This last system, in conjunction with banking-commission surcharges and the advance collection of interest, raises the cost of money well above what it appears. As an example, let us imagine a bank that discounts a three-month duplicata of NCr$15,000, declaring charges of 2.5 percent per month, 1 percent being interest and 1.5 percent commissions. However, the bank requires the borrower to keep one-third of the value of the duplicata on deposit during the three months. The interest, collected in advance, is 7.5 percent on NCr$15,000, or NCr$1,125. The borrower actually receives the value of the duplicata less interest, less the tied deposit, or NCr$8,875. Thus the effective cost of the amount received is 12.7 percent per quarter, or 4.2 percent per month in terms of simple interest. Sometimes the tie is established in terms of different maturity dates: the bank grants a three-month loan guaranteed by a two-month duplicata, the proceeds of which are deposited obligatorily for one month, until the liquidation of the operation. The

[3] It is interesting that the Bank of Brazil itself normally collects effective interest much greater than the 12 percent per year of the usury law.

practical result is the same: the elevation of the effective rate of interest well beyond what it appears.

In the last analysis, all these devices were imposed by the market, since with the high rates of inflation registered it would be impossible to equilibrate the supply and demand for credit with nominal interest rates of only 12 percent per year. In spite of these devices, interest rates stayed below the rate of inflation until 1964. The persistence of negative real rates is explained by several factors: the money illusion of many borrowers, the fact that an accelerating inflation almost always surpassed expectation, and particularly the banks' habit of lending money almost entirely on the basis of the discount of short-term duplicatas. This habit naturally acted as a curb on access to credit. It is only in 1965 and 1966, with the decline in the pace of inflation, that real interest rates (doubled by some banks) became positive.

It was perfectly normal and even desirable, from the point of view of equilibrium in the credit market, for nominal rates to rise well beyond the limits of the usury law during inflation. The distortions in the banking system resulted not from this adaptation, but from its unequal nature: loan rates rose considerably, but deposit rates stayed at the convention limits. The abnormal difference between the two rates, sustainable only in a period of violent inflation, naturally led banks into cutthroat competition for the public's deposits, which became an exceptionally profitable commodity. Thus developed one of the most curious examples of inefficiency generated by competition. According to the best principles of the adjustment of marginal cost to marginal revenue, the number of bank agencies multiplied, innumerable deposit accounts with small balances and a rapid turnover were opened, excessive employment of personnel took shape, and so forth. Consequently, banks began to have very high operating costs — suffice it to say that today few of them are able to lend money for less than 2 percent per month in nominal terms. These cost increases are difficult to reverse in the short run because of labor legislation, excessive fixed investment in buildings and luxurious installations, and so forth. Today this is one of the most difficult structural problems hindering monetary stabilization. The commercial banking system today is reasonably well adapted to 30 or 40 percent annual inflation — but not to stable prices, since real interest rates charged on loans would become unbearably high.

CREDIT AND FINANCE CORPORATIONS AND MEDIUM-TERM CREDIT

In the middle of the last decade, with the specialization of commercial banks in short-term discount operations, practically no supply existed of private medium-term finance for periods of from six months to two years. With the development of the durable consumer-goods industry and the consequent proliferation of installment plans, a quite intense demand for this type of credit was created. After a period of difficulties, the problem was solved by the creation of the so-called "credit and finance companies," which, using certain legally permissible devices, succeeded in attracting something equivalent to the public's time deposits (with the name duly changed to escape the usury law), paying for them at rates well above the 12 percent annual limit. These resources served as the basis for six- to twenty-four month loans.

The first device invented by the credit and finance companies was the "share accounts" (*contas de participação*). In essence, share-account companies performed the functions of deposits and loans, in the terms of articles 325–328 of the Brazilian Commercial Code. These companies can be formed by a simple private contract without prior registration, which makes them extremely flexible and exempt from the bureaucratic obstacles to the formation of other types of company. Accordingly, the credit and finance companies created share funds, with themselves as ostensible partners and the public as silent partners. The resources thus obtained were applied in new share-account companies with the fund's borrowers, the latter entering as ostensible partners and the fund as silent partner. Only the names changed: deposits and loans were now called share-account companies. But the name change circumvented the usury law, since the remuneration of share accounts was considered profit, not interest.

Three factors caused the gradual extinction of this device during the first few years of the 1960's. First was the appear-

ance and popularization of a much more ingenious and convenient service, the system of *letras de câmbio* (bills of exchange).
Second was the fact that depositors' profits were subject
to the schedular tax on profit income, and to the progressive complementary tax on total net personal income. Since
these gains were in fact illusory, and generally well below the
rate of inflation, their taxation was a strong disincentive. Third,
several court opinions cast doubt on the legality of substituting
share-account operations for loans by the finance companies.

The system of bills of exchange appeared near the end of
1959 and gained immense popularity in the next few years. In
general, the borrower exchanged his duplicatas or promissories
for letras de câmbio, which were drawn by him and accepted
by the credit and finance company. The maturities of the letras
de câmbio were staggered so that the expiration of each one
was preceded by that of an equal or greater sum of the borrower's duplicatas. The credit and finance company thus guaranteed the payment of the bills it accepted by the expirations
of the paper it received. In this operation the company did not
charge interest — which would make no sense in this case —
but only an acceptance commission.

Up to that point the borrower had merely exchanged
duplicatas and promissory notes for bills of exchange. However, these bills are negotiable on the stock exchange: thanks
to the prestige of the credit and finance companies' acceptance,
it was possible to sell the bills at a discount (deságio) in the
capital market. In this way, the borrower obtained the money
he needed. (In practice, a company that specialized in placing
credit instruments and was generally affiliated with the credit
and finance company bought the borrower's bills and resold
them to the public.)

For the buyer of the bill, the discount replaced interest,
circumventing the usury law once again. Thus a one-year bill,
sold for 76 percent of its face value (that is, at a 24 percent
discount) yielded its purchaser an implicit interest of 24/76 —
31.6 percent per year. The borrower from the credit and finance
company who had traded his duplicatas and promissories for
bills of exchange paid this implicit interest indirectly, plus the
income and stamp taxes and the acceptance, brokerage, and
placement commissions.

The popularity of the system resulted from two factors: in part from the convenience of the operation for the credit and finance companies, which linked the maturity of the bill to that of its respective guarantees; but especially from the preference shown the bill by the public, which saw in it a simple mechanism of protection against inflation that was tax-exempt for the buyer, who was not even required to identify himself to the company or the government. (The income tax on the discount, created in 1963, was paid only by the borrower. The rates charged were 15 percent in the first half of 1963, 25 percent in the second half of 1963 and all of 1964, 15 percent again in 1965, and 16.5 percent in 1966.)

The system of discounting bills was practically eliminated by a provision of the Capital Markets Law (Law 4728, July 1965) making it obligatory, in all bills issued after January 1, 1967, to identify the recipients of the discount, and requiring them to declare it as personal income. But this law too was circumvented. The law allowed the credit and finance companies to emit bills with monetary correction — a posteriori correction tied to the official coefficients of inflation, and exempt from the income tax. After some unhappy experiences (particularly with Resolution 21 of the National Monetary Council, which will be described below), a new system was invented, essentially the same as the discount system, but receiving much more liberal tax treatment: bills of exchange with prestipulated monetary correction. The bills are sold at par and redeemed at a premium previously agreed on. In this system, a 40 percent income tax is levied, but only on the portion of the premium and interest in excess of the official monetary correction. In practice, the tax is very low, sometimes even nonexistent, and it is not necessary to identify the beneficiary. It is within this sytem that the credit and finance companies currently operate.

The credit and finance companies are regulated by the Central Bank, and their operations are controlled by a series of laws, directives, and resolutions. The companies must satisfy minimum capital requirements, which have varied through time, and must operate within certain limits, such as:
(1)   total asset operations may not exceed five times the capital plus free reserves;

(2) the maturity of each operation must be between six months and two years;
(3) fixed assets may not surpass 30 percent of capital;
(4) applications per client may not exceed 5 percent of total asset operations at any time;
(5) the average of applications per client may not exceed 2.5 percent of total asset operations;
(6) at least 40 percent of applications must be allocated to finance the sale of durable consumer- and producer-goods to their final users.

TABLE 5. OPERATIONS OF THE CREDIT AND
FINANCE COMPANIES
(year-end balances)

Year	Balance (million NCr$)
1959	1.3
1960	7.1
1961	13.0
1962	47.9
1963	81.4
1964	245.0
1965	695.0
1966	820.0

Source: Banco Central, *Relatório de 1966*, p. 82.

The growth of credit and finance companies is shown by the rapid increase in their operations in the last few years (Table 5). It is interesting, however, that bills of exchange almost never fully compensated their buyers for inflation. In 1960, one-year bills were sold at a 17 percent discount, which corresponded to a 20.4 percent yield, a rate considerably below the inflation of that time. From then until 1964 discounts increased appreciably, but inflation rose even faster. The peak of discounts occurred in the second half of 1964, when one-year bills were sold at 36 percent below par (56.3 percent annual yield); in that period, however, inflation was even more violent. In 1965 and 1966 the increase in prices dropped to about 40 percent per year, but discounts on one-year bills also fell to 24 percent (a 31.6 percent yield). Thus, except in special periods when bills were sold at a large discount and inflation by the maturity date fell below expectations, buyers of bills of exchange were systematically decapitalized in real terms. In fact, the success of these instruments can be explained only by the money illusion of a good part of the public, by the lack of better alternatives on the market, and by the aggressive sales policy of the credit and finance companies.

It should be noted, however, that the cost of the money to the borrower is normally very high and, at least since 1964, has been reaching rates greater than that of inflation. In 1960, when bills of exchange were beginning to become popular, effective interest charged to borrowers was about 30 percent per year, less than the rate of inflation at that time. From then on, however, the cost of money kept rising dues to the increase in discounts, the introduction of the income tax on them, and the increase in acceptance and placement commissions. At the end of 1964, credit and finance companies normally collected about 4.5 percent per month in advance from borrowers. Thus, in a six-month operation, the borrower would have received 73 and paid 100. The effective cost of the funds was 37 percent per semester, which in terms of compound interest is equivalent to 88 percent per year. For a one-year operation, with interest paid in advance, the borrower would have received 46 and paid 100: an exorbitant effective interest rate of 117 percent per year. Perhaps all this seemed natural in a year when inflation had reached 90 percent. But many operations were contracted at this rate at the end of 1964, to be redeemed in 1965, when inflation was much less intense. In this period, borrowers from the credit and finance companies had to pay extremely high real interest rates. Since 1965, with the fall in discounts and a reduction in taxes on bills of exchange, the cost of funds from the finance companies has fallen quite a bit, but it has still continued to be considerably above the rate of inflation. As this is written (mid-1967), this cost varies between 40 and 50 percent per year within the system of bills with prestipulated monetary correction.

At the beginning of the 1960's no law granted the finance companies the exclusive right to place bills of exchange with the public. This allowed several firms to place bills or promissory notes of their own acceptance on the market without the intervention of credit and finance companies. These bills, which sought to attract the public through greater discounts, made up the so-called "parallel credit market," which escaped entirely the regulation of the monetary authorities. After July 1963 (Law 4242), the parallel market was considered illegal. Nevertheless, because of insufficient enforcement and legal doubts, this market continued to operate, openly, outside the law. Its actual dissolution occurred only in 1966, because of a dramatic series of banruptcies of firms using the market.

THE LONG-TERM CREDIT MARKET

Long-term loans are virtually unavailable in Brazil, except through certain government institutions. The problem here is not the legal limit on interest rates, which always could be circumvented by some device such as discounting. The impasse results basically from uncertainty about the future rhythm of inflation. In an inflationary situation, the rate of interest that would tend to be established in a free market depends on expectations about the velocity of price increases, which for the long run is totally unpredictable. A rate of 3 percent a month in a ten-year operation can be disastrous for the borrower if prices stabilize, or disastrous for the lender if inflation explodes.

A result of this long-term credit impasse is the weakness of the Brazilian bond market. Although corporate law permits companies to issue debentures up to the total of the stockholders' equity, few firms do so. Table 6 shows corporate

TABLE 6. DEBENTURE ISSUES

Year	Value (millions NCr$)	Percent of GNP
1956	0.29	0.03
1957	0.11	0.01
1958	0.54	0.04
1959	0.88	0.05
1960	1.20	0.05
1961	0.60	0.01
1962	2.4	0.04
1963	2.2	0.02
1964	11.0	0.06
1965	31.6	0.11
1966	29.1	0.06

Source: Fundação Getúlio Vargas.

bonds issued in the period 1956–1966, in total value and as a percentage of Gross National Product. The market is very small when compared, for example, with that of letras de câmbio. Moreover, many of the debentures issued in recent years have been short-run instruments (generally one-year), sold at a discount in the manner of letras de câmbio.

From several viewpoints, the natural remedy for a shortage of long-term credit during a violent inflation is the adoption of an inflation clause — adjusting payments and unpaid balances in accordance with price indices previously agreed on. Until 1964, such readjustments were considered to be prohibited by the gold-clause law. This naturally caused the disappearance of any private supply of funds for long-term loans. The sources of supply were thus limited to government institutions like the National Economic Development Bank (BNDE), the biggest supplier of long-term loans; the Bank of Brazil; and a few regional and state institutions. Also, some international financial agencies, particularly USAID, occasionally extend long-term loans in cruzeiros. There is also a rationed supply of funds for mortgage credit, from the savings banks (caixas econômicas) and, on a small scale, from a few social welfare institutes (institutos de previdência social).

Until 1964 the cost of funds lent by these institutions was extremely low in comparison with the rate of inflation. In fact, at one time Brazil was in the curious situation of having a long-term interest rate well below the short-term rate. Obviously loans on these terms were highly advantageous to borrowers — but it was inevitable that the supply of such subsidies should be severely rationed. Since 1956, the National Economic Development Bank has had legal permission to operate with the inflation clause, but it has not done so. It has sometimes used some mechanisms of partial defense against inflation, such as receiving participation rights in companies that contracted for its loans. In general, however, the BNDE has come to act as a holding company, taking corporate securities in preference to extending long-term financing.

Since 1964, several laws have been promulgated authorizing the issuance of credit instruments and the extension of loans with a monetary-correction clause. It is still too early to judge all the consequences of this clause, the details of which will be described below. In principle, monetary correction has shown itself capable of attracting a sizable amount of low- and middle-income savings. However, many borrowers appear to be afraid to contract loans on such terms. Until now real-estate loans with monetary correction have been reasonably successful, but industrial loans have not.

THE STOCK MARKET

The Brazilian stock market is still in the early stages of development. Although all corporate stocks were officially quoted on the stock exchanges until the promulgation of the capital market law in 1965, few were traded frequently.[4] In fact, only some thirty or forty companies were normally traded to any great extent.

In principle the purchaser of stocks can receive four types of income: money dividends, stock bonuses, increases in a stock's quotation, and subscription rights. Money dividends are a direct distribution of the company's profits. Stock bonuses (popularly known as *desdobramentos*) are a distribution of new stock corresponding to increases in capital from the internal resources of the firm, either through monetary correction of assets or through the incorporation of reserves to capital. Increases or reductions in a stock's quotation result from supply and demand movements on the stock exchanges, and are influenced by the company's profitability, by investors' monetary liquidity, by alternative applications of funds, and by psychological factors. Finally, on stocks quoted above par, investors can obtain income from the sale of rights to subscribe at face value.

The evolution of the average price of the most traded stocks (the National Investment Service or S.N. index) is shown in Figure 1. Table 7 shows the index deflated by the general wholesale price index. As can be seen, quotations on th Exchange rose moderately until 1958, usually not as fast as

[4] Until 1964 all corporations, at their formation and on increasing their capital, were obliged to furnish the stock exchange with the official quotation of their stock. On the other hand, any transfer of corporate stocks should have been made through the Exchange.

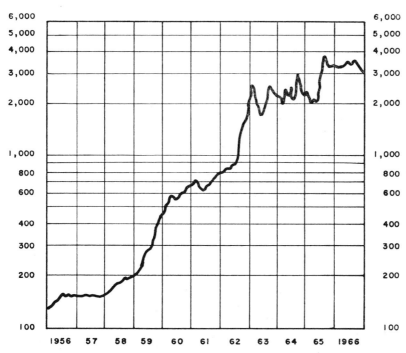

FIG. 1. Annual Index of Prices, Rio De Janeiro Stock Exchange. Source: Serviço Nacional de Investimentos and Fundação Getúlio Vargas

the general rise in prices. In 1959 and 1960, stocks rose sharply, not only in nominal but in real terms. This was a result of the creation of automatic mechanisms for the monetary correction of fixed assets (Law 3470, November 1958), which led firms to distribute numerous stock bonuses to their stockholders. In 1961 the Exchange fluctuated, principally because of the variability of credit policy. Between mid-1962 and March 1963, prices again rose in a spectacular and speculative manner, many stocks tripling and some even quadrupling in price. Since then the Exchange has been subject to intense fluctuations. Prices tended to rise in nominal terms from 1963 to 1966, which is natural during inflation, but they fell in real terms.

A few years ago, many firms were bitterly criticized for not offering their stock to the public at a time when the public had savings it was willing to invest in them. Today the situation is reversed: quite a few traditional firms have shown themselves willing to let the public in, but since stocks have risen little in recent years (they fell in terms of purchasing power) many investors prefer bills of exchange or readjustable obligations of the National Treasury. There are several factors behind this recent behavior of the stock market.

For any stock traded on the Exchange there are two potential values and one effective value. The first potential value

TABLE 7. ANNUAL S.N. AVERAGE OF STOCK PRICES
(1954 = 100)

Year	S.N. average	General wholesale price index	Real S.N. average
1954	100	100	100
1955	116	113	103
1956	137	135	101
1957	143	152	94
1958	165	170	97
1959	275	235	117
1960	529	307	172
1961	634	425	149
1962	945	651	145
1963	1982	1129	176
1964	2081	2164	96
1965	2598	3272	79
1966	3281	4452	74

Source: Serviço Nacional de Investimentos (S.N.) and Fundação Getúlio Vargas.

is the stock's share in the net worth of the firm; it is calculated by dividing the replacement cost of total net worth by the number of shares outstanding. The second potential value is the stock's expected income: the present value of its future dividends. The effective value is what the stock brings on the market. It is interesting to examine the correlation between this effective value and the potential values.

In the last few years, the effective value of stocks has apparently been well below the real value of their share in net worth. The most flagrant example was when numerous stocks fell below par at the moment that Law 4357 made monetary correction of assets compulsory. (The corrections did not take book capital completely into account; it continued far below replacement costs. And replacement costs, no matter how objective, do not enter into the considerations of the investor.)

The second potential value, capitalized expected future dividends, normally exercises considerable influence on stock prices in countries with stable currencies. The greater the profit expectations and the proportion of profits distributed, and the lower the interest rate (the standard of comparison with the investor's other alternatives), the greater this value will be. Many specialized studies have examined the normal price/profit ratio as a function of these parameters, and observation of developed markets suggests that these studies predict reasonably well.

There is no doubt that these determinants of capitalized value affect the fluctuations of the stock market qualitatively, but the quantitative effects are unpredictable. Higher interest rates, introduced by new credit instruments like the readjustable obligations of the Treasury, usually provoked a fall in the market, and vice versa. Increases in company profits and decreases in taxes on dividends cause visible rises in stock prices. Because of inflation, however, money returns on investment in stock can result only from increases in quotations, from stock bonuses, or from eventual subscription rights to stocks having a market price above par. Since the rate of inflation must be balanced against these indirect elements in appraising a stock's value, an objective calculation of long-run capitalized value is impossible.

Thus, in the Brazilian capital market, stock prices are subject to innumerable short-run disturbance factors. The most influential seems to be the level of monetary liquidity of the private sector. Stocks rise considerably when credit is easy and fall considerably when money is tight. Qualitatively, this phenomenon is normal everywhere; it could even be predicted by calculating the capitalized value of future yields, since easy credit corresponds to low interest rates, and vice versa. The problem is that the Brazilian market is oversensitive to oscillations in real liquidity. Periods of sharp stock-price rises (such as July 1962–February 1963, or the third quarter of 1965) were periods of easy money, when monetary expansion ran ahead of prices. The periods of decline (such as the second quarter of 1963, the last months of 1964, or the year 1966) were periods of tight credit, with prices rising faster than the means of payment.

It is clear that such intense oscillation is quite discouraging to the market. Several measures have been put into effect to stimulate the market. Several measures have been put into effect to stimulate the market, including the recent Decree-Law 157 (February 1967), which permits individuals to apply 10 percent and corporations 5 percent of their income tax to the purchase of new shares through financial institutions. It is possible that the market will be stimulated by such powerful incentives, but there are those who doubt the permanency of the results. In fact, it seems very difficult for a stock market to function properly in a time of violent inflation. Money dividends are by necessity distributed in percentages well below the general increase in prices, which repels many investors touched by money illusion. Stocks can yield high returns through distribution of bonuses or increase in quotations, but this evolution is unstable in the short and medium runs. One security yields another, which in turn yields another, and the end result is a type of indeterminate system. So it is not surprising that the market fluctuates violently in an inflationary period, and that investors end up preferring other financial alternatives for many reasons.

LOANS WITH MONETARY CORRECTION

Since 1964 the government has passed a series of laws designed to stimulate the use of the monetary correction clause in loans, especially long-term loans. The principal laws were:
(1) July 1964, Law 4357 created readjustable obligations of the National Treasury — federal, that is, public, debt instruments with a monetary-correction clause;
(2) August 1964, Law 4380 created the National Housing Bank and real estate bills (letras imobiliárias), and permitted monetary correction in loans for the purpose of acquiring one's own dwelling;
(3) July 1965, Law 4728 created several new types of instruments with monetary correction — debentures, bills of exchange, time deposits, and long-term certificates of deposit; the law also generalized the conditions of the monetary

correction applied to housing loans (previously limited to the percentage increases of the minimum wage).

All these laws subscribed to the principle that monetary correction merely updates values, and therefore does not constitute taxable income. The most successful of these laws up to now (mid-1967) has been the one creating the readjustable obligations of the National Treasury. Until 1964 there was practically no market for federal public debt. The government

TABLE 8. READJUSTABLE OBLIGATIONS IN CIRCULATION
(December 31, 1966)

Types		Billion old cruzeiros (million NCr)
Voluntary		
Maturity	Annual Interest	
1 year	6%	400
2 years	8%	63
more than 1 year	6%	89
6 months	no interest or monetary correction	69
Held as alternative to taxes		
Correction of fixed assets		63
Compulsory		
Workmen's Compensation Fund		
(16% per year — indefinite maturity)		59
Total		743

could incur new debt only through compulsory loans, since no one would voluntarily invest in bonds that rarely yielded more than 6 or 8 percent per year in nominal value. The readjustable obligations made public debt extremely attractive to private investors. After 1965, the government could count on the issuance of these bonds to cover most of its cash deficits, thus taking pressure off the Central Bank.

The success of readjustable obligations can be gauged from their growing balance in circulation — 59 billion old cruzeiros in 1964, 293 billion in 1965, and 743 billion in 1966. The balance in circulation on December 31, 1966, was distributed as shown in Table 8.

Undoubtedly, the popularity of readjustable obligations has partly been due to extremely powerful incentives that from several viewpoints were also very burdensome for the National Treasury. For example, in November 1965 the government issued Decree-Law 1, which gave buyers of readjustable obligations two alternatives until May 1966: they could opt either for the monetary-correction clause, or for readjustment of the value of the obligation by an increase in the dollar exchange rate, using US\$ 1 = NCr\$1.85 as the base (the decree-law was promulgated when the dollar rate was already NCr\$2.20). After May 1966 one-year obligations would yield 6 percent per year. Since the dollar was readjusted to NCr\$2.70 in February 1967, purchasers of obligations at par between February and May 1966 received a nominal yield of $\frac{2700}{1850} \times 1.06 - 1 = 55$ percent per year. This was a burdensome rate for the Treasury, since the inflation of the period did not reach 40 percent per year.

The conditions of Decree-Law 1 were extremely favorable to those who bought readjustable obligations with foreign capital. However the exchange rate varied, obligations bought before May 1966 had a guaranteed one-year yield of $\frac{2.20}{1.85} \times 1.06 - 1 = 26$ percent in dollars, since the obligations' base for readjustment was the dollar at NCr\$1.85 and the effective exchange rate was already NCr\$2.20.[5]

The system of monetary correction of real estate contracts has been in effect since 1965, based principally on the resources of public institutions (the National Housing Bank and the savings banks). In the long run the system will no doubt considerably strengthen the loan capacity of these institutions, since amortizations and interest will be received in money of constant purchasing power rather than in depreciated currency. The attempt to attract private savings through real estate bills (*letras imobiliárias*) began only recently; the first results appear quite promising. It is curious that many real estate credit companies have issued bills of three or four years on which the monetary correction is paid in cash each quarter or semester, instead of being capitalized into the value of the bill — a conspicuous concession to the money-illusion of many buyers.

---

[5] Moreover, many were acquired at discounts of up to 8 percent, which increased their yield even more.

It should be emphasized that the government has considerably strengthened the market for real estate bills by its creation in 1966 of the Guarantee Fund of Time and Service (Fundo de Garantia de Tempo e Serviço). This fund, from an 8 percent payroll tax, is intended to finance workers' indemnifications, the purchase of their own houses, and other special investments; its rotating balance is administered by the National Housing Bank. Principally because of this fund, the budget for the National Housing Bank for 1967 is rising to 800 billion old cruzeiros (NCr$800 million), which leads one to expect great activity in real estate finance.

The application of monetary correction to the bills of exchange accepted by the credit and finance companies has been unsuccessful. Law 4728 sought to stimulate monetary correction by considering only the simple discount as taxable personal income (beginning in 1967), but exempting the bills' monetary correction from the income tax. It should be noted that until that time discounts rarely yielded the full equivalent of monetary correction. The government reasoned that during a period of slowdown in inflation investors would tend to overestimate the future rise in prices, and that as a result the systems of discounts would lead to exaggerated interest rates in real terms. Instead of having borrowers correct for inflation a priori through the discounts, the government attempted to provide a means of correcting for it a posteriori through monetary correction.

The failure of the system is due to the refusal of borrowers to accept relatively short-term loans with monetary correction, since the rate of correction would be an uncertain factor in their financial programming and their cost calculations. Generally, the finance companies extended loans based on duplicatas — commercial instruments with a fixed nominal value. The borrower was repelled by the idea of discounting paper of this nature through monetary correction, and the finance company itself was confused over how to calculate the appropriate margins of guarantee. Apparently the only viable formula would be to establish a contractual type of monetary correction; this, however, would drive away the buyers of these bills.

Between March and May 1966 the government attempted a compromise by means of Resolution 21 of the National Monetary Council. The resources for financing would be obtained

through the sale to the public of one-year readjustable obligations, with complete monetary correction and 6 percent interest per year (including the exchange-rate readjustment option
clause provided for by Decree-Law 1). Through the credit and
finance companies, these resources would also be lent for one
year, with interest at 12 percent per year and monetary correction up to a limit of 12 percent. All the profits and losses
of the operation would go to the government. The system soon
began to function with great losses to the government, which
had to pay no less than 55 percent on the obligations because
of the exchange-rate readjustment option. Since the proceeds
of the sale of obligations were lent at 24 percent per year, and
since the credit and finance companies received a 10 percent
commission for acting as go-between, the intended compromise
yielded the public coffers a 41 percent loss in one year. Moreover, the finance companies collected additional interest on
the outside from their borrowers (the so-called "manikin"),
transferring part of it to buyers of the obligations via higher
discounts and keeping the rest. Foreign firms using foreign
funds to buy readjustable obligations were again favored im-
measurably over domestic firms, since Decree-Law 1 guaranteed them a yield of 26 percent in one year.

After the failure of Resolution 21 to work, the government
switched to a formula strictly equivalent to the discount device: bills with prestipulated monetary correction.[6] These
bills are issued at par and redeemed at a predetermined premium, which includes the interest and monetary correction
contracted. This system has been functioning satisfactorily.

As to the long-term instruments created by Law 4728 — readjustable debentures, certificates of deposit, and so on — there
is still very little experience in their application. In principle
there are two difficulties to the development of this market:
the fear of buyers, who avoid long-term paper because of the
risk of some change in the rules of the game before redemp-
tion; and the reluctance of borrowers to accept the monetary-
correction clause. These obstacles will probably retard the ex-

---

[6] The commercial banks have also entered the field, and are accepting time deposits of 6–8 months with prestipulated monetary
correction.

pansion of the private investment banks, which until now have been functioning principally as large finance companies.

In general, recent Brazilian experience suggests that monetary correction should be reserved for long-term operations, where one must face the problem of the unpredictability of inflation. For relatively short-term operations, such as those of the banks and the finance companies, monetary correction is a cumbersome complicating factor, introducing risks and difficulties into economic and financial calculations that can be avoided by simpler expedients, such as discounts. For long-term loans, monetary correction appears to be the only measure for coping with chronic inflation. It is, nevertheless, a measure to which there is much psychological resistance, and it cannot be implemented without considerable difficulty.

CHAPTER 6

Financial Recuperation for Economic Expansion

Octávio de Gouveia Bulhões

Given the bureaucratic slowness of the tax administration and the profitability of indebtedness when the depreciation of money is rapid, many businesses were accustomed until 1964 to remain in debt to the social welfare institutes and the Treasury. Delayed payment of tax debts, despite cumulative penalties, was the best way of increasing working capital. Thus *Conjuntura Econômica* was right in saying, in its December 1966 number, that "inflation granted a premium to those who delayed payment of taxes, until Law 4367 (July 1964) instituted monetary correction on tax debts."

But the institution of monetary correction did not aim only at controlling tax contributions. Its chief objective was to restore savings, the foundation of current production and the sine qua non of new investments.

With inflation, the government's credit had disappeared. Its reestablishment became imperative if government investments were to be freed from the exigencies of taxation. With inflation, the banking system had been swept clean of time deposits, an excellent source of cheap commercial credit. With inflation, the flotation of commercial bonds had been halted, though they are normally an excellent means of capturing resources to complement shareholder capital. During the negative real-interest phase of inflation, firms had gone excessively into debt, and they failed to reduce sufficiently their dependence on credit during the more recent anti-inflationary period.

Because of the inflation, no one ventured to purchase fixed-income securities or to hold time deposits. Capital thus loaned or deposited was quickly eroded by the workings of inflation. Once the government opted for gradualism in its fight against inflation, which meant a continuation (albeit reduced) of the rise in prices, it was incumbent upon it to offer some guarantee of the preservation of capital values, while the inflation persisted, in order to stimulate savings. Hence its recourse to monetary correction.

TREASURY SECURITIES

The burden of taxation makes it more difficult for firms to recover their investment, whether because taxation requires a greater amount of financial resources or because it reduces the buying power of consumers. Consequently, the primary condition for the economic success of government debt is an alleviation of the burden of taxation. Generally, those who acquire government bonds are in a position to supply resources not normally destined for consumption or for share capital. These funds have special requirements. They aim more for security than for income. They represent something halfway between liquidity and investment. They are reserves.

Once the Treasury, through the Central Bank, is able to inject government obligations into the market, these securities become ideal for those who need to maintain reserves or who want to hold their savings in a form with modest returns but with complete safety.

The sale of Treasury obligations with the monetary correction clause could not meet with instant success. Furthermore, upon its assumption of authority in April 1964, the government faced a country with an enormous deficiency of electric power, a dangerous scarcity of housing, and an alarming shortage of agricultural products. These were the sectors of economic activity that had suffered the deleterious effects of repressed inflation. Previous governments, frightened by the effects of an inflation they did not have the courage to eliminate, preferred to combat effects rather than attack causes. They decided to freeze the prices of electric energy, of rents, and of certain agricultural products. In 1964, a result of this procedure, there was power rationing; there were interminable queues to buy foodstuffs; and housing found itself in the midst of a paradoxical crisis, an enormous demand for living quarters combined with a complete lack of incentives for construction. In the face of these compelling circumstances, the government decided to increase taxes in order to accelerate the expansion of the electric power supply and to stimulate the construction of low-cost housing. There was no time to wait for voluntary savings, despite signs that government securities were being well received.

In a short time, these measures relieved the scarcity of electric power, permitted the initiation of construction of mass housing, made possible the expansion of agricultural production, and strengthened government credit. Today there is a market for the obligations of the National Treasury.

It is alleged that the issuance of Treasury securities has made the financing of private business more difficult. This assertion is only half true: the fragment of truth is that receipts from the sale of bonds have not yet made it possible to reduce taxes appreciably. What the charge that Treasury securities have been prejudicial to private issues overlooks is the fact that government issues have been minute in volume compared to those of the private sector; moreover, it ignores the diversification of the capital market.

If the government is successfully floating Treasury obligations, and if at the same time it is not able to reduce the demands made by taxation, government spending must be excessive. Beginning with fiscal 1965, the federal government succeeded in eliminating the deficit on current account, and budgets began to show surpluses to finance investment outlays. Thus the chief cause of inflation was eliminated shortly after the beginning of the Revolutionary Government of Castello Branco. Table 1 shows actual receipts and expenditures according to the Treasury balance for the fiscal years 1964 to 1966.

The transfers and balances are, in part, destined for the decentralized administration, for the states, and for the municipalities. The decentralized administration is composed of organizations with financial autonomy, such the railway system, the Department of Highways, the Investment Bank, and various other government enterprises. In the aggregate this group has a budget more than twice the size of the central administration's. This decentralization was put into effect in order to achieve efficiency in operations. But according to a document published by EPEA,[1] current expenses absorb more than 70 percent of receipts, the latter including the yield of taxes and transfers from the central administration. Current expenses being so high, it is little wonder that the investment program ran into deficits.

TABLE 1. TREASURY RECEIPTS AND EXPENDITURES
(*million NCr$*)

	1964	*1965*	*1966*
Receipts	1,889	3,238	5,090
Current expenses and transfers	2,018	2,656	3,752
Balances	−129	582	1,338

Source: Budget items as organized by the Ministry of Planning.

In 1966 total outlays, including investment plans, of the central and decentralized administration were calculated at 14 billion new cruzeiros, which amounted to more than 30 percent of estimated GNP for that year.[2]

With the sound purpose of reducing the current expenditures of the decentralized administration, it was established by law that the central administration could not increase its transfers to cover higher personnel costs. However, the legal limit was completely circumvented. Administrators stopped paying their financial obligations abroad and postponed indefinitely the payment of debts to domestic suppliers and contractors, thus compelling the central administration to liquidate these debts. In 1966, for example, more than NCr$150 million were paid abroad for obligations that had not been liquidated,

[1] Escritório de Pesquisa Econômica Aplicada do Ministério do Planejamento, *Programa de Investimentos Públicos, 1966*.

[2] The 1966 GNP was estimated by the Instituto de Economia of the Fundação Getúlio Vargas at NCr$45 billion.

and several hundred million cruzeiros were added to outlays in the form of special credits.

Still more serious in 1966 was the financial disorder of the states. Under the cynical philosophy of the fait accompli, the federal government was obliged to take care of several states. An appreciable part of receipts coming from Treasury securities was earmarked to alleviate the financial difficulties of suppliers and contractors caused by default on payments on their accounts by the states. If the federal government had not rescued the states, the banking illiquidity of 1966, through a breach of contract by these suppliers and contractors, would have provoked a banking crisis.

TABLE 2. VALUE OF SUBSCRIPTIONS TO
TREASURY OBLIGATIONS
December 1964 to December 1966
(million NCr$)

Obligations for a term of one year	400
More than a year	536
Total	936

Source: As in Table 1.

These facts show how far we stray from reality when we insist on the need for new investments without giving heed to the imperative of financial discipline. The country has made notable financial progress since April 1964; but much still remains to be done and consolidated.

Painstaking studies made during the past three years now permit the government to establish a scheme of investment priorities and to utilize more effectively those investments already made. The government has at its command the legal means to expedite administrative coordination, and can count on a discipline in wages that did not exist in the past. The task is far from easy. But now, at least, there is the possibility of better planning and of better execution of plans.

The government, through the Banco Central, has succeeded in placing on the market a promising sum of Treasury obligations, as shown in Table 2. The value of one-year obligations bought from December 1964 to December 1966 was NCr$400 million; longer-term obligations bought in the same period amounted to NCr$536 million. The year 1964 closed with sales of NCr$59 million, of which only 37 percent was voluntary. In 1966, 87 percent was voluntary. The success is indisputable. A comparison of these figures with figures on other financing, destined for private firms, indicates that the sale of obligations was not detrimental to the credit position of private enterprise.[3] Table 3 shows that total subscriptions to Treasury obligations in 1966 were less than 5 percent of the resources destined for firms, a modest proportion. The fact that government bonds tend to attract private individuals seeking a secure investment should also be considered.

TABLE 3. FINANCING OF INDUSTRY AND COMMERCE
(*million NCr$*)

Years	Bank loans Working capital	Investments	Letras de câmbio (real bills)	Subscription to shares	Treasury obligations
1964	3367	579	245	377	60
1965	5343	979	695	1133	315
1966	7200	1678	852	1664	561

Source: Banco Central and *Conjuntura Econômica*.

The initial issues of Treasury obligations of one-year maturity were obviously designed to arouse public attention. Receipts from the sale of such short-term securities could not replace tax receipts. The success of the short-term issues was followed by the placement of longer-term securities. Proceeds from these sales could have made a reduction of the tax burden possible had it not been for anarchy in the finances of the states and the decentralized administration.

PRIVATE-SECTOR LENDING

The relentless rise of prices after 1956, with only very short intervals of lesser inflation, finally led to the creation of a financial market alongside normal banking operations as a means of evading the limitation on interest rates established by the law against usury. The growth in sales of durable goods gave the greatest impulse to this clandestine market. Without

[3] This was pointed out clearly in the *Análise e Perspectiva Econômica Bulletin* of July 5, 1967.

it banks could not have financed these sales satisfactorily, mostly because of the violent loss of time deposits.

Since the banks could not satisfy the demand for loans for consumer durables, and also wanted to react effectively against triangular operations, they organized "finance companies." These companies, utilizing acceptances, sold *letras de câmbio* (real bills of exchange) on the market at variable rates of discount. Table 5 shows the effective rates of interest.

TABLE 4. COMMERCIAL BANK DEPOSITS
(millions NCr$)

Year	Total deposits	Time deposits	Time deposits as percent of total
1951	69	17	24.4
1952	72	27	23.9
1955	122	19	16.2
1956	147	21	14.3
1957	200	24	12.1
1960	485	47	9.8
1961	665	55	8.7
1962	1094	56	5.1
1963	1793	89	5.0

Source: Banco Central.

Until 1965, borrowers were able to endure such high rates, since rising prices offset the service on the loan. But in 1965, the rate of price increase was substantially reduced. At the outset of 1966 there was a slight quickening in the pace of inflation, followed by a return to deceleration near the end of the year. Under these conditions, the interest rates shown above became exorbitant.

Purchaser of letras de câmbio became accustomed to receiving more than 2 percent per month, and resisted a smaller remuneration. They forgot that most of the returns went to offset capital loss through the decline in the value of money. Once the rise of prices tapered off and tended towards stability, the yield on loans could not maintain its earlier level. It had to suffer a substantial decline. When monetary correction becomes small because the depreciation in the value of money is also small, there is no reason to demand a high interest rate.

Borrowers and lenders in the private market refuse to

follow the system of monetary correction used in Treasury obligations. Their objection lies in the difficulty the borrower has in making an additional payment, at the end of the loan, to compensate the creditor for capital depreciation due to inflation during the loan period. This attitude is understandable, given uncertainties about monetary policy. It is, however, quite likely that lenders will come to accept a posteriori readjustment if a point is reached at which a decisively declining rate of monetary depreciation is expected. Credit would then be granted at moderate interest rates, with a clause providing for an increase in the principal to be repaid if there should be a rise of more than 2 percent in the general price level during the life of the loan.

TABLE 5. INTEREST RATES, 1965

Term of loan in days	Monthly rate for borrower	Monthly rate for lender
180	5.0	2.6
270	5.6	2.8
360	6.7	3.0

Source: EPEA, *Situação Monetária, Creditícia e do Mercado de Capitais.*

I see no difficulty — provided the downward trend in the depreciation of money is firm — in accepting a correction in the value of the principal at the end of the term of a loan. Bankers receiving a time deposit of a minimum of 180 days could pay the depositor a reasonable interest plus a sum corresponding to the monetary depreciation occurring during the time of the deposit. In this way, the current system of 18 to 22 percent yields for lenders, which result in more than 25 percent costs to the borrower, would cease. The borrower, in turn, would accept a readjustment of the principal at the expiration of loans of more than 90 days. Without a doubt, total charges in this system would be appreciably less than 25 percent — provided, I repeat, that the government is able, as it seems to be, to continue slowing down inflation.

Bankers allege that they must demand more than 20 percent annual interest from borrowers to cover expenses. Obviously no economy with monetary stability can bear such a

preposterous rate of interest. Sr. Obregon de Carvalho, banker and well-known economist, concluded a detailed article published in the *Jornal do Brasil*, by acknowledging the following defects needing correction in the banking system:
(1) low productivity in banking services;
(2) too many banking establishments, which creates excess capacity and prevents economies of scale;
(3) rendition of unpaid services by the banks;
(4) subsidies granted to the monetary authorities by commercial banks.

All these defects are being corrected. The subsidies to which the writer refers have to do with the compulsory reserve deposits of commercial banks with the Central Bank. This monetary policy measure was long perverted during the inflationary phase because of an excess in government expenditures. A portion of financial resources was taken from commercial activities in the form of compulsory reserves and transferred to the federal government by the Central Bank. Today this no longer happens. In addition, a by no means negligible part of compulsory deposits now can yield a return, if used to acquire Treasury obligations. Moreover, time deposits are not subjected to compulsory reserve requirements. As to the other defects mentioned above, the Central Bank facilitates mergers provided by law through tax exemptions, among other ways.

Sr. Obregon de Carvalho did not mention a very important item: the reestablishment of time deposits. Table 4 showed that, at the beginning of the 1950's, 25 percent of total bank deposits were time deposits. Time deposits are stable funds. Cash reserves necessary for them are much smaller than those required by the frequent withdrawals of demand deposits. This characteristic of time deposits favors lower service costs, and their greater stability widens the range of loan uses without inflationary effects.

To the extent that time deposits increase, bankers could reduce the activities of the finance companies, transferring their operations to the banks. With the increased activity of the finance companies, commercial banks lost more than 25 percent of their loans, but none of their vast structure of services and administrative expense.

The interest rate remains high not only because lenders

and borrowers resist a posterior monetary correction, nor because banks consider it difficult to reduce their operating costs. These problems exist because the demand for credit, in the short run, is inconsistent with the trend toward price stability. Brazilian entrepreneurs grew accustomed to the heavy use of credit during the acceleration phase of inflation, when sales prices rose more rapidly than the rate of interest. Now they sense that a change is in order, but believe a reordering of their finances to be impracticable.

TABLE 6. EVOLUTION OF CORPORATE FINANCES
(1960 = 100)

	1960	1961	1962	1963	1964	1965
New fixed investment	100	130	291	389	1248	2511
Own working capital	100	155	266	537	1277	2226
Borrowed working capital	100	211	359	656	1836	2463

Source: *Conjuntura Econômica*, xv–xx.

Table 6 shows the evolution of new fixed investments, the corporations' own working capital, and borrowed capital. Between 1960 and 1963, entrepreneurs invested relatively little and resorted heavily to credit. Beginning in 1964, in the expectation of consolidation in the value of the cruzeiro, they intensified investments. Note, however, that they continued the heavy use of credit.

Individual examples are even more illuminating in showing the excessive use of credit. The president of Usiminas (Minas Gerais Steel Company), the well-known engineer Amaro Lanari, estimates the cost of production of heavy steel plate in Brazil at US$ 144.90/ton — $40.50 of which is interest and $22.90 taxes. In the United States, the cost is $107.90/ton — $1.30 for interest and $7.90 for taxes. The Central Bank classifies short-term credit as working-capital loans. These loans, considering bank credits and letras de câmbio, amounted to NCr$8 billion in 1966, or 18 percent of GNP — a very high percentage.

All these data point up the great distortions suffered by the Brazilian financial market as a consequence of intense and prolonged inflation. Inflation-control policy, especially in its final stage, requires a new process of financing.

The problem has now been defined. The solution consists of reducing loans, and increasing corporations' own working capital and shareholder capital. This is a challenge because it requires the painful work of restructuring business finances. As a first step, firms must utilize available resources to strengthen their own working capital before going ahead with new investments or expanding their operations. Firms heavily in debt must reduce loans in favor of an increase in share capital, even in the form of an induced or compulsory subscription, both of which are provided for in the income tax legislation. In this way it will be possible to reduce the pressure on the credit market in a relatively short time. The rate of interest will decline, which will favor the stock market and stimulate the supply of resources for new investments.

As long as we insist on basing the expansion of firms on short-term credit, and persist in financing public works through surtaxcs, we can be sure that inflation will always be a danger and promising economic development a dream. Impatience is not constructive. The desire for progress alone, without discipline, will lead us into frustration, for we will be destined to find more obstacles to surmount than steps to climb.

LIMITS TO THE USE OF MONETARY CORRECTION

With the goal of ensuring financial recuperation, the application of monetary correction should be limited to Treasury obligations, private credit instruments with maturity greater than one year, and time deposits of not less than 180 days.

Strictly speaking, there is no monetary correction of rents, but rather a provision to avoid the abrupt unfreezing of property incomes. It was necessary to establish limits on rental contracts — considered excessive by property owners and too liberal by tenants — in face of the enormous housing scarcity. The system of correction described above applies to construction finance, with certain specific forms for low-cost housing, as the editorial in the APEC *Bulletin* of July 5, 1967, correctly points out.

As to income tax, the exclusion of the illusory excess of income that monetary correction brings has been sought since the most acute phase of inflation. Decree-Law 62 is nothing but a complementary measure that should have been adopted long ago. The tax situation of corporations is quite curious. Calculated tax can be somewhat excessive because of the problem that the government sought to correct through Decree-Law 62, but the Treasury refrains from collecting more than 50 percent of the tax due. It leaves the remainder in the firm for reinvestment. In the current situation, this tax exemption is not sound economic practice; moreover, it is excessive. Consequently, the enforcement of Decree-Law 62 requires a reexamination of existing tax deductions.

Having made these reservations, I now transcribe the aritcle from *Conjuntura Econômica* referred to at the beginning of this essay.[4] It examines monetary correction in relation to the income tax with extraordinary perception.

In the case of the income tax payable by private individuals, the principal adaptation necessary relates to the limits of the progressive application. They will have to be adjusted periodically in accordance with the rise in prices, otherwise the tax may become unbearably heavy. Up to 1961 these adjustments were made without any definite system, occasional changes being made in the income tax law in order to lighten the progressive character of the schedules. Only after 1961 was an automatic corrective mechanism introduced, when the schedules were based on and expressed in multiples of the minimum wage. Later, Law 4506 of November 1964 adopted the new system, which is still in use, of schedules revised yearly in accordance with the monetary corrective coefficients of the Brazilian Institute of Economics.

Taxes to be paid on profits made by firms required more subtle adaptation to the inflationary process. In this case it was not so much a question of neutralizing the rates as of reviewing the usual accounting methods. The traditional system of registering book values by their nominal historical values, applied under inflationary conditions, lead to two types of illusory profits. First, depreciation funds, calculated as from the nominal values of the equipment and installations,

---

[4] *Conjuntura Econômica*, International Edition, XIII, No. 12, Dec. 1966, pp. 3–6. Some changes in the English translation have been made by the editor of this volume.

become insufficient to meet replacement requirements of the fixed assets of the enterprise, which, with inflation, have naturally become much dearer. Under such conditions, a part of the retained profits represents nothing more than complementary provisions for depreciation purposes. Second, another part of the retained profits represents a provision for the maintenance of the real value of the firm's working capital. Profits are absorbed in replacing stocks, which due to inflation have increased in price, or in preserving the real value of the firm's credits. These are illusory profits, since their reinvestment adds nothing to the firm's real assets. There is yet a third form of illusory profit, which is arithmetical, resulting from the division of a profit expressed in the currency of the present purchasing power by a book asset in the currency of a bygone purchasing power.

The adaptation of the Brazilian income tax legislation to inflation began precisely with the recognition of this arithmetical illusion. The natural solution found was monetary correction of fixed assets, permitted in certain specific cases by Law 1474 of November 1951 and Law 2862 of September 1956, and later made automatic, based on the coefficients of the Brazilian Institute of Economics, and by Law 3470 of November 1958. It should be stressed that in the beginning the law looked upon monetary correction as a kind of favor granted to enterprises and not as a simple adjustment of book values. A tax of 10 percent was imposed on the correction and it was forbidden to calculate depreciation on the corrected assets. In fact, the monetary correction served only to alert the attention of enterprises interested in distributing bonuses in shares, or in escaping the tax on extraordinary profits.

The fundamental steps toward recognizing illusory profits were taken by Law 4357 of July 1964. The monetary correction of assets, although made obligatory, saw the tax reduced by 5 percent. (Later, Law 4506 reduced the tax still further and contemplated its elimination after 1967.) At the same time permission was given to calculate depreciation based on the corrected values for equipment and installations, which automatically suppressed one of the traditional components of illusory profits. Lastly, the maintenance of working capital, the other part of the illusory profit, was provided for. Fearing a large drop in income tax revenue, the law did not go to the logical conclusion (of completely exempting illusory profits), permitting only that the maintenance of working capital could be deducted when calculating extraordinary profits. (Later, Law 4663 extended that deduction to the taxable profits of enterprises that achieved especially satisfactory indexes of productivity and stabilization of prices.) In any case, the principle was firmly established that inflation created illusory profits that in principle should be free from any fiscal burdens.

The recent Decree-Law 62, which instituted monetary correction on balance sheets, completed the adaptation of the Brazilian income tax to the inflationary process. The monetary correction referred to applies to both fixed assets and the depreciation and maintenance of working capital, by a more simple and more functional method. In short, Decree-Law 62 permits that, in each balance sheet, enterprises must effect monetary correction of determined items of their assets and liabilities (including the capital and reserve accounts), making book counter-entries in a special account titled "monetary correction of the balance sheet." This account, whenever it shows a debit balance, will indicate the nominal illusory profit attributable to inflation, which under the terms of the decree-law may be charged up to profit and loss.

Specifically, Articles 4 to 9 of Decree-Law 62 (promulgated November 12, 1966) establish that in balance sheets closed as of January 1, 1967, enterprises that are legally obliged to keep accounts may effect monetary correction in the following accounts: fixed assets, with respect to depreciations, amortizations, and so on; capital account, that is, capital, surplus, reserves, and accumulated profits or losses; and credits and commitments in foreign currency, or in national currency subject to monetary correction by the terms of the contracts.

These accounts shall be corrected in accordance with the coefficients of the Brazilian Institute of Economics (excepting debits and credits in foreign currency, which shall be corrected in accordance with the exchange rate), and the book counter-entries shall be written up in the "monetary correction of the balance sheet" account. Should this account show a debtor balance, it will indicate that inflation was the cause of the illusory nominal profits of the enterprise.

Under the terms of the decree-law, this balance may be debited in part or totally to the profit and loss account. Should the "monetary correction" account show a credit balance, inflation must have produced real profits now shown by the book accounting. Within certain limits it will be necessary to add this to the taxable profits, in accordance with the terms of the new text.

From various viewpoints, Decree-Law 62 involves important changes in the conventional criteria for accounting profits and analyzing balance sheets. The new accounting is certainly more complicated, but has the advantage of indicating real values, without the distortions of illusory profits. Its explicitness will also allow enterprises to have better control over their situations, since it prevents the decapitalization that might result from the euphoria provoked by nominal gains.

Thus we have briefly reviewed the evolution of monetary correction under the Castello Branco government. In a period of marked inflation, it is the only device — given the continuance of the usury or maximum-interest law — by which to rehabilitate savings in monetary form or restore the government securities market, to introduce rationality in the fiscal system, and to lay a basis for order in private finance.

CHAPTER 7

Corrective Inflation in Brazil, 1964-1966

Howard S. Ellis

What special significance from the economic angle attaches to the three-year period of the Castello Branco government in Brazil, from March 1964 to March 1967? The answer is that since the "Revolutionary Government" took power in the midst of a virtual economic and political collapse of the country, and was chiefly guided by economists of the highest caliber, it shows what economic measures in and of themselves — without a transformation of the society itself — can and cannot accomplish. It also shows that economic measures are not all equally meritorious. This essay is written in the hope that it will yield lessons for future policy makers who try to solve the age-old dilemma of Latin American countries: trying to achieve economic development without disastrous inflation.

March 1964 marks the end-point of upward-curving functions showing the behavior of the cost of living, of central

[1] Lawrence Fertig, in his syndicated column "Inside Business" of September 16, 1967, estimated that even the 3.2 percent inflation of 1966 in the United States involved real-value losses on savings deposits, bonds and mortgages, and insurance and pension reserves amounting to $27 billion. In addition, $25 billion was lost on the real value of life insurance policies. In total, this $52 billion loss of savings exceeded the $42 billion that was added to nominal dollar savings in all forms in 1966. This outcome cannot be greatly different from the experience of Brazil.

government budget deficits, and of the supply of means of
payment. The years between 1949 and 1958 may be characterized as "moderately inflationary," at least by Latin American
standards, with annual increments to the cost of living generally not over 20 percent. But, following the lavish expenditures
of the Kubitschek government on Brasília, and especially beginning in 1959, the percentage increments were 43, 32, 43, 61,
81, and 85. While annual growth rates in gross national product
of 7 percent or more had once led to complacency about the
simultaneous appearance of inflation and growth, the cumulative nature of inflation now revealed its inherently dangerous
character. During the first quarter of 1964, the last of the
Goulart government, inflation reached 25 percent for those
three months alone.

Meanwhile, the increment to gross national product had
become a negative 1.4 percent in 1963, the inflow of U.S.
capital into the country had ceased, and real wages – having
once risen so rapidly as to be a chief cause of government
deficits – continued a decline begun as far back as 1958. The
diversion of bank credit to support growing government deficits
was slowly strangling private business. Added to these economic woes was the ever-mounting threat of a left-wing take-
over under Goulart.

Such was the setting into which the Revolutionary Government of Castello Branco came in March 1964. Among its
greatest assets were the unassailable probity of the president,
and his desire to be guided by expert opinion. His chief guides
were two economists, the Minister of Finance, Professor Octávio de Gouveia Bulhões, and the Minister of Planning and
Economic Coordination, Roberto de Oliveira Campos.

The proclaimed philosophy of this government was "corrective inflation," which rejected an attempt at abruptly halting
all increases of money and prices, and embraced a great variety
of measures extending far beyond fiscal and monetary devices.
Since Castello Branco had promised on his accession to power
that constitutional government would be restored in three
years, the crisis had to be surmounted and long-range reforms
introduced almost simultaneously. This intense activity and its
outcome are recorded in the following pages.

THE NATURE OF CORRECTIVE INFLATION

The economists in Brazil who apparently coined the term "corrective inflation" did not and do not intend any favorable or tolerant attitude toward inflation because of possible economic gains from it. No sympathy is implied for the idea that, because of the lag of wages behind prices, inflation supplies forced saving and thus accelerates economic development. Nor is the notion involved, explicit or implicit in some "structuralist" positions, that inflation more or less inevitably attends economic development or that every approach to full employment inevitably entails inflation. "Corrective inflation" does not carry these overtones.

Indeed, one must go farther and emphasize that the originators of the concept of corrective inflation in Brazil regarded inflation as an evil — perhaps a necessary evil for the time being, but an economically costly one. These costs include the erosion of the real value of government tax income, the distortions of prices accompanied by nonproductive investment, the deterioration of mass purchasing power with resulting wage struggles, and — not least — the discouraging of voluntary saving by individuals.

Why then tolerate a continuance of inflation at all? In the first place, a gradual decrease in the rate of money creation may have fewer ill effects than an abrupt termination, at least in some circumstances. Stabilization crises are not unknown in financial history; and if such crises lead to the abandonment of the effort to control inflation, the cure is as bad as the disease.

More specifically, there are at least three justifications of gradualism. First, most severe inflations feed on central government budget deficits, and it takes time to devise and put into effect measures to balance the budget — to find new sources of revenue or improve old ones, and to plan and enforce reductions in expenditure. Corrective inflation can "buy time" for the execution of reforms, with the recognition that any continuation of inflation involves social and economic costs that must be set against potential gains.

Second, inflation distorts prices, sectoral and individual incomes, and all types of economic values. Sectors of the economy come to live on inflationary gains. Withdrawing these gains may result in the collapse of these sectors; and however socially just their demise may be, their disappearance or shrinkage may infect the whole economy and produce a general collapse.

Third, though part of the process of removing the maladjustments resulting from inflation involves *downward* revisions, another and equally important part is the *upward* revision of prices that have been artificially held down in an effort to cure inflation by curing its symptoms. Upward price revisions of this sort inevitably reduce the rate at which the movement of a general price index can be decelerated. Originally, "corrective inflation" referred to these upward revisions alone.

All of the foregoing implies that rampant inflation must be attacked along a broad front. If it is impossible or undesirable to put a dead stop to the increase of money, it is equally necessary to allow some time for the elaboration of nonmonetary measures to combat inflation. Thus corrective inflation may be understood to include the whole complex of monetary and nonmonetary measures to stem the rise of prices.

This description of the concept of corrective inflation has almost necessarily been in terms of the advantages expected of it as a deliberate policy. It has disadvantages as well. One type springs from the protracted duration of the process. With time, the risk increases of unfavorable turns of public expectations about all types of inflationary phenomena that affect commodity prices, income, interest rate, foreign exchange rate, and so on. A successful outcome of gradual disinflation may also be endangered by unforeseen (and unforeseeable) adversities. The recent history of Brazil demonstrates this fact impressively.

Finally, an important element is what Professor Albert G. Hart calls "the linkage of risks." Such linkages rest in turn on certain fiscal, financial, and other economic relationships. Professor Bulhões calls attention to budgetary linkages, like the tax on petroleum products, most of which automatically goes into highway construction.[2] Raising the rate of this tax or

[2] Octávio Gouveia de Bulhões, "O Combate à Inflação e as Vinculações Orcamentárias," *Revista Brasileira de Economia*, XX, Nos. 2 and 3, June–Sept. 1966, p. 35.

otherwise improving its net yield does nothing to restore budget equilibrium, since it merely promotes more highway construction. There are innumerable other real economic linkages through complementarity, substitution, and the like. All of these interrelations complicate the elimination of maladjustments produced by inflation.

On the other hand, the longer period allows a greater role to be played by conscious policies to promote adjustment. It can be said with some certainty that the longer the inflation has lasted, and the more intense it has become in its final stage, the greater the need for adjustments. Thus in Brazil the presumptive merits would be relatively large for a policy of gradualism.

FISCAL POLICY

Corrective inflation implies the progressive lowering of the rate of increase of the means of payment. Monetary restraint and fiscal control are both essential, but in the runaway inflation of Brazil in the 1960's it was the latter that required the more drastic action. For one thing, credit to the private sector, which is the principal domain of monetary control, had in real terms barely kept abreast of the growth of GNP. But more important, the supply of primary money, the compulsory reserves that form the basis of commercial bank loans, depends upon the size of the budget deficit. Aside from the foreign balance — a somewhat exogenous factor — the mastery of budget deficits is thus the critical factor in reducing inflation.

Should the objective of reducing deficits be attempted chiefly by reducing expenditures or by increasing revenues? While the advocate of private enterprise would emphasize fiscal economy, and the socialist or defender of state action would expand revenues, both lines of attack have to be pursued in a short-run strategy against inflation. The advocate of fiscal economy would not rejoice in the fact that federal taxes in Brazil rose from 17.7 percent of national income in 1964, to 19.2, 21.4, and 21.6 percent in the three subsequent years.[3]

[3] Ministério do Planejamento e Coordenação Econômica, *Plano Decenal de Desenvolvimento Econômico*, Tomo II, Aspectos Macroeconômicos, Volume 1, *Política Tributária*, p. 36.

TABLE 1. TAX RECEIPTS, FEDERAL GOVERNMENT
(indexes of real yield; 1962 = 100)[a]

Type of tax	1963	1964	1965	1966	1967[b]
Consumption	118	134	126	153	175
Income	70	73	99	92	127
Stamp	27	29	34	37	—
Other imposts and taxes	30	25	33	46	46
Total	245	261	292	329[c]	347[c]

Source: Plano Decenal, Política Tributária, p. 52.
   [a] Deflator: implicit PIB deflator, 1953 = 100.
   [b] The source cited is responsible for the 1967 estimates.
   [c] Slight differences in adding are due to rounding.

Nor would the equalitarian be pleased that indirect taxation, already 72 percent of the total in 1963, rose to 74 percent in 1966, despite a considerable rise in the real yield of the income tax.[4] But the objective was to reduce deficits, and this we can properly take as the point of departure.

Government Revenue

Though the government did indeed adopt several measures to limit expenditures, it was in increasing revenue that it scored its more important victories. The evolution of taxes is shown in real terms in Table 1.

Over the Castello Branco years, 1964–1966, the real yield of taxes was raised by 34.4 percent over 1963, a signal triumph considering that it was achieved during a time of substantial inflation, which automatically erodes the real yield of given taxes. The accomplishment is the more noteworthy in that the increased yield was to a considerable degree the result not of raising tax rates but of enforcement. Withholding for income tax, for example, increased from 26.4 percent in 1963 to 43.5 percent in 1966. The income tax law (Law 4357 of July 14, 1964) made tax debts subject to monetary correction, thus removing the motive for delaying the payment of taxes. Finally, the exemption of certain liberal professions and the judiciary from income tax was abolished. In 1965, a Fiscal Crimes Law made tax evasion a criminal offense and provided imprison-

[4] Ibid., p. 43.

ment for violations. Over the years 1964–1966, the Treasury's performance in increasing revenue was the single most notable contribution to the abatement of inflation.

In addition to reducing budget deficits, tax reform was directed toward the strengthening of private enterprise, that is, to a considerable extent aimed at offsetting some of the distortions produced by inflation.[5] An important measure was the elimination of the grossly unjust tax on the appreciation of nominal value of assets under inflation at the same rate as any income. A jungle of informal practices had grown up that partly mitigated this curious distortion. Law 4357 made obligatory the writing-up of corporate *fixed* capital assets, but reduced the tax on the increase of value from 10 to 5 percent; subsequently, the tax was first reduced to 2 percent and then, on January 1, 1967, abolished altogether. Law 4357, supplemented by acts of June 3 and July 14, 1965, permitted the reduction of taxable income by amounts sufficient to maintain *working* capital assets intact.

Still more fiscal measures were designed to offset other distortions attributable to inflation. Its tendency toward the "decapitalizing" of private business was partly offset by Law 4506 of November 30, 1964, which imposed an additional 7 percent tax on the distribution of profits to shareholders. The same law permitted the partial deduction (about one-third) of corporate research and development expenses from taxable income. A complex of laws and regulations (including Law 4506) sought to democratize the ownership of corporations in Brazil, and thus to compensate in some degree for the impoverishment of the middle class produced by years of inflation. Finally, excise and stamp taxes stated in monetary terms — and thus absurdly depreciated — were raised by Law 4388; subsequently two laws (4425 and 4440) increased the yield of the stamp tax by improving its administration. Postal and domestic-telegraph rates have been raised several times, but still lag considerably behind the depreciation of the cruzeiro.

[5] This account is based in large part on the *Plano Decenal* document already referred to: *Política Tributária*, chap. 5, "Adequação Tributária, e Fortalecimento da Emprêsa Privada."

Government Expenditures

In view of notorious inflexibility of government expenditures to reduction, it should not be surprising that the Castello Branco government was less successful in attacking fiscal deficits from this side than from that of tax revenue. Shortly after the government took power, it apparently seemed politically necessary (in April and May 1964) to raise the salaries and wages of civilian and military government employees by an average of 30 percent, entailing a budget cost of NCr$580 million, which in itself largely accounted for the 1964 deficit of NCr$760 million.

Among the earliest measures, adopted in 1964, aimed at reducing expenditures were Decree 53,949, which was designed to cut Federal outlays by one-third, and Decree 54,228, which limited the adjustment of the salaries of government employees to restoration of the average and not the peak) salary in real terms over the past two years; moreover, adjustments were not to be made more often than annually. By mid-1964, subsidies on imports of petroleum, wheat, and newsprint were abolished.

The year 1965 saw the introduction of two devices limiting government expenditures. Decree 55,623 (January 1, 1965) created a *Fundo de Reserva* of NCr$550 million, which was not really a fund but an accounting device. Authorized budget funds for the second half-year were actually to be used only if there were sufficient receipts in the first half-year to cover the outlay, or if expenditure in another budgetary division had been sufficiently lower than planned to cover it. A second measure, Decree 55,789 (February 23, 1965) established a financial program for the Federal government that was not to exceed NCr$3,698 million in both the regular and any supplementary budgets. The program was in general adhered to, despite a 6 percent increase in the investment program that constituted 31.5 percent of total government outlays.

In significant sectors of the transport industry, the 1964–1966 period saw substantial reductions in government subsidies both in real terms and in relation to total of budget spending, as Table 2 shows.

In the railway sector the reduction resulted from holding wages constant and increasing transport charges, though a

TABLE 2. FEDERAL GOVERNMENT SUBSIDIES IN TRANSPORT INDUSTRY
(1965 prices in millions NCr$)

Year	Railways	Shipping	Ports	Commercial aviation	Total	Percent of budget spending
1962	462	154	26	66	707	17
1963	538	137	18	36	728	17
1964	498	96	10	28	632	15
1965	328	77	12	25	442	12
1966	268	71	9	19	366	8

Source: Presidential Message to Congress on Draft Budget for 1967. Figures for 1966 are estimates.

contribution was also made by abandoning some lines. However, the figures adduced in the presidential message omit subsidies at the federal and state levels to the road program, which from 1961–1965 constituted 40 percent of public-sector expenditures and in 1966 rose to a magnitude equivalent to 133.4 percent of the federal budgetary deficit. Thus it must be said that the road-building program contributed heavily to inflation at the end of the Castello Branco regime.[6]

The Budget Deficit

Anyone dealing with public finance in Brazil is painfully aware of the complexities produced by the fact that only about one-third of central government finances is included in the formal budget. As yet the fiscal reform has not produced a unified official budget including the *autarquias*, mixed companies, and the like. The construction of something approaching an exhaustive budget is an individual enterprise. One, put together by a competent authority, João Baptista de Carvalho Athayde, is given in Table 3. It omits the completely autonomous mixed companies but is said to include about two-thirds of the field of federal finance. Other compilations differ in detail, but not on the general order of changes.

What is amply clear is that the heroic efforts of the Castello Branco government to reduce the budget deficit were indeed rewarded. The evolution of the formal union or federal

[6] On this subject see Alan Abouchar, "Inflation and Transportation Policy in Brazil," September, 1969 issue of *Economic Development and Cultural Change.*

TABLE 3. CONSOLIDATED BUDGET, FEDERAL GOVERNMENT
(millions NCr$)

	1964	1965	1966	1967[a]
1. Budget receipts	2,010	3,238	5,200	6,650
2. Current budget expenditures	2,171	2,656	3,981	5,210
3. Budget savings (2 minus 1)	−161	582	1,219	1,440
4. Capital expenditures	599	1,170	1,719	1,993
5. Budgetary balances (3 minus 4)	−760	−588	−500	−554
6. Extra-budgetary receipts (including budget transfers)	1,941	3,161	4,864	6,606
7. Current extra-budgetary expenditures	1,242	2,030	2,626	3,391
8. Extra-budgetary saving (6 minus 7)	699	1,131	2,238	3,215
9. Extra-budgetary capital expenditures	543	1,252	1,903	2,631
10. Extra-budgetary balance	156	−121	335	584
11. Total balance (5 plus 10)	−604	−709	−265	31
12. Domestic credit operations (Treasury obligations)	49	324	440	353
13. Final consolidated balance	−555	−385	175	384

Source: "Orçamento Federal e Programa de Investimentos Públicos," *Jornal do Brasil*, "Revista Econômica," Feb. 16, 1967.
[a] Provisional.

budget runs as follows for 1963, 1964, 1965, and 1966 (in semi-final form). Deficit in million NCr$ − (1963 n. a.), 760, 580, and 500; deficit as percent of GNP − 5.1, 3.9, 1.8, and 1.1; deficit as a percent of budget receipts − 54, 38, 18, and 9.6; taxes as a percent of GNP − 26.4, 29.3, 30.9, and 33.7. These figures are even more impressive when three facts are considered. First, when extra-budgetary receipts and expenditures are considered, the aggregate central government financial balance ceased to be a deficit in 1966. Second, the federal government had to assume considerable indebtedness in rescue operations on behalf of some states. In 1966 the Banco Central lent NCr$44.3 million to the official state banks, and the Treasury advanced NCr$68.5 million to state treasuries, a total of NCr$143.6 million, or nearly one-third of the federal deficit. Third, the strategy of corrective inflation involves the gradual liberation of controlled prices, which causes increases in the price and cost structure and makes it somewhat more difficult to balance the budget. For example, the tax advantages accorded to producers who agreed to limit price increases on their products entailed a loss in revenue.

The resources devoted to minimum-price maintenance for certain agricultural products should also be taken into account on the other side of the ledger, that is, inflationary forces. Credit for these purchases or loans is extended by the Bank of Brazil through its two special funds, the Department for Agricultural and Industrial Credit (CREAI) and the Department for General Credit (CREGE). Since they are considered as loans by a commercial bank, these sums are not included in the formal federal budget. But in reality they are public funds, and in recognition of this they are now controlled by the monetary authorities. Consequently, though these funds are not primary money in the sense of bank reserves created by the Treasury or Banco Central, they directly expand the total of bank credit. At the end of 1966, they totaled NCr$271.8 million. Setting this against the NCr$175 surplus in the final consolidated balance, we do indeed have a balance of about NCr$97 on the side of inflationary finance. Even this was eliminated by the close of the Castello Branco regime in March 1967 by the trend of federal finances during that year.

All factors considered, it seems evident that the realization of a positive net balance in the total financing operations of the federal government by the Castello Branco regime was a great achievement.

MONETARY POLICY

Looking at the operations of the monetary authorities from 1964–1966 at time intervals of a year and, for the time being, not probing deeply into basic causes, we see a quite favorable picture. The record is one of marked disinflation in the first two years, generally continuing in 1966.

From the angle of aggregate expansion, the developments of 1966 seem very good; similarly, it may seem that the great expansion of discounts for commercial banks and of loans to nonbank borrowers is a salutary reversal of the favoring of the government over the private sector.

However, the reversal was probably excessive. It was in

response to a great expansion of lending by the commercial banks that the monetary authorities' discounts and loans mounted so precipitously. The Banco Central itself points out that though the 32.9 percent increase in "normal credit" extended by the banks was probably justifiable, the 140.2 percent increase in "extraordinary" credit was questionable even from the angle of sound business. For this expansion of extraordinary credit the loans of CREGE and CREAI — the departments of the Bank of Brazil that make quasi-government or government-inspired loans to the private sector — were chiefly responsible.

Aside from this circumstance, however, one must concede that the evolution of aggregate money creation in 1965 and 1966 was indeed favorable. But what was the role of monetary policy itself? Three circumstances reveal that it was relatively small. In the first place, as has been shown, it was the public finance sector that scored notable successes in reducing money creation from budget deficits. In the second place, the institutional apparatus of monetary control left much to be desired. Finally, a close quarter-by-quarter examination of financial developments during the Castello Branco years shows a lamentable lack of rationale in short-run monetary management.

The Complexion of Brazilian Monetary Control

It is common knowledge that Brazil lacked a central bank for most of its history; it is possibly much less common knowledge that a strong and well-functioning center of monetary control is still very far from being realized. The Superintendency of Money and Credit (SUMOC), founded in 1945 to provide a government authority that could deal with the International Monetary Fund and carry on the national requirements of that organization, exercised monetary control in a quite limited way. Since it has the power to establish minimum-reserve requirements and to determine discount rates, SUMOC might therefore be supposed capable of effective control of the quantity of money in Brazil. But in fact this is not so. For one thing, during most of the history of SUMOC the federal deficits were so large as to render monetary control, which applies almost entirely to the private sector, impotent or nearly so. In the second place, open-market operations, the chief weapon of central banking in more developed economies, could not be employed because there was little market for government bonds with the general public. Thirdly, rediscounting for the commercial banks was not an effective means of monetary control but rather a passive mechanisim of accommodating the banks, for reasons that still persist and will presently be explained. Finally, even the prescription of minimum-reserve ratios did not prove effective because the reserves were deposited with the Bank of Brazil and were then re-lent to the Treasury.[7] Since all the conventional weapons of monetary control were useless, Brazil evolved a somewhat clumsy and only partly effective substitute: credit ceilings or quotas imposed on the private-sector lending of the Bank of Brazil. In sum, monetary control scarcely existed.

On December 31, 1964, the Castello Branco government enacted a law ostensibly creating a central banking institution. In fact, no very great changes were made in the previously existing situation, though there is some promise for change in the future. A new institution independent of the Bank of Brazil was created, the Banco Central do Brasil; it was made the repository of commercial bank reserves and was given the power to carry on open-market operations and the monetary powers that had belonged to SUMOC.

However, effective monetary control still does not exist. Though the central government's budget deficits were drastically reduced from March 1964 to March 1967, they still produced rates of inflation that could only have been completely offset by crippling the private sector. But even an incomplete offsetting was practically impossible for the available monetary apparatus. Open-market operations had to await a much wider distribution of government securities than has yet been realized, even with the modest success of the Treasury obligations. Though the prescription of compulsory reserves, joined with the discount mechanism, is potentially a fairly powerful weapon,

---

[7] It was sometimes said that if the Bank of Brazil had not lent these reserves to the government, an equal emission of banknotes would have been necessary. This is a valid statement, but it seems to ignore the fact that both procedures are equally inflationary since both supply equal amounts of primary money, that is, money usable by the banking system as reserves.

it does not seem to have been effectively utilized, or even utilized with clearly identifiable results, as the brief historical review that follows will show.

There are two probable explanations for the Banco Central's ineffectiveness. First, most of SUMOC's personnel — and hence most of its orientation, which was decidedly subordinate to the viewpoint and needs of the Treasury — were transferred into the Banco Central. Second, another new institution was created with the Banco Central, the Conselho Monetário Nacional; and the Conselho — so far at least — constitutes a rather considerable obstacle to effective monetary control. This is ascribable in part to an awkward and ill-defined division of responsibility between the Banco Central and the Conselho. In part, it is ascribable to the role the Conselho has arrogated, that of giving specific and ad hoc directives to the Banco Central on discount rates and the like, though the Conselho was probably intended merely to lay down general lines of policy. The Conselho has also felt called on to concern itself with the allocation of credit, whereas this should be a legislative (or at least a budgetary) function, not one profitably commingled with central bank concern for price levels, monetary aggregates, employment, and general development. The constitution of the Conselho does not bespeak an intention on the part of the founders to create a top-level executive organ for monetary management, but rather a judiciously balanced advisory group.[8]

The remaining orthodox instruments of monetary control are the discount rate and the quantity of discounting. Before discussing them, I should point out two characteristics of Brazilian commercial banking. One is that rediscounting with the Central Bank (or its approximate earlier equivalent, the Bank of Brazil) is seldom resorted to. Over the years 1958–1966, the portion of commercial bank reserves obtained through rediscounting has only in one or two months been as high as 20–22 percent, has often been around 13–15 percent, and has sometimes fallen below 10 percent. It seems doubtful that this portion

[8] There are nine ex-officio members — three ministers (Finance, Industry and Commerce, Planning and Economic Coordination), the presidents of the Development Bank and the Bank of Brazil, and four officers of the Banco Central — and two members appointed by the president from the commercial bankers.

is large enough to have a controlling effect on the monetary base, the volume of money usable as bank reserves. Furthermore, rediscounting is known to be utilized mostly by the smaller and weaker commercial banks; concern for their precarious situation would seem bound to restrain the monetary authority from a really firm use of the rediscount mechanism to control expansion. (It is worth mentioning parenthetically that the "discount window" of the U.S. Federal Reserve is utilized to *soften* the impact of stronger measures, such as open-market and reserve requirements on the more vulnerable banks.)

The second characteristic of commercial banking in Brazil is the prestige enjoyed by the *duplicata* (trade bill) as an instrument for public borrowing from the banks, and for borrowing by the banks (rediscounting) from the Central Bank. Indeed, this prestige is so traditional and so compelling that the Minister of Planning and Economic Coordination, Roberto Campos, referred to the "religion of the duplicata," meaning that the banks find it difficult to deny credit to the holder of "legitimate" duplicatas.[9] In such a situation it is easily imaginable that rediscounting of duplicatas may be a means of escaping from monetary control rather than of enforcing it.

Short-Run Performance of Monetary Control

It seems clear that the main cause of secular improvement in the inflation situation of Brazil in the Castello Branco years was the reduction of the budget deficit, backed by wage controls and ancillary stabilization measures. The weakness of the monetary control mechanism condemned it to a secondary role in the longer run. We turn now to an examination of the performance of monetary policy in the short run, where it has been thought traditionally to be well adapted.

Let us first consider rediscounting. Bearing in mind that these rates are always differentiated widely for different categories of borrowers, we find that despite rather marked variations in general economic barometers such as the index of industrial employment, the complex of rates was changed only twice from July 7, 1961, to January 20, 1967. Instruction 210

---

[9] There is no way of keeping one *duplicata* from being used several times over for loans from different banks.

of the extinct SUMOC established the following rates on the first of these dates for four categories of rediscounts: 4, 6, 8, and 10 percent. On January 14, 1965, with the categories somewhat redefined, the rates were set at 4, 4, 6, and 12 percent. Finally, on January 1, 1967, the rates — having been judged to be no deterrent to applications for resort to the Banco Central — were raised to 22–30 percent for normal-limit and above-limit "common" rediscounts, again with other rates for special categories.

The infrequency of change itself seems to indicate an insensitivity of rediscount policy to the economic situation; in addition, the absurd lowness of rates during inflation can scarcely have lent them any efficacy, which was recognized by the advance of rates of January 1967. Ironically enough, this sudden and strong increase came in the midst of an economic downswing.

As to the *quantity* of rediscounting, there is fairly strong evidence from the angle of monetary control that it behaved perversely; that is, instead of varying more or less inversely with the behavior of economic activity, it varied in the same direction, and sometmes to a greater degree. Thus, during the first quarter of 1965, while the index of industrial employment was declining from 100 to 75, Banco Central rediscounts fell from NCr$197.3 million to NCr$117.2 million, or 40 percent, thus probably contributing to the economic decline. In the subsequent three quarters of 1965, the volume of rediscounts conformed approximately to the changes of the index of employment — except that in the third quarter, while the index of employment rose from 45 to 55, rediscounts rose 125.9 percent.[10]

The first and second quarters of 1966 again witnessed a simultaneous rise of economic activity and rediscounting, and the fourth quarter a simultaneous fall. Only in the third quarter did rediscounts rise while employment fell, illustrating for once an opposed movement that would characterize the use of this instrument for stabilization.

The history of changes in compulsory reserves is no more

[10] See Banco Central, *Relatório 1965*, p. 5, for discount changes; for employment changes, see Ministérios do Planejamento e Fazenda, *Análise do Comportamento Recents da Economia Brasileira*, pp. 4–5.

encouraging than that of the discounting process. On September 1, 1965, reserves were increased, just at the *beginning* of a recovery from the downward course of the first semester. But during the fairly sustained recovery of economic activity from about the middle of 1965 to mid-1966, reserve requirements were *decreased* four times: on December 10 and 13, 1965; on June 6, 1966, and again on July 20, 1966. *After* the peaking-out of the recovery in midwinter 1966, requirements were again raised to the level they had been at before July 20, 1966.[11]

That the quantity of rediscounts has varied more or less directly with economic activity, and that reserve requirements have varied roughly inversely with it, may be interpreted as indicating that variations in industrial employment are the *result* of the two monetary variations. No one has really maintained this interpretation for the period under review, probably because of the difficulty of ascribing such a strong effect of money on production in a country that has been so saturated with money for decades as Brazil. Nevertheless, for a limited period—for example, the last quarter of 1966 and the early part of 1967—it does not seem implausible that the sag in activity was partly induced by credit stringency. It should be remembered that the private sector was kept under pressure, and that the real value of loans to business had barely kept abreast of the growth of GNP for a decade. It would not be surprising if this protracted process finally took its toll. Furthermore, as has often been observed, it is difficult to end an inflation without some temporary setback to production.

In retrospect, neither the rediscount rate nor the reserve requirement were generally employed, so far as can be discerned, in such a way as to prevent undue booms and collapses in industrial employment. About all that can be said of them is that they did not interfere too much with the secular disinflation ascribable to the fiscal and wage measures.

Of course, rediscounting and compulsory reserves are not the only monetary-control devices in Brazil, despite the absence of open-market operations. Control may also be exercised

[11] Data supplied by Banco Central. The September 1 reserve increases were followed by the sizable increase in the discount rates of January 1, 1967, mentioned above.

through credit ceilings or quotas. This device seems, even abstractly, a rather clumsy and crude one, but there can be no question that, at least in theory, it could impose an absolute outside limit to the expansion of credit to the private sector. It is rumored that the credit ceilings have at times been raised to accommodate this or that industry or sector of economic activity, until the ceiling lost its restraining quality. It would seem less probable that this occurred under the Castello Branco government than under its predecessors, but unfortunately there are no published records that could support this belief.

Monetary Control and Nonfiscal Phenomena

We have examined the operation of the Brazilian monetary-control apparatus from the angle of each of the separate control devices. Another approach suggests itself. Monetary control, it has been said repeatedly, is virtually impotent in the face of large budget deficits that have to be covered by money creation. By counterimplication, monetary control should attempt to offset most *nonfiscal* sources of instability. What does the record of the period under review show in this respect?

The year 1964 presents no anomalies: the expansion of paper-money issues of NCr$56.6 million was approximately equal to the consolidated budget deficit of NCr$55.4 million and the percentage rise of the cost-of-living index was about the same as the percentage rise of means of payment. Total means of payment increased considerably more than note issues: the public converted 3.5 percent of its total monetary reserves from notes into bank deposits from April to December of the year. But bank loans to the public during these months expanded in real terms only from NCr$55.6 million to NCr$60.9, which is only mildly inflationary relative to the expansion ascribable to the federal budget.

The year 1965 witnessed a violent disturbance of these relations, which partly offset the "corrective inflation" achieved on the fiscal front by the decline of the consolidated budget deficit from NCr$555 million to NCr$385 million. Bank loans leapt from their 1964 year-end value of NCr$60 million (in deflated terms) to NCr$84.9 million a year later, contributing greatly to the NCr$75.3 million increase of money in the hands of the public.

Three circumstances account for this vast increase of bank loans in the midst of the fiscal effort at restraining inflation. First was a continuance of the shift from cash to deposits on the part of the public that had been noted in 1964 but became conspicuous in 1965 because of the inflationary effect through loans. The safety and convenience of checking accounts and the fact that loans by commercial banks are based partly on the customer's deposit balance explain the fall of the cash deposit ratio from 25.8 in April 1964 to 19.0 at the end of 1965. Second, banks were possessed of a new optimism, and thinned down their reserve ratios enough — according to an analysis by Delfim Netto — to account for about two-thirds as large an increment to loans as did the increase of the reserve base.[12] Finally, during 1965, because of the strongly "favorable" turn in the foreign balance, the monetary authorities expended NCR$1,231 million on additional foreign-exchange reserves. No steps were taken to insulate the domestic money supply from this flood of reserve money from abroad.

It was Brazil's good luck to escape some of the inflationary impact of the 75.3 percent increase in the money supply in 1965. Wholesale prices rose only by 31.4 percent, though the cost of living, largely because of necessary upward corrections in rents and utility rates, rose by 65.7 percent. Part of the reason for the less than proportional price advance was the expansion of banking business and the use of bank loans in connection with harvests and stock-raising. Also, both income and transaction velocity declined by about 10 percent in 1965, apparently as a consequence of improved expectations about the future course of inflation.[13] The restraint on wage increases caused costs of production to lag behind prices. Finally, Portaria 71 (discussed below) had at least a temporary restraining influence on prices and anticipatory spending.

From a monetary viewpoint, 1966 showed an almost exact

[12] Delfim Netto, "Alguns Aspectos da Inflação Brasileira," *Estudos Anpes*, V, pp. 197–204.

[13] EPEA, *Situação Monetária, Creditícia, e do Mercado de Capitais*, Quadros IV and V, pp. 54–56.

reversal of all the conditions of 1965. Inflation continued, though the government financial deficit was brought down to a mere NCr$79 million; commercial bank loans to the public, though increasing in nominal terms by 25 percent, did not increase in real value at all. The means of payment rose by 18.8 percent; but—reversing the 1965 relation—wholesale prices and the cost of living rose by 41.4 percent. Why? There were three main causes: delayed effect of the very large money creation of 1965; poor agricultural harvests; and the playing-out of the price restraint exercised by Portaria 71. Contributing factors may have been the deficits incurred by the states and the increase of trade credit.

In reviewing A Política Anti-Inflacionária de 1965, Simonsen wrote with prophetic insight: "The question is whether the increase of real liquidity registered in 1965 may carry with it some elements of instability capable of giving origin to a resumption of inflation in the first months of 1966." [14] Indeed, any theory about normal money holdings (in real terms) would predict the eventual spending of the excess sums accumulated in 1965; and the continuance of inflation would induce persons and firms to spend their money before it depreciated. Strong evidence that the rise of prices in 1966 was partly a consequence of the creation of means of payment in 1965 is to be found in the complete stagnation of commercial-bank lending in the first four months of 1966, and its very slow recovery even through July.

Like all devices attaching the symptoms of inflation rather than its causes, Portaria 71 would be expected to gradually lose effect; and it seemed to do so in the industrial field in 1966. As to the poor harvests, it is true that the cost of foodstuffs rose less in 1966 compared to 1965 than the general cost-of-living index did; but food prices did rise absolutely and hence did contribute to the inflation of prices.

Thus there might very probably have been *some* inflation in 1966 even if there had been no increase in the means of payment. But the wholesale-price and cost-of-living increases were much higher than expected, and were popularly regarded as the greatest economic shortcoming of the Castello Branco

[14] *Jornal do Brasil, Revista Econômica,* Feb. 10, 1966, p. 16.

government. It is therefore difficult to understand why the monetary authorities chose in 1966 to extend loans to the private sector amounting to NCr$899.2 million. Neither minimum-price operations nor the conventional budget deficit were inflationary factors in 1966. The foreign balance was a very influential factor in the expansion of means of payment (NCr$724.8 million); but the net inflationary effect of monetary authority loans, even deducting the public deposits with the Bank of Brazil, was NCr$774.1 million. Thus it was a larger factor than the foreign balance in engendering inflation. The general results in the money and credit field for the years 1964–1966 are presented in Tables 4, 5, and 6.

TABLE 4. OPERATIONS OF THE MONETARY AUTHORITIES, 1964–1965

	Percentage increase 1964 over 1963	*Percentage increase 1965 over 1964*
Total volume of business	84.5	38.1
Total expansion of monetary authority loans	90.0	41.9
Financing of National Treasury	81.2	15.9
Financing of budget deficit	42.3	−15.4
Discounts for commercial banks	n.a.	−18.0

Source: Banco Central, *Relatório 1965*, pp. 49–50.

It seems quite clear from a review of the Castello Branco years that monetary phenomena responded willy-nilly not only to budget deficits, which is more or less inevitable, but to other factors to which some effective resistance should have been forthcoming. It may be that monetary control could have been effected through the Bank of Brazil's departments for loans to the private sector, CREGE and CREAI. But such loans were considered to be invested with a strong public interest, and therefore not subject to the same manipulation as commercial loans.

WAGE POLICY

The brunt of responsibility for stabilization over the Castello Branco years was borne by fiscal measures, but the containment of wages clearly takes second rank. Though wage

TABLE 5. OPERATIONS OF THE MONETARY AUTHORITIES, 1965–1966

	Percentage increase 1965 over 1964	Percentage increase 1966 over 1965
Total volume of business	46.9[a]	37.7
Increase of paper money	49.4	32.2
Loans to National Treasury	45[b]	13.6[b]
Discounts for commercial banks	−21.8	167.9
Loans to nonbank borrowers	27.6[c]	52.5[c]

Source: Banco Central, *Relatório 1966*, pp. 43–51.
   [a] Revision by the Banco Central of the figure given in its 1965 report.
   [b] These figures are not increments but total amounts expressed as percent of budget deficits.
   [c] Loans by Banco do Brasil.

TABLE 6. ANNUAL INCREASES IN MONEY AND PRICES
(*percent*)

Year	Paper money issued	Means of payment	Wholesale prices (excluding coffee)	Cost of living (Guanabara)
1964	66.9	85.9	84.1	91.7
1965	46.6	75.3	31.4	65.7
1966	30.6	18.8	41.4	41.3

Source: Banco Central.

policy eventually took on a Spartan aspect, the initial wage increase of NCr$600 million (NCr$300 million to the military in April 1964 and NCr$300 million to civil servants in June) had a devastating effect on the budget. These concessions considerably exceeded the rise in the cost of living subsequent to the last round of upward adjustment. They evidently played the major role in the 1964 budget deficit of NCr$760 million, which occurred despite heroic reductions of NCr$360 million in other government outlays. They must also have been indirectly responsible for advances in parts of the private sector.

The 1964 increases were probably considered a necessary political or economic expedient. They were immediately followed by a declaration of wage policy set forth initially in the *Programa de Ação Econômica do Govêrno*, and put into tember 1, 1964) and by Law 4725 (July 13, 1965). The principle governing the wage policy was that increases of the legal minimum wage should be calculated so as to secure the real income average of the preceding two years. Raising the minimum wage to absorb the immediately preceding peak in the cost of living, as had been done before the revolution would, it was correctly argued, have a positive inflationary effect, perpetuating a price-wage-price cycle. Later the principle was slightly modified to allow for a fraction of the rise of the cost of living in the contract year itself, and for productivity increases. Thus refined, the wage policy was adhered to consistently despite anguished outcries from public servants and labor; and the interval between adjustments was considerably lengthened in order to slow down the price-wage cycle.

TABLE 7. INCREASES IN PRICES AND MINIMUM WAGES
(*percent*)

Effective period of increase	Minimum wage (Guanabara)	Cost of living (Guanabara)
June 1963–February 1964	100	110
February 1964–February 1965	57	77
February 1965–March 1966	27	50

Source: Banco Central and Fundação Getúlio Vargas.

The wage legislation was originally applied to the public sector, with recommendations and inducements for the private sector to follow suit. After the initial wage and salary increases in 1964, it was announced that no further wage adjustments would be made for public functionaries throughout the year, and no advances were made in 1965. Indeed, a law passed by the Congress in 1965 provided as a temporary measure that part of the salaries of the highest-paid civil servants would be paid in frozen saving deposits or Treasury bonds. In January 1966 government employees were given a 35 percent salary increase, followed by another 6 percent raise later in the year. A Council on Wage and Salary Policy decides on all wage disputes in the public sector.

The government preferred to leave private-sector wages to collective bargaining rather than to freeze wage rates. Since labor contracts do not all expire at the same time, it was explained in the 1964 CIAP review, a wage freeze would operate very unequally. So far, however, as concerns minimum wages, which apply to a large mass of unskilled labor, the government formula was made mandatory in July 1965 on private firms, infractions being punishable by denial of government credit. The evolution of the legal minimum wage during the Castello Branco period is shown in Table 7.

In one case the government intervened directly in labor affairs, terminating an agreement with the Union of Stevedores and other port workers and eliminating unreasonable rules and practices, including those pertaining to overtime. A law applicable to the whole private sector directed that the so-called "thirteenth-month bonus," legally imposed under the Goulart regime and paid around Christmas, should be allocated over the whole year in order to eliminate severe inflationary pressure at one time of year.

Recent developments seem to make it clear that, though wages can still exert inflationary pressure, their influence has become a relatively minor concern.

DIRECT ACTION ON PRICES

While fiscal, monetary, and wage policies were mainly oriented — ostensibly at least — toward reducing inflation, the same cannot be said in all cases of direct influences on prices exercised by the government. Price policy on staple foodstuffs apparently had two objectives: at the producer level, to overcome a lag of prices behind inflation and thus to stabilize and increase the flow of supplies to the market; at the retail level, to ease the burden of inflation on the poorer classes of consumers. For producers, minimum prices were set by the Commission for Financing Producing (CFP); based upon these minimum prices, maximum dealer margins were fixed by the National Superintendency of Supplies (SUNAB). Corn products, rice, barley, dressed poultry, manioc meal, beans, butter, pasta, eggs, salt, cotton, fodder, and meat were the products mainly involved, but the list varied from time to time. SUNAB also controlled the retail prices of common drugs and medicines, and of tobacco products.

The *Estatuto da Terra*, the law concerned with the basic producers' prices to be set by the CFP, provided that prices should cover costs plus a 30 percent margin for the producer, but made no mention of demand. In an environment of extreme inflation, it is apparent that this policy could not deal with chronic shortages. The other objective, stabilizing prices and outputs, was also not achieved.[15] Hence, in March 1965 salt completely disappeared from the market, and milk was subject to random scarcities, and the vicissitudes of meat supply led to temporary suspension of meat-price limits in December 1965. Speculative hoarding by producers and consumers probably contributed to these gyrations, but they proceeded in part from the instability of price control itself at the hands of SUNAB.[16] On the whole, it seems doubtful that SUNAB contributed to the welfare of either producers or consumers, or reduced inflationary pressure on prices so as to permit decontrol.

Though "price control" signified SUNAB to the average citizen, the field included several other authorities. Rates for electricity were controlled by the Conselho Nacional de Águas e Energia Eléctrica. From 1963 to 1966, electric rates increased 750 percent, as compared to the following percentage increases: cost of living 450; minimum wage, 400; milk, 520; meat, 620; bread, 460; and wholesale prices, 330.[17] But it is quite probable that this represents a movement toward equilibrium for electricity, inasmuch as over the period 1955–1963 electrical rates rose by less than any of the other indexes mentioned.

Transportation rates, for which maximums were set by the Conselho Nacional de Transportes, seem at first glance to have behaved paradoxically. Railways generally did not raise their rates even to the permitted levels. This practice, which helped to perpetuate deficits, was apparently explained by the railway administrations' fear of losing business, and thus causing unemployment among railway workers.

There had been a steady rise of the railway deficit as a proportion of expenditures throughout the inflation years from 1960 to 1963, with only a trifling reduction in 1964. This deterioration was caused partly by a lag of rates behind inflation, but mostly by inflationary wage advances. The improvement in

[15] See Gordon Smith, "The Minimum Price Program," typewritten for internal circulation in EPEA.

[16] *Ibid.*, p. 22.

[17] EPEA, *Energia Elétrica*, Diagnóstico Preliminar, Jan. 1967, p. 122.

the deficit position in 1965 and 1966 can be ascribed to the stopping of such wage increases, to the raising of rates for urban communities, which account for 70 percent of the nation's passenger travel, and finally to the general increase of traffic.

The close competition of trucks and buses with rail transport indicates that not much more improvement in the deficit situation could have been secured by a faster rise of rates. The logical reform, resisted by the railway authorities, would have been to eliminate losing operations and reduce the number of employees.

In an extended sense, price control or price influencing by government goes far beyond the practices already mentioned. The adjustment of rents under the authority of the Monetary Council is a broad field of regulation, discussed below under monetary correction. Indeed, monetary correction is essentially an attempt to adjust one set of prices, including the whole complex of interest rates, to more realistic (that is, higher) levels despite the usury law. Similarly, the devaluations of November 1965 and February 1967 are recognitions of the necessity of increasing another price, the rates of exchange on foreign currencies.[18]

All of these upward revisions of prices were, of course, purchased at a cost in the battle against inflation. Thus the increase of electricity, telephone, and other public-service charges (123 percent in the first eight months of the Castello Branco regime, followed by another 66 percent in the first half of 1965) produced an unavoidable inflationary effect by shifting the cost of these services from the taxpayer and the general

[18] Devaluation, of course, is necessary to restore the exportability of domestic products and the domestic production of artificially stimulated imports. Thus devaluations could be regarded as part of a policy of "corrective inflation," that is, restoring intermarket equilibrium. But there are so many ways in which devaluations can actively contribute to inflation, "unless monetary and fiscal restrictions are applied so as to minimize the indirect price-enhancing effects of devaluation," that it seems preferable not to regard devaluation as itself a part of corrective inflation. These quotations are from the excellent statement in *Inflation in Latin America*, Subcommittee on American Republics Affairs of the Committee on Foreign Relations, United States Senate (Washington, D.C.: G.P.O., 1967).

public to the user of the services. A similar shift attended the gradual decontrol of livestock and milk prices at the producer level in the autumn of 1966. It is said that these increases and the increase in rent produced half the rise of the cost of living in Guanabara in 1966.[19]

Industrial goods are also subject to direct government action on prices. These were made the object of a voluntary system, designed to arrest inflation and inflationary expectations, set forth in the famous Portaria 71 of February 23, 1965, and in several subsequent decrees and laws. According to this legislation, industrial firms that promised not to raise the prices of their products within the year by more than 7 percent without the permission of SUNAB were granted various favors. Among them were enlargement of foreign exchange rations for imports and reduction of compulsory deposits on imports, extension of the limits on credits granted to the firm by the Bank of Brazil, and reduction of the income tax. As time went on, a special agency, the National Committee to Encourage Price Stability (CONEP) was established to administer the program; rewards for stabilizing prices were generally increased, though the directives establishing these rewards unfortunately became harder to interpret.

CONEP claimed that Portaria 71 and related legislation (including Decree-Law 38) would eliminate increases in prices based on anticipated cost increases, make entrepreneurs less willing to accept increases in prices of cost goods, establish more precise cost-accounting, and eliminate superfluous operations.[20] Some of these benefits may have resulted from the program, but it was not generally successful. The cost and demand data necessary for a rational administration of the permitted price increases were not available, and the staff of CONEP was much too small to cope with the problem. Aside from the havoc probably wrought by arbitrary interference with the price system, it is possible, as Samuel Morley has shown, that inflation was actually intensified through adverse supply reactions to restraints on sale prices in the cases of firms experiencing rapidly expanding demand, and of firms

[19] CIAP, country review of Brazil, 1966; Minister Campos' statement.

[20] The CONEP position was set forth in an internal memorandum.

204
HOWARD S. ELLIS

with rising relative-cost schedules.[21] A better means of using business motivation to counter inflation would be, as he argues, a system of bonuses for expanding production. But the limitations on cost and demand data would still be a formidable obstacle.

All things considered, price control does not seem to have been one of the successes of the Castello Branco stabilization effort.

MONETARY CORRECTION

Capital markets are probably the most sensitive sector of the economy inflation. For one thing, the main type of money in Brazil and in most developed countries, that based upon demand deposits, is itself a credit phenomenon, and the gradation to time deposits and to near-moneys is almost imperceptible. Moreover, real rates of interest based on the productivity of capital do not typically rise above 10–15 percent per year; hence rates of inflation of that magnitude – often regarded as mild – may reduce the real return on productive capital to zero or negative amounts. This occurs much less frequently in ordinary commodity and service markets.

In matters pertaining to money and capital, the degree of sophistication of the individual or firm probably plays a greater than average role in determining the economic impact of inflation. The man on the street, in the factory, or on the farm does not understand these matters very well; even if he did, he would not know what to do about them. But bankers, brokers, foreign exchange operators, and managers of large firms quickly become aware of the money illusion fallacy; moreover, they are better able to defend themselves by using devices to avoid the erosion of monetary purchasing power. Indeed, their sophistication in perceiving and countering the results of inflation may even turn it greatly to their profit.

Private Measures

This seems to have been true of commercial banks, which apparently prospered in the Brazilian inflation. As is generally

[21] Samuel A. Morley, "Thoughts on the Revision of Decree-Law 38," typewritten memorandum for EPEA, June 1967.

known, interest in excess of 12 percent has been illegal since the days of President Vargas (Decree-Law 23,501, November 27, 1933). But even by the time that inflation had reached a 12 percent annual rate, the banks had invented several ways of circumventing the law: by oral understandings with borrowers by which they paid sums in excess of the interest stipulated in writing; by adding various commissions and ostensible costs to the nominal interest charged; by requiring a large unspent balance from the deposit resulting from a loan, and so on.

The banks were not equally inventive on behalf of their depositors, and new firms grew up rapidly in the extreme phases of the Brazilian inflation to capture savings from the commercial banks. The Sociedades de Crédito, Financiamentos e Investimentos offered letras de câmbio at whatever discount was necessary, without actually violating the usury law.[22]

These and many other devices grew up spontaneously, without any more overt assistance from the government than an unzealous enforcement of the usury law. This widespread, automatic correction may account for the fact that the *Programa de Ação Econômica do Govêrno* of the Castello Branco regime did not include any explicit measures on interest rates. However, the spontaneous adjustments were far from producing a satisfactory situation in the capital markets. While the banks were paying depositors 3–6 percent per year, they were charging borrowers 4 or 5 percent or more per month, and the letras de câmbio were furnishing capital to businessmen at rates as high as 90–100 percent per year.

The inadequacy of spontaneous market defenses against inflation is clearly revealed in a study by Affonso Vitule of the investment alternatives open to the Brazilian public from the end of World War II through 1965.[23] For the letras de câmbio the average real yield was negative, by varying amounts running as high as 2.6 percent per month, from September 1961 to the end of 1965, except for ten months in late 1964 and

[22] For a fuller treatment of this subject see the essay by Professor Simonsen, chap. 5 above.

[23] Vitule, Ellis, Martins, and Moura, *As Opções do Investidor, o Financiamento das Emprêsas, e as Decisões da Política Monetária,* I, mimeographed (EPEA, March 1967).

early 1965 when positive yields were achieved varying from
.07 to 1.52 percent per month. During the same period, the
Treasury's *letras de importação* generally gave negative real
returns, with only scattered months showing positive values.
As an escape from inflation the purchase of dollar foreign
exchange was more or less successful, depending on the skill
of the investor in guessing the dates of cruzeiro devaluation.
Only a few common stocks yielded a positive return to the
investor who was well-informed or lucky enough to have purchased them.

Government Measures

In view of these imperfections, the Castello Branco government instituted measures that may be lumped together
under the term "monetary correction," despite considerable
diversity in their purposes. The Emergency Tax Reform (Law
4357 of July 16, 1964) made mandatory the upward monetary
valuation of business assets to correct for the undervaluation
ensuing from inflation. Here the motive was to induce investment in fixed and circulating capital by putting a realistc
price on these assets and by reducing and finally eliminating
the illogical levy of income tax on upward revisions of the
book value of assets. The same law applied monetary correction to tax debts, including arrears of social security. Most
important, however, was the application of monetary correction to central government bonds of three to twenty years
maturity — a drastic attempt to rehabilitate government credit —
basing the adjustment on the timing and degree of change in
the legal minimum wage. A month later, another law (4380 of
August 21, 1964) applied a similar monetary correction to
real estate contracts and mortgages; and it was soon extended
by the famous Tenancy Law (4494 of November 25, 1964) to
rent on urban buildings, including dwellings.

The Capital Markets Law (4728 of July 14, 1965) included an important provision (Article 28) permitting commercial banks to accept deposits and make loans with monetary correction. This provision was interpreted by various
laws, decrees, and resolutions that generally provided an upward gradation of rates from 18, 19, and 20 percent per year
on six-month, nine-month, and twelve-or-more-month time de-

posits; while the rate on loans was established at 30 percent per year. These are prestipulated monetary corrections and do not depend on the actual subsequent course of inflation.

In general, private finance was averse to monetary correction applied after a loan or deposit matured, unless a ceiling on the possible correction was agreed on in advance. This arrangement proved to be the felicitous solution of a conflict between the government and the Sociedades de Crédito e Financiamento. These intermediaries were issuers of the popular letras de câmbio, which were used to evade the usury law by being sold at whatever discount was considered necessary to offset the anticipated inflation. The government argued that this practice built the anticipated inflation into the present, and it was determined to outlaw a priori discounting of letras de câmbio. But the stipulation of a maximum correction seemed to avoid this criticism; and letras remain one of the most popular investment channels, although the preestablished maximum correction seems scarcely to differ from the discount device.

Monetary correction was eventually extended to the various central-government special lending funds, such as FINEP, FINAME, and FUNDECE. Thus it applied to virtually all government debt, and covered much of the private sector.

Evaluation

An evaluation of monetary correction may well begin with its contribution to the policy of corrective inflation. There seems to be no doubt that this contribution was a valuable one, even aside from the policy's effect in normalizing markets. Voluntary subscriptions to the readjustable obligations of the National Treasury (ORTN) made up 37 percent of total subscriptions in 1964, 63 percent in 1965, and 84 percent in 1966. According to the Banco Central, "the high yield paid on these securities — 46.15 percent per year for one one-year bonds maturing in December 1966 — was the factor most important for their success."[24] The close association between voluntary public purchases and gross yield shows not only that the government bond market could be successfully stimulated by mone-

[24] Banco Central, *Relatório 1966*, p. 15.

tary correction, but also that this entailed a fiscal cost to the public, since total budget deficits were simultaneously being reduced by increased tax income. Thus, the introduction of ORTN, and the subsequent extension of monetary correction to all types of federal debt, could be taken as an earnest of the government's intention to control inflation.

In the case of the correction of urban rents, which was apparently intended to minimize income dislocations due to inflation, the limited evidence available indicates that movements in rentals were tending to conform more closely to those of the cost of living. In Rio, the ratio of change in the rent index to change in the cost of living index dropped from 2.5 in 1965 to 1.8 in 1966; in São Paulo, the ratio dropped from 1.4 to 1.1. Some lag in adjustment would of course be inevitable, since indexes and rent payments proceed by discrete time intervals.

Another aim of monetary correction was to reduce the greatest distortion inflation caused in the Brazilian capital market: the enormous gap between the interest rates paid to savers and the rates charged to borrowers in the private sector. Apparently the government intended to apply a posteriori monetary correction to banks and other financial intermediaries, as it had to ORTN and to rents. But since a posteriori correction is applied after a loan matures, the debtor bears the full risk of inflation, a condition generally unacceptable and even intolerable to private concerns. The government and the private sector settled on keeping a priori correction for letras de câmbio, but applying a fixed maximum, as discussed above. Given the unwillingness of private business to adopt a posteriori correction, and the prevalent fears of what would happen were the usury law simply repealed, this seems to be a practicable solution. At any rate, the lender-borrower gap is closing, at least from the creditor's side. During 1966, the Rio market for six-month letra de câmbio rose from a 2.31 percent monthly interest rate to 2.63 and during the first half of 1967 to 2.94.[25]

Monetary correction was put into effect by the Castello Branco government with vigor and imagination. It removed some of the grossest inequities in rentals, laid the foundation

[25] *Boletim Diário da Bolsa de Valores do Rio de Janeiro.*

of a broader market for government bonds, and started a movement to narrow the lender-borrower interest gap.

CAPITAL MARKETS POLICY

Several measures were introduced over the years 1964–1967 to improve capital markets and increase the flow of savings and investment.

The long-awaited Capital Markets Law (4728 of July 14, 1965) was conceived as a sort of Magna Carta for capital in Brazil. It gives the Monetary Council and the Banco Central functions comparable to the Securities Exchange Commission in the United States. It lays the groundwork for protecting the security-buying public and minority stockholders. It attempts to provide adequate disclosure of corporate financial structure and other information necessary to the potential investor. It also establishes principles for the reformation of the stock exchanges, and establishes new bases for mutual funds and investment banks. Finally, several sections are aimed at the "Democratization of Capital," that is, increasing participation in the ownership of the *sociedades anônimas*.

All of these measures are designed to make the holding of financial claims more widespread and more attractive, thus backstopping other anti-inflation policies by increasing the relative share of more stable components than holdings of money in private and corporate portfolios. In stimulating voluntary saving, the law is anti-inflationary and developmental, but its benefits will be slow of realization.

Monetary correction was not the only policy the Castello Branco government designed to close the gap between borrowing and lending interest-rates. Among the others were:

(1) Reducing the rate of inflation, which caused the spread in the first place.

(2) Reducing the tax on letras de câmbio, which should increase the gains of the purchaser, usually the general public saver.

(3) Abolishing interest on demand deposits, which raised bank costs without securing dependable savings.

(4) Abolishing the stamp tax in favor of the lighter tax on

financial transactions, thus presumably raising the net
return to savers without added cost to borrowers.

(5) Resolution 15 of the Banco Central, which offered the
option of holding 40 percent of the compulsory reserves
in government bonds with monetary correction to banks
that would lend initially at 24 percent per year and reduce
this rate by 1.5 percent every quarter.

Several of these measures obviously have a rather limited
effect; the conclusion is doubtless correct that fundamentally
the interest gap can be narrowed only by reducing inflation
and by the laborious process of squeezing the costs of the banks
and other financial intermediaries.

An exhaustive treatise would have to devote another chapter to government lending and investment as integral parts of
the program to promote saving and productive investment. As
to public lending, in the three years of the Castello Branco
government no less than seven new institutions or funds were
created. These were in addition to the quantitatively very significant semipublic funds administered by the Bank of Brazil's
Office of General Credit (CREGE), which lends to commerce
and industry, and its Office of Agricultural and Industrial
Credit (CREAI), which lends chiefly to agriculture, though
some of its resources go to industry. A mere enumeration of the
titles of the new funds will have to suffice as an indication of
their purposes: National Fund for Rural Refinancing (FNRR);
Fund for the Democratizing of Firms (FUNDECE); Fund for
Financing the Acquisition of Industrial Machinery and Equip-
ment (FINAMEF, later reorganized as FINAME S.A., a mixed
company, whose stock is owned mostly by the Development
Bank); the Program for the Financing of Small and Medium-
Size Businesses (FIPEME); Fund for Financing the Study of
Projects and Programs (FINEP); Fund for the Financial Pro-
motion of the Use of Fertilizers and Mineral Supplements
(FUNFERTIL); and, finally, Fund for the Development of
Productivity (FUNDEPRO).

The special funds' share in government investment rose
from 18 percent in 1964 to 38 percent in 1967. Since they are
supposed to eliminate financial bottlenecks and permit under-
takings with potentially high productivity, one may presume

that the special funds have been responsible for above-average contributions to the GNP by the private sector.

CONCLUSION

The Castello Branco government was frequently criticized as being prone to the enactment of new laws and regulations; and the reader has no doubt discovered that the accusation does not lack substance. Scarcely a day passed without decrees and regulations slightly or significantly shifting the economic scenery; scarcely a month passed without major new laws. All of this change confused and exasperated the public and the business community; but what is important in summing up the performance of this government is not the number of legal changes, but the net balance of economic gain or loss.

The judgment here is favorable to the Castello Branco government — very favorable indeed, considering its immediate antecedents and the usual quality of junta governments in Latin America. On its advent to power in March 1964 this government inherited an inflation running at an annual rate of 140 percent; at the end of its term in March 1967 the annual rate had been reduced to 35 percent without any catastrophic wave of unemployment. The groundwork had been laid for salutary developments in savings and investment, including foreign capital. Monetary control had not been achieved but had been launched on an upward course; and the tax system had been rationalized and made more equitable. From the angle of cyclical stability, however, monetary policy was considerably less successful.

For many solid accomplishments, fiscal policy and fiscal administration were chiefly responsible, followed closely by a wage policy whose harshness seems to have been a practical necessity in the short run. Unfortunately not much was accomplished in the way of orderly relative prices or price-level stabilization by the various types of direct price controls and incentives. Monetary correction made a positive contribution to the general effort at stabilization and to the restoration of normal markets, but it was ineffective enough to indicate that it is not possible to render inflation harmless by such devices.

This essay has consistently referred to the Castello Branco government impersonally, since the focus has been on actions and policies rather than personalities. Of course, the government *consisted* of personalities, whose courage, honesty, imagination, and judgment made it succeed. But that would be another story.

CHAPTER 8

Brazilian Agricultural Policy, 1950-1967

Gordon W. Smith

This is an essay on the "style" of Brazilian agricultural policy since 1950. There is no pretense of exhaustiveness; indeed, several important aspects of agricultural policy are treated only briefly or not at all. Rather, I attempt to analyze what has been the principal orientation of Brazilian agricultural policy: reliance upon market incentives to achieve the expansion and modernization of agriculture.

The approach is through a sequence of policy cases in four areas:

(1) Investment in marketing facilities, designed in good part to improve price incentives to farmers and thus expand production. This was the keynote of agricultural policy throughout the 1950's.

(2) Subsidization of the use of modern inputs, primarily fertilizers and farm machinery. In the 1950's this took the form of exchange-rate subsidies and tax exemptions, while in the 1960's subsidized credit has been the principal means of lowering their cost.

(3) A massive increase in credit granted to agriculture for

AUTHOR'S NOTE: I would like to express my gratitude to my colleagues Joel Bergsman, Donald Baerresen, and especially Samuel A. Morley for many suggestions and helpful criticisms. Professor Reuben Buse of the University of Wisconsin first stimulated my interest in fertilizer subsidies, and a paper he prepared for USAID on the subject served as the point of departure of my analysis.

cultivation expenses by official banks at markedly negative rates of interest. This emphasis came to the fore primarily between 1960 and 1965.

(4) The effective implementation of a minimum-price program for basic commodities (excluding coffee, sugar, and cocoa). This began only in 1963 during the Goulart government, chiefly in response to a continuous rise in real agricultural prices since 1958, climaxed by the supply crises of 1962–1963.

The common characteristic of these policies is their attempt to increase production and productivity through higher profitability and reduced risk in farming without an initial increase in final prices to consumers. Certain undeniable gains have been achieved through this orientation. As in most underdeveloped countries, a significant proportion of Brazilian agriculture responds to price incentives. We will see, however, that market-oriented policy instruments have often been overrated in their effectiveness in achieving announced goals and that they suffer severe limitations when combined, as they are, with completely inadequate government activity in other areas, such as education. If Brazil is to reduce the ever-widening gap between industrial and agricultural per capita incomes, the emphasis of policy must change from the manipulation of market incentives (although they certainly should not be abandoned to direct action on structural factors retarding the modernization of agriculture: poor rural education, ineffective research and extension, and perhaps even the land tenure structure.

The next section analyzes what I believe to be the causes of this reliance upon market incentives. Then I turn to an examination of the four cases. Throughout I will be referring to policy as it has applied to the nontraditional exports and food products or to inputs. Coffee, cocoa, and sugar constitute special cases that will not be examined.

Market Incentives

According to theory and the experience of other countries,[1] the following factors subject to policy decisions are among the

[1] See David Hapgood (ed), *Conference on Productivity and Innovation in Agriculture in the Underdeveloped Countries* (Cambridge,

most important in determining productivity and production in agriculture:

(1) Education and training.
(2) Quality and quantity of research and extension.
(3) Land tenure structure and work relations in the country-side.
(4) Availability and cost of credit.
(5) Prices of inputs and outputs, and their stability.

The first three groups concern mainly structural or non-market factors, while the last two involve the operation of the market. Brazilian policy has concentrated on market incentives, especially on (4) and (5). Even the recent land-reform law relies principally upon an extremely complex progressive tax to force inefficient large landowners to sell their holdings. We turn to a brief description of government activity in the nonmarket areas, followed by a discussion of the basic reasons for reliance upon market incentives.

Education

An indication of the extremely low priority that education in the countryside has received appears in Table 1. Not only is the normal educational level of people working in agriculture extremely low (in 1960 less than 10 percent of persons active in agriculture had completed the primary course of four years), but worse still, there has been no real tendency for significant improvement. Agricultural trade schools, which might be expected to have some importance in a country where 50 percent of the active population is engaged in agriculture, are insignificant.[2] There has been talk of mass training courses for farmers, but thus far little has been done concretely. The payoff to education and training in Brazil seems to be high. In spite of

Mass.: Massachusetts Institute of Technology, 1965); *Agriculture in 26 Developing Nations* (Washington, D.C.: U.S. Department of Agriculture, Economic Research Service, Foreign Agricultural Economic Report No. 27, 1965); and for an interesting quantification, Zvi Griliches, "Research Expenditures, Education, and the Aggregate Agricultural Production Function," *American Economic Review*, LIV, 6 (Dec. 1964), pp. 961–974.

[2] See *Plano Decenal de Desenvolvimento Econômico e Social* (hereafter cited as *Plano Decenal*), *Diagnóstico de Educação* (II) (Rio de Janeiro: Ministério de Planejamento, EPEA, 1966), pp. 124–125.

TABLE 1. EDUCATIONAL LEVEL OF PERSONS 10 YEARS OF AGE
AND OVER IN AGRICULTURE, 1950 AND 1960 [a]
(Groups by percent of total)

Formal Education	1950	1960
Three years or less	95.00	92.30
At least primary (four years)	7.70	5.00
At least junior high school (eight years)	.24	.22
At least high school (eleven years)	.06	n.a.

Source: 1950 — Censo Demografico; 1960 — Ministerio do Planejamento e Coordenação Econômico, Plano Decenal, Educação e Mão de Obra, Rio
de Janeiro, 1967.
  [a] Comparisons are not exact: the 1950 census asked only the level of the
     highest course completed; the 1960 census, the number of years of
     study completed. There have been several changes in the length of
     primary schooling.

this, low priority has been given to both the quantity and
quality of education, but the statistics indicate that agricultural
and rural areas have suffered the most neglect.[3]

Research and Extension

Research and extension have fared somewhat better, particularly in the state of São Paulo, where the Agronomic Institute at Campinas and the extension network of the Casas da
Lavoura are among the most effective in Latin America. These
are state organizations, however, that serve the richest and
most advanced agriculture in Brazil.

At the federal government level, research in technical
agricultural problems has been ineffective and on a small scale.
In 1965, the number of research technicians working in the
five institutes that carry out the Ministry of Agriculture's research program was actually smaller than in São Paulo's
Agronomic Institute —424 compared to 547.[4] Quantity comparisons do not tell the whole story, however. As a rule, experi-

  [3] The problem is more complex, of course, then merely increasing
expenditures on education in rural areas. There is a strong tendency for
people who receive education in rural areas to emigrate to the cities.
  [4] Data obtained from Secretaria da Agricultura, São Paulo, and
Departmento do Pesquisas Agronômicas of the Ministry of Agriculture.

ments undertaken in the institutes are routine, little related to the needs of the farmers or to the possibilities of diffusion. Because of low salaries and morale, it has been difficult to attract good people, and many technicians have several outside jobs. Most experiments are not published, and this aggravates the problems of diffusion, criticism, and motivation. Finally, coordination between research and extension have been practically nonexistent. There is no doubt that the research program has been given low priority by the federal government, and as a result it has contributed little to the development of Brazilian agriculture.

The same can be said for direct federal extension services. However, since the early 1960's federal funds have assisted the growth of the Brazilian Rural Credit and Technical Assistance Association (ABCAR). This is a semiprivate extension organization, modeled on the Farmers' Home Associations of the United States. Beginning with Minas Gerais in 1948, it has been established jointly by several state governments and the American International Association, a Rockefeller organization. In 1966, ABCAR became the sole instrument of extension at the federal level. It operates through groups such as the 4-S Clubs [5] and combines instruction on new techniques with small loans to ease their introduction. Given its independence from normal bureaucratic rules, it has been able to pay higher salaries and attract better people. Studies of the operations of ABCAR in Minas Gerais, where it is best developed, indicate that it has had significant effects on the rate of adoption of new techniques, and on productivity.[6]

In spite of its rapid growth, ABCAR remains an organization of rather limited scope. In 1965, for example, 126,933 persons participated in the meetings of ABCAR, and there were 53,292 members of its various organizations.[7] While these figures

[5] Sabedoria, sentir, servício, e saude — knowledge, feeling, service, and health.

[6] See Clifton R. Wharton, Jr., "The Economic Impact of Technical Assistance: A Brazilian Case Study," *Journal of Farm Economics*, XLII, 2 (May 1960), pp. 252–267; Erly Dias Brandão, *Princípios de Administração Rural que Interessam a um Programa de Extensão e Crédito Supervisionada* (Vícosa, Minas Gerais: 1958), pp. 44–88.

[7] *Plano Decenal, Diagnóstico Preliminar Educação* (11), p. 247.

understate the impact of the organization, since its approach is to train leaders in the community to teach others, total participants still numbered no more than 1 percent of the persons active in agriculture.

Another measure of its scope is the number of technicians working in the field. Although ABCAR is the principal extension instrument in sixteen of Brazil's twenty-three states, it had only 1,005 technicians in the field compared to São Paulo's 873. Finally, in 1964, ABCAR received only 0.6 percent of total federal government expenditures on agriculture and marketing, Cr$1,400 million of a total of 222,548 million. SUNAB, essentially an ineffective price control organ, spent 3,971 million during the same year.[8]

The prospects are for increasing support from the federal government, but until very recently extension has not been a prime instrument of federal government policy.

Land Tenure

Little need be said about direct action in the fields of land distribution and the regulation of labor or working relations. In 1964, a land reform law finally passed Congress, the so-called Land Statute (*Estatuto da Terra*). It relies on complex progressive taxation to force large landowners to use their land productively or sell it. Thus far, plans for land redistribution have been limited to socially critical areas, such as the sugar zone in Pernambuco, the Baixada Fluminense of the state of Rio de Janeiro, and the colonial areas of Rio Grande do Sul. In the last two areas, the aim is to eliminate the *minfúndio* (very small property) through consolidation, removing most of the *minifundistas* to newly settled areas. The pace of the program has been very slow, and it is problematic if significant changes in the land tenure structure will be effected by the program of the Brazilian Agrarian Reform Institute (IBRA), which has charge of administering the Land Statute.

Factors Behind the Reliance on Market Incentives

It should be clear by now that Brazilian agricultural policy has given little weight to improving the human factor in agri-

---

[8] Ministério do Planejamento e Coordenação Econômico, *Balanço Orçamentário Consolidado do Govêrno Federal, 1964* (Rio de Janeiro: 1965).

culture, to generating and diffusing new information to producers, or to operating directly upon the structure of land distribution. Rather, in so far as it *has* sought to accelerate agricultural development, it has tended to rely principally upon market incentives. Why is this so?

The most important factors involved seem to be the short-time limit with which economic policy has been made in Brazil; the relative neglect of agricultural problems except in times of crisis; the poor quality of the federal bureaucracy concerned with agricultural policy; and finally, broader political decisions, which have deemphasized education in general and have ruled out land reform as it is traditionally understood.

Economic policy in Brazil has normally been biased toward quick results. The presidential term is five years, but an incumbent begins to lose power after three as the problem of succession advances to the fore. Self-succession is forbidden by the Constitution, and political parties, with little programmatic content, cannot be counted on to continue policies from one term to the next. The interruption of longer-term policies, including investment programs, is a normal fact of life in Brazilian politics. Hence, there is a strong tendency to choose programs having quick payoffs that can be rapidly put into effect. This partly explains the preference for market incentives. Subsidies and taxes, credit expansion, even price guarantees can be effective in a relatively short period of time, but structural changes have considerably longer gestation periods. Market incentives, in a word, are more flexible and better adapted to the necessities of Brazilian politics.

The short-time horizon in agriculture is in turn related to the general neglect of agricultural problems that has characterized Brazilian economic priorities until very recently.[9] The principal policy goal until 1964 was undoubtedly rapid industrialization with a minimum of urban unrest. Agriculture assumed high priority only when its performance appeared to

[9] See Werner Baer, *Industrialization and Economic Development in Brazil* (Homewood, Ill.: Richard D. Irwin, 1965), pp. 150–163; "Fifteen Years of Economic Policy in Brazil," *Economic Bulletin for Latin America*, IX, 2 (Dec. 1964), pp. 171–172; Thomas E. Skidmore, *Politics in Brazil, 1930–1964* (New York: Oxford University Press, 1967), pp. 164–182.

interfere with these other goals. Hence, policy changes have often stemmed from short-run food-supply crises which jarred the government out of inactivity. Crises require instruments that can be rapidly introduced and have a rapid short-term payoff. It is natural that policy makers would turn to market incentives. Three of the four policy emphases we will examine were directly tied to food shortages in the cities. The need for investment in marketing facilities came to the fore in 1951– 1954, when severe production losses occurred in distribution channels at the same time that real food prices were rising almost 20 percent in São Paulo.[10] Agricultural credit was expanded rapidly only after a similar supply crisis in 1959. The expansion was accelerated as food prices continued to rise in 1961–1963. Moreover, it was only in 1963 that the minimum-price program for basic commodities began to be seriously implemented.

Market incentives also require less technically trained manpower to design and administer. Indeed, little special knowledge of agricultural problems is required. Market incentives are appropriate to the dearth of trained specialists in Brazil, and to the generally poor quality of the federal bureaucracy most directly concerned with agriculture, the Ministry of Agriculture. The turnover of high-echelon personnel is enormous and makes continuity in policy nearly impossible.[11] The tendency has long been to establish new agencies outside the ministry to deal with new problems, precisely because of its low quality and its unwillingness to attempt an internal general reform. The new agencies, in turn, have usually deteriorated rapidly in quality, and the further diffusion of power has aggravated the problem of coordination in agricultural policy.

Thus, the short-time limits of Brazilian economic policy, the neglect of agriculture, and the ineffective agricultural bureaucracy seem to be the main factors behind the reliance on market incentives to the near exclusion of action to modify structural problems in Brazilian agriculture. We turn now to an analysis of the success of this orientation in four cases.

[10] According to the São Paulo cost-of-living index, the best available for that period.

[11] There were, for example, five ministers of agriculture between April 1964 and April 1967.

MARKETING INVESTMENT

Marketing inefficiency has long been considered one of the chief hindrances to the development of Brazilian agriculture. In the 1950's, improvement in marketing performance became the keynote of declared agricultural policy, indeed almost a panacea for the problems of the primary sector. A report submitted by Klein and Saks in 1954 (*O Problema de Alimentação no Brasil*) on the problems of distribution concluded that Brazil produced all the food she needed, but was losing a substantial proportion of it, perhaps 25 percent, in the marketing process. Exploitation of the consumer and producer by the middleman was common, in conjunction with physical losses in distribution, greatly depressed farm incomes, and increased final prices. The key, then, to satisfactory agricultural development was to be improved marketing, especially in the transportation and storage processes.

A somewhat more sophisticated version of the same theme appears in the reports submitted by the Joint Brazil-United States Economic and Technical Commissions.[12] They argued that marketing imperfections and inefficiencies, rooted in poor transportation and storage and in middleman oligopsony, had absorbed price stimuli deriving from increasing consumer demand in the early 1950's. Thus, it was maintained, the lag in food production that had appeared at that time did not arise because of rigidities in farmers' responses to demand stimuli, but rather because all the demand stimuli had been absorbed in higher distribution margins. Hence the sector requiring government action was primarily distribution, and the principal remedies were thought to be infrastructure investment in transportation and storage facilities, combined with more credit for farmers.

Partly as a result of this thinking, investment in transportation, storage, and other marketing facilities was the principal instrument for agriculture in the Kubitschek government's *Pro-*

[12] See, for example, Joint Brazil-United States Economic Development Commission, *The Development of Brazil* (Washington: Institute of Interamerican Affairs, Foreign Operations Administration, 1954), p. 24; and by the same group, *Brazilian Technical Studies* (1955), pp. 415–432.

grama de Metas.[13] Even today, many competent technicians in Brazil assert that the principal agricultural problems reside in a poor marketing system, although this idea is rightly becoming less common.

One should not, of course, depreciate the importance of improved distribution in the modernization and expansion of agriculture. When substantial inefficiencies are present, as they are in Brazil, the returns to marketing investments and reforms can be substantial and fairly rapid. But two aspects of this

TABLE 2. DEVELOPMENT OF FEDERAL, STATE, AND
COUNTY ROAD NETWORK
(kilometers)

Year	Total	Federal		State		County
		Total	Paved	Total	Paved	All roads
1952	302,147	12,315	n.a.	51,032	n.a.	238,800
1956	465,868	22,859	2,900	59,593	1,234	383,416
1960	468,048	32,402	8,675	75,875	4,028	359,771
1965	803,068	36,170	13,039	99,568	13,507	667,330

Source: Alan Abouchar, *Diagnostic of the Transport Situation in Brazil* (Rio de Janeiro: EPEA, 1967), p. 47.

policy emphasis are important from the present standpoint. First, the transportation and storage situation was allowed to deteriorate to the point where lags in the effective food supply could plausibly be attributed to distribution problems. This reflects the low and derivative priority accorded agriculture and the crisis nature of much agricultural policy. Secondly, it is important that for some time, at least, marketing investment to improve the operation of the price system was considered sufficient to meet the most severe agricultural problems as perceived by policy makers.

It is impossible to appraise the impact of the transportation and storage investments in quantitative terms. Certain qualitative conclusions can be drawn, however. The transportation-storage problem was extremely serious in the late 1940's

[13] See "Fifteen Years . . . ," pp. 171–172.

and early 1950's.[14] Low farm prices and oligopsonistic markets were the result, especially in the more recent settled regions (for example, western Minas Gerais, Goiás, and Paraná). Most of the bottlenecks have been eliminated in the Center-South of Brazil, largely through public investment in roads and storage and private expansion of marketing facilities in response to high profits.[15] This has been accompanied by a definite downward trend in marketing margins through wholesale in much of the region.

TABLE 3. COMMODITIES TRANSPORTED BY RAIL,
HIGHWAY, AND COASTAL SHIPPING
(ton–kilometers)

Year	Railroads	Index	Highways	Index	Coastal shipping	Index
1950	8,828	100	10,817	100	9,237	100
1955	9,337	106	23,100	214	11,320	123
1960	12,078	137	42,556	393	14,546	158
1963	15,342	174	62,056	574	15,445	167
1965	18,800	213	71,600	662	14,000	152

Source: Abouchar, *op. cit.*, p. 4.

Not only did the greatly expanded and improved road network (see Table 2 and 3) reduce direct costs of transportation,[16] but for several food products it made possible the decentralization of marketing away from large market centers that had enjoyed an advantage as hubs of rail networks or as ocean ports (for example, São Paulo, Pôrto Alegre, and Rio de Janeiro). Decentralization in turn tended to reduce margins on several products, notably rice, by increasing the degree of competition and creating more direct marketing channels from

[14] See *Brazilian Technical Studies*, pp. 415–432, for vivid descriptions of some of the worst bottlenecks.

[15] The Center-South region includes Espírito Santo, Minas Gerais, Goiás, Mato Grosso, and all states south of them.

[16] Although rail and coastal shipping rates are generally lower than truck-freight charges, when handling, pilferage, delays, and other risks are included most merchants believe the truck to be more economical. See Gordon W. Smith, *Agricultural Marketing and Economic Development: A Brazilian Case Study* (unpublished Ph.D. thesis, Harvard University, 1965), p. 221.

TABLE 4. FARM PRICE IN ASSEMBLY MARKETS SERVING SÃO PAULO
(as percent of São Paulo wholesale price, 1965–1966;
Louisiana farm price as percent of New Orleans
wholesale price)ª

Food	Areas serving São Paulo 1965–1966 [c]	Louisiana rice, 1953–1956
Rice[b]	50–60	52.5
Corn	74–75	
Beans	83	

Source: Brazilian data — Divisão de Economia Rural, São Paulo, and Bôlsa de
Cereais, São Paulo. U.S. data — Nicholas M. Thuroczy, *Marketing Margins for Medium Grain Rice*, (U.S. Department of Agriculture, Agricultural Marketing Service, Marketing Economics Research Division),
Marketing Research Report No. 444, p. 21.
  ª Margins are unweighted averages of farm and wholesale prices during
the principal farm marketing months. Hence they do not include margins due to increases in price while the commodity was in commercial
channels.
  ᵇ Rice margins appear high because of weight losses in milling. When
these are taken into account, farm prices are 75–80 percent of wholesale price.
  ᶜ Wholesale prices for São Paulo do not include the 6 percent turnover
tax in effect at that time. Producing areas cover parts of São Paulo,
Minas Gerais, and Goiás.

producer to final consumer.[17] Calculations of margins through
wholesale for rice, corn, and beans in 1965 and 1966 for several
producing areas in the Center-South showed them to be quite
reasonable and not far from similar margins in the United
States (see Table 4).

Federal government participation in the construction of
other marketing facilities was more restricted, but still significant in many areas. Of the total storage space for 12,400,000
tons of food and agricultural products existing in 1964,[18]
497,000, or 4 percent, had been financed by the National Economic Development Bank (BNDE), principally to state-operated public warehouse companies.[19] If warehouses used primarily for coffee stocks are excluded, space financed by BNDE
reaches approximately 7 percent of the total for 1964. Perhaps
more indicative is the fact that, of the total increment of ware-

[17] *Ibid.*, pp. 217–298.

[18] According to a tabulation of IBGE data made by the Brazilian
Warehousing Company (CIBRAZEM).

[19] BNDE, *Exposição Sôbre o Programa de Reaparelhamento
Econômico — 1965* (Rio de Janeiro: 1966).

houses and silos during 1956–1960, 56 percent has been financed by the BNDE.[20]

This total fell far short of the 800,000-ton target envisaged by the Programa de Metas, perhaps because it became clear that the storage problem had been considerably over-simplified. Instead of being filled with produce that would otherwise have rotted, the new storage tended to be grossly underutilized. In 1961, for example, if all produce received by BNDE-financed warehouses and silos had been in storage at one time, only 70 percent of total space would have been filled.[21] Poor location was a problem in some cases. But more important, planners had failed to reckon with the structure of marketing of storable food products. On the one hand, middlemen normally seem to possess sufficient private space without recourse to state companies. On the other hand, many farmers in the areas with the most underutilized warehouses, for example in the northeastern state of Pernambuco, are unable to store. They must sell immediately after harvesting to liquidate debts with middlemen and usually do not possess the means of transporting their produce to centrally located storage units. Finally, for reasons that are not clear, the government failed to take steps facilitating the discount of warehouse receipts with banks. This would have required a reform in warehouse regulations or subsidized credit from public sources, or both. As it was, private banks had little interest in discounting warehouse receipts, with their greater physical and price risk, when they could easily exhaust their lending capacity through mercantile loans.

Even today, these problems have been only partially resolved. Thus, though state-built or state-financed storage facilities were beneficial in many areas, their impact was generally minuscule in relation to the changes provoked by transportation investment. And although improvements in marketing structure have made considerable contributions to agriculture in many areas, primarily in the Center-South, they appear to have fallen far short of expectations.

[20] "Fifteen Years . . . ," p. 172; BNDE, *op. cit.*
[21] Paulo de Carvalho Vasconcellos, "A Armazenagem no Brasil e o Problema de Abastecimento," *Revista do BNDE*, I, 2 (April–June 1964), pp. 134–144.

SUBSIDIZATION OF THE USE OF MODERN
INPUTS: FERTILIZERS

We turn now to another important policy instrument of
the period, the subsidization of the use of modern inputs. This
is a particularly interesting case, since it involves the efficacy
of transfer payments in modernizing technology. Much work
has been done on measuring the response of farmers to product
prices in underdeveloped countries. The response to price stimuli on the input side is, if anything, more important.

In Brazil subsidies took the form of preferential import
exchange rates, freight rebates, and tax exemptions during the
1950's, and were especially favorable to fertilizers. In the 1960's
the principal instrument has been highly subsidized loans for
the acquisition of these inputs.

Only the fertilizer subsidies, by far the most important,
are analyzed here. Before examining the case itself, it is useful
to examine the three factors on which the economic success of
an input subsidy depends: the elasticity of the input's use with
respect to lower prices; the excess of marginal social productivity of the input over marginal social costs; and the shift in
the input demand function arising from past experience with the
input's use.

In combination, these factors would imply that subsidies
will induce greater use of fertilizers, that it pays socially to use
more fertilizer, and, most important for agricultural development, that farmers learn about the benefits of fertilizer by using
it, thereby permanently increasing its consumption, even after
subsidies are withdrawn.

Now it is not obvious, a priori, that any of these elements
should be substantial in a country with the high fertilizer prices
of Brazil, and with the low educational and technical-assistance
levels available to most Brazilian farmers. If the first and third
factors are unfavorable, the subsidy becomes primarily an income transfer with little impact on the use of fertilizers. And if
marginal social costs exceed marginal social productivity, a subsidy could only reduce total net output.

What follows shows that the apparent response to lower
prices of fertilizer consumed per hectare *was* quite significant
in the period 1954–1961. At the same time, there was a large
shift in the fertilizer/hectare demand function, seemingly due

in good part to lower fertilizer prices. This lends support to the learning-by-doing thesis. Thus the first and third conditions appear to have been satisfied. Furthermore, I will show that the apparent real net returns to increases in fertilizer consumed per hectare in crops were positive. The rate of return appears to have been substantial, although considerably below that obtained in the United States at a comparable period in the development of fertilizer use. Thus the second condition appears to have been fulfilled in Brazil in 1954–1963.

Since policy makers have often chosen to employ subsidies instead of increasing investment in, say, the human factor, I will also examine the conditions under which this choice may be economically valid. Finally, although successful as far as it went, the subsidy approach has had severe limitations, which will be highlighted.

Forms of Fertilizer Subsidies

The bulk of fertilizers consumed in Brazil is still imported, and domestic sources supply the greater part of the market only for phosphates.[22] Thus exchange-rate and tariff policies have been important in determining prices paid by farmers for fertilizers.

In the period 1947–1953, Brazil maintained a highly overvalued exchange rate through quantitative import controls. Preferences were theoretically granted to agricultural inputs, but today it is impossible to verify the extent to which this was actually the case. In late 1953, however, a complex system of multiple exchange rates was introduced that continues to this day (December 1967) with considerable simplifications and consolidations in 1957, 1961, and 1966–1967. Fertilizers were granted highly favorable treatment within this system until 1961. In addition, ineffective specific tariffs were replaced in 1957 by a highly protectionist ad valorem system. Nonmixed fertilizers, the bulk of fertilizer imports, were made tariff-exempt. This markedly favorable exchange-rate and tariff treat-

[22] Although considerable import-substitution of fertilizers occurred after 1953, fertilizer imports in 1963 were still 77.2 percent by value of total supply. BNDE, *Mercado Brasileiro de Fertilizantes* (Rio de Janeiro: 1965), p. 20.

ment shows clearly in Table 5, which presents the average annual effective exchange rates, including tariffs, for several important categories of both imports and exports. To the exchange preferences must be added exemptions from federal and state sales taxes instituted in 1957–1958, and highly preferential rail freight rates and port fees. Most of these are still in effect.

Finally, in 1966, direct subsidies were introduced again with the creation of the Fund for the Financial Promotion of the Use of Fertilizers and Mineral Supplements (FUNFERTIL). It operates primarily through interest rebates on bank loans for the purchase of fertilizers. This has meant even more highly negative interest rates on loans to agriculture by official banks, perhaps as great as 25 percent when inflation reaches 30 percent per year.

What has been the rate of implicit subsidy to fertilizers through the exchange-rate mechanism? To answer this question we must know the *opportunity cost* of foreign exchange, which measures the *social cost* of the fertilizer dollar. Clearly, the "free market equilibrium" rate is irrelevant for this problem, involving, as it did, only small reallocations. The most defensible alternative is the export rate for agricultural exports excluding coffee and cocoa. This represents fairly closely the marginal export rate actually paid. If domestic resources were allocated more or less in equilibrium with this exchange rate, it would measure the opportunity cost of obtaining additional dollars. With the constant changes in price relationships, the sluggishness of the reallocation process, and the substantial imperfections of resource allocation, this is unlikely to be the case. But in the absence of shadow prices generated by some elaborate programming model, it seems to be the best indicator.[23]

Thus the difference between the marginal export rate and the fertilizer rate will be taken as the measure of subsidization through the exchange mechanism, and the export rate, rather than the fertilizer rate, should be used to calculate the cruzeiro opportunity costs of additional fertilizer consumption.

[23] Results obtained using this marginal agricultural exchange rate do not differ significantly from those obtained with the total import plus effective tariff exchange rate.

Table 5. Effective Exchange Rates Including Tariffs[a]

	(1)	(2)	(3)	(4)	(5)	(6)	(7)	(8)
Year	Exports	Imports	Imports plus tariffs	Exports excluding coffee	Agricultural exports excluding coffee and cocoa[b]	Industrial capital goods	Agricultural capital goods	Fertilizers
1953	20.8	19.1	21.0	22.5	22.1	18.9	19.0	19.0
1954	27.5	33.8	35.2	27.0	27.2	32.6	31.2	30.0
1955	38.3	46.1	47.8	41.3	43.3	45.7	46.4	39.7
1956	40.3	58.0	59.6	44.9	48.5	59.9	63.0	45.3
1957	43.6	58.1	59.9	53.0	53.8	55.7	56.8	44.8
1958	51.3	76.4	85.9	65.4	71.4	92.6	96.0	57.1
1959	85.4	117.4	131.3	114.2	131.7	127.2	152.3	92.1
1960	115.9	137.6	152.7	159.8	178.8	146.0	177.5	103.8
1961	174.7	205.0	229.5	245.5	259.3	243.4	234.8	155.7
1962	253.0	346.9	386.5	370.0	372.4	449.9	419.8	344.8
1963	390.8	526.0	584.4	553.3	561.9	707.5	660.2	527.5
1964	823.4	984.1	1082.6	1210.0	1210.0	1329.4	1125.2	977.0
1965	1388.6	1760.6	1950.9	1874.0	1874.0	2183.5	2108.6	1750.4

Source: Columns (6) and (7) from Samuel A. Morley, "Import Demand and Import Substitution in Brazil," in this volume. Columns (1), (2), (3), and (8) computed directly from data supplied by IBGE. Column (4) from EPEA, *Diagnóstico do Comércio Exterior* (mimeographed), Rio de Janeiro, 1966. Column (5) computed from data supplied by the Setor do Comércio Exterior of EPEA.

[a] Columns (1), (2), (3), (6), (7), and (8) are calculated as averages of actual dollar values divided by cruzeiro-value total tariffs paid. Columns (4) and (5) are effective exchange rates weighted by time in effect; and products are aggregated by export quantities.

[b] Sugar, cotton, tobacco, rice, corn, peanuts, soybeans, and beef.

Trends in Fertilizer Prices and Consumption, 1950–1965

Partly as a result of the subsidies described above, the 1950's saw a large decline of fertilizer prices in relation to crop prices as measured by São Paulo state indices, the only ones available for the period (see Table 6). This fall was accompanied by a more than fourfold increase of apparent fertilizer consumption in Brazil from 1952 to 1960.[24] At the same time, rough calculations of fertilizer consumption per hectare in crops indicate an almost 90 percent increase in the intensity of fertilizer use from 1950–1952 to 1960 (see Table 6). When fertilizer prices returned to their pre-1953 levels, fertilizer consumed per hectare in crops fell back, but it appears to have stabilized at levels 60 percent above those in effect before the decline. This behavior strongly suggests that lower prices were the prime mover in the pattern, although other factors correlated with lower prices played some part. It also suggests that there was substantial learning by doing.

Easier credit for farmers may have stimulated the use of fertilizers. But if this were an important factor, one would have expected the fertilizer/hectare ratio to have continued its increase in the 1960's when credit was expanding most rapidly. It did not. Better and more productive varieties of cotton, corn, and coffee probably raised the marginal productivity of fertilizers, and this must have contributed to the shift in the fertilizer demand function. The expansion of technical assistance to farmers was also a factor in some areas. Increases in land values in older areas, such as São Paulo, may have led to the substitution of fertilizer for land. And so forth.

Ideally, one would want a correctly specified fertilizer demand function including such variables as these. Lack of data and difficulties in correctly specifying the adjustment over time make demand-function estimation unfeasible in this case. Inspection of Table 6, however, does strongly suggest that much of the change in fertilizer intensity is due to lower prices for the several years after 1952.

We turn now to the question of whether it paid Brazil to increase fertilizer intensity in the period 1954–1963.

---

[24] From 72,875 to 304,497 tons of nutrient elements according to IBGE, *Anuário Estatístico do Brasil*, various issues.

Costs and Benefits of Higher Fertilizer Consumption, 1954–1963

In estimating the social costs of more intensive fertilizer use, I treated *all* deviations in the internal price index of fertilizers from the index of the marginal export exchange rate (the opportunity cost of foreign exchange) as if they had arisen from a *hypothetical* subsidy program. That is, in the absence of the hypothetical subsidy,

$$P_f = E_x$$

TABLE 6. INDEX OF APPARENT CONSUMPTION OF FERTILIZERS[a]
(fertilizer price deflated by São Paulo crop price)

Year	Index of fertilizer price divided by index of 19 crop prices (1948–52 = 100)	Index of fertilizer price divided by index of coffee price (1948–52 = 100)	Index of apparent fertilizer consumption per hectare in crops (2-year moving average)[b] (1950–52 = 100)
1950	106	72	
1951	95	89	
1952	93	90	
1953	67	67	100
1954	74	49	112
1955	83	70	127
1956	80	76	139
1957	71	72	152
1958	69	108	179
1959	54	100	178
1960	63	111	189
1961	88	161	187
1962	90	166	160
1963	98	144	168
1964	109	117	164
1965	153	212	156
1966	107	n.a.	n.a.

Source: Price indices — Divisão de Economia Rural, Secretaria da Agricultura, Estado de São Paulo (cited as Divisão de Economia Rural). Fertilizer consumption — IBGE, *Anuário Estatístico do Brasil*, various issues. Area in crops — *Censo Agrícola*, 1950 and 1960.

[a] Imports plus domestic production, in tons of nutrient elements.

[b] The hectare in crops figure is an interpolation and extrapolation of the 1950 and 1960 Agricultural Census figures, using the implied annual geometric growth rate of 4.5 percent. While crude, this seems preferable to using annual estimates supplied by the Ministry of Agriculture, which are notoriously inaccurate and involve considerable double-counting.

where P_f is the internal price index of fertilizer and E_x is the marginal export exchange rate index, $1953 = 100$. Thus, the rate of this hypothetical subsidy is given by the equations below.

$$P_f = (1 - s)E_x$$
$$s = 1 - P_f/E_x$$

The main reason for this approach is that real fertilizer price changes resulted from forces other than the actual subsidies described above. The most important of these was a decline of about 15–20 percent in the dollar import prices of fertilizers after 1953.[25] Changes in margins may also have been a factor.

With the data available it is impossible to determine how much prices fell because of actual subsidies and tax exemptions alone. One approach, then, is to treat all deviations in internal prices from the marginal export exchange rate as if they were due to an implied hypothetical subsidy. This "simulation" also gives a better picture of what subsidies could have accomplished in 1954–1963 had there been no windfall to Brazil in the form of lower world market fertilizer prices.

The "simulation" assumes, then, constant 1953-dollar fertilizer import prices, and marketing costs proportional to the actual cruzeiro import price. Under these assumptions, the total social cost of fertilizers consumed is

$$TC_t = (V_{\$t}) (E_{xt}) + m(V_{\$t}) E_{ft}$$

where TC = total social cost,
m = mark-up margin = 125 percent of actual cruzeiro import prices,[26]

[25] With $1953 = 100$, dollar import-prices fell to a low of 77 by 1960 and had risen again to 86 by 1965. This is based upon a year-by-year Laspeyres chain index computed by the author, with import quantities as weights. The primary data were supplied by IBGE, Laboratório Estatístico.

[26] Based on 1965 average annual markups of São Paulo prices over import price, which varied between 107 and 117 percent. The figure was arbitrarily increased to allow for transportation costs to the interior from the city of São Paulo. (Price data are from the Divisão de Economia Rural, Secretaria de Agricultura, Estado de São Paulo, hereafter cited as Divisão de Economia Rural, and Laboratório Estatístico, IBGE.)

$V_s =$ constant 1953-dollar value of imports and domestic production,

$E_x =$ marginal export exchange rate, and

$E_f =$ average effective fertilizer exchange rate.

From this formula, the social costs of increasing fertilizer consumed per hectare over 1950–1952 averages can be derived as [27]

$$\frac{TC_t(y_t)}{(100 + y_t)}$$

where $y =$ the percentage increase of fertilizer/hectare over 1950–1952 averages.

For estimation of benefits to society from more intensive use of fertilizer I used the aggregate-production function for Brazilian agriculture estimated by the Getúlio Vargas Foundation from a 1962–1963 cross section of 2,500 farms.[28] This non-restricted Cobb-Douglas function shows a .04 elasticity of gross output with respect to fertilizers (chemical and organic) consumed. This coefficient compares with .10–.11 estimated by Zvi Griliches for the United States during 1949–1959 (using states as basic units), and .18 for Sweden, where, as in the Brazilian study, farms were the unit of observation.[29]

---

[27] If $F_t =$ total fertilizers consumed in year t, and $F_o =$ total consumption of fertilizers in year t had fertilizer/hectare remained constant at 1950–1952 levels, then $F_t = F_o(1+y)$, where $y =$ the percentage increase in fertilizer/hectare divided by 100. Thus, $F_t = F_o + yF_o$. And $(yF_o/(1+y)F_o = yF_o/F_t = y/(1+y)$, the percentage of total fertilizers consumed due to increases in fertilizers/hectare. Strictly speaking, the average exchange rate over the discrete increment of foreign exchange required by more intensive fertilizer use should be used in calculating opportunity costs. However, fertilizer imports never exceeded 1.6 percent of total dollar imports (1960), and the proportion of total imports due to greater intensity in fertilizer use was never more than .75 percent. Thus the bias introduced by our using the *marginal* export rate should be quite small.

[28] For further details see *Projections of Supply and Demand for Agricultural Products of Brazil* (Rio de Janeiro: Getúlio Vargas Foundation, Brazilian Institute of Economics, May 1967), two volumes.

[29] See Zvi Griliches, "Research Expenditures, Education, and the Aggregate Agricultural Production Function," *American Economic Review*, LIV, No. 6 (Dec. 1964), p. 966; Earl O. Heady and John L. Dil-

Several criticisms can be made of the Brazilian function.[30] If anything, it appears to *underestimate* the response to fertilizers in Brazil, since in all individual state production functions where fertilizers were significant at at least the 5 percent level (three of seven), the coefficient was .06–.07. Chemical fertilizers alone should also show a higher coefficient than the total-fertilizer variable used by the Getúlio Vargas Foundation.

In any case, the increase in gross agricultural output due to more intensive use of fertilizer can be derived from this production function as shown below.[31]

$$\triangle Q_t = [Y/(1 + Y)] Q_t$$

where Q_t = the gross product of agriculture, $Y > 0$, and

$$(1 + Y) = \left[\frac{(\text{fertilizer/hectare})_t}{(\text{fertilizer/hectare})_{1950\text{-}1952}} \right] .04$$

Total benefits and costs calculated in this fashion appear in Table 7. They show an average product of fertilizer 2.75 times

lon, *Agricultural Production Functions* (Ames, Iowa: Iowa State University Press, 1961), p. 613.

[30] For example, fifteen independent variables were included; no attempt was made to reduce multicollinearity by eliminating the scale factor; no variables were included to reflect regional differences, education, technical assistance, and so on.

[31] $Q_t = XF_t^{.04}$ where Q_t = total agricultural gross product

X = product of all other terms of the production function

F = total fertilizer consumed

$$F_t = F_0 \left(\frac{H_t}{H_0} \right) (1 + i) \text{ where } H = \text{total area in crops and}$$

$$o = 1950\text{–}1952 \text{ and}$$
$(1 + i) = (F_t/H_t) (H_0/F_0)$, the index of fertilizer consumed per hectare, 1950–1952 = 100

Thus $Q_t = Q_t' (1 + i)^{.04} = Q_t' (1 + y)$

where Q_t' = level of production in year t had there been no increase in F/H, i.e., had $(1 + i) = 1$ • $(1 + y) = 1$. $(1 + i)^{.04}$, $y > 0$.

$$\triangle Q_t = Q_t - Q_t' = \left(1 - \frac{1}{1 + y} \right) Q_t = \frac{y}{1 + y} Q_t$$

TABLE 7. COSTS AND RETURNS FROM GREATER USE OF FERTILIZER PER HECTARE
IN CROPS COMPARED WITH 1950–1952 AVERAGES[a]
(billion 1954 cruzeiros)[b]

Year	Cost of increasing fertilizers per hectare in crops	Gross benefits of increasing fertilizers per hectare in crops	Net benefits
1954	.14	.75	.61
1955	.46	1.62	1.16
1956	.65	2.21	1.56
1957	.96	3.06	2.09
1958	1.53	4.31	2.78
1959	1.55	4.49	2.95
1960	2.17	5.21	3.04
1961	1.97	5.54	3.57
1962	1.51	4.38	2.87
1963	2.35	4.87	2.53
Total	13.30	36.44	23.14

Sources of basic data: Dollar value of production and imports — BNDE, *Fertilizantes*, p. 20. Exchange rates — Table 5 above. Gross product of agriculture — *Revista Brasileira de Economia*, XX, No. 1 (March 1966).

[a] Columns may not add to totals due to rounding.

[b] Deflated by the implicit price deflator for agriculture, computed from data in *Revista Brasileira de Economia*, XX, No. 1 (March 1966).

greater than the average social costs for the period as a whole. More intensive use of fertilizers, even when calculated at their opportunity cost, had substantial rates of return in Brazil. Even had dollar prices remained constant, the net benefits from more intensive fertilizer use would have been 175 percent of total costs.[32] Thus the second precondition for a successful subsidy — that the input pays socially — appears to have been fulfilled in Brazil during the 1950's and early 1960's.

The Efficiency of the Subsidy Method

Was the subsidy, however, an efficient means of increasing agricultural net output? Or could government funds paid out

[32] It is somewhat reassuring that a feasibility study on the expansion of fertilizer production in Brazil reached gross benefit/cost ratios of 2.3–2.8 for the increases it envisaged from 1963 to 1970. The study employed response functions derived from agronomic experiments. See *Estudo Técnico-Econômico Sóbre a Exequibilidade de Aumento na Fabricação e Uso de Fertilizantes, Calcário e Sais Minerais no Brasil* (a report presented to the Ministry of Agriculture and ARDO/USAID/Brazil, 1964), p. 221.

in subsidies have been used better in investment projects, say, in education? Obviously the question is meaningful only if budget constraint prevents projects with rates of return higher than the social discount rate from being realized, which is probably the case in Brazil. Indeed there are strong constraints on reallocations within the budget itself, so that policy makers may reduce unproductive government consumption in personnel to increase investment only with great difficulty.

So let us imagine the following situations facing policy makers in the 1950's. Taxes cannot be increased; more inflation cannot be tolerated. The agricultural budget is fixed, and within it the expenditures on personnel and other consumption items. A fixed amount equal in present value to the hypothetical subsidy is set aside to "develop" agriculture. How would the fertilizer subsidy have compared with potential investments? To put it more precisely, what would the rate of return on the investment have to be to make it a more attractive use of the same subsidy funds?

The rate of time discount is assumed given either by the decision makers' preferences (more likely) or by their notions of the marginal rate of time preference in the private sector. Now, the essential difference between the subsidy and an investment is that the former does not initially reduce aggregate current consumption. It is a transfer that can be thought of as increasing the efficiency of the price mechanism. Hence we must compare the present value of the net benefits of subsidy-induced fertilizer use with the present value of the investment net of the present value of the cost of the investment. The latter, by assumption, is the present value of the hypothetical subsidies paid. Thus, if the fertilizer subsidy is to be preferable to the investment

$$\Sigma_t (R - C)_t > B - \Sigma_t S_t$$

$(R - C)_t =$ present value of gross returns minus costs of increased fertilizer consumption per hectare in year t.

$B =$ present value of the investment.

$S_t =$ present value of subsidy paid in year t.

It follows that

$$1 + \frac{\Sigma_t (R - C) t}{\Sigma_t S_t} > \frac{B}{\Sigma_t S_t}$$

The left-hand side of the inequality for the period 1954–1963, using the concept of hypothetical subsidies, is presented in Table 8,[33] along with the internal rates of return on investment that would yield the same present value ratio as the subsidy. The table shows that the policy maker would have been indifferent, for example, between the hypothetical fertilizer subsidy and an investment with a 23.6 percent internal rate of return, if the social rate of time preference had been 10 percent.

TABLE 8. 1 + Ratio of Present Value of Net Benefits from Increased Fertilizer Consumption per Hectare to Present Value of Subsidies Paid 1954–1963[a]

Rate of time preference (percent)	100% of increased fertilizer intensity due to subsidy		50% of increased fertilizer intensity due to subsidy	
	$1 + \dfrac{\Sigma(R-C)t}{\Sigma S_t}$	Internal rate of return (percent)[b]	$1 + \dfrac{\Sigma(R-C)t}{\Sigma S_t}$	Internal rate of return (percent)[b]
10	2.87	23.6	1.93	18.4
15	2.94	29.6	1.97	24.0
25	3.10	41.7	2.05	35.4

Source:

[a] For methods of estimation see note 31 to this chapter.

[b] Compounded annually. It was calculated from $\dfrac{X}{(1+i)^9} = 1 + \dfrac{\Sigma(R-C)t}{\Sigma S_t}$, where X = the undiscounted value in year 9 of a dollar's investment in year 0, and i = the rate of time discount. R (the internal rate of return) is given by solving $X = (1 + R)^9$.

Because relatively more benefits than subsidies occur in the earlier years, the internal rate of return on investment required to make it preferable to the hypothetical subsidy actually increases with the rate of time preference. Thus even if only 50 percent of the increased use of fertilizers per hectare was due to subsidy-induced lower prices, an investment would

[33] The rate of subsidy was defined as $S = (1 - P_f/E_x)$, where P_f = index of internal fertilizer prices, and E_x = index of marginal export exchange rate, both with 1953 = 100. This rate was then applied to what total opportunity costs would have been without the subsidy. That is, total subsidy = $(V_\$)$ (E_x) $(2.25)S$, with $V_\$$ being the total constant dollar value of imports and production, and 2.25 being one plus the markup over import prices.

have required 35 percent annual internal rate of return to be preferable to the subsidy when the rate of time preference reached 25 percent. At lower rates of time preference, of course, investments begin to appear relatively more attractive.

These calculations show well the strong points of the hypothetical subsidy to policy makers with high rates of time preference and short-time horizons: it acts rapidly, it does not reduce consumption, and the payoff is relatively high. Under any rational budgetary procedure, obviously, investments should be increased not at the expense of productive subsidies, but through reduced government consumption or higher taxes, or both.

Limitations

The limitations of the subsidy approach appear quite clearly in this fertilizer case. At the end of the period under consideration, and in spite of the increases we have examined, less than 5 percent of Brazilian farmers used fertilizers.[34] Lower prices primarily benefited the technologically most advanced producers, leaving the great bulk still far behind. The narrow impact of the hypothetical subsidy is reflected in several other ways. While the rate of return of fertilizer/hectare was quite good, the total impact was small in the period 1954–1963, never exceeding 2 percent of net agricultural output in any year. Furthermore, rough calculations using the production function coefficient show that fertilizers in 1960 were still being used far below the social optimum. In spite of this, fertilizer consumed per hectare fell in 1962–1963, when private returns moved closer to social levels with an increase in fertilizer prices. It is evident that most farmers who could profitably use fertilizers if they had the know-how and technical assistance are not touched by the subsidy method.

Thus an input subsidy should be thought of primarily as a useful instrument to increase productivity in the more advanced segments of agriculture, while other policies, such as rural education, must bear the principal burden of "transforming" agriculture.

[34] See *Estudo Técnico* . . . , p. 31.

CREDIT EXPANSION TO AGRICULTURE

In the early 1950's, it was estimated that only 18 percent of the total outside financing obtained by agriculture was supplied by institutional sources. The remainder came from private sources, chiefly merchants and processors (62 percent).[35] As a rule, the farmer committed his crop for sale before harvesting in order to get credit from the merchant. This greatly reduced potential competition among buyers during the harvest months and facilitated the operation of noncompetitive oligopsonies. Besides these depressing effects on farm prices, lack of credit was also held to be an important factor inhibiting investment and expansion in agriculture, especially in the basic food crops.

It is not surprising, then, that one of the principal policy instruments used by most governments since 1950 has been an increase in official bank loans to agriculture, at highly negative real interest rates.[36] Indeed, agriculture has received much more favorable treatment on this score than industry — even during the Kubitschek years.[37]

All important indicators reflect this policy. The proportion of agricultural production units that obtained Bank of Brazil loans rose from 1 percent in 1950 to 4 percent by 1960, and to 14 percent in 1964.[38] The total value of loans to agriculture from official banks almost doubled in real terms from 1953 to 1964, while those to noncoffee uses increased even more. The

[35] Klein and Saks, *O Problema da Alimentação no Brasil* (Rio de Janeiro: Comissão de Desenvolvimento Industrial, 1954), p. 75.

[36] Nominal interest rates, including commissions, charged by the Bank of Brazil on agricultural loans have never exceeded 19 percent per year, while inflation above 40 percent has been the rule since 1959. Before 1965, nominal interest rates were probably below 12 percent, including commissions.

[37] During the Kubitschek period, noted for its industrialization bias, the real value of loans to industry by the official banks (excluding BNDE) rose 8.2 percent, compared to agriculture's 28.2 percent (the deflator being that implicit in GNP). Since 1963, loans to agriculture have surpassed those made to industry.

[38] *Crédito Agrícola no Brasil* (preliminary version, Rio de Janeiro: EPEA, 1966), p. 43.

TABLE 9. TOTAL REAL LOANS TO AGRICULTURE BY BANK OF BRAZIL

| | Real loans to agriculture by official banks[a] (billion 1953 cruzeiros) | | Total agricultural loans by official banks as percent gross agricultural product |
Year	With coffee	Excluding coffee	
1953	11.9	n.a.	9.6
1956	11.5	8.2	8.9
1960	14.7	13.2	10.1
1961	19.1	17.9	12.8
1962	21.0	19.5	11.6
1963	20.3	19.7	12.7
1964	21.5	20.1	12.0
1965[b]	16.4	15.6	n.a.

Source: Banco Central, Relatório de 1965; Revista Brasileira de Economia, XX, No. 1 (March 1966).

[a] End-of-year balances, deflated by Conjuntura Econômica's general price index (No. 2) recalculated to exclude coffee. This index is a weighted average of the wholesale price index, the Guanabara cost-of-living index, and the index of construction costs.

[b] Low totals for the year reflect credit restrictions under the Castello Branco government's anti-inflationary program.

rise in official bank loans as a percentage of gross agricultural product has been less impressive but still significant (see Table 9).

Finally, illustrative of the use of subsidized credit to stimulate the use of modern inputs is farm machinery. In the period 1953–1966, the real value of Bank of Brazil loans for the acquisition of farm machinery (mainly domestically produced tractors) more than quadrupled; in 1960–1966, it alone more than tripled.[39] Loans granted in 1966 for this purpose reached over US$ 50 million. All these credit series accelerate their growth after 1960. This appears to have been caused by the recognition that all was not right with agriculture, as reflected by the strong rises in agricultural prices after 1958 (see page 245 below).

It is difficult to evaluate the impact of this credit expansion

[39] Nominal value of loans granted for acquisition of farm machinery as given by the Bank of Brazil Relatórios were deflated by the São Paulo index of prices paid by farmers for farm machinery computed by the Divisão de Economia Rural. In 1948–1952 NCr$, these loans rose from 250,000 in 1953 to 312,000 in 1960 to 1,099,000 by 1966.

on agriculture. It is not clear, for example, to what extent bank finance merely substituted for other forms (say, the borrower's own savings) no longer attractive during rapid inflation. Greater credit availability does appear to have reduced the importance of the merchant-moneylender system. But the operating system of the Bank of Brazil is full of defects, and in most cases the credit is not supervised, or tied to very meaningful technological standards. Until now the government has relied on farmers themselves to direct the use of the funds made available. Thus an important opportunity to link subsidized credit to extension and technical assistance has been lost.

THE MINIMUM-PRICE PROGRAM FOR BASIC CROPS

The last case we will examine is the minimum-price program for basic commodities: rice, cotton, corn, peanuts, soybeans, manioc flour, and dry edible beans in the Center-South region, adding sisal to the group of support-products in the North and Northeast.[40] The program operates through government purchases and nonrecourse loans to farmers and processors (but not pure middlemen). There are no restrictions on the production or marketing of support crops. The history of this program is a good example of the short-run, crisis orientation of Brazilian agricultural policy. Not only was the program, on the books since 1951, effectively implemented only after the 1962 food supply crises; since that time it has been manipulated from year to year in an attempt to influence the short-run supply situation of support products.

The next section examines briefly the nature of the potential benefits to underdeveloped countries of a price-support program. Then a short history of the Brazilian program is presented. The main part of this case study analyzes the impact of the attempts since 1962 to influence production through annual manipulation of support prices announced in advance of planting. Analysis of supply response functions indicates that minimum prices have not significantly affected production decisions for the principal food products where manipulation

[40] Sugar, coffee, and cocoa have their own special and separate programs.

was attempted. The chief implication is that support prices, to
be most effective, must be guided by the longer-term objectives
of reducing price risk and uncertainty in Brazilian agriculture.

Price-Support Payoff in Underdeveloped Countries

Agricultural price-support programs, through government
purchases and sales out of stocks, can reduce effective supply
and price fluctuations. The resultant potential benefits are of
two types. First, if executed properly, these compensating purchases and sales will increase the efficiency of the carry-over,
which tends to be especially poor in underdeveloped countries.[41] The improvement in the distribution of supplies through
time should raise both consumer welfare and farm incomes,
partly at the expense of private speculators.[42]

The side effects of this type of program may be more important for agricultural development. The risk and uncertainty
of agricultural activities will be reduced, and this should stimulate production and increase the willingness of farmers to
adopt new techniques. A U.S. Department of Agriculture study
of agriculture in twenty-six developing countries found, for
example, a negative correlation within the sample between
changes in the magnitude of aggregate harvest-to-harvest price
fluctuations and the aggregate rates of growth in productivity.[43]
While no causation can be inferred from the correlation alone,
there are sound theoretical reasons for expecting lower price
risk and less uncertainty to encourage production and the use
of modern inputs requiring money outlays.

But risk reduction for agriculture will not be costless to
society and could generate negative net benefits.[44] Besides
administrative costs, net returns depend heavily upon the system of price-fixing. The higher the support price, the greater
is the stimulus to agriculture, but the greater also is the potential cost to society through misallocation of resources and permanent accumulation of stocks. Some scheme of price-fixing

[41] See John Williams Mellor, *The Economics of Agricultural Development* (Ithaca, N.Y.: Cornell University Press, 1966), p. 201.

[42] See Gordon W. Smith, *op. cit.*, pp. 32–44.

[43] U.S. Department of Agriculture, *op. cit.*, p. 100 f.

[44] Mellor, *op. cit.*, pp. 208–210, has an interesting discussion of
some aspects of this point.

based on expected yearly or longer-term equilibrium levels seems indicated, allowing some range of price fluctuations to cover storage costs. For commodities normally exported, the future equilibrium price would be tied to yearly or longer-term world-market price expectations. Cotton, soybeans, corn, and perhaps peanuts fall in the category for Brazil. Prices for the other crops could probably best be set as some percentage of past moving averages of market prices. The price-support system would then act as a future market accessible to a considerable proportion of producers.[45]

Since the principal benefits from this system arise from a reduction in risk and uncertainty, it is important that the program itself avoid erratic and sudden change. This has not been the case in Brazil.

A Brief History of the Brazilian Minimum Price Program

The minimum price program was created for all practical purposes in 1951, with Law 1506.[46] In spite of this law, minimum prices in the 1950's were normally fixed safely below market levels and were announced halfheartedly only after the planting had been completed. As a result, the only significant purchases before 1963 were of cotton during the 1952–1953 harvest (see Table 10).

The most important reason for the neglect of the program is clear: the problems of agriculture were not considered serious enough at that time to risk the higher food and raw material prices to consumers in the short-run that might have resulted from effective price supports.[47] All of this changed with the strong rise in agricultural prices that began in the late 1950's, culminating in the food-supply crises of 1962 (see Table 11). Agriculture was suddenly a "bottleneck sector," the number one priority of the 1963 Plano Trienal. The Plan argued that land reform was the basic solution. The more pragmatic

[45] Brazil has no active futures markets for agricultural products, although sales for forward delivery are common.

[46] The Production Finance Commission (CFP), which administers the program, was created in 1943 but remained inactive until 1952.

[47] Inadequate storage and poor organization in the field were contributing but secondary factors, since they could have been rectified in a relatively short period of time.

TABLE 10. PURCHASES OF AGRICULTURAL PRODUCTS UNDER
THE MINIMUM-PRICE PROGRAM
(metric tons)

Year	Corn	Rice	Beans	Cotton	Peanuts	Soybeans	Manioc flour
1952–1960	2,451	0	13,708	442,759	0	0	17,302
1961	296	43,927	21,779	346	0	5	0
1962	0	6	0	0	0	0	0
1963	657,573	0	23,981	8,224	69,048	0	46,810
1964	61	1,738	64,000	2,373	0	0	24,101
1965	422,008	1,695,106	91,552	0	0	0	43,408
1966	Negligible for all products						

Source: Comissão de Financiamento da Produção, A Política Nacional de Preços Mínimos (Rio de Janeiro, 1966).

TABLE 11. WHOLESALE PRICES OF AGRICULTURAL
PRODUCTS DEFLATED BY THE GENERAL PRICE
INDEX, BOTH EXCLUDING COFFEE [a]
(1949–1953 = 100)

1957	99.1
1958	96.4
1959	97.4
1960	106.4
1961	106.2
1962	111.3 [b]
1963	107.3
1964	104.2
1965	95.0
1966	101.3

Source: *Conjuntura Econômica.*
   [a] The general price index was recalculated excluding coffee.
   [b] Actual price increases are underestimated in this figure, since low ceiling prices rather than high black-market prices are included for rice and beans for Feb.–Nov. 1962.

response of the Goulart government was to expand credit to farmers and to activate the minimum-price program in an effort to stimulate basic food production in the short-run. Relatively high minimum prices for 1963 were fixed for rice, corn, and beans, the principal food crops covered,[48] and for the first time the government made a strong effort to set up an effective operational network in the interior. This beginning set the tone for the subsequent operation of the program.

At the risk of some oversimplification, these principles appear to have guided the program from 1963–1967. Minimum prices were now fixed before planting in all years in order to influence production decisions. The prices themselves fell into two groups. Cotton supports have been set roughly somewhat below world prices to preserve Brazil's competitive position, approximating an annual forward equilibrium system. Peanut

[48] When announced in September 1962, real minimum prices in 1965 cruzeiros (using *Conjuntura Econômica's* general price index No. 2) were 13,382 for rice, 22,584 for beans, and 7,220 for corn, all in sacks of sixty kilos. Previous annual peaks for São Paulo farm prices (annual averages in 1965 prices) were 16,957 for rice, 27,030 for beans, and 6,325 for corn.

TABLE 12. MINIMUM PRICES AND PRICES PAID TO FARMERS[a]
(São Paulo, 1953 cruzeiros)[b]

	Rice		Corn		Beans	
Year	Price paid to farmers[b]	Minimum price[c]	Price paid to farmers[b]	Minimum price[c]	Price paid to farmers[b]	Minimum price[c]
1962	305	174	111	92	827	303
1963	318	198	62	68	400	212
1964	227	207	101	98	268	230
1965	128	115	72	74	248	151
1966	219	139	69	71	438	213

Source: Prices paid to Farmers taken from Divisão de Economia Rural, computed from monthly averages. Minimum prices from Table 10.

[a] The price paid to farmers in São Paulo is the average of monthly prices, March–September for rice, April–September for corn and beans, deflated by the price index for that year. The minimum price is set in August or September of each year to be paid during the following crop year. The minimum prices for 1962, 1963, 1965, and 1966 are deflated by the price index for the year in which they were paid. The minimum prices set in 1964 for 1965 were increased 28 percent (the rise in prices from September 1964 to February 1965) to take into account the government's (unfulfilled) promise of adjustment for inflation before the harvest.

[b] Deflated by *Conjuntura Econômica's* general price index, recalculated to exclude coffee.

[c] Computed from monthly minimum.

prices have normally been set as a function of cotton prices, since cotton is its main substitute in production.[49] Rice, corn, and beans, the most important food products in the program, have suffered more erratic treatment. Their real support prices have been changed annually, apparently as a function of the internal market situation at the time of planting. The higher the current real market prices, the higher the support price. Table 12 shows this relation clearly.

This strongly suggests that minimum-price incentives were turned on and off to stimulate production after small harvests and to deter production after a good year. Whatever the motivation, the movement of minimum prices was perverse; they were raised when past market stimuli would already have led to increases in planned production (say for 1965), and they

[49] The real minimum price of cotton explains 90 percent of the variation in the real minimum price of peanuts from 1963 to 1967.

were lowered when low market prices would in themselves generate considerable production declines (as in 1966).[50]

When fixed before planting, minimum prices have often
been quite high. Normally, however, they have been eroded by
inflation before the harvest, so that the effective protection
has been much less than farmers might have expected. The
Castello Branco government recognized this defect, and in

TABLE 13. REAL MINIMUM PRICES FOR 1965–1966 HARVEST IMPLIED
BY THE PROMISE OF READJUSTMENT FOR INFLATION
(1965 cruzeiros per sack of 60 kilos)[a]

Commodity	Minimum Price	São Paulo farm price	
		1964	1965
Rice	9,600	10,321	6,215
Corn	10,700	11,390	10,388
Beans	4,550	4,949	3,792

Source: Divisão de Economia Rural and CFP.
  [a] Minimum prices are for consumption centers (that is, São
  Paulo, Rio de Janeiro, Belo Horizonte, Brasília, Curitiba, and
  Pôrto Alegre), adjusted by the increase in the *Conjuntura
  Econômica* general price index, September 1964–February
  1965, or 28 percent. The deflator employed is the same index.

September 1964 announced a major change in policy: minimum prices were fixed effective for two years, to be adjusted
both annually and before each harvest by "indices of monetary
correction," that is, for inflation. The implied protection for
the three food products was considerable (see Table 13), especially for the more distant producing regions, such as Goiás
and Rio Grande do Sul, for which the same minima were in
effect as for São Paulo.[51] In actuality, adjustments were made

[50] If longer-term disequilibria were involved, the movement would
make more sense. It is impossible to infer anything, however, about
long-run price trends from these year-to-year movements. Indeed, two
factors seem to explain price movements fairly well during 1962–1967:
the weather and farmers' response to past market prices.
[51] Minimum prices are fixed at the same level for all the ports
and several so-called consumption centers. These range from Brasília in
Goiás to Pôrto Alegre in Rio Grande do Sul. Prices paid in the interior
are calculated after freight and handling-charge deductions. Market
prices in the more distant producing regions would normally be 10–20

only to the extent they did not price Brazil out of the world market in the bumper harvest year of 1965. Even so, massive purchases of rice were necessary, 30 percent of the total crop. Since then, no promises of readjustment of preannounced prices have been made.

After some bullishness in 1963–1965, then, the program for the three food products returned to relative timidity as upward pressure on agricultural prices eased. Much lower prices were fixed for 1966, followed by some increase for 1967. The extent of this retreat seems unjustified. First, most stocks accumulated during 1965 were sold at a considerable profit during the small harvest year of 1966. The price program was working exactly as it should have, supporting prices in bumper crops and selling from stocks in smaller crop years. More important, the decision to cut back on minimum prices seems to have been based upon an erroneous analysis of their effect on production in Brazil for these products. It was believed by many that the bumper crops of 1965 were due in good part to the rather high minimum prices announced before planting in 1964, and that if these prices were continued overproduction would persist. This seems to be incorrect, as is shown in the analysis of the impact of preannounced minimum prices on production.

The Impact of Preannounced Minimum Prices, 1963–1967

Brazilian farmers respond positively to changes in market prices for their products.[52] But did they also respond to preannounced support prices? Was the government able to guide production through the minimum-price program? Based on the analysis of several supply response functions, the answer seems to be that preannounced minimum prices have been the main determinant of peanut and possibly cotton supply from 1963 to 1967, but that their effect was negligible in rice, corn, and

percent below those in São Paulo. Minimum prices tend to be the same, thus guaranteeing places like Goiás greater direct price protection.

[52] See, for example, Antônio Delfim Netto et al., Agricultura e desenvolvimento no Brasil (preliminary version, São Paulo: Estudos ANPES No. 5, 1966); and several mimeographed reports by Sergio Brandt et al. (Sao Paulo: Divisão de Economia Rural, 1964).

beans, the products that the government attempted to influence most.

Two approaches were used. First minimum-price variables were explicitly included in the supply functions and tested for their significance. Given the possibility of mis-specification and the likelihood that minimum-price parameters varied over the period, I also used another test for the food products: Was actual supply in 1965, the year with the highest promised minimum prices for rice, corn, and beans, significantly different from that predicted by supply response functions excluding minimum-price variables?

Except for rice, all functions were estimated for the state of São Paulo for the years 1954–1967. Not only are these the only data in Brazil sufficiently accurate for this type of analysis, but if preannounced prices were a significant influence, this most commercial of Brazilian agricultures should show their influence. Since rice suffered the greatest overproduction in 1965, the conclusions from São Paulo were also checked for this product in Rio Grande do Sul (Brazil's chief rice-producing state) and the Center-South region as a whole.[53]

Most of the functions initially estimated were of the Nerlove adjustment model variety, which allows for lags in the adjustment to new production equilibria.[54] Area planted, a proxy for planned production, was the dependent variable in

[53] See the Data Appendix for a discussion of the data and deflation procedures.

[54] See Marc Nerlove, *The Dynamics of Supply: Estimation of Farmers' Response to Price* (Baltimore, Md.: Johns Hopkins University Press, 1958). The model is as follows:

$$\text{Prod}_t - \text{Prod}_{t-1} = Y(\text{Prod}_t^* - \text{Prod}_{t-1})$$

Where Prod_t^* = desired production in year t, Y is the coefficient of adjustment and Prod_{t-1} = actual production in year $t - 1$.

$\text{Prod}_t^* = a + bp_t^* + CZ \ldots$, where p_t^* = expected price in $t = p_{t-1}$, and Z is another variable influencing supply.

Solution of these three equations yields the model's reduced form:

$$\text{Prod}_t = aY + bYp_{t-1} + cYZ \ldots + (1 - Y)\,\text{Prod}_{t-1}$$

Thus from the lagged production coefficient we can determine the coefficient of adjustment, and from bY the long-run price coefficient, b. The algebra of the derivation of the function in logs is identical.

all functions. In the absence of an accurate weather index, this is probably the best one can do. For some products, log functions give better results. In the log form, the coefficients are estimates of the elasticities of supply response.

Two specifications of the influence of minimum prices within the adjustment model were tested, the "total guidance" model and the "risk reduction" model. In the total guidance model, minimum prices replace lagged market prices as the main determinant of supply during 1963–1967. Since minimum prices may be held with greater certainty by farmers, dummy variables were included to permit different coefficients for "expected" prices for the two periods: 1954–1962 without preannounced minimum prices, and 1963–1967 with them. Under this hypothesis, the supply function becomes:

(1)

$$A_1^t = a + b_1 pmp_1 + c_1 dpmp_1 + b_2 pmp_2 + c_2 dpmp_2 \ldots \\ + eA_1^{t-1} + ft$$

$pmp =$ for 1954–1962: real price paid to farmers, lagged one year; for 1963–1967: real minimum price

$1 =$ product the supply of which is being estimated

$2 =$ substitute product

$d =$ dummy variable $= 0$ for 1954–1962; $= 1$ for 1963–1967

$A^t =$ area planted crop 1 in year t

$t =$ year; 1954 $= 0$

The coefficients of pre-announced minimum prices are then $b_i = c_i$, and of lagged market prices, b_i. If the c_i are not significant, the response to both sets of prices will be the same. In all cases, minimum prices fixed before planting were deflated by the São Paulo general farm price index (excluding coffee) for the following year, when the crop was sold. This assumed that farmers anticipate inflation perfectly — a better assumption than that they suffer from complete money illusion. It still introduces a strong possibility of errors in variables.

The "total guidance" model is likely to represent reality well only if experience shows farmers that minimum prices are a significantly better predictor than lagged market price. Preliminary analysis showed this to be the case only for cotton and peanuts (see Table 14).

For other products we would look for a different effect. Expected price might now become a weighted average of lagged market price and minimum price. This specification rapidly increases the number of independent variables and consequent multi collinearity, especially if the price coefficients are allowed to change through the inclusion of dummy variables. For these reasons, I used what might be called the "risk reduction" model. The price variables continue to be lagged

TABLE 14. MINIMUM PRICES AND LAGGED MARKET PRICES AS PREDICTORS
OF CURRENT MARKET PRICES — SÃO PAULO[a]

| Commodity | $P_t = a + \Sigma_{i=1}^{3} P_{t-i}$ | | $P_t = a + b$ *minimum price*$_t$ | |
| | 1954–1967 | | 1963–1967 | |
	R^2	Significance level of F	R^2	Significance level of F
Cotton	.36	.25–.50	.98	.005
Peanuts	.27	.25–.50	.54	.10–.25
Rice	.34	.25–.50	.26	.25–.50
Corn	.50	.10–.25	.12	.50–.75

[a] P_t = price paid to farmers in harvest months of year t, deflated by general index of São Paulo farm prices excluding coffee. Minimum price = preannounced price, deflated by following year's farm price index.

market prices. Minimum prices here act chiefly to reduce downward price risk. A rough proxy for this effect is the ratio of real preannounced minimum prices to real lagged market prices. The higher this ratio, the lower is the risk of outcomes below expected (lagged market) prices. Under these assumptions, the supply response function becomes:

(2)
$$A_1^t = a + b_1 p_1 + b p_2 + c_1 pmm_1 + c_2 pmm_2 \ldots + d A_1^{t-1} + et$$

p   = real lagged price paid to farmers
pmm = ratio of real preannounced minimum prices
        to p for 1963–1967; = 0 for 1954–1962

Other symbols are as in equation (1).
Basically, then, three expected price models will be examined: the lagged market price model, the total guidance model, and the risk reduction model.

Peanuts and Cotton, São Paulo [55]

São Paulo is the leading producer of cotton and almost the only producer of peanuts in Brazil, two close substitutes in production. These are the most serious candidates for the total guidance model, because minimum prices have done much better in predicting changes in market prices than have lagged market prices (see Table 14). This appears to be due to two sets of factors. Cotton minimum prices are based on rough (and apparently valid) expectations of export prices, while peanut prices are fixed in function of their close substitute. Thus, they tend to represent future equilibrium prices, especially when large changes are involved. Of some importance, too, is the fact that the oligopsony which dominates the market for both products has used minimum prices as the basis of its purchase price, quite apart from the relationship of the price to world levels. Market prices, then, tend to be set not by competition but in the battle over minimum prices in which processors and producers' groups participate energetically.

As it turned out, the total guidance model works quite well for peanuts, while no model is satisfactory for cotton. We turn first to the estimates for peanuts. The lagged market price model gives a good explanation of area planted in the rainy season crop [56] for peanuts during 1954–1962, a period in which minimum prices were fixed after planting in most years. (The t statistic appears beneath the estimated coefficient. The constant was less than its standard error for all peanut functions, and was therefore excluded in reestimations. Suppression of the constant renders the R^2 meaningless, as usually calculated and understood in economic models. Hence this statistic is not presented.)

(3)
$$A_{pea}^t = 1.508^{(1)} P_{pea} - 1.259^{(1)} P_{cott}$$
$$(5.34) \qquad (-3.13)$$

[55] See the Data Appendix for a fuller description of the prices, area, and deflators used.

[56] See the Data Appendix for a discussion of the rainy- and dry-season harvests and the reasons for estimating only the rainy-season crop.

$$+ .781^{(1)} A_{pea}^{t-1} + .051^{(2)} YR$$
$$(4.08) \qquad (2.37)$$

$F(4, 5) = 24.84^{(1)}$ D.W. $= 2.71$

All in natural logs except YR

$A_{pea}^t =$ area planted in rainy season crop, year t, 1,000 hectares

$P_{pea} =$ real farm price of peanuts, rainy, dry season harvests, in year t–1, 25 kilos

$P_{cott} =$ real farm price of cotton, in year t–1, 15 kilos

$YR =$ Year $= 0$ in 1954

$(1) =$ significant at 1 percent level
$(2) =$ significant at 5 percent level
$(3) =$ significant at 10 percent level

One-tailed tests are used for prices and lagged areas. These conventions will be used henceforth.

The lagged market price function does very badly, however, in predicting area planted in 1963–1967, and when reestimated for the whole period, 1954–1967, gives substantially different and poorer results:

$$(4)$$
$$A_{pea}^t = .609^{(3)} P_{pea} - .200_{cott}^P + .654^{(2)} A_{pea}^{t-1} + .030 YR$$
$$(1.80) \qquad (-.42) \qquad (2.71) \qquad (.97)$$
$$F(4, 10) = 14.96^{(1)} \qquad D.W. = 1.69$$

The two price elasticities are much lower, and neither is significant at the 1 percent level. The structure of supply has obviously changed.

Estimates of the total guidance model for 1954–1967 indicate that the principal structural change was the introduction of preannounced minimum prices:

$$(5)$$
$$A_{pea}^t = 1.428^{(1)} PMP_{pea} - 1.190^{(1)} PMP_{cott} - .118^{(1)}$$
$$(7.26) \qquad (-4.95) \qquad (-4.68)$$
$$MP_{cott} + .801^{(1)} A_{pea}^{t-1} + .045^{(2)} YR$$
$$(7.01) \qquad (2.86)$$

$$F(5, 9) = 60.48^{(1)} \quad \text{D.W.} = 2.39$$

$$\text{PMP}_{\text{pea}} = \text{real price of peanuts in year } t\text{-}1, 1954\text{-}1962$$
$$= \text{real minimum price of peanuts in year } t, 1963\text{-}1967$$

All in natural logs

$$\text{PMP}_{\text{cott}} = \text{same variables for cotton}$$

$$\text{MP}_{\text{cott}} = \text{minimum price of cotton in year } t, 1963\text{-}1967$$
$$= 0, 1954\text{-}1962$$

The expected price coefficients in equation (5) return approximately to their 1954-1962 levels, but are more highly significant than in equation (3). The fit again becomes quite satisfactory. In passing, the very high price elasticities — both greater than one — should be noted. If one accepts the lagged area coefficient at face value as (1 — the coefficient of adjustment), long-run price elasticities exceed 5.

On the other hand, risk-reduction functions for peanuts performed no better than the original lagged market price model. Thus, there are strong indications that preannounced minimum prices have replaced market prices as the main determinant of supply changes in peanuts. The switch does not appear to have greatly affected the magnitude of the coefficients. The significance of the cotton minimum price coefficient does suggest, however, that the cross elasticity with cotton is somewhat higher when preannounced minimum prices become expected prices. No dummy variable was included for the minimum price of peanuts because of the high correlation (.95) between the two sets of minimum prices during 1963-1967.[57]

[57] Orthogonal regression, using as the peanut minimum-price variable the residuals of the regression of the minimum price of peanuts on that of cotton (1963-1967), seemed justified in this case, because peanut prices have in fact been set as a function of cotton prices. The coefficient of the residuals, however, was not significant at the 10 percent level (one-tail test) and was excluded in the final form.

We could be more confident in these conclusions had they been confirmed by the cotton supply-response functions. This was not the case. For no model of area planted in cotton was the *F* statistic significant at the 1 percent level. While the guidance model gives slightly better fits for 1954–1967 than the alternatives, the differences are not significant.

The most likely interpretation of these facts seems to be that preannounced minimum prices have substantial effects on planned cotton production.[58] So close observers of São Paulo agriculture are convinced. This is confirmed indirectly by the results of the peanuts guidance model. Two other facts seem to make all estimations of the area response for cotton unsatisfactory: rapid technological progress in the crop, for which data adequate for inclusion in the supply functions does not exist; and increasingly dubious area and production data for cotton from São Paulo.[59] Both factors tend to generate poor fits and insignificant price coefficients for cotton.

Rice

The government bought 30 percent of the rice crop in 1965, and these large purchases were an important consideration in the subsequent retreat of the program. The supply analysis indicates, however, that preannounced minimum prices have had little or no effect on supply. Table 15 presents the three area-response models for São Paulo. In this case, the lagged area coefficient was not significant at the 10 percent level, and was excluded. That is, adjustment to expected prices appears to be immediate. In addition, averages of price paid to farmers in the previous two harvests were used as expected prices in the market price model. This is a plausible hypothesis for a crop with large price fluctuations, and did give considerably better results.

Again, it is interesting to note the relatively high price elasticities in the lagged market price model. São Paulo agriculture appears highly responsive to expected price. No additional

[58] See, for example, "Etudo Para os Precos Minimos da Safra 1965/66," *Agricultura em São Paulo*, XII, No. 5–6 (May–June 1965), pp. 8–9.

[59] See the Data Appendix.

TABLE 15. SUPPLY-RESPONSE FUNCTION FOR RICE — SÃO PAULO

Variable (all in natural logs except YR)	Model		
	Lagged market price	Total guidance	Risk reduction
C = constant	3.928[2] (2.312)	6.120[1] (3.503)	4.162[3] (1.890)
P_r = average price of rice paid to farmer previous two harvests, 60 kilos	1.011[1] (5.875)		.707[2] (2.427)
P_c = average price of corn paid to farmers, previous two harvests, 60 kilos	−.711[2] (−2.258)		−.381 (−1.012)
MP_r = minimum price of rice, announced before planting, 60 kilos		1.256[2] (2.410)	
MP_c = minimum price of corn announced before planting, 60 kilos		1.344[3] (−2.217)	
$PMM_r = MP_r/P_r$			−.578 (−1.333)
$PMM_c = MP_c/P_c$			.576 (1.410)
$PMP_r = P_r$, 1954–1962 $= MP_r$, 1963–1967		.245 (1.274)	
$PMP_c = P_c$, 1954–1962 $= MP_c$, 1963–1967		−.261 (−.663)	
YR = trend, 1954 = 0	.052[1] (3.899)	.013 (.710)	.032[3] (1.837)
R^2	.89	.89	.92
F	df(3.10)=27.82[1]	df(5.8)=14.12[1]	df(5.8)=19.29[1]
DW	2.24	2.56	2.77

explanatory power is gained by introducing minimum-price variables for 1963–1967. Indeed, the lagged market price model is statistically most significant, judging from the F test. In neither the guidance nor the risk reduction model can any faith be put in the significance of the two minimum-price coefficients, because of high multicollinearity between the corn and rice variables (each moves from 0 in 1954–1962 to a positive number in 1963–1967). Probably as a result, in the risk reduction model, the coefficients of PMM's have the wrong sign, while market-price elasticities are reduced substantially, and that of corn becomes insignificant. In the total guidance model, the expected price variables (PMP) actually become insignificant for rice and its substitute corn. Because of these problems of multicollinearity, the F test seems to be the best indicator of the additional influence of minimum prices. Under this criterion, the lagged market price model continued after 1962 to be the "best" specification.

There is a good possibility that *neither* of the minimum price models are correct. Indeed, the sensitivity of all of the coefficients to the specification suggests the possibility that minimum price effects are being absorbed by the variables of the lagged market price model, including the trend. Another approach was indicated. The lagged market model was reestimated excluding observations for 1965, the year when promised minimum prices were highest and when farmers were most confident in their implementation. Then the area planted in rice for São Paulo was "predicted" for 1965 and the significance of the difference between the prediction and area actually planted was determined. The predicted area was 991,000 hectares, the actual area 1,065,000 hectares, and the t statistic for significance of the difference .60.[60] Although actual area planted was larger than predicted, the difference is statistically negligible.

The evidence, then, is that preannounced minimum prices have probably had little or no influence on planned production in São Paulo. This also appears to be the case for Rio Grande do Sul, Brazil's leading rice-producing state, and for the Center-

[60] See J. Johnston, *Econometric Methods* (New York: McGraw-Hill, 1963), pp. 131–133.

South region as a whole, where the following supply-response functions were estimated, both in logs.[61]

Rio Grande do Sul

$$A_t = 1.62 + .26 P_{t-1}^{(2)} + .47 (A_{t-1}) + .016 YR$$
$$(2.17) \qquad (1.68) \qquad\qquad (1.33)$$
$$R^2 = .84 \qquad F(3, 7) = 12.38^{(1)} \qquad D.W. = 1.39$$

where A_t = natural log of area planted in 1,000 hectares (rough rice, 50 kilos).

P_{t-1} = natural log of lagged price paid to farmers, rough rice, 50 kilos, 1953 cruzeiros deflated by *Conjuntura Econômica's* General Price Index.

YR = trend, 1952 = o.

Years included: 1952–1962.

Source of data: Instituto Rio Grandense do Arroz, *Anuário Estatístico do Arroz, Safra de 1964/65.*

Center-South Region

$$\triangle A_t = .034 + .21 \triangle P_{t-1}^{(1)} + .28^{(3)} (\triangle A_{1-t})$$
$$R^2 = .52 \qquad F(2, 14) = 7.58^{(1)}$$

$\triangle A_t$ = change in natural log of area, in 1,000 hectares t − 1 to t.
$\triangle P_{t-1}$ = change in natural log of price per ton t − 1 to t, in 1947 cruzeiros, deflated by *Conjuntura Econômica's* General Price Index.

Years included: 1947–1964.

Source of data: *Anuário Estatístico do Brasil*, various issues.

The following percentage errors in predicting area planted from these functions were encountered:

	Rio Grande do Sul	Center-South
1963	.9	—
1964	1.4	—
1965	−6.4	2.8

[61] See the Data Appendix for a brief discussion of data and the deflator. In both functions, area planted shows a strong trend, creating serious problems of multicollinearity with the trend variable. This probably explains the insignificance of both their coefficients in Rio Grande do Sul, and is the reason for estimation in first differences for the Center-South.

None of the differences are significant at the 5 percent level, although the 6.4 percent underprediction for Rio Grande do Sul in 1965 is significant at the 10 percent level. Thus the results for these two regions also suggest very strongly that pre-announced minimum prices have had little or no effect on the planned production of rice.

Corn and Beans

No supply models I estimated for corn were satisfactory, while only the lagged market-price model for beans appeared to be plausible. Thus only the significance of differences between actual and predicted supply in the year 1965 were tested for these two products.

For the corn prediction I used the following production-response function estimated by Sergio Brandt and others of the Divisão de Economia Rural.[62]

$$\text{Production}_{corn}^t = 10.644 - .112^{(3)} \, (\text{Price}_{corn}^{t-1}) + .941^{(1)}$$
$$(\text{Production}_{corn}^{t-1}) - .515^{(3)} \text{YR}$$
$$R^2 = .83$$

where production is in millions of sixty-kilo sacks and price is in 1948–1952 cruzeiros per sixty-kilo sack, deflated by São Paulo farm price index, including coffee. The years from 1949–1963 are included.

Predicted corn production was 3.8 percent greater than that actually realized in 1965,[63] statistically insignificant, in spite of high minimum prices fixed for corn.

Beans is the least commercial of the crops examined here. It is produced mainly by small subsistence farmers who sell their surpluses. In spite of this, prices do a good job of explaining area planted in beans during the wet season in São Paulo,

[62] Sergio Alberto Brandt *et al.*, *Estrutura da Oferta de Milho no Estado de São Paulo* (mimeographed, São Paulo: Divisão de Economia Rural, 1964).

[63] The drought in 1964 caused unusually low corn yields. Hence, I used 1964 area planted and the average of yields in 1963 and 1965 to calculate the "planned" 1964 corn production variable (Prod_{t-1}) for use in the 1965 prediction.

$$\text{Area}^t = 248.124 + .197^{(1)} \text{ (Price beans}^{t-1}) - .178^{(3)}$$
$$(6.121) \qquad\qquad\qquad (1.870)$$
$$\text{Price rice}^{t-1}) - 1.208^{(1)} \text{ (Price corn}^{t-1})$$
$$(-5.357)$$
$$R^2 = .92 \qquad F(4, 6) = 17.25^{(1)} \qquad D.W. = 2.80$$

Area in thousand hectares.
Price of beans = average May–August before planting.
Prices of rice and corn = average previous year's harvest.
All prices = 1948–1952 cruzeiros/60 kilos, deflated by São Paulo general farm price index excluding coffee.
Years included. 1954–1964.
As one would expect with this crop, there is no evidence that preannounced minimum prices have influenced planned production. Actual area in the 1965 wet season crop was only 1.8 per cent greater than that predicted by the supply function, a statistically negligible difference.

Thus, as with rice, there is little evidence that corn and beans have been affected to any degree by the upward and downward manipulation of minimum prices. If this is true of São Paulo, Brazil's commercial agricultural state, it must hold a fortiori for other areas.

Conclusions

Why has there been this dichotomy in the effects of preannounced minimum prices? For beans in São Paulo and for other products in more backward regions, there is a real problem of information: many farmers are unaware of the minimum price program. This certainly will have to change if the program is to improve. But for rice and corn in São Paulo and rice in Rio Grande do Sul lack of information does not appear to have been a leading factor. Rather, it seems that uncertainty with respect to the program itself has probably kept producers from adjusting their production to minimum prices. First, they know that real minimum prices will be changed from year to year as the government sees fit. This eliminates any longer-term security such a program could give. They also know, by experience, that unlike cotton and peanuts, changes in minimum prices have not forecast changes in market prices any better than lagged market prices. The only possible effect, then, would have been through a reduction of downward annual price risk. This apparently has not been sufficiently great to stimulate production in the short run.

The performance of the total-guidance model for peanuts points to the potential power, however, of forward equilibrium pricing in the more commercial agricultural areas of Brazil. If the government can effectively predict prices, and if this is proven by experience, farmers will begin to adjust their production to preannounced minimum prices. Uncertainty and its consequences would therefore be considerably reduced. Fairly accurate predictions may be possible only for export products. Forecasts are much more difficult for such products as beans and rice, for which Brazil probably does not have a comparative advantage. Even so, effective uncertainty and risk could be substantially reduced ex post and ex ante by government purchases and sales to limit the range of price fluctuations. This range could be based on moving averages of past market prices.

The analysis suggests that an effective minimum price program would yield considerably more benefits than costs. Further study of the administrative problems involved in such a program is necessary for a definitive answer. What we have seen clearly in this case is that price support policy, although motivated in Brazil by short-run considerations, can be effective only if guided by long-term objectives.

FINAL CONSIDERATIONS

Thus, reliance on the market mechanism and selective traditional economic incentives has characterized the style of agricultural policy in Brazil from 1950 to 1967. The policies we have examined attempted to raise agricultural output by increasing profitability without raising consumer prices (marketing investment, subsidized credit), to increase productivity through subsidies on modern inputs, and to stimulate production by reducing uncertainty about agricultural prices. All policies have had their payoffs, especially, it seems, investment in transportation facilities and subsidies to fertilizer use. With changes, credit and minimum price policies could no doubt contribute much more to agricultural development.

The problem has been excessive reliance on traditional

market incentives. This is, I have argued, the style of a government that wants quick results but has very limited technical and administrative skills with which to achieve them. Traditional economic incentives are flexible, and their payoff, if any, tends to be rapid. They are also relatively less intensive in the scarce human factor than, say, rural education and land reform.

We have also seen that the introduction and implementation of market-type incentives has often been triggered by short-run crises. Agriculture in Brazil has been considered primarily as an intermediate industry, producing food and raw materials for the final product, industrialization. Agriculture has been practically ignored except when its performance has appeared to hinder industrialization significantly. Periodically, however, harvests fail and agricultural prices rise steeply. It was this type of crisis that led to the marketing investment programs in the early 1950's. A similar but more acute crisis in the early 1960's motivated the activation of the minimum price program and an acceleration of the growth of official bank credit to agriculture. We have seen the origin of this crisis leave its mark upon implementation. Thus, credit was expanded willy-nilly with little attempt to link it with innovation and productivity. Minimum prices for food products were moved up and down in an unsuccessful attempt to influence food production. In both cases the efficiency of the market incentive instrument was considerably reduced because of the short-run and crisis objectives behind the policy.

Even had they been more effectively implemented, the impact of these market incentives would have been quite limited, because of the lack of effective policies dealing with the structural problems of Brazilian agriculture. Lower fertilizer prices influence only 5 per cent of Brazilian farmers. Minimum prices are known by perhaps 10 per cent (according to USAID-USDA estimates in Rio de Janeiro). The mass of farmers are left behind. The Castello Branco and Costa e Silva governments have both recognized the need for decisive action to improve the human factor in agriculture and to increase the level of technical assistance. There are encouraging signs that the time horizon may be increasing. The bureaucracy dealing with agriculture remains a formidable obstacle, however, to a more productive policy.

APPENDIX

DATA AND PROCEDURES USED IN THE
SUPPLY RESPONSES ESTIMATES

All area and farm price data were supplied by São Paulo's Divisão de Economia Rural. These data are by far the best available in Brazil. Figures on production and area planted have been estimated four times a year since 1954, based on a stratified sample of 2,000 farms. This sample is better for some crops than for others. As a result, cotton has been the object of much concern in recent years, since the sample no longer appears to represent the geographical distribution of production accurately.

Prices used in the functions are generally arithmetic averages for the months preceding planting, since monthly marketing figures are unavailable. The choice of deflators is difficult. Ideally such a deflator would include the prices of both inputs and consumption goods purchased by farmers. Such figures are not available. I chose the general index of farm prices in São Paulo, excluding coffee, for two reasons. First, many substitute products cannot be included directly in the supply-response function. Deflation by this index allows for other substitutes indirectly. Secondly, prices of their products probably give farmers a good part of their idea of the rate of inflation. Other indices available, such as cost-of-living and whole-sale-price indices, represent conditions in Rio de Janeiro and the city of São Paulo, and include many components irrelevant to farmers, such as urban rents and bus fares.

Minimum prices in every case are those fixed in August or September before planting. These were deflated by the following year's general farm price index. This assumes that farmers expected no readjustment and anticipated inflation perfectly, a strong assumption, but inclusion of variables reflecting farmers' expectations of the rate of inflation was not feasible. Readjustment was promised by the government before the 1965 harvest. I assumed that farmers took this promise at its face value, and thus prices fixed in September, 1964, were adjusted upward by 28 percent, the rate of increase in the *Conjuntura Econômica* general price index for September 1964 – February 1965. As noted in the text, adjustments did not approach this level, and for rice *no* adjustment was actually made. Thus I assume that farmers' expectations were frustrated in this case.

For all products, I used the most common grade or type specified in the minimum price decrees. Minimum prices are fixed not for the interior, but for the ports and centers of consumption (Brasília, Belo Horizonte, São Paulo, Curitiba, and Pôrto Alegre). Minimum prices paid in farm areas are net of handling and freight expenses to the nearest consumption center and are thus somewhat lower. No series of minimum prices in the interior exists, and there is no point for our purposes in arbitrarily adjusting minimum prices downward. The total guidance model allows the coefficient of minimum price to be lower than that of lagged market price. The coefficient of the risk reduction variable, the ratio of real minimum price to real lagged market price, depends primarily upon changes in the ratio and not upon its level. Thus no serious distortions appear to be introduced by using minimum prices in the consumption centers rather than those paid in the interior.

Data on rice from Rio Grande do Sul, gathered through an annual rice census in the state, were supplied by the Rice Institute of Rio Grande do Sul (IRGA). Prices paid to farmers are averages of actual prices paid to farmers for the whole crop, weighted by amount sold. The data appear to be excellent. Irrigated rice in Rio Grande do Sul currently has no substitute in production. Hence, I used *Conjuntura Econômica's* general price index No. 2 as the deflator. This is a weighted average of the wholesale price index, the cost of living for Guanabara, and the cost of construction index.

Data for the Center-South come from the Ministry of Agriculture and IBGE. The quality of this data is much poorer, and they can be used only with serious reservations.

Finally a word on the rainy-season dry-season harvest for beans and peanuts. Unlike the other products examined, these two are double-cropped. The rainy-season planting occurs in September-October, with the harvest in December-January. The dry-season planting occurs in December-January with harvesting in April-May. Once the decision is made to plant the rainy-season crop, the option in December is primarily to produce further or let the ground lie fallow.

I found it impossible to obtain satisfactory supply results for the dry-season crop of either product, primarily because of the difficulty of determining *which* month's prices are important. In any event, the wet-season crop is larger than the dry for both crops. If preannounced minimum prices affected planned production, it should show at least in the rainy season.

CHAPTER 9

Brazil's Participation in LAFTA, 1962-1965

Donald W. Baerresen

In response to the apparent success of the European Common Market, the major countries of Latin America have banded together in the Latin American Free Trade Association, to promote trade among themselves. LAFTA began functioning on August 1, 1961. Its original members, and those representing LAFTA for this study, were Argentina, Brazil, Chile, Ecuador, Mexico, Paraguay, Peru, and Uruguay.[1]

Intra-LAFTA trade is to be promoted by lowering and eventually eliminating tariffs among member countries. At present, however, tariff concessions are being granted more slowly and with more difficulty than is desired, which causes great concern for LAFTA's future. Suggestions for change have been many, ranging from converting LAFTA into a common market (that is, imposing common external tariff barriers) to dividing LAFTA into groups of a few countries each, to disbanding LAFTA completely.[2]

[1] In this study, the term "LAFTA" refers to the body of doctrine and agreements that constitute the legal and political framework of the association. In addition to the LAFTA group of countries, there is another trading association in Latin America known as the Central American Common Market, composed of the five Central American republics.

[2] At the Punta del Este Conference of April 1967, it was agreed to establish by 1985 a common market that will include all Latin American countries.

Brazil is LAFTA's most important member, since it is the largest in population, area, national income, and foreign trade. The viability of LAFTA, or a similar association, thus depends significantly on the willingness of Brazil to participate. Brazil's willingness, in turn, depends on the benefits of such an association to Brazil.

The rationale for LAFTA is that participating countries benefit from attainment of LAFTA's prime objective, increased trade among member countries. The purpose of this study is to determine whether Brazil benefited from membership in LAFTA during the period 1962–1965. I shall examine developments in Brazil's trade with the LAFTA region in relation to LAFTA's objective, and especially to exports of Brazilian manufactured products to the LAFTA region.[3] If LAFTA should be disbanded or significantly changed in the future (as is now envisaged), Brazil's experience with it can aid in forming Brazilian policy on new trading arrangements.

For a proper perspective of Brazil's participation in LAFTA it is important to understand the policies and pressures that led Brazil to join in forming it. I shall therefore briefly review developments in Brazil's international trade and pattern of economic growth following World War II before going on to explain the form of analysis employed in this study, present the specific results of the analysis, and draw general conclusions.

BRAZILIAN FOREIGN TRADE AND ECONOMIC DEVELOPMENT[4]

At the end of World War II, Brazil appeared to be in a favorable position economically. Substantial international reserves had been accumulated during the war because of strong demand for Brazilian exports, while imports had necessarily been limited by restriction of international trade, and by con-

---

[3] The term "LAFTA region" is used to indicate collectively all LAFTA countries excluding Brazil.

[4] A fuller treatment of this subject is found in Escritório de Pesquisa Econômica Aplicada, Ministério do Planejamento e Coordenação Econômica, *Diagnóstico Preliminar de Comércio Internacional* (Rio de Janeiro: Nov. 1966).

centration on war production in the traditional manufacturing countries. After the war, there was a large increase in Brazilian imports, resulting at first from the release of pent-up demand occasioned by wartime deprivation, and then from the increasingly lower prices of imports compared to domestically produced goods and services. For example, between 1945 and 1953 Brazil's exchange rate was held constant, and there were no significant increases in related taxes; but the cost of living more than doubled, thereby reducing the relative price of imports in terms of Brazilian money.

In the meantime, however, exports came to be hampered by competition from new suppliers (notably in Africa) of Brazil's traditional export products. Also, rising internal costs, coupled with the fixed exchange rate, were reducing export profits. These developments led to trade deficits that caused severe balance-of-payments pressures. At first the trade deficits were offset by decreasing foreign reserves. Next, commercial, and later intergovernmental, loans were obtained. When it appeared that the trade deficits were potentially of a persistent, long-run nature, quantitative and monetary import restrictions were imposed. Brazil then began an extensive series of devaluations that raised the exchange rate from 18.38 cruzeiros to the U.S. dollar in 1953 to Cr$2,700.00 per dollar in 1967.

After each tightening of restrictions or devaluation there was some improvement in the balance of payments until the internal rate of inflation rose sufficiently to nullify the corrective influence of the new measure. And so the process has continued, with balance-of-payments pressures arising not only from trade deficits, but also from the need to repay past loans.

During the years following World War II, Brazilian participation in world trade has fallen, in part because of the gradual return of the traditional major trading countries to their former positions. There has been no significant change in the composition of Brazilian exports, but there has been in the composition of imports. Consumer goods have decreased, while production goods — both capital equipment and raw materials — have risen, a result of the massive program of Brazilian industrialization, which began on a large scale in 1955. This program is often referred to as one of import substitution, since the pressure of recurring balance-of-payments problems was a major factor in motivating Brazil to industrialize in order to obtain, through local production, the types of goods for which import demand was being restrained. The wish to promote economic development through industrialization, rather than by investing to expand export receipts (and thereby foreign exchange to buy desired goods), was also a factor. Pessimism about achieving adequate development through emphasizing exportation was nurtured by memories of the Depression of the 1930's, for which dependence on international markets was blamed, and also by apparent stagnation in the growth of exports, and by the type of economic philosophy being promulgated by the United Nations Economic Commission for Latin America.[5]

Industrialization was thus chosen as Brazil's path of development. Barriers were placed against importation of products competing with domestically supplied manufactured goods, and exportation of some raw materials was limited in order to provide cheap inputs to local producers. Foreign capital and technology were encouraged. Importers of inputs required for industry were granted concessions through special credits and lower tariffs. Development of the internal market was emphasized (an additional factor in the decline in Brazil's share of world trade); however, in spite of the effort toward self-sufficiency, Brazil's dependency on imports increased. The ratio of Brazilian imports to gross national product rose in real terms. Moreover, many imports came to be essential to the industrial process; their reduction would have induced a multiple reduction in domestic production. Thus, Brazil's need to import increased because of industrialization.

Exports provide about 90 percent of Brazil's foreign exchange receipts. Allowing for external price changes and so on, the capacity to purchase imports with Brazil's exports was only slightly larger by the period 1959-1960 than it had been in the period 1947-1948.[6] By 1961, it was obvious that Brazil's exports had not developed apace with the rest of the economy,

[5] As an example of this philosophy, see Raúl Prebisch, "The Economic Development of Latin America and its Principal Problems," in ECLA, *Economic Bulletin for Latin America*, VII, No. 1, Feb. 1962.

[6] *Diagnóstico Preliminar do Comércio Internacional*, p. 55.

and that industrialization was becoming increasingly dependent on imports, for which exports were needed to earn foreign exchange. Also apparent was the desirability of obtaining a wider market for Brazilian industrial products than was available domestically.

Economic development through concentration on industrialization produces a dependency on exportation for another reason than the need to obtain foreign exchange for necessary imports. After absorption of the internal demand provided by blocking competing imports, further domestic industrial growth is limited to the rate of increase in the portion of national income available to purchase locally supplied industrial products. Exportation of those products is therefore necessary if industrialization is to increase faster than related internal demand, and thereby remain the impelling factor in development. Through exportation, industrial production achieves increased economies of scale faster than would be possible by relying solely on expansion of domestic consumption. These economies permit early reduction in prices to the domestic consumer of products being exported. Exportation thus allows increased purchase of the products at home, both because of lower internal prices and because of the increased income generated by the exports. Exports of industrial goods can therefore stimulate the growth of industrial production, for both domestic and foreign markets, at a pace faster than the growth of the national economy; and in this way industrialization can continue to stimulate economic development.

By 1961, however, manufacturing costs were generally higher in Brazil than in countries that had industrialized earlier — as is shown by the necessity of maintaining high import barriers to protect Brazilian industry. Although this condition might have discouraged direct competition by Brazil in the world market,[7] the formation of LAFTA offered a possibility for exportation of Brazilian manufactured products to a

[7] When revenue derived from exportation need cover little more than the marginal cost of those goods exported, while *all* additional costs for total production are covered from sales in the domestic market (which is reserved for local producers), it could be possible to compete on the world market by means of dual pricing.

more limited market. By simulating trade among a restricted group of countries, an organization such as LAFTA may well provide a necessary "transitional stage" in the process of a member country's industrialization. This transitional stage occurs after the period in which a country's manufactured products can be sold profitably only in its own highly protected market, and before the period when its manufactured products can be sold profitably under conditions of free trade. I shall now turn to an examination of the extent to which Brazilian participation in LAFTA has perpetuated Brazil's economic growth through industrialization by permitting exportation of manufactured products to the LAFTA region.

METHOD OF ANALYSIS

The task of determining LAFTA's effectiveness in developing Brazilian trade — particularly, exportation of Brazilian manufactures — with the LAFTA region is a complex one, for such trade is influenced simultaneously by forces arising from internal policies and conditions in the member countries. LAFTA, being only a trading association, has little capability to influence or offset these policies, or most of the other forces affecting trade, which include changes in tastes, national income and its distribution, credit, administrative procedures and discretion, exchange rates, internal taxes and subsidies, and governmental expenditures. In addition to LAFTA tariff changes, Brazilian trade with LAFTA members is strongly influenced by these forces — not only those originating in Brazil and other LAFTA members, but also those from non-Lafta countries with which Brazil and the other members trade. It is impossible to isolate these other forces, or to estimate the extent to which they affect Brazilian foreign trade, and we are thus unable to isolate, or to estimate precisely, the extent to which LAFTA tariff changes affect Brazilian trade. Nevertheless, we can obliquely approach some conclusions about the influence of LAFTA on Brazilian trade by determining, first, whether LAFTA has been ineffective in sufficiently stimulating Brazil's intra-LAFTA trade, and, second, what LAFTA's possible influence is on the composition and balance of this trade. First I will examine the extent to which Brazil's trade developments have been consistent with LAFTA's objective of promoting intra-LAFTA trade, then the makeup of Brazil's LAFTA trade in the light of LAFTA's possible influence, as determined in the first step.

Brazil's trade developments will be considered consistent with LAFTA's objective when Brazil's trade with the LAFTA region in a given period increases more, or decreases less, than Brazil's trade with non-LAFTA countries. In particular, variations in Brazil's LAFTA trade will be compared with changes in Brazil's total world trade, and in trade with non-LAFTA countries in Latin America (which are grouped under the heading "Other Latin American Countries" in tables, and hereafter designated in the text as the "OLA" region).[8]

In this analysis, Brazilian exports are broadly classified in three categories: (I) primary materials, (II) general food and beverage products, and (III) manufactured products. Together these categories account for over 99 percent of total Brazilian exports.[9]

[8] This group includes Bolivia, Venezuela, Costa Rica, Guatemala, Haiti, Honduras, Nicaragua, Panama, Dominican Republic, El Salvador, Dutch Antilles. As explained above, Bolivia and Venezuela are not here considered as LAFTA members.

[9] Statistical data employed in this study were obtained from the Serviço de Estatística Econômica e Financeira (SEEF) of the Brazilian Ministry of Finance, which is responsible for collecting and publishing official data on Brazil's international trade.

The relationship between the export classifications used in this study and those used by SEEF is as follows:

Categories used in this study	SEEF Classi- fication	SEEF Code Numbers	Example of Product Types
I Primary materials)	Class II	(20000–29999)	Hides, wood, minerals, cotton, jute
II (General food and beverage products)	Class IV	(40000–49999)	Cereals, coffee, fruits, cocoa
III (Manufactures)	Class V	(50000–59999)	Chemicals, drugs
	Class VI	(60000–69999)	Machinery, vehicles, and related parts

For categories I and II, I shall compare trends in Brazilian exports to the LAFTA and the OLA regions. Total Brazilian exports do not provide a useful basis for comparison in these categories because of special marketing arrangements outside LAFTA for some products (coffee, minerals, and so forth) that strongly influence Brazil's total trade figures. However, for category III Brazilian exports to the world and to the OLA region serve as bases for comparing trends of Brazilian manufactured exports to LAFTA.

For the purposes of our export analysis, conditions in the OLA region are probably closer to those of the LAFTA region than conditions in any other group of countries. Variations in freight costs should be similar in the two regions, and the composition of imports, the domestic economies, and the stages of development of the countries within each region are roughly parallel. Absolute differences in effective import demands between the two regions are not important, since the analysis rests on comparison of relative trends.

An example may help illustrate the value of such a comparison. Suppose that during a certain period Brazil's category I exports to the LAFTA region rose 10 percent, while Brazil's exports to the OLA region increased 5 percent. For this situation we can say that the development of Brazilian exports conforms to what would be an effective influence by LAFTA on Brazilian trade. It should not be assumed that tariff reductions by LAFTA countries were responsible for this change, but it can be said that the pattern of change of Brazilian exports is consistent with LAFTA's objective, and that the export side of Brazil's intra-LAFTA trade has grown.

To evaluate LAFTA's possible influence on Brazil's total balance of trade with the LAFTA region, I also compare trends in Brazil's LAFTA imports with total Brazilian imports. The

Class VII (70000–79999)   Tires, textiles, refined and formed metals, polished stones (i.e., manufactures are classified according to main raw material employed)

OLA region is not a satisfactory basis for import comparison, since Brazilian imports from this region are dominated by petroleum and its derivatives, the importation of which is subject to special Brazilian policies.

Although Brazil's trade developments may be consistent with the basic LAFTA objective, this can lead to a deficit in Brazil's LAFTA trade. Both the exports and imports of Brazil could have a greater increase relative to the LAFTA region than to other regions, but if the import increase exceeded the export increase the result would be a LAFTA trade deficit for Brazil.

Some LAFTA countries could gain either temporary or permanent advantages at the expense of other participating countries through lucky or astute bargaining for tariff reductions. Accordingly, some countries may be able to expand their exports to the LAFTA region more than do other countries — which means that the additional exports gained by some countries represent additional imports for others. It cannot, of course, be expected that all LAFTA countries will constantly maintain favorable or neutral trade balances with the region. It must be expected that at least for periods of one or two years a country may experience trade deficits with the region. Some country or countries must have deficits if others have surpluses. Nevertheless, perpetuation of a LAFTA trade deficit should indicate, to the country suffering this deficit, the need to examine the possible adverse influence of LAFTA, and possible alternatives for acquiring improved trading conditions within the region.

It is not the purpose of this study to pass judgment on whether a LAFTA trade deficit (or surplus) experienced by Brazil was harmful or beneficial to it, but only to indicate when and in what direction Brazil's LAFTA trade balances may have been influenced by LAFTA. My analysis of Brazilian participation in LAFTA is based on a year-by-year evaluation for the period 1962–1965. Although LAFTA began operating in August 1961, it is unlikely that its influence on Brazilian foreign trade could be discerned for the latter half of that year. The analysis therefore begins with 1962, the first full calendar year of LAFTA's operation, and goes through 1965.

Venezuela became a member of LAFTA on October 1,

1966. On October 24, 1966, Bolivia officially expressed its desire to enter LAFTA and will probably attain this objective during the middle of 1967. These alterations — and their antici-pation — in LAFTA's structure preclude extension of our pres-ent means of comparison to include 1966 in the analysis.

Yearly changes in Brazilian trade are measured from two bases: the average for the six-year period from 1955 to 1960, and the preceding year. Thus for any given year a particular trade development is evaluated by a pair of changes. These changes sometimes show movements in opposite directions, and often vary considerably in degree. For this reason I used a weighting system to reconcile conflicts that arose from using two bases of measurement. The "1955–1960" base was con-sidered more important, and was assigned the weight of .7 to reduce possible distortions in trade trends caused by irregular yearly movement. However, the "previous year" base (weighted by .3) permits the inclusion of short-run trends deserving con-sideration. For example, measuring a change from the "1955–1960" base may show a decline, while measuring the change from the "previous year" base may show an increase. This in-crease over the past year might reflect a substantial recovery from a depressed position in recent years, and therefore de-serve some credit in determining the overall trade trend. Admittedly, the weighting distribution is arbitrary, and arises from my subjective evaluation of the comparative significance of the measurements used in the analysis. Mention is made where appropriate when conclusions different from those cited in the text result from varying the weight for the "previous year" base between .5 and .3.

RESULTS OF ANALYSIS

Consistency of Brazilian Trade Developments with LAFTA's Objective

(1) *Exports.* Table 1 shows the division of Brazilian ex-ports into the three main categories, and according to the re-gions used in our analysis. This table shows that for the years 1962 and 1964 Brazilian trade development were consistent with LAFTA's objective for all export categories. For these two

years in all categories L > O, signifying that Brazilian exports to the LAFTA region rose more or fell less than Brazilian exports to the OLA region. Also, during 1962 and 1964 Brazilian exportation of manufactured products (category III) increased more relative to the LAFTA region than to the world (L > W).

Brazilian trade developments for 1963 seem to have been

TABLE 1. BRAZILIAN EXPORTS (MAJOR CATEGORIES) TO LAFTA AND
OLA REGIONS AND TO THE WORLD

Year	Category		LAFTA	OLA	World	Comparison
	I	$	25.8	3.1	387	
		a	−35.2	−82.4		L > O
		b	−38.0	−64.4		
1962	II	$	39.3	.1	792	
		a	−13.6	−90.0		L > O
		b	−43.4	−75.0		
	III	$	10.5	1.2	33.2	
		a	22.1	50.0	− 6.7	L > O & W
		b	239.7	9.1	127.4	
	I	$	27.8	1.5	397	
		a	7.8	−51.6		L > O
		b	−33.2	−82.8		
1963	II	$	39.0	.2	968	
		a	− .7	100.0		O > L
		b	−43.8	−50.0		
	III	$	8.8	4.4	37.3	
		a	−16.2	266.7	12.3	O > L > W[a]
		b	183.9	300.0	155.5	
	I	$	42.6	.3	432	
		a	53.2	80.0		L > O
		b	2.4	96.6		
1964	II	$	56.1	.2	921	
		a	43.8	0		L > O
		b	−19.2	−50.0		
	III	$	33.4	5.7	70.0	
		a	279.5	29.5	46.7	L > O & W
		b	977.4	418.2	379.5	
	I	$	56.9	.2	487	
		a	33.6	−33.3		
		b	36.8	97.7		O > L[b]
1965	II	$	69.8	.1	987	
		a	24.4	−50.0		L > O
		b	.6	−75.0		

TABLE 1. BRAZILIAN EXPORTS (MAJOR CATEGORIES) TO LAFTA AND
OLA REGIONS AND TO THE WORLD

Year	Category		LAFTA	OLA	World	Comparison
III	$		68.6	5.0	109.5	
	a		105.4	12.3	36.1	L > O & W
	b		2,112.9	354.5	650.0	

Source: Calculated from data obtained from Serviço de Estatística Econômica e
Financeira, Ministério da Fazenda do Brasil.

Key: $ — million US$ F.O.B.
       a — percent change from previous year
       b — percent change from related average for 1955–1960
       L = LAFTA region; O = OLA region; W = world (i.e., total Brazilian
       exports)
       [a] L > W when weight of item a > .5.
       [b] O > L when weight of item a > .48.

inconsistent with LAFTA's objective. Although L > O in category I (primary materials), O > L in the other two categories — particularly in the important category of manufactured products. If we consider only total exports (not shown in the table) to these regions, then the result is: W > L > O; and L > O only when the weight of the "previous year" base is less than .31. Because of Brazil's special interest in promoting exportation of manufactures to the LAFTA region, and the comparative weakness of this accomplishment in 1963, one must conclude that LAFTA did not satisfactorily stimulate Brazilian exports in that year.

In 1965, Brazilian trade developments were opposite those of 1963: O > L in category I, and L > O in categories II and III. In terms of total exports, L > O and W. Especially impressive in 1965 were Brazil's exports of manufactured products to the LAFTA region. The increase in category III LAFTA exports was significantly greater than similar exports to the OLA region and to the world. By 1965, manufactured products had assumed an important share of total Brazilian exports to the LAFTA region — rising from a share of 2.7 percent for the period 1955–1960 to 35.4 percent in 1965. This increased importance of manufactured exports to the LAFTA region was sufficient in 1965 to allow the trade trend in this category to more than offset the trade trend of category I exports. On balance, 1965 developments of Brazilian exports were consistent with LAFTA's objective.

TABLE 2. BRAZILIAN IMPORTS FROM LAFTA AND THE WORLD

Year		LAFTA	World	Comparison
	$	128.6	1,475.0	
1962	a	184.5	1.0	L > W
	b	1.8	7.7	
	$	163.9	1,486.8	
1963	a	27.4	18	L > W
	b	29.8	8.5	
	$	168.0	1,263.5	
1964	a	2.5	−15.0	L > W
	b	33.0	− 7.8	
	$	190.4	1,096.4	
1965	a	13.3	−13.2	L > W
	b	50.8	−20.0	

Source: As in Table 1.

Key: $ — million US$ C.I.F.
a — percent change from previous year
b — percent change from related average for 1955–1960
L = LAFTA region; W = world

(2) *Imports.* Imports and related changes are shown in Table 2, which shows for all years under review (1962–1965) L > W, indicating that Brazilian imports from the LAFTA region increased relatively more than total Brazilian imports, which is consistent with LAFTA's objective.

Brazil's Trade Balance with the LAFTA Region

Table 3 shows Brazil's exports to and imports from the LAFTA region, together with the related percentage changes of these trade flows. As shown in this table, Brazil had a negative trade balance with the LAFTA region for the first three of the four years under review. Furthermore, in 1962 and 1963 imports increased relatively more (according to measurement from both bases) than did exports.[10] As previously noted,

[10] It might be argued that a deficit in the trade balance arises because of increased transportation and related charges. In 1962, the proportion of these charges to the total C.I.F. value rose 7 percent for Brazilian imports from Argentina (the only LAFTA country for which the related data are available) and 0.9 percent for Brazilian imports from the world. These figures indicate that the adverse affect on Brazil's LAFTA trade balance may have resulted from a relative increase of

LAFTA was ineffective in 1963 in stimulating Brazilian exports to the LAFTA region, which contributed to Brazil's LAFTA trade deficit that year.

There was substantial expansion of Brazilian exports to the LAFTA region in 1964 and 1965, and for these two years exports increased relatively more than imports.[11]

TABLE 3. BRAZILIAN TRADE WITH LAFTA REGION

| | Value (million US$) | | Percent change from base | | | | Expansion relatively greater for |
| | | | Preceding year | | 1955–1960 average | | |
Year	Exports	Imports	Exports	Imports	Exports	Imports	
1962	76	129	−20.0	184.5	−33.9	1.8	imports
1963	76	164	0.0	27.4	−33.9	29.8	imports
1964	133	168	75.0	2.5	15.7	33.0	exports
1965	197	190	48.1	13.3	71.3	50.8	exports

Source: As in Table 1.

Brazilian trade developments for both imports and exports were thus consistent with LAFTA's objective in 1962, 1964, and 1965. In 1962, Brazil had a trade deficit with the LAFTA region that cannot be attributed to LAFTA's ineffectiveness in stimulating Brazilian exports to the region — although this stimu-

transportation and similar charges placed on Brazilian imports from the LAFTA region. For 1963, the opposite conclusion can be drawn, since for that year these charges on imports from Argentina dropped 11 percent, while for imports from the world these charges increased 12 percent.

[11] Measurements from both bases lead one to the same conclusion about trends in Brazil's LAFTA trade balance for 1965. However, for 1964 the overall conclusion is less obvious. Based on the preceding year, 1964 export expansion greatly exceeded that for imports; based on the 1955–1960 average, exports increased relatively less than imports. Reconciliation of these results (according to our weighting system) shows that the overall increase in exports was relatively greater than that of imports. The notable export recovery based on the previous year more than offset the understated change that results (as in this situation with the 1955–1960 average) from using a base with a value that lies between the starting and ending values of the year for which measurement is being made. Our conclusion for 1964 would be reversed only if the result from measuring according to the "previous year" base was weighted less than .19.

TABLE 4. PARTICIPATION OF MANUFACTURERS IN TOTAL BRAZILIAN EXPORTS
TO LAFTA AND OLA REGIONS AND THE WORLD
(percent)

Region		1955-60	1961	1962	1963	1964	1965
LAFTA	a	2.7	8.6	13.9	11.6	25.1	34.7
	b			61.6	−16.5	116.4	38.2
	c			414.8	329.6	829.6	1185.1
OLA	a	10.5	17.6	27.3	70.5	90.6	91.2
	b			55.1	158.2	28.5	.7
	c			160.0	571.4	762.9	768.6
World	a	1.1	2.5	2.7	2.7	4.9	6.9
	b			8.0	0	81.4	40.8
	c			145.5	145.5	345.5	527.3
Comparison				L>O&W	O>L&W	L>O&W	L>O&W

Source: As in Table 1.

Key: a = percent of total Brazilian manufactures exported to the region.
  b = percent change in participation from preceding year.
  c = percent change in participation from average for 1955-1960.
  L = LAFTA region; O = OLA region; W = world

lation can be considered "too small" in relation to that received by imports. In 1964 and 1965, trends of Brazil's trade development led toward a trade surplus with the LAFTA region. On the other hand, Brazil's 1963 trade deficit with the LAFTA region was aggravated by LAFTA's failure to stimulate Brazilian exports.

Brazilian Manufactured Exports to the LAFTA Region

Table 4 shows the percentage share of manufactures in Brazil's total exports to the three regions used in our analysis.

TABLE 5. COMPOSITION OF BRAZIL'S MANUFACTURED EXPORTS TO
LAFTA AND OLA REGIONS AND THE WORLD
(percent of total exports)

Manufactured exports by class[a]		Years				
		1955–60	*1962*	*1963*	*1964*	*1965*
LAFTA	V	19.9	10.3	15.4	5.5	3.4
	VI	46.1	70.6	58.3	35.2	31.8
	VII	28.0	15.5	20.5	56.4	62.9
OLA	V	20.7	15.9	2.4	1.8	4.4
	VI	16.2	40.4	64.6	64.6	69.0
	VII	55.2	30.7	29.5	28.1	20.3
World	V	62.3	44.6	44.5	25.1	13.2
	VI	13.7	36.1	28.4	26.1	26.4
	VII	19.9	16.3	23.6	45.9	57.5

Source: As in Table 1.
  [a] Manufactures are subdivided by class according to the SEEF system outlined in footnote 9 in the text. The three classes shown here make up about 95 percent of the manufactured products exported by Brazil.

For all of these regions, this share increased markedly from 1962 through 1965. Moreover, the share in exports to the LAFTA region rose relatively more than to the other regions for three of these four years (where $L > O$ and W). Thus, except for 1963, the trend in the composition of Brazil's exports to the LAFTA region was consistent with LAFTA's providing an effective mechanism for stimulating exportation of Brazilian manufactures within the region.

During 1962–1965, the composition of Brazil's manufactured exports to the LAFTA region changed significantly, as is shown in Table 5. Most notably, there was a drop in the share of machinery and vehicle (Class VI) exports. This drop was contrary to the trend of Brazilian Class VI exports to the OLA region; and considerably greater (in terms of relative change) than the decline of Brazilian Class VI exports to the world. There are, of course, many possible explanations for this change, but the degrees of divergence from the trends of the two regions of comparison suggest that the cause might lie within LAFTA itself. It seems particularly important to examine tariff concessions granted in the past by the other LAFTA countries in order to determine whether Brazilian industries supplying Class VI exports have obtained opportunities for entry into the LAFTA market equal to those of other Brazilian manufacturing industries. If not, then future tariff bargaining by Brazil might be directed toward correcting this imbalance — unless, by forgoing tariff concessions for this class of exports there is a more than compensating gain obtainable from tariff concessions for exports of other classes.

CONCLUSION

From the results of the analysis above, I conclude that the development of Brazilian trade in 1962, 1964, and 1965 was consistent with LAFTA's objective of increasing intraregional trade, and that LAFTA successfully stimulated exportation of Brazilian manufactured products in those years. However, LAFTA seems to have been ineffective in fulfilling these conditions for Brazil in 1963. Furthermore, I find that LAFTA's influence most likely contributed toward a deficit in Brazil's trade with the LAFTA region in 1962 and 1963, and a surplus in 1964 and 1965. It would seem that, on balance, Brazil probably benefited from participating in LAFTA for the period 1962–1965, at least with respect to development of Brazil's trade with the LAFTA region. This development, it is worth noting, contributed to the continuation of industrialization as the prime motive force in the process of Brazil's economic growth.

CHAPTER 10

Import Demand and
Import Substitution in Brazil

Samuel A. Morley

This paper is an attempt to provide usable and useful import demand functions for Brazil. In any developing country, imports are a key economic magnitude, yet in Brazil little work has been done to quantify the forces that generate or restrict the demand for foreign goods. In 1953 a set of quantitative restrictions on imports was replaced by a price-based scheme that used tariffs and multiple rates to ration a limited amount of foreign exchange in a way favorable to development. At the same time Brazil was undergoing a period of rapid industrialization in which import substitution was a major stimulus to investment. From the point of view of policy and external equilibrium, it is therefore both possible and interesting to try to determine the relationships among movements in in-

AUTHOR'S NOTE: I would like to express my deep gratitude to Dr. Jose Tavora and Dr. Francelino de Araujo Gomes of IBGE, Dr. Joaquim Mangia of CPA, and Dr. Cori Acioli of SEEF for their help in assembling and interpreting the basic statistics on imports. I want to thank Maria de Conceição Tavares, Paul Clark, Donald Baerresen, and Albert Fishlow for their encouragement, intellectual and personal. Finally, without the dedicated work of Maria Lourdes da Silva, Jose Kremnitzer, and Jair Mascarenhas the empirical parts of this study never could have been completed.

come, relative prices, imports, and the domestic production of import substitutes.

The principal econometric implications of our work are the significance of relative prices and the derived prediction that without special measures imports will probably grow by 6 or 7 percent per year, somewhat more than the rate of income growth that generated the prediction. In other words, even if Brazil is able to achieve the 4 or 5 percent rate of growth of exports that her government projects, she still will have to make special efforts to increase the domestic production of such more substitutable imports as refined petroleum and wheat. The derived price elasticities derived, like those in comparable studies in other countries, are statistically significant, but low. Thus, devaluation is not likely to be very effective as a short-run remedy for balance of payments deficits. A good deal of doubt has been cast on the interpretation of regression results in the analysis of import demand, but we will try to show that the special conditions needed to make such an analysis meaningful are fulfilled in the Brazilian case.

In the first part of this essay we consider the econometric problems associated with import-demand functions and defend the procedure for the case of Brazil. Alternative forms for perfect and close substitutes are presented. In the second part some results are presented. The third part contains aggregations of these results and predictions for various rates of import substitution and growth.

Let us now have a brief look at the import record since 1953. Appendix tables 4 and 5 (see the Statistical Appendix, pp. 312, 313 below), give the basic import data used in this study. They show an absolute and a relative growth of imports of capital goods, at the expense of consumer and intermediate goods, in the Kubitschek industrialization before 1960, then a steady decline partly due to the decline in total investment. Since 1962 there has been a fundamental change in import behavior in the country, with all components either falling absolutely or growing at a reduced rate.

In this relatively depressed period, imports seem to be a residual whose demand is more than proportionately affected by changes in economic activity. This is consistent with Harberger's observation that internal supply and demand functions may shift asymmetrically in a period of relative stagnation.[1] Demand is held down by an anti-inflation program or some other economy-wide adjustment, but potential industrial supply, or capacity, still is shifting outward because of past investments. Such a shift would reduce imports even though total demand was unchanged.

IMPORT-DEMAND FUNCTIONS: SOURCES AND SIGNIFICANCE OF BIAS

During the 1950's there was a good deal of controversy in the literature over the meaning and significance of regression estimates of price and income elasticities for imports for which national substitutes are available. Measured price elasticities for most countries were low or insignificant, and writers like Orcutt and Harberger have shown that this was probably due to errors in measurement, excluded variables, or the difference between the short and the long run rather than the irrelevance of the price mechanism as a determinant of import quantities.[2] By and large the problems they raise are common to any demand analysis. If the independent variable, price, is positively correlated with upward shifts in the demand function (aside from those caused by included variables), evidently the measured price elasticity of demand will be biased downward (Harberger's case). Orcutt showed that if internal and external sources of supply were combined for a standard demand analysis, the measured price elasticity would be biased downward where they were random or positively correlated shifts in the demand and supply curves. The same problem would occur if there were errors in the measurement of price.

It seems incontestable that there is a positive correlation between price and excluded shifts in demand curves in any

[1] Arnold Harberger, "A Structural Approach to the Problem of Import Demand," *American Economic Review*, XLIII (May 1953), pp. 148–159.

[2] *Ibid.*; Harberger, "Some Evidence on the International Price Mechanism," *Journal of Political Economy*, LXV (Dec. 1957), pp. 506–521; George Orcutt, "Measurement of Elasticity in International Trade," *Review of Economics and Statistics*, XXXII (May 1950), pp. 117–132.

standard internal market. But this may not be true in the import market for a country like Brazil whose demand is a small fraction of world supply. The supply curve in such a situation is probably perfectly elastic, so shifts in demand will raise only the amount imported, not prices. Even if there were positive correlation, the importance of the bias depends on the relative size of shifts in the supply and demand curves. When both shift very little, any shift or error in the measurement of price makes single-equation regression analysis a poor approach. However, if the supply curve shifts a great deal, the relative importance of demand shifts is diminished. While no one can say exactly how big a relatively "big" shift in the external supply curve would have to be to render the bias of excluded variables in the demand function unimportant, the fact that in Brazil the observed price in cruzeiros has more than doubled for all import categories since 1953 (tripled for manufacturers) suggests that supply shifts are large relative to those of demand. Therefore we may safely use the single-equation regression technique.

Shifts in the *external* supply facing a country are a necessary condition for estimating import-demand functions. For with exchange rate and international prices both stable, any shift in *internal* demand or supply shifts only the import demand schedule and traces out the relevant portion of the external supply curve. Imports will rise or fall with constant prices, and it obviously will not be possible to estimate a demand curve.

Turning now to Orcutt's point of the bias resulting from either positive or random shifts in import demand and supply, it is our contention that these shifts in Brazil were neither random nor obviously positive. Consider Figure 1, which graphs import demand and supply for a substitutable commodity.

Line AB is the import-demand curve. Its slope equals the sum of absolute values of the slopes of the internal supply and demand curves. Imports at any point on it are equal to the horizontal difference between those two curves. The case of nonsubstitutes is the special case where internal supply is zero and the import and total demand functions are identical.

Let us now trace out the various possible shifts over time and examine the resulting bias.

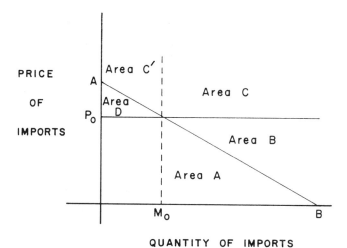

QUANTITY OF IMPORTS

Fɪɢ. 1. Import Demand and Supply for a Substitutable Commodity.

Changes in Internal Conditions, International Supply Constant

Here the original price, P_0, is maintained; and shifts in either national demand or supply, by moving AB horizontally, simply trace out the relevant portion of the fixed international supply curve. Regression analysis is useless since the variation in supply that is a necessary condition is not fulfilled.

Falling International Supply Curve

If the international supply curve falls over time successive observations fall in the area below the original price line. If internal supply and demand both shift by an equal amount in each period — the total increase in internal demand just matched by internal supply at the new price — then the shifts in international supply trace out the demand curve for imports without bias. If the underlying demand curve shifts more than supply, observations will lie in area B, and any aggression will overestimate the price elasticity of import demand. Conversely, if supply shifts more than demand, the import-demand curve will fall. Successive observations will lie in area A, and regression analysis will underestimate import-price elasticity. Parenthetically, the case of equal growth rates of internal demand and supply, under our assumptions about the international supply, will result in observations in area B, since where there are imports they too must be growing. For as long as this trend continues, there will be upward bias in regression estimated elasticities.

Rising International Supply Curve

The internal price of imports is rising, as a result either of world conditions or of changes in the relative cost of foreign exchange due to balance of payments problems. As in case B, if internal demand and supply shift by equal absolute amounts, so that the import-demand curve is unchanged, changes in international conditions will trace out that demand curve exactly, and regression analysis is appropriate and unbiased. If demand rises relative to supply, observations lie in area C, while if the reverse happens observations are in D. Area C should be subdivided, however, according to whether imports rise or fall. Assuming that the curves are linear, it can be shown that if the rise in import prices is more than the shift in demand divided by the sum of the slopes of internal supply and demand in absolute values, then imports will fall, and successive observations will lie in the area C', to the right of curve AB and to the left of the original quantity of imports, M_0. C' describes the economy in which demand rises faster than internal supply, but the rise in import prices is sufficiently rapid to lower the quantity of imports. A glance at the graph shows that in area D bias is upward, and in C it is downward.

Orcutt asserted that the most likely configuration of national and international conditions would be positive shifts in demand and supply resulting in observations in either area A or C, depending on whether the disturbance was a recession or a boom. This would cause downward bias in estimated price elasticities. This sort of analysis seems justified for the United States but not for Brazil. Prosperity and depression in the United States are likely to be reflected by her trading partners because of her sheer size, but in Brazil the internal cycle has been independent if the state of her major suppliers. Her boom period was practically continuous from 1953 through 1962, and was followed by stagnation. This internal picture is accompanied by almost continuously rising relative prices for both capital and consumer goods, and a rise followed by a decline for intermediate goods. In the pre-1962 period, when demand shifts may have been positive, there is some reason to expect the Orcutt pattern of downward bias. Since we were interested in getting an upper bound for the price elasticity, we arbitrarily chose income elasticities and made them somewhat higher than those observed in other countries. We are thus including a substantial amount of outward shift in import demand, and raising the likelihood that unexplained shifts will be negative (in area D) where regression bias is upward. After 1962 there was undoubtedly a leftward shift in the import-demand curve that occurred with rising prices for imports. In other words, internal and external conditions were moving in opposite directions, which tends to give an upward bias to regression estimates. The point is that the shifts in the demand for imports were neither random nor necessarily positively correlated with those in supply; and therefore they would not appear to result in a systematic predictable source of downward bias.

Our defense of regression analysis has rested on the relative size of demand and supply shifts and their probable negative relationship to each other. If this rationale is admitted, we can now get on to considering the appropriate regression form for different types of goods. There are fundamentally two different classes of goods: in the first, imports and national products are perfect substitutes, but Brazil is not self-sufficient at the going price; in the second, imports have close but not perfect substitutes produced in Brazil. For the latter, imports can be expressed as

$$M = a \left(\frac{p_1}{p_2} \right)^b \left(\frac{p_2}{p_0} \right)^c y^d$$

$P_R = \dfrac{p_1}{p_2} =$ relative price of imported and national commodities

$P_N = \dfrac{p_2}{p_0} =$ price of Brazilian goods of relevant category relative to the general price index

$y =$ demand variable

The elasticity b is the elasticity of imports, subject to the condition that the price of national substitutes is held constant relative to the overall price index. The sum of the own and the cross elasticity, c, can be interpreted as the reaction of imports and national goods. The rationale for putting the second price term in the demand function is to test the hypothesis that only relative prices of imports and close substitutes are relevant to import demand.

Where imported and national products are perfect substitutes, the appropriate price is the price of the national good relative to other national substitutes. An alternative procedure that can be used where internal supply is exogenous, as it probably is for agricultural crops and government industry, is to estimate total demand directly and derive imports as the difference between it and domestic supply. An approximation is an index of domestic output put directly into the import-demand function in place of domestic relative prices. These indices were significant in capital goods, nonmetallic intermediate goods, and wheat, but not in any other category.

In most categories there were problems of multicollinearity, especially among income, relative prices, and the substitution variable. This is not surprising, since during the period of rapid growth in Brazil during the 1950's the capacity to import was stagnant, causing the relative price of imports to rise in all categories. This *was* an incentive for much internal industrial growth but it also led to absurd direct estimates of income elasticities, another reason for choosing these elasticities directly. In making this choice we were guided by international comparisons, budget studies, and our desire to get an upper bound to overcome downward bias in estimated price elasticities.

REGRESSION RESULTS

Table 1 shows some regression results for the principal import categories other than fuel and wheat. These categories contain a mixture of perfect and imperfect substitutes, but the fit of the regressions is fairly good despite the aggregation problem. The relative price of imports, $\frac{P_2}{P_1}$, is negative and significant in all but one case, though the elasticities are smaller than might be expected. The inclusion of an industrial substitute variable helps the nonmetallic intermediate and capital

TABLE 1. REGRESSION RESULTS

Metallic Intermediate

$$[1] \quad M = -1.88 + \underset{(1.12)}{.45}I - \underset{(.38)}{1.08}P_R - \underset{(.32)}{1.43}P_N + \underset{(.35)}{1.3}Y \qquad \begin{aligned} R^2 &= .70 \\ D.W. &= 2.50 \end{aligned}$$

$$[2] \quad M = -2.42 + \underset{(1.14)}{1.62}I - \underset{(.62)}{.99}P_R - \underset{(.33)}{1.67}T_1 + \underset{(.45)}{1.3}Y \qquad \begin{aligned} R^2 &= .66 \\ D.W. &= 2.08 \end{aligned}$$

Nonmetallic Intermediate

$$[3] \quad M = -.02 + \underset{(.50)}{.80}I - \underset{(.23)}{.25}P_M - \underset{(.21)}{.61}T_2 + \underset{(.11)}{1.2}Y \qquad \begin{aligned} R^2 &= .91 \\ D.W. &= 1.99 \end{aligned}$$

Capital Goods

$$[4] \quad M = 3.4 + \underset{(.70)}{2.28}I - \underset{(.30)}{.59}P_R - \underset{(.18)}{1.15}T_1 + \underset{(.29)}{.74}P_C \qquad \begin{aligned} R^2 &= .96 \\ D.W. &= 2.03 \end{aligned}$$
$$\underset{(.34)}{}$$

$$[5] \quad M = .91 + \underset{(.37)}{1.58}I - \underset{(.22)}{1.27}P_R \qquad\qquad\qquad \begin{aligned} R^2 &= .80 \\ D.W. &= 1.75 \end{aligned}$$

Consumer Nondurables

$$[6] \quad M = -5.8 - \underset{(.79)}{1.19}P_R - \underset{(.36)}{.99}P_N + \underset{(.28)}{1.3}Y \qquad\qquad \begin{aligned} R^2 &= .77 \\ D.W. &= .82 \end{aligned}$$

Consumer Durables

$$[7] \quad M = -2.8 - \underset{(.48)}{.69}P_R - \underset{(.30)}{3.73}P_N + \underset{(.52)}{1.8}Y \qquad\qquad \begin{aligned} R^2 &= .88 \\ D.W. &= 1.98 \end{aligned}$$

For equations [1]–[3], [6]–[7], fit statistics are on transformed dependent variable, $\dfrac{M}{Yd}$.

All data in logs, imports in billions of 1953 dollars.
P_R = Price of imports divided by price of Brazilian substitutes.
T_1 = Metallic goods industry.
P_N = Price of Brazilian substitutes divided by general price deflator.
P_M = Price of imports divided by general price deflator.
T_2 = Weighted average of textiles, chemicals, and paper.
P_C = Relative price of final and intermediate goods.
I = Gross fixed investment in billions of 1953 CR$.
Y = GNP in billions of 1953 CR$.
Figures in parentheses are standard errors.

goods sectors, which suggests that a significant portion of imports are direct replacements of national products. In almost all cases it is necessary to use independent information on the income elasticity of demand, since income is so closely correlated with industrial output and relative prices as to make the estimated elasticities absurd.

Intermediate or Producer Goods

The principal determinants of imports of intermediate products have been income, fixed investment, and the growth of national industrial substitutes. Relative prices of imports have not been very important, even in metals. In metallic goods, domestic investment seems to have stimulated domestic production as much as imports. Regression [2] shows the effect of investment on imports when national production is assumed to be constant. But the Brazilian production of metallic goods is closely correlated with investment ($r = 8.1$). Thus, as regression [1] shows, the net effect of investment, after allowing for the stimulus to domestic metal production, is small and insignificant.

The price coefficients in regression [1] suggest that imports and national production are complements rather than substitutes. By its definition, if the coefficient of P_N is negative and greater in absolute value than that of P_R, this implies that the underlying cross-elasticity of imports with respect to national prices also is negative. As domestic metal prices rise, imports fall. This implication is consistent with the specialized character of metal imports. Basic metals that can be produced in Brazil are no longer imported; imports consist of high-quality steels and other metals, such as zinc, copper, and aluminum, that are necessary complements to Brazilian metal goods in many final products.

Unfortunately there is evidence that the direct price coefficients are overestimated. There is little doubt that the demand for imports has been shifting downward since 1963. But the exchange rate has continued to reflect the overall rate of inflation so that relative import prices have remained at their 1963 level. In terms of our first graph, the observation points have been moving back along a line such as P_0 in Figure 1, giving an upward bias to the regression-estimated price elasticity. As a crude check we made a two-point elasticity estimate using as the two points the averages of 1954–1955 and 1962–1963. This gave a +.44. Our conclusion was that relative prices of imports are not a very useful predictor in this category, despite the significant statistic.

For nonmetallic intermediate goods we applied the same general model with a very much better overall fit. Investment is significant both with and without the appropriate domestic industrial index, which is reasonable since the two series are quite independent. Conceivably, investment is acting as a proxy for the overall level of activity, since its fall after 1963 is very important in explaining the steep drop in imports after that date.

The relative price of imports is small and not significant. The data suggest that this is due partly to the difference between the short and long run. Prices rose during the exchange shortage of the 1950's. While this had some short-run effect on imports, it apparently was more important as an incentive for investment in domestic capacity. As the latter came on stream, the same external conditions of price and income caused a drop in imports. Technically the demand curve for imports was falling, and its variance appears to have been too large relative to the movement in relative prices to estimate the price relationship satisfactorily. As a rough measure of the long-run price effect, assuming that the changes in prices "caused" the increase in domestic production that resulted in a decline in imports, we made the same two-point price-elasticity estimate described above for metals. This gave −.83, which though larger than the regression estimate is still small. Relative import prices are apparently not an important factor in the demand for intermediate goods in Brazil. They are insignificant in non-metals, and explain no more than 11 percent of the variation in the estimate for metallic imports between 1954 and 1965.

Capital Goods

The correlations for capital goods are the best of any class. Relative prices, investment, and national production are all significant and have the proper sign. However, one must be careful in using the results. Paralleling what we have seen for metals, the coefficient of investment in regression equation [4] shows the effect on imports of a 1 percent increase in capital formation with domestic industrial production held constant. But there is a close relationship between investment and domestic metal production, so that if we drop the latter variable, we reduce substantially the effect of the former. To use equation [4] in predicting the reaction of imports to investment, one must remember to include the increase in domestic industry derived from that investment. For metals, the net effect of investment on imports was insignificant. Here that is not so. Capacity was not sufficient to supply short-run increases in demand economically, so that investment had a significant direct effect on imports as well as on domestic production.

In the long run, the influence of domestic supply can be seen by comparing import fractions for years of equivalent investment. In 1954, for example, an investment rate of 17 percent required an import component of 34 percent; in 1961 roughly the same rate had only a 24 percent import component.

Turning now to the price estimates, we see a substantial difference between equations [4] and [5], a result of the strong correlation between relative prices and domestic production of substitutes. Domestic industry is built and substitution takes place when imports become more expensive. In equation [5] the price variable acts as a proxy for domestic industry, and its coefficient could be thought of as the long-run price elasticity, whereas equation [4] shows the short-run effect with capacity held constant. This interpretation is confirmed by the two-point price elasticity of -1.38 estimated for 1954–1955 and 1963–1964. Therefore, if one is willing to assign primary cause to the price variable, he could predict that the long-run effect of a 1 percent increase in import prices would be a fall of about 1.3 percent in imports of capital goods.

Another interesting result of the regressions shown in Table 1 is the positive and significant role of P_C, the relative price of final goods. P_C is an index of the relative prices of foreign and Brazilian consumer and intermediate goods. When the index goes up, it means that there is an incentive for import subtsitution requiring investment. The P_C index should therefore be positively related to both investment and imports of investment goods. Thus, changes in relative prices for final goods may simply change the composition of imports in the short run. While imports of the final goods in question may fall, imports of capital equipment to build the substitutes increases.

Consumer Goods

The work on consumer goods is preliminary in that further improvements could be made by disaggregation, and perhaps by application of stock-demand models. For nondurables the fit statistic is misleading, since in the years after 1962 there is almost no relation between the fitted and the actual values. The reason appears to be the 1963 economic downturn, simultaneous with a decline in relative import prices. The data suggest an inward shift in the demand curve due undoubtedly to capacity growth and stagnant demand. When this occurs with falling prices it tends to cause poor fits and to lower the estimated price elasticity. Accordingly, the regression result is substantially less than the long-run elasticity estimated by the same two-point procedure we described earlier. This estimate, which assigns all the effects of all other variables to relative prices alone, is −1.71. To improve the fit and the Durbin Watson of this regression we experimented with various indices of domestic production of consumer nondurables. None added significantly to the explanation. Our choice of an income elasticity of 1.3, which may appear high, was based on the composition of imports, principally luxury fruits, whiskey, drugs, books, and textiles, for which such an elasticity does not seem unreasonable.

The consumer durables regression has a much better fit, though the small size of the price coefficient is suspect. In part this appears to be a result of the small size of this category, which gives great weight to a sudden upturn in automobile imports in 1958 and 1959. In those years average prices rose because of this change. Dropping 1958 from the figures raised the price coefficient to −.78, but it was no longer significant. As an alternative estimate, a simple regression using only P_R gave a price elasticity of −2.6 with an r^2 of .60. This corresponds well with our two-point estimate of −2.99.

Equation [7] implies that national and imported goods are complements, since the underlying cross-elasticity between P_N and imports is negative. This may reflect the fact that a substantial part of the imports in this class are components, such as parts for television sets, refrigerators, and autos.

Fuels and Wheat

Since the remaining two categories, fuels and wheat, are the most homogeneous of our import categories, they can be looked at as a test of the perfect substitute model (Table 2). Even here, however, there is an aggregation problem. Each category is composed of both crude and refined products — crude oil and gasoline, wheat and flour. The substitution process began at the final stage, and this actually increased the demand for imported raw material. As imports of refined products fell, those of crude rose to supply the new refineries. Therefore, to use an industrial-production or price variable in the prediction of imports, one must aggregate across final and intermediate products to capture the reduction in the total value of imports caused by the shift within the category to less expensive crude products.

Aside from the straightforward model using relative internal prices to predict imports implied by this approach, one could conceive of a two-step demand function, with final demand for the refined product being a function of income and price. If Brazilian production of both crude and refined could be thought of as independent of this year's price, imports of refined then follow as the difference between total demand and Brazilian supply, which in turn determines the total need for crude as a proportional input. Again taking Brazilian crude as exogeneous, and converting to value terms, should give an accurate estimate for imports. The basic assumption of this approach, an exogeneous supply, is not unreasonable. Wheat depends on last year's planting and weather conditions, and flour is no longer imported in significant quantities. Fuel production is chiefly in the hands of a government enterprise whose decisions do not appear to be governed by market considerations.

The installation of refining capacity in Brazil lowered the demand for imported refined but increased the demand for crude. There was a net saving in foreign exchange, however, since the derivative of imports with respect to Brazilian refining will be negative whenever $K < 1/1.04$, which was the case throughout the period.

TABLE 2. RESULTS FOR PERFECT SUBSTITUTES

Fuel

$$[1] \; \hat{R} = \underset{(.036)}{.51} + \underset{(.066)}{1.34Y} \qquad \begin{array}{l} R^2 = .97 \\ D.W. = 2.25 \end{array}$$

$$[2] \; R = \underset{(.14)}{.85} + \underset{(.16)}{1.73Y} - \underset{(.13)}{.33P_0} \qquad \begin{array}{l} R^2 = .98 \\ D.W. = 1.55 \end{array}$$

$$[3] \; C = \underset{(.009)}{.009} + \underset{(.13)}{1.04R_B} \qquad \begin{array}{l} R^2 = .998 \\ D.W. = 1.59 \end{array}$$

$$[4] \; M_0 = -\underset{(.08)}{.29} - \underset{(.05)}{.685P_0} + 1.2Y \qquad \begin{array}{l} R^2 = .95 \\ D.W. = 2.39 \end{array}$$

Wheat

$$M = 5.80 + \underset{(.18)}{.29Y} - \underset{(.13)}{.40Q} - \underset{(.17)}{.43P_{WF}} \qquad \begin{array}{l} R^2 = .84 \\ D.W. = 1.31 \end{array}$$

P_0 = Price of fuel relative to GNP deflator.
M = Log imports in million 1953 dollars.
R_B = Brazilian refined in hundred million barrels.
C = Total crude consumed in hundred million barrels.
$\hat{R}$ = Log of total consumption of refined in hundred million barrels.
P_{WF} = Price wheat relative to price of food.
Q = National wheat production.
M_0 = Imports of fuel in billions of 1953 dollars.
For fuel the two-step procedure gives excellent results. The derived demand for imports using equations [1] and [2] is

$$M = P_R(R-R_B) + P_R K (1.04R_B + .009 - C_B)$$

where K is the ratio of the price of crude to refined.
P_R is the price of refined.
R_B is Brazilian refined in barrels.
C_B is Brazilian crude in barrels.
R is consumption of refined in barrels.

In the standard formulation for fuels, there was a high correlation between domestic crude and refined production and domestic prices. Therefore, the best single equation was [4], in which price was the only independent variable. The price coefficient should be interpreted as a long-run elasticity, however, because the close correlations just noted between production and relative prices are more the result of a long-term uptrend in both series than of year-to-year fluctuations. For short-term predictions of imports, equations [1] and [3] should be far more dependable.

For wheat we had to rely on a direct estimation procedure, since no reliable information of Brazilian flour production exists. As in fuels, the price to be used is the price of the product relative to its substitutes, not the relative foreign and national prices. The price elasticity seems reasonable within the range of observations, and alternative estimations gave very similar results. The low elasticity of imports with respect to national supply is a reflection of the fact that about two-thirds of the wheat used in Brazil is imported. If the regression is to be believed (and there is some doubt about the data on national wheat production in the early years), as long as national production grows at more than three-fourths of the rate of income growth, wheat imports will be constant or declining.

SOME IMPLICATIONS

We are now in a position to gather up some results and look at their implications. The overall import elasticities constructed with 1966 weights are:

Aggregate Import Elasticities

Relative price	Income	Investment	Brazilian output	Brazilian prices
−.63	+1.18	+.85	−.77	−.31

To get the output elasticity we assumed equal growth in all domestic substitution indices, an approximation that can be made more interesting by simulation with different rates for each sector. For example, our fuel equations tell us that an increase in output of 1 percent from 1966 levels will reduce the import of fuel products by approximately U.S.$4 million or 1.7 percent. The investment elasticity was calculated using equation [5] and therefore gives the effect on imports of a 1 percent increase in investment, holding domestic industry constant.

A more fruitful way to use the regression results is to project the total import bill, or alternatively the yearly growth rate of imports, under different assumptions about the growth of income, prices, and domestic substitutes. To construct Table 3 we calculated the five-year compound growth rates for income, prices, and substitutes, applied these to 1966 levels, and solved the resulting set of equations for imports by category in 1971. The summation across all imports gave us the basis for the average yearly growth rates shown in Table 3. The number in the top left-hand corner of the table, for example, predicts that imports will grow at a yearly rate of 7.8 percent if income and domestic substitutes grow by 5 percent per year to 1971 and relative prices fall by 1 percent per year.

Table 3 clearly shows the sensitivity of imports to the rate of growth of the economy. Under our assumption about the investment rate, raising income growth from 5 to 6 percent means a 2 percent increase in the growth of imports. Only partly off-

TABLE 3. HYPOTHETICAL YEARLY GROWTH RATES
OF IMPORTS — 1967–1971 [a]
(percent)

Yearly growth in income	*Change in Relative prices*	*Yearly growth of domestic substitutes*			
		5	6	7	8
	−1	7.8	7.0	6.3	5.5
5	0	7.5	6.8	6.0	5.1
	+1	7.3	6.6	5.7	4.9
	−1	9.8	9.1	8.4	7.7
6	0	9.6	8.9	8.2	7.4
	+1	9.5	8.7	8.0	7.1
	−1	10.9	10.2	9.5	8.8
7	0	10.7	10.0	9.2	8.5
	+1	10.5	9.8	9.0	8.2

[a] The investment growth rate is assumed to be equal to the rate of growth in income (capital-output ratio constant). Wheat production is assumed to grow at a constant 3 percent per year. All growth rates are instantaneous, that is, the import growth-rate equals the difference between logs of imports in 1971 and 1966 divided by five.

setting this, each 1 percent increase in domestic industry reduces mport growth by .7 percent. By looking down the diagonals, one can see that at equal growth rates of domestic capacity and income there will be tendency toward increasing imbalance in the foreign sector, which is no more than a reflection of the difference between the aggregate elasticity of domestic substitutes and the sum of the income and investment elasticities. If Brazil chooses a "slow growth" path of 5 percent per year, her domestic industry will probably be growing at around 6 percent; at a more dynamic rate of 6 percent, the industrial sector, which will lead the advance if the past is any indication, will undoubtedly have to reach 8 percent annual growth. Either way, imports will be growing faster than the expected rate of growth of exports.[3] In the past, Brazil managed to achieve a high rate of growth of income while holding imports virtually constant by both raising relative prices and having domestic substitutes growing at much higher rates than we have used in the simulation. Brazilian production of crude grew at 21 percent per year, refined at 9 percent, chemicals, textiles, and paper at about 12 percent, and metals at 7 percent.[4] Our first simulation result suggests that some equivalent development strategy will have to be devised for the future to bring foreign exchange resources into balance with import demands.

Another conclusion emerging from Table 3 and the preceding analysis is that the effect of relative prices, while significant, is small. This is not statistical illusion. The simultaneous appearance in the last years of the sample of rising or constant relative import prices and falling demand should offset whatever bias is present in earlier years. To check we measured the total long-run effect of price changes on imports by arbitrarily assigning all the variation in the import ratio $(\frac{M}{Y})$ to changes in relative prices; the resulting overall price elasticity was still less than one.[5]

The reason for this historic insensitivity to relative prices is not difficult to find. The bulk of Brazilian imports is producer goods, either capital or intermediate. Given the inflationary environment it is possible to pass along price increases, so demand curves for such goods are probably inelastic over the relevant ranges. Also, the effort to reduce imports by domestic production usually meant expanding imports of some input to the newly produced good. Increasing Brazilian oil refining

[3] The Brazilian government recently predicted this export growth to be around 5 percent. Government of Brazil, Ministry of Planning, *Plano Decenal*, I, Part 1 (Rio de Janeiro, 1967), p. 57.

[4] Growth rates were calculated over the following years: crude, 1957–1963; refined, 1956–1965; nonmetals, 1955–1963; metals, 1953–1964.

[5] The estimator for each category was the difference in the logs of the dependent variable divided by the difference in the logs of relative prices. 1966 weights were used for aggregation, and the final elasticity was −.92.

necessitated greater imports of crude. Building domestic productive capacity meant increased imports of capital goods. Thus, reducing the import coefficient is a lengthy process, but if, while it takes place, import prices are rising rapidly (an average of 3.75 percent per year over 1954–1963), the result is going to be a low price elasticity for imports, however measured.

To put it another way, Brazil can reduce its import bill three and one-half times as much by raising the domestic output of metal goods, chemicals, and oil by 1 percent as it can by raising the relative cost of imports by the same proportion. This would be partly offset by increases in the imports of raw materials and capital goods needed to produce this extra output. Needless to say, the appropriate policy to deal with a balance-of-payments deficit depends on the relative cost of export expansion, import substitution or changes in relative prices, or reduced overall growth. Our result is no more than an explicit estimate of the trade-off between the last three alternatives.

STATISTICAL APPENDIX

Since the data used in the regression analysis are not generally available outside Brazil, and since the price and tariff indices are new, both are given in the five tables which follow this Appendix. Data on imports were taken from a sample maintained by the Statistical Laboratory of the Brazilian Census Bureau (IBGE). This sample has a coverage varying from 94 percent to 83 percent and is complete for wheat and fuel.

In constructing a price index for imports we were faced with a fundamental conceptual problem: which price to use, that of potential or that of actual imports. Theoretically, in an aggregate import class, there may be some goods which are not imported at today's relative prices. Tomorrow their price may fall just far enough so that they start being imported. If their price is above the average of their import category, this will result in a rise in the average price index constructed using actual imports. If one had the data, the theoretically proper price index for an import would use the total available world supply of goods, weighted by the proportion of total Brazilian income spent on that good. Since we did not have such data, we decided to use the price of goods actually imported rather than to try to approximate the theoretically more attractive index. This can be justified on two grounds. First, to do such an approximation one is forced to assume that the dollar prices of all such goods are constant, since one has no way of collecting price information on such a variety of goods. But this is a bad assumption, for prices of raw materials have fallen by as much as 35 percent, and manufactures have risen by the same amount since 1953.

The second justification for basing our prices on actual, not potential, imports is that there is not much chance that new goods, once price differentials had caused them not to be imported, would become competitive over the years of our investigation. Imports in every class became steadily more, not less, expensive as a result of the exchange shortage. The average price of imports more than doubled relative to the general price index, so this source of bias should not be too significant. The only instance where this is not so is automobiles. In 1958 and 1959 a prohibitive import classification was replaced by relatively lower tariff protection and there was a sudden burst of importation of cars which raised the average dollar price of consumer durables.

Given the fundamental decision to base our price indices on actual rather than potential imports, we had three components to measure: the exchange rate, the tariff rate, and the dollar price index. The first and last were taken directly from the worksheets of the Statistical Laboratory of the Brazilian Census Bureau.

Tariff Rates. Tariff rates, however, presented a problem. Since tariff collections are shown only according to a noncomparable classification of imports, an averaging procedure of the published tariffs on the individual products within each import category [1] became necessary. Clark and Weisskoff [2] made a complete record of the

---

[1] For tariff rates see Abilio Corrêa, Lahire Nobre, J. C. Magalhães, *Manual de Atualização de Tarifa das Alfândegas* (Rio de Janeiro, 1964).

[2] Paul Clark and Richard Weisskoff, "Import Demands and Import

goods in the IBGE sample by their tariff code classification, and then recorded the tariff rate for each one. For any import item with more than one good and consequently more than one tariff rate, they took a simple average to get a single tariff rate. For the nine import categories, the average tariff rate was then defined as the weighted average of tariff rates for the products in the class, the weighting being according to share of imports in 1962. This estimate had to be adjusted for exemptions. Rubber, wheat, and coal paid no tariffs because national production is still insufficient to satisfy demand.[3] Another group of products — lead, asbestos, aluminum — are exempt provided a certain proportion of national production is used along with the imported product.[4] Still a third broad category of goods, chiefly capital goods imported by state enterprises or judged to be beneficial to Brazil, was granted special exemption from tariff payment. To adjust the published rate for exemptions, I reclassified the IBGE sample into the tariff code and calculated estimated collections by section. Where there were wide divergences stemming from this cause, such as in the capital goods and metal sections 15–17, the tariff was reduced proportionally to make 1962 estimated and actual collections equal.

After this adjustment was made, hypothetical tariff collections were still far too high. One reason for this lay in the averaging procedure used for the import items with more than one good and more than one tariff rate. What was needed was a weighted rather than a simple average of the several tariff rates included, because it generally is the case that high tariff levels discourage imports. Since our index is to be the price of goods actually imported, a simple average overstates the level of tariff protection. Wherever the adjustment between the simple and the weighted average tariff appeared to change the overall average significantly, I used a

Policies in Brazil," (AID, Feb. 1967) and "Technical Appendix A" (AID, Sept. 19, 1966).

[3] See the testimony of Dr. Mangia in Câmara dos Deputados, *"Comissão Parlamentar de Inquérito para investigar os resultados da reforma pela Lei No. 3.244"* (Brasilia, April 20, 1966), p. 27.

[4] See notes 39 and 162 in the Tariff Manual.

weighted average, based on the proportion of foreign exchange bought for each product for the year 1962.[5]

When these correction procedures were complete and all legal changes in tariff rates had been incorporated, I applied the new rates to actual tariff collections for 1958, 1962, and 1965. For both the first and the last year a still substantial discrepancy in section 17 (transportation equipment) had to be adjusted, after which estimated and actual collections differed by less than 5 percent for all three years. Furthermore, the average rate in each class did not appear to show too much deviation over time, and it became feasible to make a linear interpolation of the observed rates for 1958, 1962, and 1965 rather than recalculate the actual average for the intervening years. Finally, for each year the average tariff rate was adjusted downward by the difference between total estimated and total actual collections.

Port Charges and Other Additional Taxes. As Paul Clark has pointed out,[6] the importer is faced with a number of additional direct charges: 5 percent on CIF value for the *taxa de despacho aduaneiro*, 5 percent on CIF value for the port assessment tax, 2 percent on CIF value for the dispatcher's commission, 5 percent of net ocean freight charges for the merchant marine improvement tax, and 1 percent on customs charges as a warehousing fee. If one assumes that freight costs about 20 percent of the CIF value of the import, then the total extras amount to 13 percent of CIF value plus 1 percent of tariff charges. However, these extras cannot simply be added to average tariffs because they are not charged to goods exempt from tariff payments.[7] As an estimate I reduced the 13 percent by the proportion of tariff-paying goods to total imports in each class and then added 1 percent of the previously determined average tariff rate. These total taxes were then added to the adjusted average tariff and the total converted to cruzeiros using the

[5] The difficulty with this weighting procedure is that there are no data of imports by tariff classification. However, I approximated this by observing the Certificado de Cobertura Cambial (CCC) purchases for each item and weighting accordingly.

[6] Clark, "Import Demand," p. B2.

[7] Interview with Dr. Joaquim Mangia.

fiscal rate for each year. For each class this calculation gives the number of cruzeiros per dollar that must be paid in import taxes to buy one dollar of exchange.

Financial Charges. From 1961 until mid 1965, the Superintendencia de Moeda e Crédito (SUMOC) required importers to make an advance deposit whose cost in terms of interest forgone must be added into the other importation costs. I relied here upon the work of the Foreign Trade Sector of the Escritorio de Pesquisa Econômica Aplicada (EPEA), except for the year 1965 when they appear to have seriously understated the interest cost.

The total desagios per dollar are 1961, 39.52; 1962, 105.66; 1963, 192.65; 1964, 404.74; 1965, 300.16.[8]

Brazilian Price Indices. The Brazilian price indices used are intended to represent the price movements of Brazilian goods capable of being substituted for imports. They are subject to at least two objections on this score, the very rough correspondence between the composition of the imports in any class and the domestic index, and the substantial imported component influencing or included in many domestic price indices. Where these objections hold, the final price index will not show the divergence between domestic and imported prices it is intended to measure. In any case, the indices were constructed using various indices from the *Conjuntura Econômica.* In every case the weighting was according to the percentage of the corresponding imported good in the IBGE sample in 1962.

The figure for nondurable consumer goods is a weighted aver-

[8] For 1965 I assumed that the financial charge for advance deposits must have risen at the same rate as the implicit deflator, that is, at an annual rate of 50 percent. This has to be adjusted for the removal of the system at the end of October 1965, and for the change in the advance deposit requirement from an average of 76 percent in 1964 to 50 percent in 1965. I took the desagio for 1964, Cr$75.47, inflated by 1.5 for the rise in the cost of living, deflated it by .667 for the lowering of the deposit requirement, and deflated it again by .83 to reflect the cancellation of the system before the end of the year. This gives Cr$146.00, to which I added the estimated *encargo financeiro* of Cr$154.16 to give the result shown above.

age of thirteen subindices, including drugs, textiles, books, and various foods.

The figure for durable consumer goods is Index 5 (Furniture and Utensil) from the Guanabara cost-of-living index.

The fuels figure is a weighted average of the national prices of coal, gasoline, and oil.

Metallic intermediate goods is a weighted average of seven metal indices.

Nonmetallic intermediate goods is a weighted average of thirteen products including paper, sulfur, caustic soda, grains, rubber, leather, and alcohol.

Construction materials is Index 64 from the *Conjuntura Econômica*.

The index for all other capital goods is Index 63 (metals and metal products) from the *Conjuntura Econômica*.

APPENDIX TABLE 1. TARIFF AND FINAL EFFECTIVE
EXCHANGE RATES
(Cr per US$)

| Year | Consumer goods | | | | Intermediate goods | | | | | |
| | Nondurable | | Durable | | Fuels[a] | | Metallic | | Nonmetallic | |
	T^b	E^c	T^b	E^c	T^b	E^c	T^b	E^c	T	E
1953		20.6		19.1		18.8		18.9		19.3
1954		36.4		45.2		28.8		37.2		36.8
1955		49.2		72.0		46.7		56.7		50.4
1956		61.2		95.7		49.2		74.7		64.6
1957		67.7		97.6		52.4		68.2		56.8
1958	36.7	136.8	73.9	200.7	50.6	113.1	18.8	132.8	27.9	127.6
1959	54.1	216.1	111.8	281.8	76.5	179.4	21.1	207.8	33.0	178.9
1960	55.1	250.4	109.6	331.7	75.0	182.6	24.3	223.0	39.0	205.9
1961	149.1	390.2	191.1	448.6	103.9	313.3	52.6	290.9	87.0	298.9
1962	212.3	572.3	314.7	664.8	142.5	476.5	100.5	442.5	170.2	509.6
1963	349.3	901.0	494.7	1,052.7	203.5	697.6	167.7	675.8	274.8	795.3
1964	698.8	1,710.6	967.8	1,975.7	376.4	1,360.7	332.9	1,240.6	532.7	1,465.1
1965	816.5	2,608.1	1,256.2	3,079.5	646.3	2,442.5	459.1	2,185.1	685.9	2,424.1

APPENDIX TABLE 1. TARIFF AND FINAL EFFECTIVE
EXCHANGE RATES—(Continued)
(Cr per US$)

Year	Construction materials		Agriculture		Capital goods				Wheat	
					Industry		Transportation			
	Tᵇ	Eᶜ	Tᵇ	Eᶜ	Tᵇ	Eᶜ	Tᵇ	Eᶜ	Tᵇ	Eᶜ
1953		18.9		19.0		18.9		19.0		18.8
1954		34.2		31.2		32.6		46.0		24.5
1955		45.0		46.4		45.7		50.9		25.5
1956		59.3		63.0		59.9		64.7		30.8
1957		56.7		56.8		55.7		63.1		51.7
1958	34.8	116.5	14.1	96.0	21.0	92.6	16.1	93.4		64.3
1959	36.6	158.0	17.0	152.3	23.6	127.2	15.8	104.8		99.7
1960	44.7	181.8	18.4	177.5	28.9	146.0	18.8	149.8		100.0
1961	84.5	265.7	45.7	234.8	58.3	243.4	63.0	236.0		222.1
1962	155.5	515.0	89.9	419.8	109.9	449.9	134.4	509.5		357.6
1963	246.1	784.9	151.2	660.2	173.9	707.5	221.4	755.0		560.6
1964	465.0	1,443.4	303.4	1,125.2	329.0	1,329.4	404.6	1,293.3		1,110.6
1965	719.1	2,481.9	354.2	2,108.6	474.0	2,183.5	636.5	2,259.4		1,866.6

ᵃ includes gas tax.
ᵇ T = average tariff in Cr$ per U.S.$. See appendix text for aggregation procedure.
ᶜ E = average exchange rate + tariff + financial and port charges. Appendix text describes the derivation of each component.

APPENDIX TABLE 2. PRICE INDEX OF IMPORTED GOODS

Year	Consumer Goods		Intermediate Goods			Capital Goods		Capital Goods			Wheat	Total
	Non-durable	Durable	Fuel	Metallic	Non-metallic	Construction	Agriculture	Industry	Transportation	Aggregate capital		
1953	100.0	100.0	100.0	100.0	100.0	100.0	100.0	100.0	100.0	100.0	100.0	100.0
1954	97.0	91.6	91.7	94.3	93.6	91.0	97.5	105.4	81.4	96.6	80.4	92.9
1955	89.2	93.8	91.7	103.7	97.0	94.0	99.3	104.6	83.4	97.5	76.0	93.6
1956	79.5	82.6	98.9	114.4	93.0	114.0	94.7	98.1	71.4	90.5	68.1	90.8
1957	91.0	87.6	103.8	99.6	92.1	131.8	104.8	103.6	70.8	93.6	65.1	92.2
1958	69.3	87.1	95.9	82.2	84.7	107.9	100.1	112.6	63.2	90.0	66.7	86.4
1959	63.5	64.7	89.7	69.6	78.9	105.8	86.1	119.1	53.5	84.2	64.6	80.3
1960	59.9	78.7	81.6	98.0	75.8	93.8	95.3	107.4	94.0	102.4	63.3	83.7
1961	57.8	61.0	77.3	90.1	74.8	115.4	109.2	104.3	95.8	89.1	66.6	79.6
1962	60.5	66.6	72.0	80.0	73.5	131.1	110.6	114.7	128.3	115.5	66.1	88.1
1963	63.2	72.7	70.1	69.9	74.8	65.8	102.6	119.4	108.0	104.5	67.8	83.6
1964	63.4	96.3	66.3	77.8	75.7	122.9	119.6	128.4	111.3	121.8	72.3	90.5
1965	58.2	101.8	64.8	91.7	78.8	114.2	129.3	138.9	120.0	129.3	65.1	93.4

APPENDIX TABLE 3. RELATIVE PRICES[a]

(1953 = 100)

Year	Consumer Goods		Intermediate Goods			Aggregates				
	Non-durable	Durable	Fuel[b]	Metallic	Non-metallic	Consumer goods	Capital goods	Intermediate goods	Wheat	Total
1953	100.0	100.0	100.0	100.0	100.0	100.0	100.0	100.0	100.0	100.0
1954	137.4	164.1	108.3	141.3	142.4	142.0	143.3	126.3	87.8	129.7
1955	147.7	191.2	121.3	190.6	168.6	155.9	168.1	148.9	65.9	147.7
1956	142.3	202.9	122.9	186.7	167.5	153.6	159.9	152.7	55.2	144.9
1957	166.9	197.2	109.8	175.1	132.1	172.6	145.9	131.8	87.8	135.3
1958	184.5	373.6	197.6	185.8	220.8	220.3	163.2	209.4	99.5	180.3
1959	187.1	263.7	201.1	160.9	153.7	209.7	144.2	193.6	148.7	170.7
1960	162.1	270.1	171.8	210.3	147.2	180.6	196.1	166.3	145.7	176.5
1961	169.2	222.1	158.1	187.9	160.6	179.1	242.8	156.9	163.9	178.8
1962	176.2	245.0	177.6	143.4	179.8	188.3	334.0	160.0	261.5	240.2
1963	182.3	220.1	140.5	109.2	152.0	207.3	239.9	126.3	167.9	180.3
1964	155.0	268.8	134.8	104.3	149.7	169.2	289.5	134.2	182.5	201.8
1965	140.9	270.9	126.4	127.3	156.6	155.1	306.3	131.4	143.3	201.8

[a] Relative Price = Effective exchange rate times price index of imports relative to price index of comparable Brazilian goods.
[b] includes gas tax.

APPENDIX TABLE 4. VALUES AND INDICES OF
VALUE OF IMPORTS
(million 1953 US$)

Year	Consumer goods				Fuel	Index	Intermediate goods			
	Nondurable	Index	Durable	Index			Metallic	Index	Nonmetallic	Index
1953	105.5	100.0	27.9	100.0	244.4	100.0	80.9	100.0	194.0	100.0
1954	123.9	117.4	41.4	148.4	290.4	118.8	152.2	188.1	330.1	170.2
1955	115.9	109.9	23.8	85.3	298.0	121.9	77.1	95.3	257.7	132.8
1956	119.4	113.2	23.8	85.3	297.3	121.6	84.6	104.6	286.5	147.7
1957	114.6	108.6	31.5	112.9	271.0	110.9	109.3	135.1	295.8	152.5
1958	85.1	80.7	35.4	126.9	298.0	121.9	81.8	101.1	279.0	143.8
1959	82.7	78.4	40.8	146.2	288.3	118.0	84.6	104.6	294.0	151.5
1960	105.5	100.0	25.0	89.6	321.8	131.7	106.9	132.1	343.4	177.0
1961	118.9	112.7	35.2	126.2	324.2	132.7	118.3	146.2	354.9	182.9
1962	137.2	130.0	29.0	103.9	334.3	136.8	140.3	173.4	392.9	202.5
1963	152.4	144.5	33.7	120.8	346.2	141.7	218.0	269.5	409.7	211.1
1964	143.2	135.7	17.8	63.8	363.3	148.6	121.3	149.9	318.0	163.9
1965	141.6	134.2	16.1	57.7	327.5	134.0	117.1	144.7	304.6	157.0

APPENDIX TABLE 4. VALUES AND INDICES OF
VALUE$ OF IMPORTS—(Continued)
(million 1953 US$)

Year	Construction materials	Index	Agriculture	Index	Capital goods			
					Industry	Index	Transport	Index
1953	72.5	100.0	46.0	100.0	245.5	100.0	114.2	100.0
1954	87.9	121.2	108.0	234.8	273.8	111.5	152.3	133.4
1955	51.1	70.5	45.6	99.1	200.0	81.5	135.4	118.6
1956	21.1	29.1	44.2	96.0	178.3	72.6	146.9	128.6
1957	28.8	39.7	71.3	155.0	255.3	104.0	291.8	255.5
1958	29.2	40.3	57.4	124.8	224.0	91.2	341.8	299.3
1959	40.8	56.3	35.9	78.0	253.0	103.1	445.6	390.2
1960	42.3	58.3	84.7	184.1	239.1	97.4	246.1	215.5
1961	61.9	85.4	57.5	125.0	322.1	131.2	142.1	124.4
1962	35.0	48.3	47.7	103.7	312.0	127.1	86.4	75.7
1963	92.7	127.9	45.9	99.8	248.2	101.1	85.6	75.0
1964	23.8	32.8	35.3	76.7	176.5	71.9	61.8	54.1
1965	26.4	36.4	32.1	69.8	133.6	54.4	35.4	31.0

APPENDIX TABLE 5. IMPORTS BY MAJOR CATEGORIES
(values in million 1953 US$)

Year	Consumer goods			Intermediate goods			Capital goods			Wheat & flour			Total import value
	Values	Quantum index	% total import value	Values	Quantum index	% total import value	Values	Quantum index	% total import value	Values	Quantum index	% total import value	
1953	133.4	100.0	10.1	519.2	100.0	39.4	478.2	100.0	36.3	185.7	100.0	14.1	1316.6
1954	165.3	123.9	9.5	766.7	147.6	43.9	622.0	130.1	35.6	192.4	103.6	11.0	1746.4
1955	139.7	104.7	9.9	627.5	120.8	44.4	432.1	90.4	30.6	212.8	114.6	15.1	1412.1
1956	143.2	107.3	10.4	667.7	128.6	48.7	390.5	81.7	28.5	169.2	91.1	12.4	1370.6
1957	146.1	109.5	8.9	674.8	129.9	41.3	647.2	135.3	39.6	165.2	88.9	10.3	1633.3
1958	120.5	90.3	7.5	658.6	126.8	41.0	652.4	136.4	40.6	174.2	93.8	10.8	1605.7
1959	123.5	92.6	7.0	670.4	129.1	37.8	775.3	162.1	43.8	202.7	109.1	11.4	1771.9
1960	130.5	97.8	7.5	773.3	148.9	44.4	612.2	128.0	35.1	225.6	121.5	12.9	1741.6
1961	154.1	115.5	8.8	798.4	153.7	45.7	583.6	122.0	33.4	209.6	112.9	12.0	1745.7
1962	166.2	124.6	9.5	866.5	165.1	49.3	481.1	100.6	27.4	244.5	131.6	13.9	1758.3
1963	186.1	139.5	9.9	974.7	185.6	51.9	472.4	98.8	25.2	243.1	130.9	13.0	1876.3
1964	161.0	120.7	10.4	803.6	153.1	51.8	297.4	62.2	19.1	291.5	156.9	18.7	1553.5
1965	157.7	118.2	11.7	750.5	143.1	55.7	227.5	47.6	16.9	210.2	113.2	15.7	1345.9

Part IV

CHAPTER 11

A Retrospect Over
Brazilian Development Plans

Roberto de Oliveira Campos

The purpose of this essay is to describe, and insofar as is feasible to appraise, Brazilian planning efforts in the postwar period. There has been a steady expansion in the area covered by planning, and increasing sophistication in the application of techniques. But though formulation has remained inadequate, the gravest difficulties have occurred in implementation, which has been spotty and discontinuous. Development planning has certainly not been very successful in preserving political stability and administrative continuity, and has been enormously hindered by the socially restless and unstable political environment that has been part and parcel of Brazilian development in the last decade.

Throughout this study the word "planning" will be used rather loosely to cover both sectoral micro-planning and more integrated macro-economic planning. It would be indeed desirable to establish a stricter terminology. By degree of increasing concreteness, we might perhaps distinguish between a mere declaration of principles, a development program, and a development plan. For the first, there would be only a broad statement of development strategy and goals. A development program would encompass, in addition to definition of goals, assignment of sectoral or regional priorities and the formulation of incentives and disincentive policies related to the chosen priorities. A development plan would build on these elements and go further by specifying a time schedule for implementation, by designating a chosen agent (government or private enterprise), and by allocating financial and material resources. The word "project" would be reserved for operational detailing of programs or plans.

A national development program can be complemented by partial plans (state, regional, or sectoral) and, of course, would have to be implemented by individual projects. A national or comprehensive development plan, satisfying the foregoing definitional conventions, would require institutional arrangements closely approaching an authoritarian central-planning framework, and would accordingly be more easily attained, using David Apter's terminology, in societies of the autocratic or mobilization model than in societies of the reconciliation or consensual model.[1]

Desirable as those semantic refinements might be, current practice in Brazil is to use the word "plan" to cover a wide array of disquisitions, ranging from project-detailed sectoral plans to rather vague listings of objectives. A notable exception was the Programa de Ação Econômica do Govêrno (PAEG), drawn up in 1964 as the emergency program of the Castello Branco government, which refrained from using "plan" terminology, precisely because of the precarious quantifications of targets and the limited area of coverage.

THE PITFALLS OF BRAZILIAN PLANNING EXPERIENCE

Although implementation of successive plans in Brazil has been volatile and discontinuous, there has been continuity in the effort to formulate plans at national and regional levels. Starting with very limited coverage — a few key areas of government expenditure — their scope has gradually been expanded to encompass sectoral planning of industry, in which the main agent was private initiative, as well as macro-economic aspects, such as monetary, fiscal, and exchange policies.

[1] See David Apter, *The Politics of Modernization* (Chicago: University of Chicago Press, 1965).

Strongly voiced opposition to the idea of planning as being harmful to capitalistic development or involving socialist and authoritarian connotations subsided to the extent that it became politically imperative to pay at least lip service to planning schemes. *Planejamento*, as a catchword, became something of a mystique, looked upon with a mixture of eagerness and naiveté. Thus Juscelino Kubitschek (1956–1961) reaped considerable political dividends from his Programa de Metas; Jânio Quadros was led to establish a Planning Commission in May 1961; "Jango" Goulart sought to win respectability with business groups and the middle class through his Plano Trienal, only to abandon it listlessly when political results seemed unrewarding.

The revolution of March 1964, under President Castello Branco, carried the process further by a total commitment to the idea of planning as an instrument of rationalizing governmental action and of establishing a reasonable degree of administrative coherence and continuity. The debate on the relevance of planning in a context of inadequate statistics, political instability, and unreliable forecasting is thus largely confined to a narrow circle of liberal economists or traditionalist business groups, while at all governmental levels, both federal and state, there is formalistic and uncritical acceptance of the need for planning. This is true though the bureaucratic implementation mechanism is hardly adequate, and the possibility of obtaining political consensus is usually confined to broad objectives that do not imply a valid operational commitment by the political parties.

It might be well at this point to glance at the main obstacles and objectives to meaningful plan formulation and implementation. Those difficulties fall into three groups: ideological, technical, and institutional.

The Ideological Debate

The ideological controversy — abated nowadays but pursued in earnest during most of the postwar period — centered on the compatibility of comprehensive or overall planning with capitalist dynamics based on private enterprise and the market economy on the one hand, and the process of democratic political bargaining on the other. It is clear that the existence of incompatibilities is a function of the comprehensiveness of the planning, of the methods for resource allocation, and of the nature of the implementation machinery. In political democracies — and this is true also of authoritarian regimes with a strong private sector — even the most comprehensive national plans are merely indicative so far as the business sector is concerned, and often coordinating rather than mandatory in relation to state or regional subdivisions.

Contrary to what happens under socialist regimes, planning in both developed and developing countries of the Western world suffers severe constraints deriving from reliance on private enterprise for the bulk of economic activity, consumer sovereignty and nonregimentation of labor, and formulation of policy by compromise and political bargain rather than by the normative power of a central planning authority.

While there are limitations on the degree of planning consistent with the preservation of a nonsocialist pattern of growth, the resort to planning need not necessarily betray, as some Brazilian liberals would have it, a perverse socialist bent. Planning, in a loose sense, is in itself politically neutral. It can open the door for socialization, by fostering excessive government control and orientation of economic life. But it can also be used to strengthen private initiative — by replacing spotty and disruptive government intervention with purposeful policies, by clarifying the respective fields of action of government and private initiative, and by indicating overall targets of growth and establishing incentives for entrepreneurial action. Much of the debate in Brazil between the "interventionists" and the "liberals" on the need for and the dangers of planning — the interventionists supposedly authoritarian and the liberals true democrats — carries little meaning *in abstracto* and becomes relevant only in the light of ideological commitment and operating methods. Practically all of the recent plans (the Plano Trienal of the Goulart regime, which might be suspected of leftist-socialist leanings, is no exception) have laid emphasis on strengthening the private sector, and since there is no compulsory discipline of implementation, the interventionist argument carries little weight. In fact, such disruptive "socializing" interventions as have occurred in the last few years though enlargement of the area of governmental operation well beyond the managerial capabilities of the bureaucracy occurred in spite of, rather than because of, the intervention of the planners.

The Technical Factors

Perhaps more relevant to the appraisal of Brazilian planning efforts since the beginning of World War II is a review of the formidable technical problems that bedevil the planners. These difficulties are, of course, common to all developing countries and, so far as the foreign trade sector is concerned, to any form of planning in an open economy; but they are particularly relevant in the Brazilian context. A cursory listing of these obstacles would include:

(1) statistical deficiencies, of such fundamental data as employment figures, investment of the private sector, and interindustry relations;

(2) scarcity of experienced planners;

(3) the large sige of the agricultural sector, in which planning is difficult because of the proliferation of small units, not to mention weather and climatic factors; and

(4) the importance of the foreign sector (exports and capital inflow), which is subject to sharp fluctuations, particularly in the case of trade, because of the dependence on a narrow range of price-unstable exports.

The Institutional Problems

The institutional obstacles to comprehensive national planning are:

(1) The existence of autonomous political subdivisions. When those units have substantial financial and economic weight of their own, as well as the capacity to raise investment funds by taxes or borrowing, it is hardly possible to subject them to the constraints of central planning. The only practical alternative is to try to coordinate federal with regional plans.

(2) The inadequacy of the implementation machinery. Though plans are conceived by technicians, they have to be implemented through the bureaucratic machinery, which in Brazil partakes of the nature of the "prismatic" bureaucracy,

bent on achieving status rather than performance, and does not easily comply with the rational goals of the Weberian Western bureaucracy, with its rational approach and specialized structures.[2]

(3) Lack of consensus-building political machinery. Afflicted by personalism and factionalism, the traditional political parties proved incapable of the consensus-building effort needed to create a political commitment to specific planning goals, and a fortiori to the continuous implementation of the planning goals. After the 1964 revolution, two measures were taken for institutional reform: first, the abolition of the traditional personalist and factionalist parties and their replacement by a national two-party system, which would presumably render easier the achievement of party discipline in support of government plans or programs; second, the revocation of the power of Congress to increase budget expenditures, which had made any consistent financial planning impossible. The latter measure was complemented by the constitutional requirement of submission by the Executive to Congress of multi-year investment budgets.

(4) Political instability. Given the fact that, for lack of consensus-building machinery, plans represent little more than a personal commitment of the chief executive, the instability of leadership plays havoc with planning efforts. From 1961 to 1966 there were no less than four presidents — Quadros, Goulart, Castello Branco, and Costa e Silva — each succession involving substantial changes not so much in general goals as in specific priorities and techniques of implementation. Some economists and social scientists express utter skepticism at the relevance of planning efforts in an unstable political context, but others recommend a more limited planning approach built on "islands of rationality."[3]

[2] Fred Riggs, *Administration in Developing Countries, The Theory of the Prismatic Society* (Boston: Houghton-Mifflin, 1964).

[3] See Robert T. Daland, *Brazilian Planning* (Chapel Hill: University of North Carolina Press, 1967), p. 216; also Albert Hirschman, *Journeys Toward Progress* (New York: Twentieth Century Fund, 1963), chap. 4.

EARLY ATTEMPTS

The first planning efforts in Brazil date from World War II, and were prompted mainly by the shortages and bottlenecks attending the war economy. International cooperation was mobilized chiefly to improve the transportation system and ease access to raw materials. The focus of planning efforts was then the newly created Departamento Administrativo do Serviço Público (DASP); a number of administrative technicians there had received training in public administration and budgeting, several being sent abroad, notably to the United States, for special studies in administrative techniques. The first three investment plans prepared in Brazil — the Plano Qüinqüenal de Obras e Reaparelhamento da Defesa Nacional (1942), the Plano de Obras (1943), and the SALTE Plan (1946–1950) — had their origin in ideas of the DASP technicians. During the war period, international cooperation was also resorted to for limited planning efforts. These were the Taub Mission in 1942, a group of engineers who drew up a 10-year investment priority program that never materialized; and the American Technical Mission (Cooke Mission) in 1943, which made recommendations for sectoral development of transport, fuel, textiles and minerals, chemicals, and education, without quantification of the required investments.

The 1946 Constitution, written in terms of political and economic liberalism as a reaction against the Vargas regime, makes no mention of planning, but the seeds of regional planning were planted through the earmarking of 3 percent of federal tax revenues for the economic development of the Amazon and an equivalent amount for investment in the depressed areas of the Northeast.

The SALTE Plan, drawn up during 1946 and 1947 and presented to Congress by President Dutra in 1948, was by far the most meaningful of these efforts, but even so it was little more than a listing of government expenditures in four fields — health, food supply, transport, and energy. Approved by Congress in 1950, the SALTE Plan had only spotty implementation.

The first approach to macro-economic policy formulation is traceable to the Abbink Mission (Joint Brazil-United States Technical Commission). The U.S. advisors were led by John

Abbink, whose Brazilian counterpart was Octávio Gouveia de Bulhões (Finance Minister of the Castello Branco Government). By the time the Abbink Mission began its work (1948) there was increasing awareness of the problem of inflation as well as of balance-of-payments pressures. Policy recommendations were drawn on both counts, together with proposals for railroad rehabilitation and tariff reform.[4]

THE "BOTTLENECK" APPROACH

Of much greater significance for the history of Brazilian planning was the work of the Joint Brazil-United States Development Commission, created in December 1949 and operative from 1950 to 1953. On the Brazilian side, the technicians were headed by Dr. Ary Torres, directed by a coordination committee composed of the Ministers of Finance, Foreign Affairs, Agriculture, and Transportation and Public Works. The foreign technicians, who included both U.S. experts and technicians of the World Bank (the main financing agency), were headed first by Burke Knapp and later by Ambassador Merwin Bohan.

The major contributions of the Joint Commission were developing the "bottleneck" approach for identification of priority investment areas; sparking the establishment of the National Economic Development Bank (BNDE), which was to be the agent for channeling foreign funds and raising (through a tax and compulsory loan mechanism) funds needed for local expenditure on the investment plans; and applying locally the technique of feasibility studies and project formulation for both public and private investments.

The "bottleneck" approach, rudimentary as it was, set the stage for the later upgrading of the planning process through the successive stages of the "growing points" approach of the Programa de Metas, 1957–1960 (formulated by the BNDE and the Development Council); the framework planning approach of the Plano Trienal, 1962, and the Programa de Ação Econômica do Governo (PAEG), 1964–1966; and finally the

[4] For a good summation of early planning attempts, see Daland, op. cit., pp. 26–34.

comprehensive planning and model-building approach of the Plano Decenal, completed in the last days of the Castello Branco government.

In the bottleneck approach the priorities are in a sense predetermined. Given supply shortages of transport and power leading to underutilization of existing industrial facilities and a high rate of spoilage of agricultural production, the natural emphasis would be on investments designed to improve the overall output capital ratio of the economy and to exercise a disinflationary effect. The Joint Commission thus formulated its criteria for projects: they should lead toward the elimination of bottlenecks or the creation of basic conditions for economic growth; they should be complementary to, rather than substitutes for, private investments; they should be susceptible of reasonably quick implementation; and they should be financeable by noninflationary means.[5]

The basic planning of the Joint Commission, particularly in port and railroad rehabilitation, was to guide for almost a decade the work of the BNDE. The old tradition of budget allocations for public works unsupported by detailed project studies gave way gradually to cost-benefit and marginal-social-productivity studies, leading to a rapid development of the techniques of project formulation and appraisal in both the public and in the private sectors.

THE "GROWING POINTS" APPROACH

The "growing points" approach to planning, dating from the creation of the BNDE in 1952, was to reach its full maturity a few years later with the work of the National Development Council, established in 1956 during the Kubitschek regime. The Council included cabinet members and chief monetary authorities (such as the superintendent of currency and credit and the president of the Bank of Brazil); the president of the BNDE was ex-officio secretary general and provided secretarial and technical services from the BNDE staff.

As the work of the Joint Council neared its end and it

[5] *Report of the Joint Brazil-United States Technical Commission* (Washington, D.C.: Department of State, publ. 3487, June 1949), p. 79.

drew up projects for the elimination of the most obvious bottlenecks, the need was felt for a more sophisticated approach. No
comprehensive planning could realistically be undertaken because of the difficulties of political coordination on a national
basis, statistical deficiencies, and the utter inadequacy of government technical machinery. It was, moreover, felt that
private entrepreneurship, given appropriate stimuli, had a
sufficient growth impulse, particularly in the field of import
substitution, to dispense with complex globalization efforts.

While the bottleneck approach focused on the removal of
obstacles created by the inadequacy of the infrastructure of
public services, the growing-points approach aimed at identi-
fying "impulse sectors." It raised two problems of priority:
priority within sectors, and the allocation of resources between
the infrastructure and the directly productive projects. At that
time questions of regional imbalance between the South and
the North, which were later to assume dramatic importance
and fully engage governmental attention, were still in the
background; the approach was strictly in terms of economic
rather than political or social productivity. The most urgent
priority seemed to be to bring into full utilization investment
facilities in the Center-South, which, despite a buoyant inflationary demand, could not operate fully because of power
and transport shortages — in contrast to the situation in the
Northeast, where Paulo Afonso power remained underutilized
because of sluggish private industrial investment in the area.

THE NEW PLANNING AND
PROGRAMMING MACHINERY

It might be instructive to survey briefly the debate that
preceded the enactment in June 1952 of the BNDE legislation.
As a result of the work of the Joint Development Commission,
two considerations emerged.

(1) The existence of "bottlenecks" in the infrastructural services created a gap between marginal private productivity and
marginal social productivity. In the absence of conscious effort
by taxation or borrowing to reorient savings from private use
in the direct productivity sectors to the bottleneck sectors, continuation of the previous pattern of investment would only

aggravate problems by adding to the demand for the provision of basic services, which were unable to attract the desired amount of public and private investment.

(2) There was need for an agency to coordinate the implementation of the Joint Commission projects and to act both as a channel for foreign loans and as a provider of local counterpart financing.

Once the creation of the BNDE was decided upon, the main questions were how to raise the internal counterpart resources, and what should be the institutional nature of the funds. A compulsory loan scheme was judged preferable to the alternatives of a straight tax and a voluntary loan. A voluntary loan scheme would be unrealistic in view of the unattractiveness of fixed-yield bonds in an environment of inflation. As for taxation, it was feared that the nonreimbursable nature of tax receipts would weaken the Bank's determination to resist political pressures favoring low-priority or uneconomical projects. Conversely, the repayment obligations inherent in the compulsory loan mechanism would compel the Bank to adopt stricter measurements of the economic return of the instruments, even though it was recognized that the inflationary erosion of the bond value in the course of time would in any event imply a "disguised taxation" component.

The compulsory loan scheme was enacted in the form of a surcharge on income-tax payments, levied over a five-year period, for reimbursement in the succeeding five years; later it became a permanent feature of the tax system, and was eventually replaced by a straight-tax approach. Another point of debate was whether there should be earmarking of resources for specific sectors through the compartmentalization of funds (an approach later taken in the creation of the railway, merchant marine, electricity, and highway funds), or whether the Bank should act as a general development fund, able to shift resources according to changing priorities and needs. While the specificity of destination of resources would be politically more palatable to Congress in pinpointing special areas of application and restricting executive discretion, flexibility seemed imperative, and the "general development fund" concept was finally written into the basic statutes of the BNDE.

Priority Criteria of the BNDE

At the time BNDE operations began, a number of studies on priority criteria and project selection had been carried out both by private industry (Confederação Nacional da Industria), and by the Comissão de Desenvolvimento Industrial, a mixed body of government officials and representatives of industry and trade that served as an advisory organ to the foreign exchange and import control authorities. Three broad criteria were adopted. First, the so-called structural criterion covered projects capable of promoting vertical integration of industry either by putting local raw materials to use or by simulating production of raw material and intermediate products. Second was the foreign exchange criterion, by which preference was given to projects capable of alleviating balance-of-payments pressures through either import substitution or export promotion. Last, the conjunctural criterion was an omnibus classification applying to projects alleviating supply shortages.

The basic BNDE legislation established some statutory priorities, while leaving open an area of discretionary priorities, under such general headings as "basic industry" and "agriculture." The statutory priorities were both sectoral (reflecting the bottleneck approach) — railway and maritime transport, electric power, cold storage, warehousing — and regional. Twenty-five percent of the yearly tax resources were to be invested in the less-developed areas of the country.

Because of their relevance to all subsequent planning efforts, the priority criteria of BNDE deserve a somewhat more detailed discussion. They were established for the appraisal both of priorities between sectors and among projects within each sector. In general, sectoral priorities are easier to determine, since the cross-elasticity of substitution between sectors is low (while substantially higher for projects within the sector), and also because complementarities are more reliably assessed between sectors than between alternative projects.

The sectoral priorities in the BNDE were appraised in the light of:

(1)   inadequacy of domestic production in relation to current

demand, as indicated by the value of imports and their elasticity of demand and absorption of hard currency;

(2) prospective supply inadequacy in the light of continued growth of demand;

(3) net positive effects of investment in the balance of payments;

(4) need for government financial assistance because of low direct monetary profitability of a sector or high capital/output ratio resulting from technical lumpiness or in divisibility; and

(5) repercussion of sectoral expansion on utilization of available resources (domestic raw materials and so forth).[6]

The specific project priorities in turn were decided through the application of the conventional cost-benefit analysis, attention being given, inter alia, to the following:

(1) The Bank was to regard itself as residual lender and refrain from financing very profitable projects that could raise funds in the private market.

(2) Preference was to be given to projects involving technological innovation capable of raising sectoral productivity.

(3) Preference was also to be attached to projects permitting economies of scale.

(4) The capital structure of the project was to be taken into account, preference being given to an "open" rather than a "closed" composition of the capital, and to projects which, *ceteris paribus*, would involve a greater degree of participation by nationals.

Simultaneously with the technical development and initial implementation of the growing-points approach, a modest beginning at macro-economic planning was made through the work of a Joint Group of BNDE and the Economic Commission for Latin America (ECLA). The plan produced contained useful elements for future work, and was based on the following sequential steps:

a. Diagnosis of past rates of growth.

b. Projection of the spontaneous growth trends.

---

[6] This concept is equivalent to Hirschman's "backward linkage." See Albert Hirschman, *The Strategy of Economic Development* (New Haven: Yale University Press, 1958).

c. Projection of investment needs for alternative *planned* rates of growth.

d. Sectoral projections of demand.

e. Projection of exports.

f. Determination of the required import-substitution effort.

g. Residual determination of foreign exchange needs to be covered by capital imports.

The planning of the Joint Group presented the same short-comings as earlier attempts. It was "planning from above," unrelated to the existence of specific projects and entrepreneurship. The problem of compatibility was conveniently passed over, no recommendations being made on concrete monetary, fiscal, and foreign exchange policies designed to avoid inflation, raise fiscal resources, and assure the necessary export effort. On the technical side, demand projections were based mainly on income elasticities of demand, ignoring price effects because of technical difficulties of measurement.

Although representing a substantial improvement in planning technique, the work of the Joint Group, lacking a concrete policy formulation, never reached practical application.

THE PROGRAM OF GOALS (*PROGRAMA DE METAS*)

Drawn up as the joint work of the BNDE and the Development Council, the Programa de Metas of the Kubitschek regime represented the culmination of the growing-points approach, and also documented its pitfalls and deficiencies. It involved essentially the following elements:

1. Quantitative production goals backed by detailed specific projects (railway, electric power, etc.).

2. Quantitative production goals based partly on projects under study (example, steel development).

3. Nonquantified statement of the priorities attributed to expansion in certain fields (heavy machinery and electrical industries).

4. Formulation of a list of incentives to be given to private enterprise to attain production goals, later followed by approval of specific projects submitted by industries (motor-vehicle industries, ship-building, etc.).

The secretary general of the Development Council made an attempt in 1956 at complementing the sectoral planning by framework planning, in terms of broad monetary and fiscal policies, through the presentation of a development-with-stability program, which was not accepted by the Minister of Finance largely because it involved a drastic reform of the exchange rate system. A similar objective was pursued later, through the Plano de Estabilização Monetária, approved by the executive in October 1958 but subsequently abandoned because of political difficulties in the implementation of anti-inflationary measures.

The history of the planning efforts so far indicates that sectoral plans, involving the expansion of individual sectors and conveying the impression of an activist government, presented considerably more attraction than comprehensive formulation requiring difficult measures to raise noninflationary resources and to assure compatibility of objectives. Comprehensive macro-economic planning, raising more clearly the problem of compatibility of goals and limitation of resources, was indeed considerably more difficult technically and considerably less attractive politically. The Programa de Metas was reasonably successful in fulfilling most of its specific goals; but predictably enough, because of government reluctance to face up to vigorous monetary and fiscal policies and to maintain realistic exchange rates, it led to an aggravation of inflationary pressures and to a major foreign exchange crisis. It acted undoubtedly as a consensus-building factor around the theme of industrial development and contributed to the political viability of the Kubitschek government. But as later experience would demonstrate, it also started major economic distortions that bedeviled succeeding governments faced with accelerating inflation and acute balance-of-payments pressures.

THE PLANO TRIENAL

The next stage in the development of Brazilian planning was the Plano Trienal, prepared toward the end of 1962 by Celso Furtado for the Goulart administration. The Plano Trienal benefited from the considerable material and research accumulated by the Planning Commission (COPLAN) under the leadership of Dr. Bulhões Pedreira during a brief interlude of the parliamentary regime in late 1961 and early 1962. Substantial work had been done in consolidating the public sector budget, in formulating financial programs and the basic legislation for specific sectors such as power and highway development, and in stimulating sectoral planning within individual ministries by the establishment of liaison officers with CO-PLAN.

The Plano Trienal can be described as an attempt at framework planning because it added to the sectoral plans — the technique of which had been fairly well mastered by the BNDE as the Development Council — some elements of a macro-economic formulation. It recognized the problem of compatibility (promoting growth *versus* combating inflation), drew up a short-run stabilization program, and dealt with foreign exchange policy and, rather sketchily, with wage policy. It also stressed the need for basic reforms — agrarian, banking, fiscal, and administrative.

Though it fell short of the quantification and precision required by macro-economic models, and was less minute than the Program of Goals in the micro-planning of individual sectors, it broadened the scope of planning by covering some areas in greater detail, such as education and agriculture. It also began to deal with the problem of regional imbalance, while the Program of Goals concentrated largely on the infrastructure and on industrial investments in the Center-South region.

In most cases, quantitative sectoral goals were stated; in others merely an indication of the priority ranking of investments was given. But the major distinctive feature of the program was the attempt to integrate sectoral policies with broader economic magnitudes in terms of overall rate of growth, anti-inflationary exchange rates, and wage policies.

The Plano Trienal was extremely short-lived. Used by Goulart as a political instrument to win the allegiance of middle-class conservative elements, it was soon abandoned when it became clear that the maintenance of an anti-inflationary wage policy and the elimination of consumers' subsidies to spare resources for investment would result in short-term social tensions and unpopularity, while the concessions of the plan to orthodox recipes for economic stabilization irritated the radical wing of the Labor Party.

THE PROGRAMA DE AÇÃO ECONÔMICA DO GOVÊRNO

When the revolution first took over after the downfall of Goulart in March 1964, conditions were most unpropitious for the resumption of planning efforts. There had been a breakdown of social and bureaucratic discipline and an almost complete collapse of governmental statistical machinery. Under those circumstances the policy directives of President Castello Branco were to formulate an emergency program of action for the period 1964–1966, directed chiefly at combating inflation and correcting price distortions; to proceed with the modernization of the economic and social structure by the enactment of reforms; to institutionalize the planning machinery and restate the system of budget formulation and implementation through an administrative reform; and to initiate the process of long-range planning.

The PAEG advanced one step further than the Plano Trienal by a closer integration of monetary, fiscal, exchange rate, and wage policies. Given the deterioration of both the administrative machinery and the statistical apparatus since the Plano Trienal, the PAEG laid greater emphasis on a clear definition of basic policies.

Its five stated goals were (1) to abate the rate of inflation with a view to restoring reasonable equilibrium by 1966; (2) to accelerate the rate of economic growth interrupted in the period 1962–1963; (3) to alleviate sectoral and regional inequities and tensions created by social imbalance, through improvement of social conditions; (4) to assure, through investment policy, adequate conditions for productive employment, so as to absorb the expanding labor force; (5) to restore balance-of-payments viability.

Renouncing the more pretentious verbiage of "planning" in favor of the more modest "program of action," the PAEG thus states its scope:

"This program does not purport to represent a 'global plan of development,' but simply a program for coordinated governmental action in the economic field. Global quantifications are utilized purely in an indicative sense. The endeavor was thus to formulate a development strategy and a program of action for the ensuing two-year period, during which foundations would be established for a longer term and more organic system of planning."[7]

It lists instruments of action, comprising a set of basic economic and financial policies, deals with sectoral targets and programs, and announces policies concerned with social productivity.

Perhaps the major accomplishment of the PAEG lies not so much in the attainment of specific goals as in the major concentrated effort that was made in the direction of institutional reform and modernization. Those reforms were to be economic and social (fiscal, agrarian, and housing) and instrumental (banking and administrative).

Great attention was also given to improvement of the financial planning machinery; budget ceilings were introduced as an instrument of budget formulation; and a consolidated budget of the public sector was prepared and presented to the Congress together with the central administration budget. More important than that, the Central Bank began to implement monetary policies through the so-called "global monetary budget," including the complex of money flows resulting from fiscal revenues and expenditures, credit expansion to the private sector, financing of autarquias and states, as well as the balance of operations relating to the coffee and foreign exchange accounts controlled by the monetary authorities. For the first time, also, a wage policy was clearly outlined and vigorously implemented.

Major advances in institutional reform and modernization were made:

(1) Credit markets were reorganized and the capital market regulations were completely reformulated. Adjustable treasury bonds have been floated to encourage savings despite the residual inflation.

(2) Tax legislation was revised more realistically to abolish in-

[7] See *Programa de Ação Economica do Govêrno, 1964–1966* (Rio de Janeiro: Nov. 1964), pp. 15–16.

come tax on purely nominal inflationary profits; tax evasion was curtailed by the monetary upgrading of fiscal debts and by enlarging the area of withholding taxes; and the entire tax system was streamlined through the simplification of a complex array of taxes. By constitutional reform, the distribution of taxing power between the different levels of government was reorganized and the cumbersome system of state turnover taxes was replaced by taxation on the basis of value added.

(3) The policy of rate making for public entities was revised to allow for full coverage of operational expenditures and to move in the direction of self-financing of expansion, particularly in relation to electric power and telecommunications, while a more realistic pricing policy permitted a substantial reduction in railway and merchant marine deficits.

(4) The exchange system was simplified through the virtual abolition of subsidies, multiple rates, and exchange deposits.

(5) A housing bank was organized, and a corrective currency depreciation factor applied to rent and house-buying contracts, with the object of stimulating investment in the housing field.

(6) The stability-of-employment provisions detrimental to labor efficiency, which hampered the mobility of labor, were replaced by a system of financial insurance of the labor force through bank deposits made by employers for the benefit of employees, thus channeling vast resources to the housing bank.

As for specific goals, there was variable success in implementation. A spectacular recovery in the balance of payments, through a substantial accumulation of reserves in 1965, forced a much higher degree of monetary expansion than was originally planned for, with a correlate setback in the time schedule for the containment of inflation; the reorganization of the Superintendencia do Desenvolvimento do Nordeste (SUDENE) and the effective application of the fiscal incentives for the depressed areas resulted in perceptible progress in the correction of regional imbalances between the Northeast (whose economy grew over the years 1964–1966 at an average yearly rate of 7 percent, contrasting with a modest 4 percent average in the South). Much slower progress was made in the control of inflation. The cost-of-living index in the state of Guanabara declined from 87 percent in 1964 to 45 percent in 1965 and 41 percent in 1966. The latter was much less favorable than originally hoped for, reflecting the excessive monetary expansion in 1965 arising from the accumulation of exchange reserves as well as the poor performance of the food-producing sector due to climatic factors. Growth recovery was also slower than expected. Real product rose by 3.1 percent in 1964, 4.7 percent in 1965, and 4.3 percent in the year 1966, which showed a considerable upturn in industrial production but an unsatisfactory performance by agriculture. The lag in the recovery of investment, both national and foreign, was due to the initial uncertainty about the continuity of economic policies, the effects of credit control and monetary restraint policies, and the normal lead time for reformulation of shelved projects. By 1967, most of the price distortions had been corrected, several basic sectors (housing, power, telecommunications) had recovered substantial capacity to invest because of realistic price and rate policies, and substantial stimuli had been given to the agricultural sector through the improvement of the minimum price system and the subsidizing of fertilizer consumption by the farmers. The stage was set for a much better growth performance.

Much attention was given, during the period of implementation of the PAEG, to the improvement of the environmental conditions for planning by three sorts of measures.

1. reorganization of the statistical machinery;
2. institutionalization of the planning effort by the creation of a Ministry of Planning in charge of overall coordination, and of secretaries of planning in each of the individual ministries;
3. reformulation of the budget-making machinery.

The budget-making function was centralized in the Ministry of Planning and, through constitutional amendments, the executive was directed to submit to Congress pluri-year investment budgets. The traditional deformation of governmental action programs through pork-barrel appropriations in Congress was effectively curbed by a constitutional limitation on the congressional power to raise expenditures.

In an attempt to obtain some degree of private participation in the planning process, an Advisory Council (CONSPLAN) was created in March 1965, comprising representatives of industry, business, and labor as well as of the press and academic professions, with the function of formulating suggestions for planning, as well as of reviewing and criticizing governmental plans.

Contrary to other governments which had paid lip service to planning in the expectation of reaping short-term political benefits, the Castello Branco government had a profound commitment to the concept of planning as an instrument of national mobilization of resources for economic and social development. This permitted the implementation of most of the basic measures for institutional modernization recommended in the PAEG, and set the stage for the next planning effort, conceived as a long-run strategy for development.

THE TEN-YEAR PLAN FOR ECONOMIC AND SOCIAL DEVELOPMENT

While the PAEG was essentially a strategy for the transition period, President Castello Branco felt acutely the need for a much more systematic long-term planning effort, subject, of course, to continuous revision and updating, but with sufficient perspective and lead time to guide the decision-making process. It was hoped that the formulation of long-term development strategy and pluri-year investment budgets would help in assuring a certain degree of administrative continuity.

The Ten-Year Plan completed in the last days of the Castello Branco government was prepared by the EPEA, a special organization within the Planning Ministry in charge of long-range planning, with the technical assistance of experts from the University of California and of individual technicians seconded by the U.N., the O.A.S., and several European governments.

It comprises a perspective plan, in which goals are stated and a development strategy formulated for the ten-year period 1967–1976, and a five-year investment program, under which capital formation budgets are set forth at three levels:

(1) Regular budgets, covering the central administration of the federal government, autonomous agencies, and mixed capital companies, which provide for all the estimated investments of such bodies;

(2) Specific budgets for state and municipal government investments within the sectors specially examined under the

plan, which represent 80 to 90 percent of capital formation to be undertaken by states and municipalities;

(3) The investment forecasts of private enterprise, within those sectors specially mentioned under the plan (housing, steel, nonferrous metals, mechanical and electrical engineering, chemicals, infrastructure, building, communications, electric power, and mining).

The investment program is to be revised and updated through yearly operational plans.

For the decentralized sector of the economy (private enterprise and noninfrastructure investment by state and municipal authorities), the plan is indicative in nature, but market projections are presented to serve as guidance for decision-making, without however a quantification of production and investment goals; and there is a qualitative listing of the sundry incentives — in the fiscal, credit, and tariff fields — that the federal government is willing to give for the expansion of individual sectors.

The level of concreteness of the plan varies according to the degree of government control over the investment process. For this purpose, the sectors where the government has total or partial control of the instruments of production or wishes to assure a certain level of production (the steel industry, for instance) are defined as public or mixed. For those sectors, which encompass the infrastructural services of power, transport, and communication, as well as the metallurgical, mining, and chemical industries (and with important limitations arising from technical complexities or multiplicity of producers, agriculture and mechanical and electrical industries) — the plan includes at least projections of final demand for internal consumption and/or exports; goals for internal production and/or import needs; quantification of the main inputs (including whenever possible skilled manpower); investment programs, with an indication of direct sources of financing (public, private, external); locational choices for the investment; identification of the main projects and suggestion for evaluation criteria.

In all other cases, that is, in relation to the noncentralized sectors of the economy (mainly consumers' goods industries) there will be market demand projections for the guidance of entrepreneurs and a qualitative definition of those incentive instruments in the fiscal, credit, exchange, and tariff fields which the government is willing to use. However, no attempt will be made to establish precise production goals or investment allocations.

The major advances of the Ten-Year Plan over past efforts lie in three directions. First, greater attention is paid to social sectors, particularly education. What educational planning had been done previously was based largely on demographic growth data, leading to ineffectual rigidity in the distribution of educational investment. The new approach was based on manpower studies, the planning of investments being therefore much more closely related to the actual demand for specialized manpower. Very detailed attention was also given to investment in housing, both as a social stabilizer and a major instrument in creating employment.

A second advance is the detailed attention given to agriculture because of the relevance of the improvement of agricultural productivity in controlling inflation and in assuring balance-of-payments validity.

The decisive technical contribution of the Ten-Year Plan is, however, the micro-economic planning and model-building approach. Most of the earlier attempts were but collections of micro-plans. For the first time the Ten-Year Plan related the sectoral plan to a broader framework of monetary, fiscal, and foreign-trade policies. Several alternative strategies were analyzed and consistency tests applied to determine the compatibility of the growth objectives with the stabilization objective, the employment objective, and the preservation of balance-of-payments viability.

THE ROAD AHEAD

The main obstacles to a successful denouement of plans have been largely of an institutional nature — political instability and the inadequacy of the bureaucratic implementation machinery. While plans were formulated by a Weberian bureaucratic elite, they had to be implemented by a traditional bureaucracy much more status-seeking than achievement-conscious. This would indicate that a very first condition for successful planning—which should have been obvious but has in fact been sadly overlooked—is administrative reform. Moreover, whereas planning was supposed to be helpful as a political instrument for consensus-building, leading therefore at least to an attenuation of political instability, no such result was in fact attained. It is true that the political viability of the Kubitschek regime was at least partially enhanced by the development mystique of the Program of Goals. On the other hand, President Goulart was quite unsuccessful in utilizing the political potentialities of the Plano Trienal. Actually the plans never represented a political allegiance of the parties, but rather a personal commitment of the presidents, pursued with only cursory interest by President Goulart but representing a much deeper involvement for President Castello Branco. This points to a need for better communication. Planning from the top has to be replaced by planning by participation, involving a much greater degree of communication both within the government machinery and with the public at large.

An attempt is in fact being made to broaden the public involvement in plan formulation. The CONSPLAN mechanism, of which mention has been made, had precisely that objective. In the formulation of the Ten-Year Plan much stock was placed, at least for sectoral planning, on the Coordination Groups that merged federal, state, and regional planners, representatives of autonomous public entities, and delegates of private enterprise. The device of Coordination Groups is a rough imitation of the French system of regional and functional "comités du Plan."

In addition to greater communication with the private sector, there must be interdisciplinary communication. Planning in Brazil, though affecting the entire social and political structure and depending for implementation on the administrative apparatus, has been so far the special preserve of the economist. This is one of the reasons why insufficient attention has been given, except perhaps in the Ten-Year Plan, to social aspects. It is quite clear that a much bigger role in planning must be given not only to sociologists and political scientists, but also to public administration experts.

Considerable progress was made during the Castello Branco administration toward improving the institutional framework of planning: the creation of the Ministry of Planning; the device of pluri-year investment budgets, the abolition of Congressional discretion in raising expenditures; the elimination of splinter and factionalist parties always ready to jockey for position and political favor and uncommitted to any concrete government programs.

Despite those improvements, formidable issues remain unsolved in the Brazilian travail of development planning. Two of the most difficult are in the nature of broad decisional conflicts.

There is first the conflict between stability and development. Artificial as it may be, the fortuitous conjunction of accelerating inflation with substantial development in the postwar period, right to the end of the Kubitschek period, led many people to believe that inflation is a necessary accompaniment, if not a causal factor, in development. This runs contrary to the international experience and is also belied by the Brazilian experience of the early sixties when acceleration of the inflation rate was accompanied by economic stagnation and even retrogression (in 1963). The core of the problem lies in the short-run measures of monetary and fiscal restraint to combat inflation, which are likely to provoke temporary unemployment and decline in output of some sectors which have been overexpanded on the basis of inflationary prices and demand expectations. A by-product of this is the temptation of mistaken diagnosis. As output falls in the disinflating sectors, unit costs rise and there is pressure to discontinue efforts to curb overall demand inflation, the argument being that the nature of the inflationary pressures has changed from demand-pull to cost-push. The painful readjustment of production to a pattern more consistent with stable monetary conditions — which shears off speculative inventory-building as well as the demand for durable goods as a substitute for money — causes major political attrition and leads often to a premature abandonment of stabilization programs under the compelling slogan of "saving the country from stagnation." The history of the Brazilian economy in the last fifteen years has been a sad alternation of half-hearted stabilization programs, promptly discarded as the unavoidable shock of temporary unemployment and recession unleashed political pressures, with spurts of *desenvolvimentismo* that soon collapsed in the fact of balance-of-payment bottlenecks and internal social tensions, which rehabilitated temporarily the political acceptability of anti-inflation measures. One of the services that the macro-economic and model-building approach of the Ten-Year Plan can render is to bring into clear focus the compatibilities or inconsistencies in alternative rates of growth and the complementary objectives of monetary stability and balance of payments viability.

The second major decisional conflict centers on the issue of nationalism versus the absorption of foreign resources. It has long been recognized that the passionate pull of nationalism can be a major force in mobilizing energies for development and conditioning the masses for the required sacrifices. On the other hand, it tends to foster irrational patterns of behavior, rendering more difficult the absorption of technology and leading to an uncritical rejection of foreign investment before local sources of savings are mobilized to fill the gap. In the light of historical experience, the Brazilian brand of nationalism has shown more intoxicating capacity than mobilizing energy, and has rendered virtually impossible the adoption of rational policies for the development of national mineral resources.

Apart from the decisional conflicts, the major problems that are likely to be faced by Brazilian planners, if one tries to foresee the fate and shape of future efforts, will be the high rate of endogenous population growth, the near exhaustion of the import substitution propellant of economic growth, and political instability.

The high rate of population growth (3.1 percent per year) imposes a great strain on investment resources and limits the choice of the investment mix, which has to be slanted in so as to be less favorable to the labor-saving techniques now so dominant in Western technology. Brazil is at that phase of the population-growth curve where the decline in mortality is far from offset by a decline in fertility rates. Yet obstacles to the adoption of modern family-planning methods include religious, sentimental, and even misplaced economic or military preconceptions. Some business groups identify a high rate of population growth with a rapidly expanding market, or visualize it as a convenient source of cheap labor; military groups, on the other hand, oblivious of preconditional investments in the infrastructure, defend the demographic explosion as a welcome contribution to the occupation of the empty areas of the Amazon basin.

A second perturbing factor is the fact that the easy, almost spontaneous growth era of the 1950's, based on import substitution, is nearing its end. Those import replacement efforts now needed lie in fields requiring greater capital intensiveness and more sophisticated technology. Development planning now has to be geared to expansion of the internal market and to competitive export-oriented industries, obviously a more difficult task than planning for the needs of a known and captive preexisting market.

But essentially the victory or defeat of the planners will hinge on a much more satisfactory solution than has hitherto been found to the problem of maintaining popular communication and assuring political allegiance to the plans. The vague political mystique of planning must give place to a consensus-building effort. During the Castello Branco regime the environmental conditions for planning have been measurably improved through administrative reform, the institution of the two-party system, the affirmation of budgetary discipline against congressional free-spending pressures, and reinforcement of federal powers through the requirement of presentation of plans as a condition of grants-in-aid and through limitations placed on the borrowing authority of the states in the capital market. But the fact remains that the problem of depersonalizing the plans, to assure their continuity through successive administrations, is far from solved.

A melancholy illustration of this is the recent fate of the Ten-Year Plan. Bequeathed by Castello Branco to the Costa e Silva administration, which took over in March 1967, it was promptly consigned to oblivion as part of the image-building effort of the new government; it was replaced by a new Plano Trienal, which did little more than incorporate the first three years of the investment program, and abandoned the conceptual structure, sacrificed the long-term perspective, and blurred the compatibility tests inherent in the model-building approach of the Ten-Year Plan.

Unless greater success is attained by the planners in converting planning from the top into a more effective consensus-building instrument for political stability, the summation given by Albert Waterston in his broad review of planning in under-developed countries will remain, perhaps sadly, true:

". . . when a country's leaders in a *stable* government are strongly devoted to development, inadequacies of the particular form of planning used — or even the lack of any formal planning — will not seriously impede the country's development. Conversely, in the absence of political commitment or stability, the most advanced form of planning will not make a significant contribution toward a country's development."[8]

[8] Albert Waterston, *Development Planning: Lessons of Experience* (Baltimore: Johns Hopkins Press, 1965), p. 6.

CHAPTER 12

Public Investment Allocation
and Pricing Policy for Transportation

Alan Abouchar

This paper is concerned with allocation of investment and rational pricing policy in Brazilian transportation.[1] The need for rational criteria in this sector is underscored by the major economic role played by public investment in transportation, which has accounted for about 25–30 percent of gross national fixed capital formation in recent years. In the past, however, this investment has usually been made to serve the narrow causes of entrenched bureaucracies and private business interests rather than the national economy as a whole. Total public investment[2] in the various modes of transport from 1961 to 1965 is shown in Table 1.

[1] The interested reader may consult the author's *Diagnostic of the Transport Situation in Brazil*, published 1967 in mimeographed form by EPEA, for additional details on most issues discussed here.

[2] Unless otherwise specified, all costs in this paper are calculated in terms of October 1965 prices. The appropriate exchange rate is Cr$2,200 per U.S.$ 1.00. The official rate was changed from Cr$1,850 to Cr$2,200 per U.S.$ 1.00 in November 1965. This change was a response to an accomplished fact of domestic inflation, and the later exchange rate is believed more representative of the October situation. Finally, values are converted to new cruzeiros (NCr$), each of which is equal to 1,000 old cruzeiros.

TABLE 1. PUBLIC INVESTMENTS IN TRANSPORTATION, 1961–1965

Investment	Roads[a]	Railroads[b]	Maritime[c] transport	Civil[d] aviation	Total
Million NCr$	3,731.1	968.8	475.5	102.3	5,267.7
Percent of total	70.9	18.2	9.0	1.9	100.0

[a] Includes federal, state, and county expenditures on investment, maintenance, and administration.
[b] Includes investment in Federal Railway Network, S.A. São Paulo state-owned railroads, and Companhia Vale do Rio Doce, as well as construction expenditures by the National Railroad Department (DNEF).
[c] Includes investments by ports and all federal autarkies and mixed companies, as well as federal transfers for private ship construction.
[d] Airports only.

This study is divided into four parts. The first contains a brief comparative analysis of the investment mechanism in the three most important types of economy — mature market economy, Soviet-type economy, and underdeveloped market economy — and concludes that for at least the more advanced members of the latter group, such as Brazil, a policy of non-subsidized transportation is appropriate. The second section develops this view further and shows its implications for Brazilian transport prices. The third section reviews existing pricing policies for the major modes of transport, all of which are seen to be seriously inadequate either in indicating demand for the mode and the need for investment in it, or in generating funds to provide service, or both. The last section indicates the main lines of necessary change.

NATIONAL INVESTMENT DECISION-MAKING CRITERIA

Just as too little investment in transport can retard the nation's economic growth, so can too much deprive other sectors of needed funds that might contribute to faster growth. It is the latter — or if not overinvestment, at least incorrect choice of investment projects — that frequently is the greater danger. Many factors combine to promote this. First, there is a strong belief in transportation as a catalyst of economic development, which leads to a too uncritical acceptance of investment proposals. Next, even when projects are acknowledged to be economically unfeasible, they are often justified on political, humanitarian, or strategic grounds that close inspection might reveal to be chimerical. Third, there is the notion that transport is unique among the transformation and production sectors, that it is indispensable, and that its investment is not to be measured by the same rod as the others — a notion given added currency by lumping transport together with water supply, sanitation, education, and public health as social overhead capital, with the implication that any investment at all in this sector is desirable.[3] It is one thing to recognize these stimuli towards overinvestment, however, and another to provide adequate criteria to which transport investment should be tied. What, then, should be used as the standard for transport investment decisions?[4] How much should be invested in transport, and how should it be distributed within the sector among alternative technologies? Are the criteria relevant to other countries also appropriate for Brazil?

The correct approach to transport investment in an economy such as Brazil's can best be determined against the background of Brazilian planning philosophy and in relation to investment-allocation procedures in other economies. Brazilian planning constitutes an attempt to foresee and provide for the underlying trends in an essentially capitalistic economy with a very large public sector; and to rationalize the investment of the public sector, which includes many mixed private-public production enterprises (the *companhias mistas*) as well as education, public health, a great deal of civil construction, and most of the transport sector. It will be useful to divide these investment targets into three different groups, whose investment-allocation criteria may differ from one economy to another.

[3] Apropos of this point see George Wilson's insightful remarks in the first and last chapters of Wilson *et al.*, *The Impact of Highway Investment on Development* (Washington, D.C.: Brookings Institution, 1966).

[4] We are not concerned here with investment in local county roads. While consistency would also require exclusion of the suburban lines in the rail network, they are included for reasons of administrative convenience and their large capital component. As will be seen shortly, they constitute the only important exception to the price policy developed here.

The first group includes education, public health, and other social overhead such as water supply; the second consists of industry, agriculture, and services such as retail and commerce; and the third is transport.

It is extremely difficult to determine a sound economic criterion for investment in the first group. This is true in any economy — an advanced market economy like the United States, a centrally planned socialist economy like the U.S.S.R., or a developing market economy like Brazil. We can only proceed from the desire to permit a given proportion of the population to achieve a certain educational level, for example, and see whether the cost of such a policy can be borne at the present stage of economic development. Likewise, it is difficult to assign a value to public health programs, sanitation, and water supply, and to analyze the return from alternative investment choices. Again we must proceed from politically or socially dictated targets and investment availability, taking account of other investment needs and the level of growth.

The difficulty of attaining rational investment for the second group varies. In the United States such decisions are left for the most part to private initiative, which reacts to market signals. Since these signals more or less accurately reflect prevailing consumer preferences, investment allocation in this economy may be said to be rational in the sense of being consistent with final demand patterns. In the socialist economy decisions to invest in individual sectors within this group are based on the planners' preferences for certain production mixes. However, a given production mix is not necessarily consistent with the desired growth rate for the economy as a whole, a target also set by the planning board. Hence, what may be a rational investment pattern in a socialist economy for this group from one point of view may be irrational from another. In the Brazilian economy such decisions are also difficult, but as long as planning policy tends to focus more on the overall growth rate rather than on the production mix, and as long as the possible benefits of international trade are not lost to view, there is reason to hope for greater rationality among the sectors in this group than has at times prevailed in the U.S.S.R.

It should be easier to plan investment rationally in the third group, the transport sector, in Brazil than in the other types of economy (in Brazil it should also be easier to plan rationally for the third group than for the first two). In the United States the diversity of use of the transport network complicates analysis of the yield from transport investment and of the allocation of costs. U.S. transport serves as an intermediate production input, a final consumption good (automobiles), an intermediate good for consumers, and a large military input. External economies are extended beyond the transport sector by, for example, providing a clear way for power transmission lines, or by flood control in river development. In a Soviet-type economy transport use is more homogeneous, and production goals have historically reflected strategic needs, permitting transport investment decisions to be made in terms of the planners' own production preference pattern. That is, transport has been an intermediate good required as an input for production; its investment could be efficiently planned primarily in terms of its contribution to the desired final production mix, with no special considerations required for possible sources of intermediate and final consumer transport demand. One conclusion of the major study of Soviet transportation to date is that such efficiency was achieved in the U.S.S.R. by keeping investment at relatively low levels while the output indicators of the sector soared.[5] But, as noted above, the planners' preferences may be irrational or inconsistent with a maximal growth rate, creating an irrational demand for transport through incorrect location and other factors. As I have shown elsewhere, a severe, artificially inflated transport demand can be the result, with the consequence that investment in transport may be irrational from the viewpoint of the economy as a whole.[6]

The relative homogeneity of transport use in Brazil — as a method of moving freight and passengers by common carrier, for the most part — should simplify analysis of investment in Brazilian transport, because the comparative absence of private automobiles facilitates cost allocation on the major transport mode; because transportation, as an intermediate good

[5] Holland Hunter, *Soviet Transportation Policy* (Cambridge, Mass.: Harvard University Press, 1957).

[6] Alan Abouchar, "Rationality in the Prewar Soviet Cement Industry," *Soviet Studies*, Oct. 1967.

entering the production process, can be priced, and its demand can be projected, according to market conditions, just like any other industrial input; and because common-carrier movement of passenger traffic can also be priced and projected according to market conditions. The essential point of these considerations is that the external economies of the Brazilian transport network are slight, and except in a very few cases can be disregarded.

INVESTMENT ALLOCATION AND PRICING POLICY

Most pricing schemes advocated for transport systems or subsystems are based on one or more of the following principles: average cost, marginal cost, support of infant industries or regions, and value of service.

Average-Cost Pricing

Under this system the long-run average cost incurred by each user class of a mode of transport is distributed over that class. Examples of user classes are bulk mineral shippers on the RFFSA, or large truck. If the basic facility is already operating and is being properly maintained so that high replacement costs are obviated, that is, if the facilities truly represent sunk costs and have a zero opportunity-cost, they need not be reflected in average cost and only variable capital and operating costs (including maintenance of permanent facility) must be covered. The first point to note about this pricing principle is that the total real economic cost of operation and capital is recovered from the final users, the shippers.

The problem usually arises that different user classes are responsible for different components of the costs associated with the basic permanent facility. For example, a highway designed for a given automobile capacity requires certain standards; the addition of heavy trucks requires a deeper base and thicker pavement. If a road is required for automobiles in any event, a reasonable approach is to allocate to trucks the incremental costs of their road requirements.[7] If, as in Brazil,

---

[7] Various attempts at incremental cost imputation have been made in the United States. One such study is Allen R. Ferguson, "A Marginal

trucks and buses are the main traffic, most or all of the road cost would be allocated to them under this system. The truck share should then be distributed among the trucks in accordance with weight and distance traveled, or some other composite indicator of the burden they impose on the road.

By charging the users the full cost of service, average-cost pricing avoids the price distortions introduced through the granting of subsidies and the consequent misallocation of traffic among modes; distortions in the trade-off between private transport costs and scale economies or regional resource differentials would also be avoided.

Marginal-Cost Pricing

Industries such as power generation, transportation, and other public utilities are generally declining-cost industries over a long range of output. Over this range the long-run marginal-cost curve lies below the long-run average-cost curve. Since capital costs are usually high, these industries are frequently local or regional monopolies; hence economies of scale can be attained. The downward-sloping demand curve facing the monopolist cuts the marginal-cost curve at a lower price than that at which it cuts the average-cost curve, and at a greater volume of output. If such industries produced at the higher level (lower price) their revenue would not cover their cost. To avoid this, they tend to produce at the lower level of output where price equals average cost. It has often been argued that such industries should be required to produce at the higher level, since as long as people are willing to pay a price for a service in excess of its marginal production cost, there is a net contribution to social welfare. The firm would then be reimbursed from public funds for the deficit that would ensue. If a public agency provides the service, the deficit is simply paid for through general tax revenues.

Several problems arise in any attempt to institute marginal cost pricing. The main difficulty is that we cannot usually determine marginal cost and usually fall back on something like variable cost. There is a tendency to consider more and

Cost Function for Highway Construction and Operation," *American Economic Review*, May 1958.

more of the variable components as fixed costs — the large work staff on the railroads, for example. Once the precedent is set for pricing below full average cost, intensive pressures are set up to reduce rates further and to extend the principle to other activities. Frequently this leads to regional mislocation and to the rendering of parallel transport services.

Support of Infant Industries or Regions

It is sometimes argued that enough traffic to pay the average unit cost of a system cannot be expected for several years after the system is completed. Later, traffic will grow enough to pay total costs, including opportunity capital costs, without raising user charges, which when service begins reflect a subsidy. The lightly traveled Belém-Brasília highway, where there are no tolls to compensate for the lower user payment (contributed via the fuel tax) than on the other roads, would seem to be an example of infant-region pricing. A variant on the theme is the granting of special low rates to encourage the users of a service while their new industry develops. This is the justification sometimes offered for various low railway rates, such as that for cement at certain distances.

Frequently nontransport benefits, such as are alleged to accrue to the settlers along the Belém-Brasília road, are claimed to justify a road. But it is forgotten that even sharing the road cost between transport and nontransport objectives would leave the cost per migrant extremely high. If a main goal of a road project is population relocation, that goal can be reached much more cheaply by building a settlement near already existing towns and building short road connections. Another objection to infant-industry or infant-region pricing is that it is difficult to limit its application. For example, if a Belém-Brasília road is justified well ahead of need, why not also a direct Belo Horizonte-Belém connection?

Value-of-Service Pricing

Value-of-service pricing is often invoked for pricing individual services on a mode of transport whose joint costs cannot be apportioned over all individual services. These costs are imputed disproportionately to the more valuable commodities, which can afford to pay higher rates. Value-of-service pricing may be justified as long as the costs in question are in reality joint costs rather than incremental costs required by the low-value services, and as long as the pricing does not become abusive; for these reasons, the circumstances in which it can be justified are much more limited than is frequently believed. For example, iron-ore traffic on the Central do Brasil railway accounts for about two-thirds of the line's cargo traffic. In this case it would be inappropriate to set the iron-ore rate to equal only the cost of fuel, equipment, and direct labor, and to neglect maintenance and administration costs on the grounds that these must be incurred in any event.

The usual result of value-of-service pricing is that cargoes that can support a higher rate because of their higher initial value transfer to modes more appropriate to their needs. For example, if manufacturers must pay high rates on railroads that are slow and have high terminal costs because of the reloading necessary for door-to-door delivery, they will divert their freight to highway transport, which has advantages in these respects. The railroad will then be left with the less remunerative traffic, the traffic that cannot afford to pay high rates.

Pricing and Efficient Recourse Allocation

In light of the pricing principles just outlined, and given the nature of Brazilian transportation, which acts primarily as a common carrier of cargo and passengers in intercity movement and has few external economies, the appropriate investment criterion for the transport sector should be the willingness of users to pay the full costs of a system, including the cost of its further capital expansion. By "full costs" are meant costs that will vary over a long period. For example, if no further expansion of the permanent fixed facilities in a transport mode is envisaged, "full cost" means the cost of equipment, labor, fuel, and other materials, and maintenance of the permanent facilities (including necessary minor improvements). If the mode is being expanded, on the other hand, the capital costs of this expansion must be included in calculations of full cost.

The pricing policy advocated here means that all public revenues for transport operation and investment must be collected from direct users of the service (including a limited amount from owners of abutting properties), rather than from federal subsidy. Care should be exercised to prevent earmarked property taxes from exceeding the benefit received by property owners over and above the benefits that they receive as shippers, for which they pay through regular channels. It is all too easy to overstep the appropriate property tax levels and create inequity and inefficiency, a point to which I will return.

The policy outlined above also means that one mode of transport must not be made to subsidize another. We should interpret this statement narrowly, regarding each important class of users of a type of transport as an individual mode. Then there can be no justification for subsidizing heavy trucks, one mode of transport, by imposing high taxes on gasoline users, who in very large part are owners of cars, a second mode of transport that uses a very small portion of the road network.[8] To argue that equality between total automotive fuel collec-

[8] Strictly speaking efficiency considerations would require us to consider each combination of narrow weight class of (loaded) vehicle and individual road as a separate user class or mode of transport for the determination of user charges, the main variables in the second factor being differential maintenance costs and the extent of the improvement to be undertaken; similarly, for railroads, each combination of commodity and railroad line (or major stretch of line) would be charged differently. For trucks it is administratively quite difficult and costly to adhere to the self-support principle for all user classes so defined. The obvious way to handle the problem would be through the use of roadside scales and toll booths. But when the road being improved is small and the improvement modest (drainage betterment, for example), collection costs could easily amount to more than the improvement cost. Since much of the investment in Brazilian roads will continue to be of this nature, the toll system cannot be generally applied (this would not preclude a single high-specification road from being paid for through tolls, however). Accordingly, it seems advisable to treat the intercity road network as a single unit with expansion and improvement costs distributed over all relevant traffic, grouped into four or five main classes in proportion to use.

It is relatively easy for the railroads to charge different rates to allow for the costs of handling different commodity groups (today different rates are charged for different commodities but they appear to depend more on other factors than differential handling costs). But to vary rates on different individual lines in relation to their renovation and maintenance

tions and total road expenditures implies the absence of a subsidy and establishes the existence of efficient pricing in the
road transport sector would be like maintaining that equality
between total costs and revenues of the transport sector as a
whole mean that rail-service prices are equal to costs. The
railroads, of course, are subsidized (to a much greater extent
than is indicated by the present 60 percent operating deficit,
which does not adequately reflect most capital investments),
and thus introduce a serious element of inefficiency. For most
rail services the policy cannot be defended simply by reference
to the existence of deficits in other countries, an apology recently adduced in extenuation by the incoming president of
the Federal Railway System.[9] Nor should industry, usually the
final beneficiary of the transport subsidies, be permitted to
develop and locate inefficiently. The locational rule for industry
is ultimately very straightforward: if scale economies of production are enough to pay total real transport costs, concentration should be encouraged; if they cannot, it should not be.
Infant-industry or infant-region petitions for exception to this
rule should be examined very carefully, and the granting
authority should be satisfied that the properly discounted benefits from such proposals exceed their correctly calculated
costs.

A deviation from full-cost pricing might be made in certain exceptional cases. For example, if the economic costs of
relocating the people in a given area are high and if the people
have no urge to leave, the minimum-cost policy, and the one
consistent with maximal social welfare, might be to subsidize
cheap transport services in the area. In this case, however,
great care must be taken to keep the subsidy from being extended to other groups. The problem of suburban traffic, espe-

costs would be extremely difficult, and would discourage through traffic.
Regional variation might prove feasible, however. The discrepancies
between cost incidence and the pricing policy here presented, some of
which can be taken into account, are in any event minor when con-
trasted to the sources of gross inefficiency in the present system of
revenue collection and allocation in the railroad and highway systems.

[9] See "RFF não pede sacrifício mas sim o máximo esfôrço," *Jornal
do Brasil*, April 5, 1967, p. 7. The theme is a recurring one in Brazilian
railroad circles, and usually appears in any discussion of the industry.

cially around Rio, is of this nature, and presents the only compelling case for significant subsidy in Brazilian transportation
today. Full-cost pricing here would divert many travelers to
buses, overburdening the roads and resulting in high short-
term new construction costs or encouraging resettlement in the
central city, requiring high urban overhead costs. These, at
least, would appear to be correct conclusions, although sufficient data for a thorough analysis of the problem have not been
assembled. Similarly, military considerations and national security may require the construction of some apparently "uneco-
nomic" transport facility, although this justification is often
somewhat fanciful and is probably applied too liberally. What
the policy does require is that where transport services are
provided at prices below full relevant cost the reasons should
be made very clear; the total cost of alternative actions, such
as population resettlement, should be sought; and care should
be taken to ensure that the subsidy is not extended beyond
the area of application originally intended.

Our analysis of pricing to this point has stressed resource
allocation through the market. However, there is a second
mechanism by which a full-cost user charge can promote rational
investment allocation within the transport sector, and between it
and the rest of the economy. This mechanism is the generation of
investment funds internally rather than at the expense of other
sectors whose need might be equally great, one logical consequence of confronting limited investment capacity and excessive
investment demand. As an alternative to such a confrontation an
inflationary deficit-financing policy might be pursued. Indeed
this has been the rule in the past, with the federal deficit ranging
between 7 percent and 35 percent of total federal expenditures
in the 1952–1966 period while the price level was rising more
than sixtyfold. As I show elsewhere, one of the most important
factors in the formation of this deficit has been the transport
sector deficit, which from 1961 1965 amounted to over 60 percent of public-sector expenditure in transport and over 95
percent of the federal deficit.[10] While any activity marked by

[10] Alan Abouchar, "Inflation and Transport Policy in Brazil,"
Economic Development and Cultural Change, September, 1969. Not all
the transport deficit shows up directly in the federal deficit, since the

greater expenditure than revenue might be considered to have an inflationary effect, no one would suggest that deficit activities such as public health or education should on these grounds be reduced, since they afford benefits to the society as a whole beyond those received by the direct participants. Transportation, however, is an activity in which the beneficiaries can be specified, and should therefore bear the financial burden.

Highways, which have accounted for about 40 percent of federal and state transport expenditures in recent years, provide an apt illustration of the problem. Only about half of the funds for highways have been generated within the highway sector of the economy (and of this half a disproportionately large share by automobile users), with the result that the highway program has either forced a reduction in investment in other sectors (even though the return on such investment might have been greater than investment in roads) or, if no reduction was made, promoted the pace of inflation by increasing the government deficit. Either result is the more lamentable because it is avoidable. The demand for truck transport, a derived demand depending on the demand for final products, is relatively insensitive to changes in trucking costs; since the necessary user-charge increases implied by full-cost pricing would have been insignificant when compared to the value of the goods moved, around 3–4 percent on average, a large increase in highway investment revenues could have been generated within the sector. State and federal deficits in the railroad sector could have been reduced considerably, or eliminated, although at the cost of shifting labor costs to the economy at large, by terminating unwarranted investment projects and cutting back operating levels and costs. The elasticity of demand for the services of the RFFSA is probably around 0.7 to 1.0 at present prices, which would indicate an increased revenue from small rate increases. But the necessary rate increases are not small. As we will see shortly, the indicated increase is well over 200 percent, and this would proba-

former reflects some state deficits as well. The state deficits are financed in part by federal loans and in part by deferment of payment for services. The second possibility also has an inflationary effect by raising the velocity of money.

bly reduce demand so much that actual revenue would fall. Operating costs should fall almost proportionately, however. Since the new rates would be set at average cost for the relevant activities, the deficit would be eliminated. However, although it should no longer be charged to the railroad sector account, a large deficit activity would continue for some years as excess railroad labor was prematurely retired and pension costs rose.

RAILROAD PRICE POLICY

Recent Financial History

The deficiencies in the pricing of railroad services can best be appreciated against the background of recent railroad financial history.

The last year that the consolidated railroad sector showed an operating profit was 1945, and in recent years very heavy losses have been suffered. Most of these losses, which in 1963 totaled NCr$157 million, or 65 percent of total expenditures, arose on the Rêde Ferroviaria Federal, S.A. (RFFSA), a federal autarky that handles about 60 percent of the traffic on Brazilian railroads and contains about 60 percent of total route mileage. The RFFSA deficit amounted to 73 percent of total expenditures. The deficit on all the other railroads came to 37 percent of expenses. (Only two railroads did not incur a deficit between 1961 and 1963, the insignificant, privately owned Perus-Pirapora and the very important Vitória-Minas ore line, which showed an operating profit of about 10 percent in 1963.)

The large deficit of the RFFSA, shown in Table 2, is covered by the federal budget. In 1957, the first year of RFFSA operation, it amounted to 25 percent of the total federal budgetary deficit. It rose to 40 percent in 1958 and 46 percent by 1965, an important inflationary force in the period.

In addition to the subsidy required to cover its operating deficit, the RFFSA has been receiving a substantial subsidy in the form of an allotment of 11 percent of petroleum tax revenues. The latest legislation reduces this share to 9.4 percent, but it now extends past 1972, the year at which it was to expire under earlier legislation. The new level represents

TABLE 2. OPERATING REVENUES, EXPENDITURES, AND
DEFICIT OF THE RFFSA
(million current NCr$)

| | | | | Deficit as percent of | |
| | | | | Expendi-tures | Total federal budgetary deficit |
Year	Revenues	Expenditures	Deficit		
1957	8.9	18.9	9.9	52.4	24.9
1958	9.4	20.0	10.6	53.0	40.0
1959	11.3	25.9	14.6	56.4	27.2
1960	13.5	32.8	19.3	58.8	24.8
1961	20.1	56.8	36.6	64.4	28.1
1962	29.6	95.6	65.6	68.6	23.4
1963	51.6	189.0	137.4	72.7	27.2
1964	91.6	321.6	230.0	71.5	32.8
1965	182.2	452.5	270.3	59.7	46.0
1965[a]	195.6	485.9	290.2	59.7	46.0

Source: *Anuário Estatístico da RFFSA*, 1963, 1964, 1965, 1966; *Estradas de Ferro do Brasil, Suplemento da Revista Ferroviária*, 1964. p. 113.
[a] at October 1965 prices

a 530 percent subsidy to the RFFSA.[11] Further subsidies are contained in the financing of imported railroad equipment.

Finally, the railroad sector as a whole has been receiving an additional capital allocation in the form of new-line construction undertaken by the National Railway Department. This investment has reached NCr$880 million in the postwar period.

In view of supplementary expenditures in the railroad sector not reflected in the annual operating statement, the average cost cannot be calculated from the total operating cost. An attempt to determine average Brazilian railroad traffic costs, including an annual capital cost for equipment and mainte-

[11] Briefly, the law attempts to promote the development of the various modes of transport through tax rebates. Economic efficiency would require that these rebates correspond to the tax revenues originating in the mode. However, the RFFSA in the past has accounted for consumption of only about 2 percent of refined petroleum products, and since about half its consumption is fuel oil and half is diesel, taxed at lower than average rates, it has accounted for a disproportionately small share of tax revenues, perhaps 1.5 percent. Its 11 percent share therefore represented a subsidy of over 600 percent of its tax contribution.

nance but excluding any annual charge for the basic permanent facility, which is so old as to be fully depreciated with
zero opportunity cost, resulted in average cost estimates of 3.4
centavos per ton-kilometer and 3.8 centavos per intercity passenger-kilometer. The average suburban passenger-kilometer
cost was estimated to be 1.4 centavos.[12] Applying these cost estimates to the traffic breakdown actually recorded for the RFFSA
in 1965 implies a total cost for the system of NCr$625.7 million
in that year. Comparing this with the actual revenues of the
RFFSA system on the comparable basis shown in the last row
of Table 2 indicates an average subsidy of 69 percent, the average charge amounting to only 31 percent of average cost, which
is very far below the marginal cost of railroad operations as it
might be calculated by almost any conceivable method.

A brief review of the rate structure will show that the railroads have been motivated almost exclusively by the desire to
generate traffic at any cost to increase their share and maintain
the appearance of indispensability. That is, recognizing that in
present transport conditions the value of railroad services is
low, and that the traffic will not bear rates anywhere near the
railroads' out-of-pocket costs, rates are set at unconscionably
low levels.

The Rate Structure

The Brazilian freight rate structure has historically been
differentiated according to specific railroad, commodity, and
distance. The basis for differentiation among railroads and
commodities has not alwuys been apparent and the frequent
changes in the application of various rate schedules have no
obvious explanation. This is illustrated by the rate schedules
for nine important agricultural products during the period
1959–1965. Only two of these products, beans and rice, had the
same intermediate schedule in all seven years. Three commodities — coffee, manioc flour, and timber — had schedules that
were sometimes higher than and sometimes the same as the
intermediate schedule. In no two successive years of the period

---

[12] Abouchar, *Diagnostic* . . . , p. 29. The heavy ore traffic on
the Vitória-Minas line was excluded from the calculation, since it represents very special circumstances and is isolated from the rest of the
national system.

1962–1965 did coffee occupy the same position with respect to the intermediate schedule. The remaining four commodities — cotton, fats and oils, wheat flour, and sugar — had schedules which were sometimes higher and sometimes lower than the intermediate beans-rice schedule. Since 1964, the disorder among commodities has been lessened.

The examples just cited indicate the railroads' failure to take account of costs in setting rates; changes in cost patterns from one year to the next simply could not be abrupt enough to explain the random pattern of rate changes. An even greater disregard of costs may be seen in the special rates for iron ore, cement, and timber, which accounted for 34 percent of the total ton-kilometers of traffic on the RFFSA in 1965. These rates are shown in Table 3 along with the highest and lowest general cargo rates, given for comparative purposes. It must be kept in mind that even these general cargo rates are far below the railroads' direct operating costs, not to mention the total variable cost including equipment. To see this, it is sufficient to note that if the highest short-haul cargo rates had been applied to all cargo traffic and the highest short-haul passenger rates to all passenger traffic in 1964, and if traffic levels could

TABLE 3. RATE STRUCTURE, SELECTED IMPORTANT
COMMODITIES, RFFSA RAILROADS

Distance Kilometers		General rate schedules		Special rate schedules		
		Highest	Lowest	Iron ore	Lumber	Cement
100	a	4.344	3.495	2.647	2.930	3.495
	b	2.52	1.68	.60	1.63	1.67
	c	100	100	100	100	100
600	a	16.509	11.652	5.851	11.076	10.829
	b	2.02	1.41	.99	.81	.60
	c	80	85	164	50	36
800	a	20.561	14.496	7.805	12.722	12.046
	b	2.02	1.41	.94	.13	.09
	c	80	85	157	8	5
2000	a	44.884	31.588	19.499	14.085	20.741
	b	2.02	1.41	.99	.09	1.07
	c	80	85	164	5	64

Source: RFFSA, *Tarifa Geral da RFFSA*, March 1966.
Key: a = NCr$ per ton.
        b = Incremental rate per ton kilometer (centavos).
        c = Incremental rate index (incremental rate at 100 kilometers = 100).

be assumed to hold constant, even then there would have been
an operating deficit of 32.5 percent in that year.

The rate on iron ore — which accounts for about 20 percent
of RFFSA ton-kilometers — appears to be set to equal the cost
on the Vitória-Minas, the large line of the Companhia Vale do
Rio Doce, a mixed enterprise that handles about 80 percent of
the nation's export ore. The Vitória-Minas is a gently sloping
line with low costs. The Central, over which the RFFSA ore
flows from Minas Gerais, runs through mountainous terrain
with steep grades. The Vitória-Minas shows a 10 percent profit
on its operations; the Central incurs a 70 percent loss (ore
accounts for about two-thirds of its freight traffic). The low rate
on the Central, then, seems to have been set with a view to
holding export ore through Rio (via the Central) at the same
price as that shipped by the CVRD over its own line through
Vitória. Adoption by the Central of a more cost-oriented rate
structure would see the loss of most of this ore to the port of
Vitória, further north.

It would seem obvious that the Central rate should not be
taken into account in planning Brazilian exports. However,
terms of reference for feasibility studies for ore export often
accept the continued export of ore over Central tracks as a
datum, although it would obviously be cheaper for Brazil's ore
exports to be consolidated through Vitória either from the deposits of the CVRD itself or, to keep active the other producers
with excellent deposits in Minas Gerais, by extending the Vitória-Minas.

The rate on cement behaves in a markedly strange fashion.
The incremental rate falls by two-thirds at 500 kilometers and
again by six-sevenths at 800 kilometers. It then rises five-fold
at 1,000 kilometers and again by 250 percent at 1,300 kilometers. This pattern seems to be set to encourage cement shipment from producing regions in Minas Gerais to Rio. Without
these subsidies, cement from Minas Gerais could not compete
in the Rio market. This is an especially unfortunate policy
when extensive limestone deposits abound in the state of Rio.
In a situation like this it would be better to encourage imports
if it is impossible for any reason to increase production closer
to these markets.

The treatment of timber also appears to be a case of attempting to regain or retain diverted or divertible traffic. To-day, most shipment of timber is for export through the ports of Paranaguá, São Francisco do Sul, and Pôrto Alegre. In recent years much, if not most, of the traffic to São Paulo for domestic consumption has been diverted to trucks, owing to the more direct and faster routes by road. The main timber areas are in Paraná and in Rio Grande do Sul, at distances respectively of 600–750 kilometers and 800–1,000 kilometers from São Paulo. Interestingly, at 600 kilometers the incremental rate for timber falls by almost 50 percent and at 800 kilometers it falls by another 85 percent. The fact that the incremental rate is constant below 500 kilometers reflects the inelasticity of demand for rail transportation to the ports, all lumber ports being located less than 500 kilometers from the timber stands.

An attempt to raise rates closer to full variable cost, the criterion we have advocated for the railroads, would undoubtedly see the loss of much traffic. Most ore traffic would be lost to the Vitória-Minas railroad outside the federal system, much of the demand for cement shipment would not arise, and intercity passenger traffic, the rate for which has been estimated to be nearly 90 percent below variable cost, would transfer to bus and air travel. Total revenue would decline. So would the railroad deficit as costs were cut back.

It should be emphasized that the costs under discussion are variable costs and do not reflect a charge for basic permanent facilities, which are the conventional source of scale economies in railroading. Nor could it be hoped that line maintenance, which is here considered a variable cost, constitutes a large source of scale economies that could best be exploited by raising traffic through further rate reduction. The simple truth is that the technical specifications of Brazil's railroads are so poor as to preclude volume operations with their consequent scale economies in such "overhead" costs as track maintenance. For example, the average net tonnage on the RFFSA is around 5 percent of that of a train in the United States.[13]

---

[13] Variable cost, as we have defined it, includes one component that is in a sense a fixed cost. This is the large labor force — about 145,000 people on the São Paulo and federal railway systems. Now,

MOTOR VEHICLE PRICE POLICY

The unit cost of common-carrier motor vehicle transport depends primarily on the size and load of the vehicle and on the road surface. Given the average conditions of the Brazilian intercity road network, the vehicle operating costs — depreciation, interest, parts, profit, materials, labor, insurance, and fuels (less taxes) — range from 7.3 centavos per ton-kilometer for a 6-ton gasoline truck down to 3.8 centavos per ton-kilometer for a 25-ton diesel. The same costs per bus passenger-kilometer average 1.5 centavos. In the absence of direct subsidies to the trucking industry it must be assumed that these costs are covered by the shippers.

To the vehicle operating costs must be added the cost of road maintenance and administration and of new investment. Estimated maintenance and administration costs are 0.3 cetavos per ton-kilometer and 0.11 centavos per passenger-kilometer, based on recent experience. To this must be added the cost of the roads, the sector's public capital.

Several approaches to the determination of appropriate public capital costs are possible. One is to apportion the interest and depreciation on the existing network over the present traffic. This valuation may be put very conservatively at NCr$5.3 billion in 1965 by assigning values of NCr$80 thousand, NCr$50 thousand, and NCr$40 thousand respectively to the 26.5 thousand, 55.4 thousand, and 10.5 thousand kilometers of paved, graveled, and earth roads comprising the system (these values are all well below today's cost, but this is offset

while the railroads have often been accused of overstaffing, it may be instead that overstaffing is only on the order of 15–20 percent, the balance of the large force resulting simply from the very poor technical characteristics of the railroad plant. Traffic declines would then indicate how much of the labor force should be released. In any event, present legislation precludes immediate labor cutbacks, that is, outright dismissal of workers, so that the labor force represents a fixed cost in the very short run. However, in the interests of efficient traffic allocation over the long run it would be rational to retire workers prematurely and transfer the burden of their sustenance to an agency outside the transport sector. Railroad operations would then be on a more businesslike basis, on which costs could be correctly calculated. This, however, might require certain legislative changes.

to some extent by the fact that the quality of the components is inferior to that of newly constructed roads). Imputing 80.4 percent to trucks and 9.6 percent to buses [14] gives an annual road cost of NCr$797 million, of which NCr$637 million can be assigned to trucks and NCr$80 million to intercity bus traffic.

The procedure just outlined would result in a user charge averaging 200 percent more than present fuel-tax contributions. The fuel tax is the only tax that can be considered a user charge, since other levies, such as the sales tax on tires and parts, are of the same magnitude as sales taxes on most other intermediate and final goods — about 4–8 percent.

With an increase of 200 percent in user charges, total tax revenues would be enough to cover the annual federal and state highway department outlay on construction, maintenance, and administration. Thus, although the approach here has been to levy user charges as an annual charge against the existing stock, the result is the provision of enough revenue to cover the continuing road development program, consequently eliminating the inflationary effect of present financing procedures.[15]

The necessary increases for different traffic classes are shown in Table 4. As we see in line 5, present contributions for some classes are very low — as low as 10.6 percent for buses and 18.3 percent for 25-ton trucks. This implies increases of about 900 percent and 450 percent respectively for these classes. However, as we see in line 10, the required increases in user charges are small when compared with present shippers' costs (the total of direct operating and capital costs plus present fuel taxes). As shown in line 10, the largest relative

[14] These coefficients are based on recent traffic counts and weights as reported for the important state of Minas Gerais. These values leave 10 percent of the cost of the state and federal systems to be imputed to military and automobile use (the latter accounted for about 3 percent of the gross vehicle-kilometers in the study).

[15] I have not explicitly sought to impute road costs on the basis of annual outlays, since capital expenditure represents a component that will last many years and benefit future users. However, annual outlay, including capital expenditure, is sometimes used explicitly for cost imputation. This is the approach in the Ferguson study cited in note 7 above.

TABLE 4. VEHICLE COSTS, ROAD COSTS, AND
USER CONTRIBUTORS

	Trucks						Buses
	6-ton[a]	7-ton	10-ton	15-ton	20-ton	25-ton	
1. Fuel tax[b]	.81	.47	.38	.29	.25	.22	.07
2. Basic road capital cost[b]	.90	.90	.90	.90	.90	.90	.57
3. Road maintenance cost[b, c]	.30	.30	.30	.30	.30	.30	.11
4. Total road cost[b]	1.20	1.20	1.20	1.20	1.20	1.20	.68
5. Percent coverage[d]	67.3	39.0	31.8	24.5	20.7	18.3	10.6
6. Percent shortfall[e]	32.7	61.0	68.2	75.5	79.3	81.7	89.4
7. Percent medium and heavy truck and bus traffic[f]	14.6	32.6	13.0	10.9	17.0	1.8	10.7
8. Private direct operating costs[b]	7.30	6.76	5.95	5.11	4.27	3.75	1.49
9. Total present user cost[g]	8.11	7.23	6.33	5.44	4.52	3.97	1.56
10. Total user charge increase as percent of total present user cost[h]	4.8	10.1	12.9	16.6	21.1	24.7	38.8

Source: Alan Abouchar, *Diagnostic of the Transport Situation in Brazil*, EPEA, 1967 (mimeographed).
[a] Gasoline truck; all others are diesel.
[b] In centavos per unit.
[c] From Table III-5 *in Diagnostic*.
[d] Line 1 divided by line 4.
[e] 100 percent minus line 5.
[f] As percent of total traffic.
[g] Line 8 plus line 1.
[h] Line 4 minus line 1, divided by line 9.

increase for trucks amounts to only 24.7 percent of present shippers' cost, and the average truck increase can be calculated from line 10 at around 8 percent. Considering just the large trucks — 10-ton trucks and up — the user charge adjustment would raise operating costs around 12 percent. If, as seems reasonable to assume, present trucking costs account for 25 percent of the destination price of the goods shipped, this average 12 percent increase would raise destination costs by only 3 percent and could surely be passed along to the final user in almost all cases. Some of the lower value goods would revert to coastal traffic, with the consequence of lower destination costs. Since these goods would be the most important commodities in low-income budgets, a further social benefit would redound to the poor. A full-cost user policy, then, should see only a small diminution in traffic volume, perhaps 5–8 percent at most, and the public road program fund should rise almost in proportion to the user charge increase.

Inequality between price and cost always presents the threat of resource misallocation. Truck- and bus-user contributions cover only about one-third of the road costs attributable to them, while automobiles pay disproportionately more than their share, raising the possibility of serious distortion in traffic patterns and in location. As we have seen, the rail network, through rates substantially below variable costs, retains or attracts large volumes of traffic and encourages inefficient intermodal traffic allocation, as well as both overconcentration of production and expansion into new areas, by distorting the trade-off between material and processing costs on the one hand and real transport costs on the other. In the same way, the subsidy granted to truck operators distorts the relative prices facing shippers and must lead ultimately to inefficient traffic allocation and location.

Almost the whole of the federal and state road costs should be borne by trucks and buses; automotive users account for only 3–4 percent of gross ton-kilometers on the federal and state network, and this tends to be concentrated in a small portion of the system, in densities modest enough not to require the standards on passing lanes, grades, curves, visibility, and paving necessary for an intercity road transport system. Thus the fuel tax revenues contributed by automobile users — most of the gasoline tax revenues — should not be considered to be freely at the disposal of the long-distance highway grid. The trucks and buses must pay their own costs.

The low automobile density on the intercity network does not mean that the large revenues deriving from automobile traffic should be eliminated or reduced. Rather, the tax on gasoline, like other luxury excise taxes, is a form of progressive income taxation. The automobile owner is a member of the upper or upper-middle income groups, and his car size, which determines his gas consumption per kilometer, usually varies with his income. Moreover, the wealthier tend to use their cars more. Thus the gasoline tax tends to fall disproportionately on the well-to-do, and within this group in a progressive fashion, and could be considered as a general revenue-raising medium like other excise or personal-income taxes, rather than a road-user charge. In a country where income tax evasion appears

TABLE 5. FINANCIAL PERFORMANCE OF LOIDE, COSTEIRA, AND
CONSOLIDATED PRIVATE DRY-CARGO SECTOR, 1963
(thousand of NCr$)

	Loide	Costeira	Private Sector
Receipts	622.9	3,381.7	15,995.8
Expenditures	757.3	7,423.7	14,990.3
Operating profit or deficit	−134.4	−4,042.0	1,005.4
Profit or deficit as percent of expenditures	17.7	54.4	6.7

Source: Comissão de Marinha Mercante, Relatório 1964, pp. 97, 99.
Note: Receipts and expenditures include both shipping and auxiliary operations, principally stevedoring. The profit on the latter tends to be somewhat higher than that on the former.

easy and widespread, such a tax would be welcome for the ease and certainty in administering it; consideration might even be given to raise the tax on products consumed chiefly by automobiles, especially the higher grade of gasoline. Parenthetically, it is worth noting that gasoline prices in Western Europe are several times as high as in Brazil. A system of partial rebates to taxi owners and other business automobile users would help keep this impost in the nature of a surrogate income tax.

Finally, we must return to the argument that the owners of abutting lands should bear part of the cost of highway development because they are major beneficiaries of road construction. For reasons of equity, we should be reminded that in the normal situation with the usual taxation policy the entire benefit of the increased land value does not accrue to the landowner; he pays a large portion of it in capital-gain or income taxes. If there is any justification for charging him directly for the indirect benefit of the road, there would be no less basis for increasing the taxes on, say, a parking lot because the government chose to construct a public building across the street.

Besides being discriminatory, such a property-taxation policy for abutting lands would be administratively difficult — especially in Brazil's inflationary setting, where the increase attributable to general inflation would be hard to separate from the effect of the road — and would open many possibilities for corrupt assessment.

The efficiency argument against property taxation for highway development is more compelling. Suppose that such a tax policy were adopted and the entire difference between present truck-user charges and development costs were to be raised through property taxation. This difference would range from about two-thirds of the capital cost on roads of average density up to 80–90 percent on roads with moderate or low densities in the state and federal network.[16] The cost of farming the abutting lands would probably be prohibitive, and agricultural products would continue to be shipped, at great subsidy, over the long distances from the farms to the market at the terminal points of the road — unless the intervening lands had some other technical advantage, which cannot be assumed to be the general case. The situation could result that all the land along the way remained unused, or was defaulted to the state for failure to pay taxes, while there was as yet no demand for the land for urban purposes. If, however, the truckers themselves had to pay the cost of the road development and in turn charged the shippers, the intervening lands would be kept in crops, since their output would have a competitive edge in the market, the advantage being the transport-cost differential between the original source and the intervening farms.

COASTAL SHIPPING PRICE POLICY

Rates in the private coastal shipping sector have been adequate to cover expenditures and provide a reasonable profit. Rates in the two most important public sector enterprises, Costeira and Loide, which were combined in May 1966, have not. The 1963 performances are summarized in Table 5.

---

[16] This discussion excludes county roads, where automobile use would be relatively more important. On the county road system the total automobile gasoline tax contribution should be considered a user charge, and the balance could be derived from property taxation.

The losses in the public sector are due to several factors, including overmanning, inefficient operation of the large repair yards, and low utilization coefficients, the last-named reflecting both the long periods spent in the repair yards and the public firms' attempts to extend regular service to the smaller ports, which generate less traffic per call. Thus, the utilization coefficients of Costeira and Loide in 1963 were respectively 0.3 ton/dwt and 1.6 ton/dwt while that of the private dry cargo sector was 4.1 ton/dwt. This was 14 and 2.5 times as high as the public sector agencies, respectively.

The public sector deficit should be eliminated by reducing high costs such as those of its repair yard services. To the extent that the deficit is caused by extension of frequent liner service to small ports the deficit could also be reduced through raising rates on shipments originating or terminating in these ports, combined, perhaps, with some cutback in service.

The costs we have been looking at so far are the financial costs, the expenditures of the companies as they have actually been incurred. These expenditures include a fuel tax payment that in the past has been used for the development of other modes of transportation. For example, the average general dry cargo expenditure (including profit) per ton-kilometer in 1964 amounted to 1.275 centavos, of which .075 centavos was fuel tax. Adjusting accordingly gives us a total variable unit social cost of 1.2 centavos. As long as the ports are not included in the distribution of the fuel tax revenues, coastal shipping should not have to pay such taxes. Eliminating them would permit a reduction in rates.

If major port improvements are undertaken, the social cost of coastal shipping will rise, requiring a rate increase in conformity with the principle of self-support of transport modes. An investment program has recently been developed for the three important ports of Recife, Rio, and Santos, where combined international and coastal traffic is expected to reach 7.5 million tons of general cargo and 7.2 million tons of dry bulk cargo (excluding iron ore) by 1976. The total reequipment program calls for NCr$403 million divided 70–30 between the two types of cargo. Assuming similar reequipment requirements in other parts, a twenty-year equipment life, linear growth of traffic, a linear investment program, and a

10 percent interest charge, the cost per ton of general cargo is then NCr$5.58 for each arrival or departure, or NCr$11.16 per ton shipped. Once the investment program is under way, these charges should be levied at the terminal ports when cargoes are loaded and unloaded. They would then be built into the shipping rate schedules.

The traffic projection used in the foregoing calculation, 14.7 million tons of international and coastal shipping (excluding iron ore), is reasonable in view of the comparable 1964 total of 9.3 million and the fact that coastal shipping costs will still be far below those of other modes while the level of service in the ports will rise significantly. Thus, even assuming a fall in the average haul of coastal traffic, the unit cost of coastal shipping will continue to be very low, under 1.6 centavos per ton-kilometer. This is much lower than rail or road costs in terms of equivalent distance, that is, adjusting for the shorter distance of coastal shipping on any arc as compared with roads or the much longer railroad route. The average distance-adjusted costs of road and rail are 3.8 centavos and 4.4 centavos.

AIR-TRANSPORT PRICE POLICY

Air transport services are underpriced.

The air transport industry customarily receives subsidies from the federal government to cover unexpected domestic losses as well as deficit international operations, equipment purchases, and service to the interior. Total losses amounted to one-seventh of total expenditures in 1964; 85 percent of this was covered by subsidy.

Losses do not always take proper account of capital costs. That is to say, depreciation is sometimes calculated on the basis of historical rather than replacement cost.

Airport landing fees are trifling compared to the costs of operating the airports (or compared to those in foreign countries). Thus, an important cost of civil aviation is not reflected in the base on which the industry's deficit is usually calculated.

Air-transport companies are exempt from fuel taxes. Unlike the coastal shipping industry, however, civil aviation does receive a share (2.7 percent) of the fuel tax revenues. Again an important industry cost is not reflected in the usual accounts.

Self-support should be promoted through elimination of the subsidies in the next few years (together with elimination of one important reason for their formation, the 25 percent discount given government employees), introduction of uniform and realistic accounting procedures, proper landing fees, and payment of fuel taxes.

CONCLUSION

Full-cost pricing is the appropriate pricing principle for most Brazilian transport services to avoid the distortions in traffic-demand patterns that might lead to overinvestment in transport facilities, and, not incidentally, to minimize the inflationary impact of deficit investment financing. However, the existence of many serious discrepancies has been noted between prices and costs in every important mode of transport — railroad passenger and freight movement, bus traffic, truck movement, coastal shipping, and air transport. Railroads receive too little from their own users and too much from the economy at large and from road users by way of their fuel tax allocation; trucks pay too little toward the cost of road maintenance and construction; civil aviation contributes almost nothing to airport development and operation, but receives large operating subsidies; the petroleum refining industry (Petrobrás) is heavily subsidized, primarily by automobile owners, through its fuel tax allotment; and, finally, coastal shipping helps support other modes by virtue of the present fuel tax distribution. It should be noted that misallocation of fuel tax revenues has arisen as much, if not more, from the pressures of public agencies as from private interests. The important government authorities responsible for the several modes of transport — the federal railroad system, the highway and railroad department, the coastal shipping agencies, and the civil aviation agency, as well as Petrobrás — are large and firmly entrenched bureaucracies capable of exerting great pressure to maintain and increase their investment and expenditure shares, the scope of their operations, and their jobs and importance. Frequently government expertise in a transport mode is heavily concentrated in the supervisory organizations of the mode, and spending plans cannot be properly questioned and analyzed by outside agencies. It is vain to argue that the countervailing power of the several bureaucracies and the private sector will promote an allocation of resources consistent with the consumer preferences underlying the economy; there is little to show that the national highway department did anything to prevent the recent change in the distribution of the fuel tax in favor of the railroads and Petrobrás, and it is probable that those organizations supported the DNER in its subse-

TABLE 6. ESTIMATED VOLUME OF MAIN TYPES OF
INTERCITY TRAFFIC, 1963
(billion ton- or passenger-kilometers)

General cargo	69.8
Dense land traffic	11.3
Petroleum coastal traffic	6.7
Dry bulk coastal traffic	3.0
Passengers	26.8

quent effort to incorporate into the national constitution a change in the allocation of the national road fund from the 40–60 split between the federal government and the states and counties to a 60–40 split favoring the federal highway department. And, of course, little opposition was likely from the unorganized state and county interests.

Many specific directions for change in the pricing of individual transport services have been indicated above. In view of the entrenched interests that may be expected to resist such changes, it cannot be hoped to effect them immediately, but they should be adopted as a goal of national policy within a period of three to five years. How will these changes affect traffic patterns and the implied need for investment?

Part of the answer is supplied by the transport technology oriented traffic classification in Table 6. Five major classes are distinguished: general cargo, high-density land flows, petroleum between coastal cities, bulk mineral products between coastal cities, and intercity passengers.

Evidently the greatest traffic flow in Brazil is general cargo, for which motor vehicle transport is best suited since many diverse origins and destinations are involved and shipments tend to be made in small lots. The speed and relative security of motor vehicles are especially desirable for this traffic, since losses, if they occur, involve heavier financial loss than losses of the other cargoes considered. However, rail and coastal vessels do account for a share of this traffic, about 10 percent. Coastal shipping could handle considerably more if the service were improved, since its unit costs are about 70 percent lower than shippers' costs by truck. A more equitable user charge would further increase the private savings by ship.

Total commodity traffic has grown at a compound annual rate of 9 percent since 1950, and there is no reason to expect this growth to cease. General cargo and petroleum coastal traffic have shown the fastest growth; while both will continue to grow at a high rate, the former represents a much larger absolute component and will probably grow more rapidly with further industrialization. This signifies an even larger role for truck transport in the future, as well as an increased participation of dry coastal shipping if port conditions are improved. Moreover, since demand for truck transportation can be presumed to be fairly inelastic, the recommended user-charge increases should not preclude the forward planning of road investment on the basis of historical trends in motor vehicle transport activity; nor should it introduce uncertainty about the sources of investment funds.

Since there are relatively few origins and destinations in dense land traffic, this class is best suited to movement by rail or pipeline (about 3.5 percent of this traffic was moved by pipeline in 1963; another 3 percent consisted of petroleum products by rail), for which the high initial capital costs can be more easily amortized. However, most of the traffic in question is limited to a few lines. About 40 percent is handled by the Vitória-Minas and about 27 percent by the Central (and most of the iron ore included in the latter percentage would be rerouted by the Vitória-Minas if a more rational pricing policy were instituted). Moreover, traffic on the Vitória-Minas will increase fastest in the future, followed by petroleum traffic through existing pipelines and a few new ones as well. These traffic conditions, together with the high cost of line construction, argue against any major expansion or rehabilitation of the railroad system and suggest a very substantial reduction in the railroad sector's share of investment, which, as shown in Table 1, reached nearly 20 percent of total public transport investment in 1961–1965 period.

The third and fourth classes of traffic will continue to go by coastal vessel, the liquid increasing more rapidly and the dry less rapidly than total national transport demand. As noted above, the maritime sector could also play a larger role in the movement of general cargo.

Finally, the growth of passenger traffic is another stimulus to the development of motor-vehicle transport. About two-thirds of passenger traffic today moves by bus. Almost all of it would if the prices of all services were set to cover their costs, since bus prices would rise absolutely and relatively little, whereas the prices of other intercity passenger services would rise significantly. Continued subsidy of suburban rail transport, especially outside Rio, is probably desirable to avoid further congestion within the city and on its feeder roads, with the prejudicial effect on welfare that would result.

CHAPTER 13

An Intersectoral Consistency Model
for Economic Planning in Brazil

Willy van Rijckeghem

Consistency planning is concerned with the calculation of sectoral output targets that correspond to the requirement of "balanced growth." If the plan is implemented, there will then be no shortages on either commodity or factor markets. The result may not be optimal (there may be waste), but it will correspond to a set of targets imposed by the policy maker, and therefore related to the latter's preference function.

Depending on the available amount of statistical information, alternative and possibly complementary methods have been used to deal with the problem of consistency planning.

The Rule-of-Thumb Method

Rules of thumb for the expansion of industries have been devised in situations where little or no information was available. The best-known rule states that sectors must be expanded proportionately to the income elasticities of demand, obviously an inappropriate rule for industries depending mainly on intermediate demand, such as steel and chemicals. It also needs amendment for ad hoc considerations, such as import substitu-

AUTHOR'S NOTE: I am indebted to A. Fishlow and S. Morley for comments and suggestions on previous drafts of this paper.

tion, the development of export markets, and so on. More sophisticated rules, taking into account relative prices, have been worked out by Leif Johansen, but they serve mostly to show what an inordinate amount of information is required to arrive at a satisfactory rule.[1]

The Time-Series Method

Assuming that past development, as reflected in historical sectoral growth rates, has been more or less balanced, it is possible to estimate the average relationship between the growth rate of a particular industry and the overall growth rate of the economy. In addition, it is possible to introduce separate variables, such as population growth and exports, into the regression relationships. Still, the relationships may be biased by supply bottlenecks, the presence of lags and leads, measurement errors in production indices, and so on. The most serious problem is usually the shortness of the period for which data are available, with, therefore, an insufficient range for the explanatory variables.

The International Cross-Section Method

A wider range of variation is permitted by the use of international cross sections in which highly developed as well as underdeveloped economies are represented side by side. The best-known study of this type is the one by H. Chenery in which industrial output is explained as a function of per capita income and of population.[2] The method has been applied to Brazil by J. Bergsman and A. Candal in this volume. Comparing observed growth rates of the various industrial branches in Brazil with the growth rates predicted by the regression equations of the international cross-section, they found discrepancies ranging from 12 to 56 percent, with an average of 31 percent. Their calculations also show that the residuals of the relationship when applied to Brazil are not

---

[1] L. Johansen, "Rules of Thumb for the Expansion of Industries," *Econometrica*, April 1960, pp. 258–271.

[2] H. B. Chenery, "Patterns of Industrial Growth," *American Economic Review*, Sept. 1960, pp. 624–654; *A Study of Industrial Growth* (New York: United Nations, 1963).

random but follow a certain pattern over time. To the extent that these residuals are correlated with any of the explanatory variables in the regression equation, the parameter estimates are likely to be biased and therefore to lead to wrong extrapolations.

The Input-Output Approach

The so-called closed dynamic Leontief model is theoretically best suited to estimate sectorally consistent production levels. In one way or another, most recent planning models are a variant of this prototype. According to what is specified of the relationship between inputs and outputs, three different models can be constructed.

(1) *The constant average coefficients model.* This is the original Leontief formulation and still the most widely used version. Input-output coefficients, consumption coefficients, and capital-output ratios are all invariant over time. Most recent improvements aim at relaxing these assumptions.[3]

(2) *The constant marginal coefficients model.* In this type the constancy of the average coefficients is replaced by the constancy of the marginal coefficients. The only planning model which makes use of this modification so far is the Times model for Pakistan.[4]

(3) *The constant elasticity coefficients model.* This approach will be experimented with below. Elasticities will be used to relate inputs to outputs, household demand to income, and capital requirements to production. Apart from the inherent advantage of working with elasticities, especially for the consumption and production functions, this ap-

[3] Recent models using the fixed coefficients framework, but containing modifications in other directions include the Bergsman-Manne model for India; see I. Adelman and E. Thorbecke, eds., *The Theory and Design of Economic Development* (Baltimore: Johns Hopkins Press, 1967); and the Bruno model for Israel, T. Barna, ed., *Structural Interdependence and Economic Development* (London: Macmillan, 1963).

[4] W. Tims, "A Growth Model for Pakistan and Its Application," in G. F. Papanek, ed., *Development Policy: Theory and Practice* (Cambridge, Mass.: Harvard University Press, 1968).

proach offers the convenience of directly expressing the solution of the model in sectoral growth rates, which, by the nature of the model, are mutually consistent.

It is obvious that any modification of the constant coefficients assumption has to be undertaken with circumspection. The relative importance of measurement errors increases considerably as the move is made from average to marginal coefficients or, for that matter, to elasticities. This is especially true when the estimates are derived from only two observations, for example when only two input-output tables are available. It is therefore not surprising to find, as Tilanus did for the Netherlands,[5] that the forecasting ability of a system using constant coefficients was superior to the one using marginal coefficients. Still, a system which allows input-output elasticities and capital-output elasticities to differ from the value one would appear theoretically superior. Even when some of the elasticity estimates appear doubtful because of measurement errors and the like, it is still possible to use a value equal to one, leaving things no worse than in the case where *all* average coefficients were assumed to be constant.

OUTLINE OF THE MODEL

To clarify the mechanism of the model we have in mind, we describe rapidly a sequence of operations for a general *n*-sector version of the economy. For practical purposes, the sequence is here made recursive and therefore lends itself easily to decentralization and computer simulation.

(1) Determine an overall growth rate for national product, say *y* percent annually. If possible, this growth rate should be determined in a macro-economic framework, such as the Fishlow-Morley model, so that no problem of macro-economic consistency arises afterward.

(2) Determine the growth rates of consumer demand for the product of the various sectors, consistent with the overall

[5] C. B. Tilanus, "Marginal Versus Average Input Coefficients in Input-Output Forecasting," *Quarterly Journal of Economics*, Feb. 1967, pp. 140–145.

growth rate in income. We use consumption functions of the following type:

$$c_i = \beta_i y + (1 - \beta_i)\, p$$

where

$c_i =$ the growth rate of consumer demand for sector i

$p =$ the growth rate of population

The estimation of the consumption functions will be discussed below. Suffice it to mention here that the $p =$ variable was introduced to take into account the impact of rapid population growth (as it takes place in Brazil) on the structure of consumption.

(3) Determine the sectoral growth rates of investment demand, government consumption, and export demand. At this stage all these growth rates are taken as exogenous. The investment growth rates will have to be revised at a later stage in the model. As a first approximation, the growth rate of total investment as implied by the macro-model can be taken.

(4) Determine the sectoral growth rates consistent with the growth rates of final and intermediate demand:

$$s_i = \Sigma \delta_{ij} x_{ij} + \delta_{ic} c_i + \delta_{ig} g_i + \delta_{iz} z_i + \delta_{ie} e_i$$

where:

$s_i =$ the growth rate of supply of sector i

$x_{ij} =$ the growth rate of sales of i to j

$c_i =$ the growth rate of consumer demand for i

$g_i =$ the growth rate of government demand for i

$z_i =$ the growth rate of investment demand for i

$e_i =$ the growth rate of export demand for i

The required growth rate of supply in each sector is expressed as the weighted average of the growth rates of intermediate and final demand. The coefficients δ are used as the weights. They may appropriately be called product distribution coefficients, which reflect the relative distribution of supply at the beginning of the planning period.[6] The sum of these coefficients is equal to 1 for any given sector. They have to be de-

---

[6] Product distribution coefficients (also called output coefficient) have been used in the work of A. Ghosh, *Experiments with Input-Output Models* (London: Cambridge University Press, 1964); and S. B. Noble, "A Property and Use of Output Coefficients of a Leontief Model," in

rived from an input-output table. As a matter of fact, they represent an alternative way of looking at the latter.

(5) Specify the degree of self-sufficiency for each of the sectors at the beginning of the planning period:

$$s_i = \pi_i x_i + (1 - \pi_i) m_i$$

where

s_i = the growth rate of supply of i
x_i = the growth rate of domestic supply
m_i = the growth rate of competitive imports of i

The weights π_i indicate the degree of self-sufficiency at the beginning of the planning period.

(6) Determine the import substitution targets. These are expressed by a relationship between the growth rate of competitive imports and of total supply:

$$m_i = \mu_i s_i$$

If μ_i is set equal to 1, the degree of self-sufficiency will remain unchanged. If it is set at a level smaller than 1, import substitution will take place, and self-sufficiency will be increased. As a consequence, π_i weights will be different at the end of the planning period from those prevailing at the beginning. This does not affect the growth rates in the solution of the model, however, since these refer also to the situation at the beginning of the planning period.

(7) Specify the input-output elasticities, that is, the relationship between the growth rates of inputs and the growth rates of the corresponding output:

$$x_{ij} = a_{ij} x_j$$

The inputs x_{ij} are so defined that they include imported inputs as well. Substitution between imported and domestic inputs therefore does not affect a_{ij}.

(8) Substitute (7), (6), (5), and (2) into (4) and obtain a system of n simultaneous equations in n endogenous variables (the n-sectoral growth rates) in function of a set of predetermined variables:

M. Shubik, ed., *Essays in Honor of O. Morgenstern* (Princeton: Princeton University Press, 1967).

$$\begin{bmatrix} x_1 \\ \cdot \\ \cdot \\ \cdot \\ \cdot \\ \cdot \\ \cdot \\ \cdot \\ x_n \end{bmatrix} = \begin{bmatrix} \dfrac{\pi_1}{1-(1-\pi_1)\mu_1} - \delta_{11}a_{11} & \cdot \cdot \cdot \cdot \cdot & -\delta_{1n}a_{1n} \\ & & \\ & & \\ & & \\ & & \\ & & \\ & & \\ -\delta_{n1}a_{n1} & \cdot \cdot \cdot \cdot \dfrac{\pi_n}{1-(1-\pi_n)\mu_n} & - \delta_{nn}a_{nn} \end{bmatrix}^{-1} \begin{bmatrix} f_1 \\ \\ \\ \\ \\ \\ \\ \\ f_n \end{bmatrix}$$

where $f_i = \delta_{ic}\beta_i y + (1-\beta_i)p + \delta_{iz}z_i + \delta_{ig}g_i + \delta_{ie}e_i$

The vector of sectoral growth rates of production is obtained after premultiplying the vector of the weighted growth rates of final demand f_i by the inverse of a matrix, with diagonal elements equal to $\dfrac{\pi_j}{1-(1-\pi_i)\mu_i} - \delta_{ii}a_{ii}$, and with off-diagonal elements equal to $-\delta_{ij}a_{ij}$.

In the special case of complete self-sufficiency, the diagonal elements reduce to $1 - \delta_{ii}a_{ii}$. When self-sufficiency is not complete, but no further import substitution is planned ($\mu_i = 1$), the same simplified expression is obtained.

(9) Determine the sectoral growth rates of capital stock corresponding to the growth rates of sectoral outputs:

$$k_j = \tau_j x_j$$

where $k_j =$ the growth rate of capital stock of sector j
$\tau_j =$ the sectoral capital-output elasticity

The growth rates of capital stock can be translated into growth rates of gross investment using the definitional relationship (neglecting subscripts):

$$Z = DK + \sigma K$$

where $Z =$ the level of gross investment
$DK =$ the change in capital stock (net investment)
$\sigma K =$ the level of depreciation (σ is the depreciation rate)

Translating this relationship into relative changes, we obtain:

$$z = \frac{k + \sigma + Dk/k}{1 + \sigma/k}$$

When the growth rate of capital stock is a constant $(Dk = 0)$, the growth rate of gross investment becomes equal to the growth rate of the capital stock $(z = k)$. When the growth rate of capital stock is accelerating, the growth rate of gross investment will exceed the growth rate of the capital stock. For example, when the growth rate of capital stock accelerates from 6 to 7 percent, and the depreciation rate is equal to 10 percent, the growth rate of gross investment is equal to 14 percent. If all elements of the capital stock grow at the same rate, that is, when the investment mix is assumed constant, all z_{ij}, that is, the growth rates of investment in sector j using capital good i will be equal to the rate calculated above. Finally, taking for any given i the weighted average of the sectoral z_{ij} and of the z_{ic} and z_{ig}, we can determine the growth rate of total investment demand for capital goods supplied by sector i:

$$z_i = \Sigma \epsilon_{ij} z_{ij} + \epsilon_{ic} z_{ic} + \epsilon_{ig} z_{ig}$$

where z_{ij} = the growth rate of investment demand from sector j for investment goods supplied by sector i

z_{ic} = the growth rate of consumer demand for investment goods supplied by i

z_{ig} = the growth rate of government demand for investment goods supplied by i

By analogy with the product distribution coefficients, we may call the ϵ_{ij} the investment distribution coefficients, which reflect the distribution of investment at the beginning of the planning period. The calculated growth rates z_i can now be checked against the provisional growth rates assumed at stage (4) of the model. Replacing the provisional by the calculated growth rates of investment demand leads to a second-round estimate of sectoral growth rates of output at stage (8), and to a second-round estimate of growth rates of investment demand at stage (9). The system converges very rapidly.

(10) Check whether the growth rate of national product produced by the system corresponds to the growth rate assumed at stage (1). If it is the same, this means that macro-economic consistency is also assured. If it is different, this indicates that the growth rate calculated in the macro-economic framework

is not the true equilibrium growth rate. Either this growth rate or the import substitution targets may then have to be revised.*

THE CONSUMPTION FUNCTIONS

No time series are available for consumer demand for the product of the different sectors. Our consumption functions had therefore to be derived from the budget survey carried out by the Getúlio Vargas Foundation.[7] The survey presents information on per-family consumption of some twenty-two expenditure categories, family income, and family size. The following regression relationship was examined:

$$\ln \frac{C_i}{F} = a_i + \beta_i \ln \frac{Y}{F} + \gamma_i \ln \frac{P}{F}$$

where $C_i/F =$ family expenditure on products from sector i
$\quad Y/F \ \ =$ family income
$\quad P/F \ \ =$ family size

The major problem encountered in testing this function was that of multicollinearity, as family income and family size appeared to be correlated. Only for four cities (São Paulo, Rio de Janeiro, Curitiba, and Belém) and for the interior of São Paulo was the r^2 between family income and family size smaller than 0.50. For some other cities, it went as high as 0.90, making the regression results unusable. However, for the four cities mentioned above, as well as for the interior of São Paulo, the estimates obtained for β and γ were remarkably stable. We used therefore their weighted average as an estimate for Brazil as a whole. The results are shown in Table 1. Most income elasticities seem reasonable, ranging from about one-half for food to around two for investment expenditures such as the purchase of a car or the acquisition of a house or apartment.

---

* This problem is related to Chenery's well-known two-gap analysis of an economy. Macro-economic consistency requires equality of the investment-savings and the import-export gaps. When they are not equal, either the overall growth target has to be revised, or import substitution has to take place. See also the Tims model on this point.

---

[7] Fundação Getúlio Vargas, *Pesquisa Sôbre Orçamentos Familiares 1961–1962 e 1962–1963.*

The elasticities for family size are all smaller than 1, indicating economies of scale in consumption as family size increases. Negative elasticities are obtained for luxury expenditure items, such as restaurant meals, travel, own transportation, and even maintenance. The latter two can be explained by their complementarity with investment expenditures on cars and homes, which also show a negative elasticity with respect to family size.

What are the implications of these results for projecting consumer demand? By differentiating our previous loglinear functions with respect to time, we obtain an expression in growth rates as follows:

$$(c_i - f) = \beta_i(y - f) + \gamma_i(p - f)$$

TABLE 1. PARAMETER ESTIMATES FOR CONSUMPTION FUNCTION

Income elasticity (β_i)	Elasticity with respect to family size (γ_i)	Consumer budget classification	Input-output sector classification
		Current-consumption Functions	
0.52	0.63	Food prepared at home	1, 2, 26
1.03	0.00	Beverages	27
0.47	0.34	Tobacco	28
1.01	0.97	Clothing and textiles	19, 24, 25
0.46	0.99	Cleaning products	22
0.73	0.27	Personal care products	21
1.09	0.67	Household equipment	10–13, 15, 16, 23
1.27	0.00	Reading material	29
0.56	0.72	Urban transportation	32
1.94	−2.95	Own transportation	14, 18
1.32	−2.87	Restaurants	5
1.02	0.70	Amusements	5
1.12	0.48	Clothing services	5
0.77	0.26	Rents	5
0.97	0.00	Personal care services	5
0.90	0.29	Medical assistance	5
1.38	0.00	Education	5
1.01	−0.85	Maintenance	3, 7, 20, 31, wages[a]
1.74	−2.33	Travel	32
		Investment Functions	
1.98	−2.19	Housing construction	31
2.12	−3.57	New car purchases	14

[a] Wages paid for direct use of labor by households and not included in the service sector.

where $c_i = $ the growth rate of consumer demand for the
              product of sector i
    $y = $ the growth rate of national income
    $f = $ the growth rate of the number of families
    $p = $ the growth rate of population

What future relation can we expect between the growth
rate of the number of families and the growth rate of population? Because of the observed connection between family size
and family income at the cross-section level, we might be
tempted to project an increase in family size, that is, a faster
growth for population than for the number of families. Unfortunately, there are no reliable time series against which we can
test this assumption. However, census figures on the number of
people per residence, a concept closely related to family size,
show no increase in this ratio since 1940. We therefore made
the relatively safe assumption:

$$p = f$$

so that $\quad\quad\quad\quad\quad c_i = \beta_i y + (1 - \beta_i) p$

The growth rate of consumer demand for the product of sector i now depends solely on the growth rate of national income
and on population growth. Obviously, rapid population growth
will bias the structure of consumption in favor of products with
a low income elasticity.

THE PRODUCT- AND
INVESTMENT-DISTRIBUTION MATRICES

The δ- and ϵ-coefficients, which reflect the distribution of
supply for current and for investment use respectively, can
conveniently be summarized in two matrices. The product distribution matrix is presented in Figure 1.

Every element in the matrix was obtained by dividing
every transaction in a given row of the 1959 input-output table
by total supply of the corresponding sector.[8] Total supply is
defined as the sum of domestic production and of competitive
imports. The input-output table is given in Table 2. The rela-

[8] W. van Rijckeghem: *The 1959 Input-Output Table for Brazil.*
IPEA working paper, August, 1967 (mimeographed).

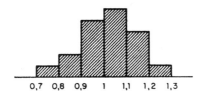

RAW MATERIALS

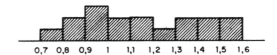

PACKING MATERIALS

FUELS AND LUBRICANTS

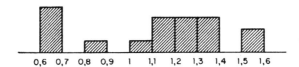

ELECTRIC ENERGY

FIG. 1 Distribution of Proportions Between Input-Output Coefficients, 1959 and 1949.

TABLE 2. BRAZIL: INPUT-OUTPUT TABLE, 1959

Sectors	1	2	3	4	5
1 Vegetable product	12,982	20,720	0	0	300
2 Animal product	24	0	0	0	345
3 Electric energy	200	102	3,772	1,200	913
4 Commerce	800	251	0	0	1,717
5 Services	6,375	1,875	1,886	47,436	16,708
6 Wastes	0	0	0	0	0
7 Fuels	1,000	0	2,037	2,000	2,000
8 Packaging	3,084	0	0	0	0
9 Extractive industry	0	0	0	0	0
10 Nonmetallic minerals	0	0	0	0	350
11 Metallurgy	3,000	1,831	0	0	182
12 Machine tools	0	0	0	0	200
13 Electrical goods	0	0	0	0	200
14 Transportation goods	200	0	0	0	997
15 Wood	0	0	0	0	150
16 Furniture	0	0	0	0	0
17 Paper	0	0	0	0	50
18 Rubber	0	0	0	0	0
19 Leather	0	0	0	0	836
20 Chemical industry	8,712	3,145	0	1,000	1,000
21 Pharmaceuticals	0	239	0	0	4,652
22 Perfumery	0	0	0	479	687
23 Plastics	0	0	0	0	30
24 Textiles	0	0	0	0	1,332
25 Clothing	0	0	0	74	1,000
26 Food	0	1,302	0	0	1,000
27 Beverages	0	0	0	0	2,029
28 Tobacco	0	0	0	0	0
29 Publishing	0	0	0	3,000	4,768
30 Miscellaneous	0	0	0	0	2,425
31 Construction	2,423	0	0	0	25,000
32 Transportation	0	0	0	9,343	807
Σ	38,800	29,465	7,695	64,532	69,678
Gross Returns to capital	215,695	84,936	9,970	160,398	227,579
Wages, salaries, and social security	80,302	15,000	1,197	55,418	86,864
Value Added	295,997	99,936	11,167	215,816	314,443
Gross product	334,797	129,401	18,862	280,348	384,121

TABLE 2. BRAZIL: INPUT-OUTPUT TABLE, 1959—(Continued)

6	7	8	9	10	11	12
0	11,205	0	11	3	560	8
0	0	0	0	1	4	0
0	0	0	70	636	1,523	147
0	15,362	3,444	184	1,670	1,946	506
0	0	0	977	3,338	6,974	2,293
0	0	0	0	71	3,862	51
0	0	0	340	4,794	4,462	315
0	0	0	55	1,828	755	169
0	4,682	0	1,387	2,354	3,705	30
85	0	3,201	0	3,666	125	80
5,225	0	6,879	48	400	40,340	11,151
0	0	0	0	2	17	368
0	0	0	3	58	102	979
0	0	0	0	0	1	6
0	0	3,743	2	30	246	282
0	0	0	0	0	0	105
1,614	0	10,555	0	25	124	2
85	0	684	0	5	32	56
0	0	0	0	4	1	20
935	42,813	0	116	1,390	1,598	208
0	0	0	0	0	0	0
0	0	0	0	0	3	0
0	0	0	1	5	51	22
679	0	7,981	0	26	161	32
0	0	0	0	0	0	0
0	0	0	0	4	45	0
0	0	0	0	1	3	0
0	0	0	0	0	0	0
0	0	0	89	286	245	123
0	0	0	0	0	13	0
0	0	0	0	0	0	0
0	0	0	469	1,716	1,310	284
8,623	74,062	36,487	3,752	22,313	68,208	17,237
0	0	0	7,346	19,113	36,223	8,564
0	0	0	4,130	11,448	19,821	7,829
0	0	0	11,476	30,561	56,044	16,393
8,623	74,062	36,487	15,228	52,874	124,252	33,630

TABLE 2. BRAZIL: INPUT-OUTPUT TABLE, 1959—(Continued)

Sectors	13	14	15	16	17
1 Vegetable product	70	52	7,387	225	514
2 Animal product	3	0	6	8	0
3 Electric energy	164	219	170	118	412
4 Commerce	1,278	712	220	672	350
5 Services	3,145	6,503	1,448	1,418	1,894
6 Wastes	10	285	58	17	1,486
7 Fuels	183	571	459	55	940
8 Packaging	493	152	104	162	295
9 Extractive industry	37	56	6	6	23
10 Nonmetallic minerals	632	355	52	187	76
11 Metallurgy	14,095	18,441	197	1,506	71
12 Machine tools	1,454	234	1	3	0
13 Electrical goods	3,759	1,472	0	12	0
14 Transportation goods	11	12,165	0	0	0
15 Wood	132	626	4,581	4,660	173
16 Furniture	464	12	0	20	0
17 Paper	78	88	19	9	12,613
18 Rubber	57	1,768	5	28	17
19 Leather	1	24	2	59	1
20 Chemical industry	824	531	219	390	1,550
21 Pharmaceuticals	24	0	0	0	0
22 Perfumery	3	0	0	0	0
23 Plastics	913	265	0	414	4
24 Textiles	176	172	37	1,194	443
25 Clothing	0	2	0	0	0
26 Food	6	8	17	4	30
27 Beverages	1	1	1	22	3
28 Tobacco	0	0	0	0	0
29 Publishing	178	211	163	134	60
30 Miscellaneous	11	0	0	0	0
31 Construction	0	0	0	0	0
32 Transportation	241	432	1,448	337	498
Σ	28,443	45,357	16,600	11,660	21,453
Gross Returns to capital	11,328	23,714	9,057	5,090	9,558
Wages, salaries, and social security	7,158	11,026	5,546	4,964	4,097
Value added	18,486	34,740	14,603	10,054	13,655
Gross product	46,929	80,097	31,203	21,714	35,108

TABLE 2. BRAZIL: INPUT-OUTPUT TABLE, 1959–(Continued)

18	19	20	21	22	23	24
4,427	311	9,141	23	405	3	19,432
0	2,085	829	4	390	0	680
122	66	731	64	36	40	1,141
259	647	1,518	466	807	104	3,121
1,451	679	4,111	2,878	1,509	720	7,501
1,493	3	18	2	0	2	588
239	107	2,217	121	153	31	1,714
183	53	3,225	2,942	1,670	111	1,386
3	19	16,001	0	9	1	30
21	61	276	2	42	8	22
346	104	522	1	0	37	18
0	0	0	0	0	114	24
0	0	32	0	0	1	0
0	4	0	0	0	0	11
1	36	106	0	4	5	0
0	0	0	0	0	0	0
1	54	573	0	0	167	4
3,581	0	35	0	0	7	24
12	2,083	0	0	0	83	35
1,118	1,007	22,355	5,552	6,727	2,106	12,087
0	0	0	53	0	0	0
0	8	5	3	37	0	31
7	32	1	0	0	331	1
1,988	123	508	0	0	275	36,751
0	0	0	0	5	0	0
0	3	275	103	18	0	83
0	1	363	64	75	10	6
0	0	0	0	0	0	0
49	44	266	125	62	28	278
0	10	0	0	0	0	0
0	0	0	0	0	0	0
258	198	1,155	272	223	51	1,189
15,559	7,738	64,263	12,675	12,172	4,235	86,157
11,569	3,092	31,626	6,544	4,329	2,619	35,561
2,714	1,935	9,886	3,814	1,472	1,134	26,291
14,283	5,027	41,512	10,358	5,801	3,753	61,852
29,842	12,765	105,775	23,033	17,973	7,988	148,009

TABLE 2. BRAZIL: INPUT-OUTPUT TABLE, 1959–(Continued)

Sectors	25	26	27	28	29
1 Vegetable product	11	82,401	2,748	1,867	0
2 Animal product	100	54,000	27	1	0
3 Electric energy	107	1,304	131	20	130
4 Commerce	1,418	2,430	430	102	620
5 Services	2,727	10,285	2,179	492	2,043
6 Wastes	17	1	0	0	0
7 Fuels	67	3,215	450	39	74
8 Packaging	735	13,784	3,330	1,466	117
9 Extractive industry	2	1,019	0	0	1
10 Nonmetallic minerals	143	190	2	0	1
11 Metallurgy	254	1	0	0	247
12 Machine tools	0	0	0	0	0
13 Electrical goods	0	0	0	0	0
14 Transportation goods	0	0	0	0	0
15 Wood	261	2	0	0	13
16 Furniture	0	0	0	0	0
17 Paper	247	1	0	279	8,260
18 Rubber	1,592	0	1	0	0
19 Leather	6,082	0	0	0	7
20 Chemical industry	219	5,234	849	27	1,086
21 Pharmaceuticals	0	1	0	0	0
22 Perfumery	0	0	0	0	0
23 Plastics	214	0	0	0	2
24 Textiles	8,998	4	0	0	95
25 Clothing	75	1	0	0	0
26 Food	2	31,638	3,122	9	1
27 Beverages	3	53	1,097	1	1
28 Tobacco	0	0	0	2,282	0
29 Publishing	138	659	135	22	461
30 Miscellaneous	54	0	0	0	24
31 Construction	0	0	0	0	0
32 Transportation	284	5,828	701	112	299
Σ	23,750	212,051	15,202	6,719	13,482
Gross Returns to capital	9,337	53,640	8,435	5,176	6,917
Wages, salaries and social security	7,185	19,296	4,313	1,272	6,555
Value added	16,522	72,936	12,748	6,448	13,472
Gross product	40,272	284,987	27,950	13,167	26,954

TABLE 2. BRAZIL: INPUT-OUTPUT TABLE, 1959–(*Continued*)

30	31	32	Σ	CF	CG
98	0	0	174,904	156,130	160
78	0	0	55,585	59,619	500
73	0	755	14,366	3,289	1,207
254	26,914	2,744	70,946	164,197	1,423
1,335	7,903	4,586	152,669	231,452	0
656	0	0	8,620	0	0
66	2,160	32,500	62,309	8,421	3,246
388	0	0	36,487	0	0
116	0	0	29,487	0	457
183	36,370	0	46,130	6,352	2,203
923	24,835	0	130,654	5,102	5,175
0	0	0	2,417	3,913	3,251
55	3,759	0	10,432	22,713	1,940
15	1,063	10,597	25,070	9,833	3,545
455	14,162	0	29,670	1,099	432
0	647	0	1,248	16,599	0
247	0	0	35,010	1,344	850
64	0	9,689	17,730	11,927	303
94	0	0	9,344	1,378	30
774	1,331	1,150	126,053	3,479	2,890
0	0	0	4,969	19,385	684
3	0	0	1,259	16,202	698
117	327	0	2,737	5,187	74
417	0	0	61,392	85,255	892
0	0	0	1,157	38,605	512
2	0	0	37,672	187,699	2,012
4	0	0	3,739	24,914	1
0	0	0	2,282	10,752	0
70	0	0	11,594	15,059	1,307
175	0	0	2,712	12,778	140
0	0	2,000	29,423	30,000	10,000
126	4,595	3,304	35,480	87,196	25,000
6,788	124,066	67,325	1,236,547	1,239,879	68,932
4,873	32,357	9,707	1,054,353		
3,615	23,000	83,422	510,704	45,923	105,589
8,488	55,357	93,129		45,923	105,589
15,276	179,423	160,454	2,801,604	1,285,802	174,528

TABLE 2. BRAZIL: INPUT-OUTPUT TABLE, 1959–(*Continued*)

Sectors	I	X	−M	PB
1 Vegetable product	6,555	11,884	−14,836	334,797
2 Animal product	10,445	391	−139	129,401
3 Electric energy	0	0	0	18,862
4 Commerce	22,730	21,052	0	280,348
5 Services	0	0	0	384,121
6 Wastes	0	3	0	8,623
7 Fuels	0	86	0	74,062
8 Packaging	0	0	0	36,487
9 Extractive industry	0	2,604	−17,320	15,228
10 Nonmetallic minerals	0	203	−2,014	52,874
11 Metallurgy	6,152	17	−22,848	124,252
12 Machine tools	41,216	151	−17,318	33,630
13 Electrical goods	20,161	11	−8,328	46,929
14 Transportation goods	61,346	91	−19,788	80,097
15 Wood	0	78	−76	31,203
16 Furniture	3,873	0	−6	21,714
17 Paper	0	0	−2,096	35,108
18 Rubber	0	35	−153	29,842
19 Leather	0	2,062	−49	12,765
20 Chemical industry	0	6,583	−33,230	105,775
21 Pharmaceuticals	0	58	−2,063	23,033
22 Perfumery	0	1	−187	17,973
23 Plastics	0	2	−12	7,988
24 Textiles	0	924	−454	148,009
25 Clothing	0	29	−31	40,272
26 Food	0	63,043	−5,439	284,987
27 Beverages	0	15	−719	27,950
28 Tobacco	0	133	0	13,167
29 Publishing	0	76	−1,082	26,954
30 Miscellaneous	1,301	56	−1,711	15,276
31 Construction	110,000	0	0	179,423
32 Transportation	0	12,778	0	160,454
Σ	283,779	122,366	−149,899	2,801,604
Gross Returns to capital				1,054,353
Wages, salaries and social security				662,216
Value added				1,716,569
Gross product	283,779	122,366	−149,899	4,518,173

tive importance of domestic production and of imports for three selected years is shown in Table 3. Although the bulk of import substitution took place between 1949 and 1959, for some sectors, especially the heavy industries and the chemical sector, the import shares continued to fall significantly after 1959 as well.

For applications of the model to the current situation, it seems therefore necessary to use the most recent coefficients available, in this case those for 1965. In principle, the same holds true for the δ-coefficients, although these are independent of import substitution, since they include domestic as well as imported inputs. The ϵ-coefficients, presented in Table 4, which reflect the distribution of investment in 1959, are undoubtedly less stable than the product distribution coefficients, and may therefore be obsolete for applications to the present situation. For none of the postcensus years, however, was information of comparable quality available.

THE INPUT-OUTPUT ELASTICITIES

For our analysis of variable input-output coefficients, we followed Shephard[9] in his distinction between materials physically embodied in the output of the consuming industry (such as agricultural produce in processed food) and those not embodied but consumed in one way or another by the equipment of production (such as coke in blast furnaces). For an embodied input, the input flow should basically be proportional to the output flow over time (assuming the product mix is not altered). On the other hand, technological efficiency in the use of fuels, for example, may well be expected to change.

For the purposes of this study, an analysis was made of the technical coefficients as implied by the 1949 and 1959 censuses. Unfortunately, the high degree of aggregation of inputs in the 1949 census did not permit a very detailed comparison. However, it did permit us to follow the distinction made above between embodied and nonembodied inputs. The 1949 census presented estimates for each industrial sector of pur-

[9] R. W. Shephard, "An Econometric Model of Interindustry Material Flows," *Econometrica*, July 1952, pp. 488–489.

chases of raw materials, electrical energy, fuels, packing materials, transportation, and other services. The last two had to be left out, because of obviously incomplete coverage. For the remaining cost elements, we divided the 1959 input-output coefficients by the corresponding estimates for 1949, and charted their distributions (see Figure 1). The results are quite interesting, for they seem to confirm an essential distinction between embodied and disembodied inputs. The distribution obtained for raw materials (typically embodied inputs) comes quite close to a normal one with its average 1, indicating that the changes in coefficients probably reflect observational errors

TABLE 3. RELATIVE IMPORTANCE OF IMPORTS
IN TOTAL SUPPLY
(Selected Years)

Sectors	$1-\pi_i$		
	1949	1959	1965
1	0.07	0.04	0.05
2	0.01	0.01	0.02
9	0.20	0.47	0.52
10	0.08	0.04	0.02
11	0.22	0.16	0.09
12	0.62	0.34	0.22
13	0.48	0.15	0.09
14	0.55	0.20	0.07
15	0.01	0.02	0.03
17	0.19	0.06	0.06
18	0.03	0.05	0.09
20	0.39	0.24	0.14
21	0.19	0.08	0.00
22	0.00	0.01	0.01
23	1.00	0.00	0.00
24	0.03	0.00	0.00
25	0.00	0.00	0.01
26	0.03	0.02	0.03
27	0.02	0.03	0.02
29	0.02	0.02	0.04
30	0.29	0.10	0.16

Source: 1950 and 1960 censuses and *Anuário Estatístico* for 1950, 1960, and 1966.
Note: The increase in the import coefficient for the mining sector (9) reflects the substitution of previously imported gasoline (now produced by the chemical sector 20) by crude petroleum.

TABLE 4. INVESTMENT DISTRIBUTION COEFFICIENTS (e_{ij})

e_{ij} i	Machinery $e_{12,j} + e_{13,j}$	Transport equipment (sector 14) $e_{14,j}$	Construction (sector 31) $e_{31,j}$
1	0.034	0.009	0.018
2	0	0	0.018
3	0.042	0	0.009
4	0.079	0.032	0.018
5	0.065	0.019	0.187
9	0.003	0	0.005
10	0.018	0.001	0.005
11	0.103	0.001	0.014
12	0.045	0	0.005
13	0.036	0	0.007
14	0.187	0.001	0.019
15	0.005	0.002	0.002
16	0.005	0.002	0.002
17	0.011	0	0.003
18	0.019	0	0.002
19	0.004	0	0.001
20	0.041	0	0.008
21	0.007	0	0.003
22	0.004	0	0.003
23	0.003	0	0.001
24	0.044	0	0.005
25	0.008	0	0.002
26	0.059	0.003	0.021
27	0.010	0.001	0.002
28	0.004	0	0.001
29	0.012	0	0.002
30	0.008	0	0.001
31	0.070	0.015	0.009
32	0.028	0.314	0.009
c	0	0.532	0.386
g	0.046	0.065	0.236
	1.000	1.000	1.000

Source: 1960 industrial and service censuses.

more than anything else. The same cannot be said, however, of the inputs of electric energy, fuels, and packing materials. The distributions of the 1959/1949 ratios correspond rather to a rectangular pattern. This does not mean, of course, that measurement errors in these coefficients were less important (on the contrary, perhaps, because of the smaller degree of

TABLE 5. INPUT-OUTPUT ELASTICITIES (a_{ij})

i	Electric energy a_{3j}	Fuels a_{7j}	Packing materials a_{8j}
9	0.98	1.25	1.00
10	1.19	0.90	1.27
11	1.01	0.86	0.69
12	0.94	1.00	1.09
13	0.81	0.93	0.95
14	0.88	1.07	1.35
15	1.02	1.38	1.16
16	0.99	1.24	1.25
17	0.62	0.94	0.62
18	0.68	0.91	0.82
19	1.72	1.50	1.53
20–23	0.90	1.03	0.61
24	1.12	1.00	1.03
25	1.10	1.29	1.23
26	1.28	1.14	1.34
27	1.00	1.37	1.57
28	0.93	1.12	1.10
29	0.89	1.00	1.21
30	0.59	1.00	1.21

aggregation), but apparently they could not hide the basic changes in the coefficients.

As a consequence, in the practical applications described below, we assumed that all input-output elasticities for raw materials were equal to 1, but we used elasticity values different from 1 for the inputs of electric energy, fuels, and packing materials. The values for these elasticities are shown in Table 5.

THE CAPITAL-OUTPUT ELASTICITIES

The elasticity formulation of the model also permits us to introduce a variable capital-output ratio for the various sectors of the economy. In the past, economic development in Brazil has been characterized by a rather low marginal capital-output ratio. It is therefore likely that the capital-output elasticities are on the whole smaller than 1. This was confirmed by an analysis of the 1949 and 1959 censuses, from which we derived elasticities for the various sectors of the economy. We analyzed information on horsepower installed and on total applied capital. The picture that emerged showed that for most sectors the capital-output elasticity was indeed smaller than 1 (see Table 6). The average lies in the 0.8–0.9 bracket, with the other sectors

TABLE 6. CAPITAL-OUTPUT ELASTICITIES (τ_i)

10	1.00	24	0.53
11	0.40	25	0.85
12	0.96	26	0.80
13	0.80	27	0.77
14	1.02	28	0.65
15	0.63	29	0.51
16	0.81	30	0.66
17	0.83	31	1.00
18	0.80	32	1.00
20–23	1.07		

more or less normally distributed around it. The total range is quite large, however, from 0.4 to 1.3.

Whether or not these elasticities will continue to be valid for the future is difficult to foresee. During the development decade of the 1950's, the Brazilian economy was obviously able to exploit economies of scale potentially available at the beginning of the period, because at that time the average size of the firms was still quite small. It seems unlikely that the same economies of scale would still be available, although it is equally impossible to tell to what extent they may have been reduced.

APPLICATION TO THE THREE-YEAR PLAN 1968–1970

In the summer of 1967, an attempt was made to use the model for some preliminary calculations related to the three-year plan 1968–1970. In the beginning of 1967 the economy had shown an acceleration in its economic growth and the question was posed whether a further acceleration to an annual

TABLE 7. SECTORAL GROWTH RATES, SECOND-ROUND ESTIMATES

sector	1	Agriculture	5.4
sector	2	Animal husbandry	5.2
sector	3	Electric energy	7.5
sector	4	Commerce	7.8
sector	5	Services	7.3
sector	9	Mining	8.0
sector	10	Nonmetallic mineral products	11.4
sector	11	Metallurgy	10.4
sector	12	Mechanical	14.4
sector	13	Electrotechnical	11.2
sector	14	Transport equipment	11.6
sector	15	Wood products	9.4
sector	16	Furniture	8.9
sector	17	Paper products	7.4
sector	18	Rubber products	8.6
sector	19	Leather products	6.7
sector	20	Chemical	7.0
sector	21	Pharmaceuticals	6.2
sector	22	Perfumes, soap	5.1
sector	23	Plastic products	8.2
sector	24	Textiles	7.1
sector	25	Clothing	7.0
sector	26	Food products	5.1
sector	27	Beverages	7.1
sector	28	Tobacco	4.8
sector	29	Printing	7.7
sector	30	Miscellaneous	8.0
sector	31	Construction	10.3
sector	32	Transportation	5.9

average of 7 percent would be possible. Calculations using the macro-economic framework indicated that, taking into account the still substantial excess capacity existing in the economy, an annual growth rate of gross investment of around 15 percent would make it possible to achieve this target. It remained to be seen, however, what this implied for the relative growth rates of the different sectors, keeping in mind the latter's import substitution targets. During a first-round calculation, we assumed that the growth rate of investment demand for each of the sectors producing capital goods would indeed be of the order of 15 percent, and we calculated the sectoral growth rates of production corresponding to this assumption as well as to the overall growth target of 7 percent. The results indicated that, for the major capital-goods sectors, the assumption of an annual growth rate of investment demand was about right, if acceleration in the growth rate of the sectors' capital stock did not exceed 25 percent. For the mechanical and electrotechnical sectors, we found that the annual growth rate of investment demand would be 16.9 percent, for the transport equipment sector it would be 13.1 percent, and for the construction sector it would be 13.4 percent. Replacing these calculated rates for the 15 percent originally assumed, we obtained second-round estimates for the sectoral growth rates of output.

The growth rates of investment demand corresponding to these estimates no longer diverged from those assumed in the second-round calculations, so that no third round was necessary. On the other hand, the weighted average of value added in the sectors, combined with a growth rate of government wage payments of 5 percent and of wages paid by households to servants of 6 percent, was equal to 7 percent. This indicated that macro-economic consistency is also ensured at this rate, as the macro-economic calculations had already suggested.*

* The precise assumptions under which the foregoing were obtained were the following: Overall annual growth rate, 7 per cent; Population growth rate, 3 per cent; Growth rate of government demand for sectors 1–32, 6 per cent; Growth rate of government wage bill, 5 per cent; Growth rates of exports, Sector 1, 5.6 per cent; Sector 9, 13.4 per cent; Sector 20, 3.8 per cent; Sector 26, 4.4 per cent; All other exports, 4.0 per cent.

Import substitution targets (μ_i): Sector 12, 1.2; Sector 13, 1.2; Sector 20, 0.7; All other sectors, 1.0; Consumption functions, Table 1; Input-output elasticities, Table 5; Product distribution coefficient, Table 2; Self-sufficiency coefficient, Table 3; Investment distribution coefficient, Table 4; Depreciation rate (σ), 10 percent.

Indexes

INDEX OF PERSONS

INDEX OF SUBJECTS